THE BERLITZ SELF-TEACHER:
ITALIAN

THE BERLITZ
SELF-TEACHER:

ITALIAN

BY THE EDITORIAL STAFF OF

**THE BERLITZ SCHOOLS
OF LANGUAGES OF AMERICA, INC.**

GROSSET & DUNLAP

PUBLISHERS   NEW YORK

INTRODUCTION

A very strange paradox exists in connection with languages and the learning of them. On the one hand, the ability to speak two or more languages reasonably well is *prima facie* evidence of better-than-average intelligence. On the other hand, learning a language is a very easy business. The proof of it is that every living human being who is not an utter idiot speaks one!

The trick lies in how you go about it. It would seem reasonable to use somewhat the same system to learn a new language as you did to acquire your own. This idea built up the Berlitz Schools of Languages from a one-room studio in Providence, Rhode Island, to a globe-circling institution with over 300 branches.

In a word, you learn to *speak* a language *by speaking it*—and in no other way. That is how the Italians do it, and that is how you learned English.

You will succeed with the BERLITZ SELF-TEACHER to the extent that you *speak*. Do not deceive yourself into thinking you have "arrived" when you find yourself able to read or translate the Italian text. You master Italian only in the degree to which you can express your ideas in it. The ability to interpret the thoughts of others is only the first step.

One way of using the BERLITZ SELF-TEACHER is to pair off with someone else, or to organize a small group. After reading over the lesson in advance for meaning and pronunciation, each student then reads aloud, direct from the Italian text. The lesson is divided into convenient portions by agreement among the students. After each student has practiced reading aloud, one of them assumes the role of instructor and questions the others from the exercises called THINKING IN ITALIAN. When all can answer these questions without hesitation, each student should invent ten or twelve new questions, based on the same or preceding lessons, and then put these questions to the others. Afterwards, answers to the exercise questions should be written out and corrected from the key in the appendix.

When a group of you are learning together, do not succumb to the "community-sing" temptation. Each student must speak individually, so that he can hear himself and the others, and profit thereby.

Make no mistake, however! This book is designed primarily for the student working alone. He must do exactly what pairs or groups do, covering each operation for himself. If you are embarrassed by the sound of your own voice, hide in the pantry! Put a sack over your head! No matter what form of defense mechanism you set up, see to it that you *speak out!* Do not mumble or whisper.

Your attention is directed to the glossary in the back of the book. Use it sparingly, if at all. With few exceptions, all the words are made clear in the lesson texts, and only occasionally have we sneaked a new one into the THINKING IN ITALIAN exercises, just to keep you on your toes.

The authors have enjoyed preparing the BERLITZ SELF-TEACHER, because they are confident that, properly used, it can provide you with a flying start toward a working knowledge of Italian—and an extra dividend of good, clean fun.

NOTE ON PRONUNCIATION

It would be most gratifying to the authors to take modest credit for having developed a lucid and easy-to-use phonetic system for this book. However, honesty compels the admission that Italian pronunciation, once you learn the fundamental values of the Italian alphabet, is extremely simple. There are no gutturals as in German, no throaty r's or nasals as in French.

This simplicity may explain the fact that singers of all nationalities have no difficulty in sounding the most difficult notes when learned with Italian lyrics.

You will gradually come to pronounce properly as you follow the text and phonetics of this book. In the meanwhile, here are a few things to watch for:

CH—has the sound of the English K.

GH—is always like G in "get".

GL—sounds like LLI in "million".

GN—has the sound of NY in "canyon".

R—trill it like an alarm-clock.

RR—trill it even more so.

SC—like SH in "shell".

SCH—like SK in "skill".

Z—like TS in front of IO. Ex: Stazione—*Stah-ts'YOH-neh*—station.

ZZ—like TZ. Ex: Pizza—PEE-*tzah*.

Otherwise, the words pronounce themselves. The stressed syllables are in capitals, the others small.

Ex: libro—LEE-*broh*.

LEZIONE PRIMA

Che cosa è questo?
Keh KOH-*zah* EH KWESS-*toh?*
What is this?

Il lapis
Eel LAH-*peess*
The pencil

la penna
lah PEHN-*nah*
the pen

il libro
eel LEE-*broh*
the book

la scatola
lah SKAH-*toh-lah*
the box

lo specchio
loh SPEHK-*k'yoh*
the mirror

la chiave
lah k'YAH-*veh*
the key

Che cosa è questo?
Keh KOH-*zah* EH KWESS-*toh?*
What is this?

È il lapis; è la penna; è lo specchio; ecc.
EH *eel* LAH-*peess;* EH *lah* PEHN-*nah;* EH *loh* SPEHK-*k'yoh; eht*-CHEH-*teh-rah.*
It is the pencil; it is the pen; it is the mirror; etc.

È questo il libro?
EH KWESS-*toh eel* LEE-*broh?*
Is this the book?

Sì, è il libro.
See, EH *eel* LEE-*broh.*
Yes, it is the book.

È questo lo specchio?
EH KWESS-*toh loh* SPEHK-*k'yoh?*
Is this the mirror?

No, non è lo specchio.
Noh, noh-NEH *loh* SPEHK-*k'yoh.*
No, it is not the mirror.

1

Che cosa è?
Keh KOH-*zah* EH?
What is it?

È la scatola.
EH *lah* SKAH-*toh-lah.*
It is the box.

È questo il lapis?
EH KWESS-*toh eel* LAH-*peess?*
Is this the pencil?

No, non è il lapis, è la penna.
*Noh, noh-*NEH *eel* LAH-*peess,* EH *lah*
PEHN-*nah.*
No, it is not the pencil, it is the pen.

NOTE to Student: All nouns are either masculine or feminine. *Il* precedes all masculine nouns. *La* precedes all feminine nouns. Exception: All masculine nouns which begin with a vowel, or the letter *S* followed by another consonant, or the letter *Z*, or *GN* are preceded by *lo* instead of *il*. The reason for these exceptions is purely phonetic.

The word *è* means "is", "it is" and "is it". The "it" is unnecessary in Italian.

la sedia
lah SEHD-*yah*
the chair

la tavola
lah TAH-*voh-lah*
the table

la lampada
lah LAHM-*pah-daṅ*
the lamp

la porta
lah POHR-*tah*
the door

la finestra
*lah fee-*NESS-*trah*
the window

il quadro
eel KWAH-*droh*
the picture

Signorina, è questa la finestra o la porta?
*Seen-yoh-*REE-*nah,* EH KWESS-*tah lah fee-*NESS-*trah oh lah* POHR-*tah?*
Young lady, is this the window or the door?

NOTE: *Questo* means "this", and is used only to indicate masculine nouns. It becomes *questa* when it indicates feminine nouns.

È la porta, signore.
EH *lah* POHR-*tah, seen-*YOH-*reh.*
It is the door, sir.

È la finestra, signora.
EH *lah fee-*NESS-*trah, seen-*YOH-*rah.*
It is the window, madam.

la parete
*lah pah-*REH-*teh*
the wall

la stanza
lah STAHN-*tsah*
the room

il soffitto
*eel sohf-*FEET-*toh*
the ceiling

il pavimento
*eel pah-vee-*MEHN-*toh*
the floor

1	2	3	4	5
uno	due	tre	quattro	cinque
OO-*noh*	DOO-*eh*	*treh*	KWAHT-*troh*	CHEEN-*kweh*

THINKING IN ITALIAN

Answer the following questions aloud; then write the answers and check them on page 281.

1. Che cosa è questo?
2. È questo il libro?
3. È questa la scatola?

4. È questa la tavola?
5. È questo lo specchio?
6. Che cosa è?

7. È questa la lampada?
8. È questa la sedia?
9. Che cosa è?

10. Che cosa è questo?
11. È questo il quadro?
12. È questo il libro?

13. È questa la porta?
14. È questa la chiave?
15. Che cosa è?

LEZIONE 2

Il vestiario
Eel vehs-tee-AH-ree-oh
Clothing

La giacca
Lah JAHK-kah
The jacket

il cappello
eel kahp-PEL-loh
the hat

il vestito
eel vehs-TEE-toh
the suit (dress)

la camicia
lah kah-MEE-chah
the shirt

la cravatta
lah krah-VAHT-tah
the tie

il soprabito
eel soh-PRAH-bee-toh
the overcoat

la scarpa
lah SKAHR-pah
the shoe

il fazzoletto
eel fah-tsoh-LET-toh
the handkerchief

la borsetta
lah bohr-SET-tah
the pocket-book

È questo il cappello?
EH KWESS-*toh eel kahp-*PEL-*loh?*
Is this the hat?

Sì, è il cappello.
See, EH *eel kahp-*PEL-*loh.*
Yes, it is the hat.

È questa la giacca o la camicia?
EH KWESS-*tah lah* JAHK-*kah oh lah kah-*MEE-*chah?*
Is this the jacket or the shirt?

È la giacca.
EH *lah* JAHK-*kah.*
It is the jacket.

il danaro	**la calza**	**l'orologio**
*eel dah-*NAH-*roh*	*lah* KAHL-*tsah*	*loh-roh-*LOH-*joh*
the money	the sock (stocking)	the watch
la gonnella	**il guanto**	**la camicetta**
*lah gohn-*NEL-*lah*	*eel* GWAHN-*toh*	*lah kah-mee-*CHEHT-*tah*
the skirt	the glove	the blouse

NOTE: The articles *lo* and *la* become *l'* whenever they precede a singular noun which begins with a vowel. Therefore, you cannot tell from the article whether a word is masculine or feminine; but bear in mind that with the single exception of *la mano*—"the hand", all nouns ending with the letter *o* are masculine, and that almost all nouns ending with *a* are feminine.

È questo il danaro o la borsetta?
EH KWESS-*toh eel dah-*NAH-*roh oh lah bohr-*SET-*tah?*
Is this the money or the pocket-book?

È la borsetta.
EH *lah bohr-*SET-*tah.*
It is the pocket-book (handbag).

È questo il guanto, signorina?
EH KWESS-*toh eel* GWAHN-*toh,*
    *seen-yoh-*REE-*nah?*
Is this the glove, miss?

No, signore, non è il guanto, è l'orologio.
*Noh, seen-*YOH-*reh, noh-*NEH *eel* GWAHN-*toh,* EH *loh-roh-*LOH-*joh.*
No, sir, it is not the glove, it is the watch.

Molto bene!
MOHL-*toh* BEH-*neh!*
Very good!

Grazie.
GRAHTS-*yeh.*
Thanks.

NOTE to Student: *Molto bene!* means literally "Very well!" but we have translated it by "Very good!" to show what its true English equivalent is in the circumstance.

6	7	8	9	10
sei	sette	otto	nove	dieci
say	SET-*teh*	OHT-*toh*	NOH-*veh*	*d'*YEH-*chee*

HINTS on Pronunciation: *G* before *e* and *i* is pronounced like "J" in "John"; elsewhere like "g" in "get".

THINKING IN ITALIAN

(Answers on page 281)

1. Che cosa è questa?
2. È il guanto o la scarpa?
3. È la cravatta o il fazzoletto?

4. Che cosa è questo?
5. È il fazzoletto o il guanto?
6. È il lapis?

7. Che cosa è questo?
8. È il vestito?
9. È il soprabito?
10. È la giacca o la camicia?
11. È il cappello?
12. È la gonnella?

Di che colore è questo?
*Dee keh koh-*LOH*-reh* EH KWESS-*toh?*
What color is this?

Nero
NEH-*roh*
Black

rosso
ROHS-*soh*
red

giallo
JAHL-*loh*
yellow

grigio
GREE-*joh*
gray

bianco
b'YAHN-*koh*
white

bruno
BROO-*noh*
brown

verde
VEHR-*deh*
green

azzurro
*ah-*DZOOR-*roh*
blue

Il lapis è bruno.
Eel LAH-*peess* EH BROO-*noh.*
The pencil is brown.

Il telefono è nero.
*Eel teh-*LEH-*foh-noh* EH NEH-*roh.*
The telephone is black.

Il libro è azzurro.
Eel LEE-*broh* EH *ah-*DZOOR-*roh.*
The book is blue.

Il guanto è grigio.
Eel GWAHN-*toh* EH GREE-*joh.*
The glove is gray.

Il soffitto è bianco.
*Eel sohf-*FEET-*toh* EH *b'*YAHN-*koh.*
The ceilin is white.

Il cappello è verde.
*Eel kahp-*PEL-*loh* EH VEHR-*deh.*
The hat is green.

NOTE: Adjectives of color, like other adjectives, must agree with their nouns in gender. Ex: *Il libro è rosso.*—"The book is red."; *La penna è rossa.*—"The pen is red."

EXCEPTION: All adjectives ending with *e* have the same form for masculine and feminine such as *verde*, etc. Ex: *Il cappello è verde.*—"That hat is green."; *La gonnella è verde.*—"The skirt is green."

Che cosa è questo?
Keh KOH-*zah* EH KWESS-*toh?*
What is this?

È il libro.
EH *eel* LEE-*broh.*
It is the book.

Di che colore è il libro?
*Dee keh koh-*LOH-*reh* EH *eel* LEE-*broh?*
What color is the book?

Il libro è azzurro.
Eel LEE-*broh* EH *ah-*DZOOR-*roh.*
The book is blue.

Che cosa è questo?
Keh KOH-*zah* EH KWESS-*toh?*
What is this?

È il soffitto.
EH *eel sohf-*FEET-*toh.*
It is the ceiling.

Di che colore è il soffitto?
*Dee keh koh-*LOH-*reh* EH *eel sohf-*FEET-*toh?*
What color is the ceiling?

Il soffitto è bianco.
*Eel sohf-*FEET-*toh* EH *b'*YAHN-*koh.*
The ceiling is white.

Di che colore è il cappello?
*Dee keh koh-*LOH-*reh* EH *eel kahp-*PEL-*loh?*
What color is the hat?

È verde.
EH VEHR-*deh.*
It is green.

È bruno il lapis?
EH BROO-*noh eel* LAH-*peess?*
Is the pencil brown?

Sì, signore, il lapis è bruno.
*See, seen-*YOH-*reh, eel* LAH-*peess* EH BROO-*noh.*
Yes, sir, the pencil is brown.

È verde il lapis?
EH VEHR-*deh eel* LAH-*peess?*
Is the pencil green?

No, signore, il lapis non è verde.
*Noh, seen-*YOH-*reh, eel* LAH-*peess noh-*NEH VEHR-*deh.*
No, sir, the pencil is not green.

È nero il lapis?
EH NEH-*roh eel* LAH-*peess?*
Is the pencil black?

No, non è nero.
*Noh, noh-*NEH NEH-*roh.*
No, it is not black.

Di che colore è il lapis?
*Dee keh koh-*LOH-*reh* EH *eel* LAH-*peess?*
What color is the pencil?

Il lapis è bruno.
Eel LAH-*peess* EH BROO-*noh.*
The pencil is brown.

È verde la scatola?
EH VEHR-*deh lah* SKAH-*toh-lah?*
Is the box green?

No, la scatola è gialla.
Noh, lah SKAH-*toh-lah* EH JAHL-*lah.*
No, the box is yellow.

È rossa la gonnella?
EH ROHS-*sah lah* gohn-NEL-*lah?*
Is the skirt red?

No, la gonnella è bruna.
Noh, lah gohn-NEL-*lah* EH BROO-*nah.*
No, the skirt is brown.

Di che colore è la camicia?
Dee keh koh-LOH-*reh* EH *lah*
kah-MEE-*chah?*
What color is the shirt?

La camicia è bianca.
Lah kah-MEE-*chah* EH *b'*YAHN-*kah.*
The shirt is white.

Di che colore è la parete?
Dee keh koh-LOH-*reh* EH *lah* pah-REH-*teh?*
What color is the wall?

È grigia.
EH GREE-*jah.*
It is gray.

Di che colore è la penna?
Dee keh koh-LOH-*reh* EH *lah* PEHN-*nah?*
What color is the pen?

È azzurra.
EH *ah*-DZOOR-*rah.*
It is blue.

È questo il telefono?
EH KWESS-*toh eel* teh-LEH-*foh-noh?*
Is this the telephone?

Sì, è il telefono.
See, EH *eel* teh-LEH-*foh-noh.*
Yes, it is the telephone.

Di che colore è?
Dee keh koh-LOH-*reh* EH?
What color is it?

È nero.
EH NEH-*roh.*
It is black.

È questa la sedia?
EH KWESS-*tah lah* SEHD-*yah?*
Is this the chair?

No, è la tavola.
Noh, EH *lah* TAH-*voh-lah.*
No, it is the table.

Di che colore è?
Dee keh koh-LOH-*reh* EH?
What color is it?

È nera.
EH NEH-*rah.*
It is black.

Di che colore è la bandiera italiana?
Dee kee koh-LOH-*reh* EH *lah* bahn-*d'*YEH-*rah* ee-tahl-YAH-*nah?*
What color is the Italian flag?

È verde, bianca e rossa.
EH VEHR-*deh, b'*YAHN-*kah eh* ROHS-*sah.*
It is green, white and red.

Di che colore è la bandiera francese?
Dee keh koh-LOH-*reh* EH *lah* bahn-*d'*YEH-*rah* frahn-CHEH-*zeh?*
What color is the French flag?

È azzurra, bianca e rossa.
EH *ah*-DZOOR-*rah, b'*YAHN-*kah eh* ROHS-*sah.*
It is blue, white and red.

Di che colore è la bandiera americana?
*Dee keh koh-*LOH-*reh* EH *lah bahn-d'*YEH-*rah ah-meh-ree-*KAH-*nah?*
What color is the American flag?

È anche rossa, bianca e azzurra.
EH AHN-*keh* ROHS-*sah, b'*YAHN-*kah eh ah-*DZOOR-*rah.*
It is also red, white and blue.

Molto bene!
MOHL-*toh* BEH-*neh!*
Very good!

Grazie, signore.
GRAHTS-*yeh, seen-*YOH-*reh.*
Thank you, sir.

A rivederla, signorina Valli.
*Ah-ree-veh-*DEHR-*lah, seen-yoh-*REE-*nah*
VAHL-*lee.*
Good-bye, Miss Valli.

A rivederla, signore.
*Ah-ree-veh-*DEHR-*lah, seen-*YOH-*reh.*
Good-bye, sir.

HINT on Good Form: Don't feel embarrassed if you don't remember the name of a person; it is quite correct, in Italian, to say: *A rivederla, signorina.*—"Good-bye, miss."

THINKING IN ITALIAN
(Answers on page 281)

1. È gialla la penna?
2. È grigia la penna?
3. Di che colore è la penna?
4. È la penna rossa?

5. È la penna verde o azzurra?
6. Che cosa è questo?
7. È il lapis?
8. Di che colore è?
9. È il lapis rosso?

10. È verde?
11. È questa la tavola?
12. È la sedia?
13. Che cosa è?
14. È la lampada?
15. Di che colore è la lampada?
16. Che cosa è questo?

17. È giallo il libro?
18. È bruno il libro?
19. È il libro nero?
20. Di che colore è il libro?

LEZIONE 4

Le dimensioni
*Leh dee-mehn-s'*YOH-*nee*
The dimensions

Il lapis nero è lungo.
Eel LAH-*peess* NEH-*roh* EH LOON-*goh.*
The black pencil is long.

La matita nera è lunga.
*Lah mah-*TEE-*tah* NEH-*rah* EH LOON-*gah.*
The black pencil is long.

TAKE YOUR CHOICE! The pencil can be called either *lapis* (masculine) or *matita* (feminine).

Il lapis rosso non è lungo,
Eel LAH-*peess* ROHS-*soh noh-*NEH LOON-*goh,*
The red pencil is not long,

è corto.
EH KOHR-*toh.*
it is short.

È lungo il lapis nero?
EH LOON-*goh eel* LAH-*peess* NEH-*roh?*
Is the black pencil long?

È corto il lapis rosso?
EH KOHR-*toh eel* LAH-*peess* ROHS-*soh?*
Is the red pencil short?

È lunga o corta la matita rossa?
EH LOON-*gah oh* KOHR-*tah lah mah-*TEE-*tah* ROHS-*sah?*
Is the red pencil long or short?

È corta.
EH KOHR-*tah.*
It is short.

È lungo il vestito nero?
EH LOON-*goh eel vehs-*TEE-*toh* NEH-*roh?*
Is the black dress long?

Sì, è lungo.
See, EH LOON-*goh.*
Yes, it is long.

È lungo il vestito giallo?
EH LOON-*goh eel vehs*-TEE-*toh* JAHL-*loh?*
Is the yellow dress long?

No, è corto.
Noh, EH KOHR-*toh.*
No, it is short.

La scatola gialla è lunga;
Lah SKAH-*toh-lah* JAHL-*!ah*
  EH LOON-*gah;*
The yellow box is long;

la scatola nera è corta.
lah SKAH-*toh-lah* NEH-*rah*
  EH KOHR-*tah.*
the black box is short.

La scatola gialla è lunga e larga:
Lah SKAH-*toh-lah* JAHL-*lah* EH LOON-*gah eh* LAHR-*gah:*
The yellow box is long and wide:

è grande.
EH GRAHN-*deh.*
it is large.

La scatola nera è corta e stretta:
Lah SKAH-*toh-lah* NEH-*rah* EH KOHR-*tah eh* STREHT-*tah:*
The black box is short and narrow:

è piccola.
EH PEEK-*koh-lah.*
it is small.

Il libro bruno è lungo e largo:
Eel LEE-*broh* BROO-*noh* EH LOON-*goh eh* LAHR-*goh:*
The brown book is long and wide:

è grande.
EH GRAHN-*deh.*
it is large.

Il libro rosso è corto e stretto:
Eel LEE-*broh* ROHS-*soh* EH KOHR-*toh eh* STREHT-*toh:*
The red book is short and narrow:

è piccolo.
EH PEEK-*koh-loh.*
it is small.

HAVE YOU NOTICED the masculine and feminine forms for the new adjectives you have learned in this lesson? *Lungo—lunga; corto—corta; largo—larga; stretto—stretta; piccolo—piccola. Grande* does not vary in the feminine because it ends with an *e.*

La finestra è grande;
Lah fee-NESS-*trah* EH GRAHN-*deh;*
The window is large;

la tavola è piccola.
lah TAH-*voh-lah* EH PEEK-*koh-lah.*
the table is small.

Di che colore è il libro grande?
Dee keh koh-LOH-*reh* EH *eel* LEE-*broh* GRAHN-*deh?*
What color is the large book?

È bruno.
EH BROO-*noh.*
It is brown.

Di che colore è il vestito piccolo?
Dee keh koh-LOH-*reh* EH *eel vehs*-TEE-*toh*
  PEEK-*koh-loh?*
What color is the small dress?

È giallo.
EH JAHL-*loh.*
It is yellow.

Il libro verde non è nè grande nè piccolo;
Eel LEE-*broh* VEHR-*deh* noh-NEH NEH GRAHN-*deh*
  NEH PEEK-*koh-loh;*
The green book is neither large nor small;

è medio.
EH MEH-*d'yoh.*
it is medium-sized.

È grande la scatola gialla?
EH GRAHN-*deh lah* SKAH-*toh-lah* JAHL-*lah?*
Is the yellow box large?

Sì, è grande.
See, EH GRAHN-*deh.*
Yes, it is large.

È grande il vestito giallo?
EH GRAHN-*deh eel vehs*-TEE-*toh* JAHL-*loh?*
Is the yellow dress large?

No, è piccolo.
Noh, EH PEEK-*koh-loh.*
No, it is small.

Di che colore è il lapis lungo?
*Dee keh koh-*LOH-*reh* EH *eel* LAH-*peess* LOON-*goh?*
What color is the long pencil?

Di che colore è il lapis corto?
*Dee keh koh-*LOH-*reh* EH *eel* LAH-*peess* KOHR-*toh?*
What color is the short pencil?

Di che colore è il libro medio?
*Dee keh koh-*LOH-*reh* EH *eel* LEE-*broh* MEH-*d'yoh?*
What color is the medium-sized book?

L'Italia è grande.
*Lee-*TAHL-*yah* EH GRAHN-*deh.*
Italy is large.

La Sicilia è piccola.
*Lah See-*CHEE-*l'yah* EH PEEK-*koh-lah.*
Sicily is small.

È grande l'America?
EH GRAHN-*deh lah-*MEH-*ree-kah?*
Is America large?

È piccolo il Perù?
EH PEEK-*koh-loh eel Peh-*ROO?
Is Peru small?

11	12	13
undici	**dodici**	**tredici**
OON-*dee-chee*	DOH-*dee-chee*	TREH-*dee-chee*

14	15
quattordici	**quindici**
*kwaht-*TOHR-*dee-chee*	KWEEN-*dee-chee*

Buona notte!
*b'woh-*nah NOHT-*teh!*
Good night!

REMEMBER THE NOTE IN LESSON 2! *La Italia* and *la America* become *l'Italia* and *l'America* because each begins with a vowel.

THINKING IN ITALIAN

(Answers on page 282)

1. È lungo il libro rosso?
2. È largo?
3. È grande?
4. È corto il libro verde?
5. È stretto?
6. È piccolo?
7. Di che colore è il libro grande?
8. Di che colore è il libro piccolo?

9. Di che colore è il vestito lungo?
10. È rosso?
11. È lungo il vestito nero?
12. È corto?
13. Di che colore è il vestito ccrto?
14. È nero o verde?

15. È la finestra larga azzurra o bruna?
16. Di che colore è la finestra grande?
17. È grigia?
18. È larga la finestra rossa?
19. È larga o stretta la finestra azzurra?
20. È grande la finestra azzurra?
21. È piccola la finestra rossa?
22. È gialla o rossa la finestra piccola?
23. È azzurra o verde la finestra grande?

LEZIONE 5

Chi è?
Kee EH?
Who is it?

Un signore,	**una signora,**	**una signorina.**
*Oon seen-*YOH-*reh,*	*oo-nah seen-*YOH-*rah,*	oo-*nah seen-yoh-*REE-*nah.*
A gentleman,	a lady,	a young lady.

Questo è il signor Berlitz;
KWESS-*toh* EH *eel seen-*YOHR BEHR-*leets;*
This is Mr. Berlitz;

questa è la signora Berlitz;
KWESS-*tah* EH *lah seen-*YOH-*rah* BEHR-*leets;*
this is Mrs. Berlitz;

questa è la signorina Berlitz.
KWESS-*tah* EH *lah seen-yoh-*REE-*nah* BEHR-*leets.*
this is Miss Berlitz.

 NOTE to Student: *Un* (masculine) and *una* (feminine) mean either "a" or "one". Therefore, whether you wish to say "a gentleman" or "one gentleman", it will be: *Un signore.*

16

È questo il signor Berlitz?
EH KWESS-*toh eel seen-*YOHR BEHR-*leets?*
Is this Mr. Berlitz?

Sì, è il signor Berlitz.   No, non è il signor Berlitz.
See, EH *eel seen-*YOHR BEHR-*leets.*   *Noh, noh-*NEH *eel seen-*YOHR BEHR-*leets.*
Yes, it is Mr. Berlitz.   No, it is not Mr. Berlitz.

È questa la signora Berlitz?
EH KWESS-*tah lah seen-*YOH-*rah* BEHR-*leets?*
Is this Mrs. Berlitz?

Sì, è la signora Berlitz.
See, EH *lah seen-*YOH-*rah* BEHR-*leets.*
Yes, it is Mrs. Berlitz.

No, non è la signora Berlitz.
*Noh, noh-*NEH *lah seen-*YOH-*rah* BEHR-*leets.*
No, it is not Mrs. Berlitz.

È questo il signor Pinza?
EH KWESS-*toh eel seen-*YOHR PEEN-*tsah?*
Is this Mr. Pinza?

No, è il signor Martini.
Noh, EH *eel seen-*YOHR *Mahr-*TEE-*nee.*
No, it is Mr. Martini.

È il signor Martini?   No, è il signor Pinza.
EH *eel seen-*YOHR *Mahr-*TEE-*nee?*   *Noh,* EH *eel seen-*YOHR PEEN-*tsah.*
Is this Mr. Martini?   No, it is Mr. Pinza.

È il signor Baccaloni?   No, ...
EH *eel seen-*YOHR *Bahk-kah-*LOH-*nee?*   *Noh,* ....
Is this Mr. Baccaloni?   No, ...

Chi è questo signore?   È il signor De Luca.
Kee EH KWESS-*toh seen-*YOH-*reh?*   EH *eel seen-*YOHR *Deh* LOO-*kah.*
Who is this gentleman?   It is Mr. De Luca.

Chi?   Il signor De Luca.
Kee?   *Eel seen-*YOHR *Deh* LOO-*kah.*
Who?   Mr. De Luca.

Chi è questa signora?   È la signora Puccini.
Kee EH KWESS-*tah seen-*YOH-*rah?*   EH *lah seen-*YOH-*rah Poo-*TCHEE-*nee.*
Who is this lady?   It is Mrs. Puccini.

Chi è questa signorina?   È la signorina Donizetti.
Kee EH KWESS-*tah seen-yoh-*REE-*nah?* EH *lah seen-yoh-*REE-*nah*
Who is this young lady?   *Doh-nee-*DZET-*tee.*
                                      It is Miss Donizetti.

Lei è il signor Tizio.
Lay EH *eel seen-*YOHR TEE-*ts'yoh.*
You are Mr. Tizio.

Io sono il signor Berlitz.
EE-*oh* SOH-*noh eel seen-*YOHR BEHR-*leets.*
I am Mr. Berlitz.

Lei è l'allievo.
Lay EH *lahl-l'*YEH-*voh.*
You are the pupil.

Io sono il professore.
EE-*oh* SOH-*noh eel proh-fess-*SOH-*reh.*
I am the teacher.

È Lei il signor Sinatra?
EH *Lay eel seen-*YOHR *See-*NAH-*trah?*
Are you Mr. Sinatra?

Sì, sono io.
See, SOH-*noh* EE-*oh.*
Yes, I am.

Sono io il signor Varvaro?
SOH-*noh* EE-*oh eel seen-*YOHR VAHR-*vah-roh?*
Am I Mr. Varvaro?

No, Lei non è il signor Varvaro.
*Noh, Lay noh-*NEH *eel seen-*YOHR VAHR-*vah-roh.*
No, you are not Mr. Varvaro.

Chi sono io?
Kee SOH-*noh* EE-*oh?*
Who am I?

Lei è il signor Berlitz.
Lay EH *eel seen-*YOHR BEHR-*leets.*
You are Mr. Berlitz.

Chi è Lei?
Kee EH *Lay?*
Who are you?

Io sono il signor Sinatra.
EE-*oh* SOH-*noh eel seen-*YOHR *See-*NAH-*trah.*
I am Mr. Sinatra.

Chi è questa signora?
Kee EH KWESS-*tah seen-*YOH-*rah?*
Who is this lady?

È la signora Roberti.
EH *lah seen-*YOH-*rah Roh-*BEHR-*tee.*
She is Mrs. Roberti.

Chi è il signor Di Bella?
Kee EH *eel seen-*YOHR *Dee* BEL-*lah?*
Who is Mr. Di Bella?

È Lei.
EH *Lay.*
You are.

Chi è la signorina Cellini?
Kee EH *lah seen-yoh-*REE-*nah Chel-*LEE-*nee?*
Who is Miss Cellini?

Sono io.
SOH-*noh* EE-*oh.*
I am.

È Lei il professore?
EH *Lay eel proh-fess-*SOH-*reh?*
Are you the teacher?

No, io non sono il professore, sono l'allievo.
Noh, EE-*oh nohn* SOH-*noh eel proh-fess-*SOH-*reh,* SOH-*noh lahl-l'*YEH-*voh.*
No, I am not the teacher, I am the pupil.

Sono io il professore?
SOH-*noh* EE-*oh eel proh-fess-*SOH-*reh?*
Am I the teacher?

Sì, è Lei.
See, EH *Lay.*
Yes, you are.

Io sono in piedi.
EE-*oh* SOH-*noh een* p'YEH-*dee.*
I am standing.

Lei è seduto.
Lay EH *seh-*DOO-*toh.*
You are seated.

La signora Magnani è in piedi.
*Lah seen-*YOH-*rah Mahn-*YAH-*nee* EH *een* p'YEH-*dee.*
Mrs. Magnani is standing.

Il signor Di Maggio è in piedi.
*Eel seen-*YOHR *Dee* MAH-*djoh* EH *een* p'YEH-*dee.*
Mr. Di Maggio is standing.

La signorina Cinzano è in piedi.
*Lah seen-yoh-*REE-*nah Cheen-*TSAH-*noh* EH *een* p'YEH-*dee.*
Miss Cinzano is standing.

La signora Rossellini è seduta.
*Lah seen-*YOH-*rah Rohs-sel-*LEE-*nee* EH *seh-*DOO-*tah.*
Mrs. Rossellini is seated.

Il signor Branca è seduto.
*Eel seen-*YOHR BRAHN-*kah* EH *seh-*DOO-*toh.*
Mr. Branca is seated.

Sono io seduto?
SOH-*noh* EE-*oh seh-*DOO-*toh?*
Am I seated?

No, Lei è in piedi.
Noh, Lay EH *een* p'YEH-*dee.*
No, you are standing.

Io sono la signora Lupino; sono in piedi.
EE-*oh* SOH-*noh lah seen-*YOH-*rah Loo-*PEE-*noh;* SOH-*noh een* p'YEH-*dee.*
I am Mrs. Lupino; I am standing.

Sono io la signora Marconi?
SOH-*noh* EE-*oh lah seen-*YOH-*rah Mahr-*KOH-*nee?*
Am I Mrs. Marconi?

No, signora, Lei è la signora Lupino.
*Noh, seen-*YOH-*rah, Lay* EH *lah seen-*YOH-*rah Loo-*PEE-*noh.*
No, madam, you are Mrs. Lupino.

Sono io seduta?
SOH-*noh* EE-*oh seh-*DOO-*tah?*
Am I seated?

No, signora, Lei non è seduta: Lei è in piedi.
*Noh, seen-*YOH-*rah, Lay noh-*NEH *seh-*DOO-*tah: Lay* EH *een* p'YEH-*dee.*
No, madam, you are not seated: you are standing.

NOTE to Student: *Il* and *la* must always precede the words *signore* and *signora* or *signorina,* except when addressing a person. Ex: *Buon giorno, signor Pinza.*—"Good morning Mr. Pinza."; *Il signor Branca è in piedi.*—"Mr. Branca is standing." *Sig., Sig.ra, Sig.na* are the abbreviations for *signore, signora* and *signorina* and are used only in business letters and addresses. Note the unusual position of the periods.

Io sono italiano.
EE-*oh* SOH-*noh ee-tahl-*YAH-*noh.*
I am Italian.

Lei è americano.
Lay EH *ah-meh-ree-*KAH-*noh.*
You are American.

Sono io americano?
SOH-*noh* EE-*oh ah-meh-ree-*KAH-*noh?*
Am I American?

No, Lei non è americano, è italiano.
*Noh, Lay noh-*NEH *ah-meh-ree-*KAH-*noh,* EH *ee-tahl-*YAH-*noh.*
No, you are not American, you are Italian.

È la signorina Albanese americana?
EH *lah seen-yoh-*REE-*nah Ahl-bah-*NEH-*zeh ah-meh-ree-*KAH-*nah?*
Is Miss Albanese American?

No, essa è italiana.
Noh, ESS-*sah* EH *ee-tahl-*YAH-*nah.*
No, she is Italian.

È il signor Berlitz italiano?
EH *eel seen-*YOHR BEHR-*leets*
*ee-tahl-*YAH-*noh?*
Is Mr. Berlitz Italian?

Sì, egli è italiano.
See, EHL-*yee* EH *ee-tahl-*YAH-*noh.*
Yes, he is Italian.

NOTE: In Italian you may say: *Io sono italiano* or simply *sono italiano*—"I am Italian." The subject is not necessary since the verb form shows who or what is acting.

16	17	18
sedici	diciassette	diciotto
SEH-*dee-chee*	*dee-chahs-*SET-*teh*	*dee-*CHOT-*toh*

19	20
diciannove	venti
*dee-chahn-*NOH-*veh*	VEHN-*tee*

THINKING IN ITALIAN

(Answers on page 282)

1. Chi è Lei?
2. È Lei americano?
3. È Lei il professore?
4. È Lei italiano?
5. Sono io il signor Berlitz?
6. Sono io il professore?
7. Sono io italiano?
8. Sono americano?
9. Arturo Toscanini è italiano?
10. È italiano Bing Crosby?
11. È Ingrid Bergman italiana?
12. È Carmen Miranda americana, francese o brasiliana?
13. Chi è americano, Maurice Chevalier o il generale MacArthur?
14. Il signor Churchill è inglese o tedesco?
15. Il signor Stalin è spagnolo o russo?
16. È Hirohito cinese o giapponese?

Qual' è?
Kwahl EH?
Which one is it?

Questo cappello è nero;
KWESS-*toh kahp*-PEL-*loh* EH NEH-*roh;*
This hat is black;

quel cappello è grigio.
kwell kahp-PEL-*loh* EH GREE-*joh.*
that hat is gray.

Quale cappello è nero?
KWAH-*leh kahp*-PEL-*loh* EH NEH-*roh?*
Which hat is black?

Questo.
KWESS-*toh.*
This one.

Quale cappello è grigio?
KWAH-*leh kahp*-PEL-*loh* EH GREE-*joh?*
Which hat is gray?

Quello.
KWELL-*loh.*
That one.

22

Questa scatola è nera;
KWESS-*tah* SKAH-*toh-lah* EH NEH-*rah;*
This box is black;

quella scatola è gialla.
KWELL-*lah* SKAH-*to-lah* EH JAHL-*lah.*
that box is yellow.

Quale scatola è nera?
KWAH-*leh* SKAH-*toh-lah* EH NEH-*rah?*
Which box is black?

Questa.
KWESS-*tah.*
This one.

Quale scatola è gialla?
KWAH-*leh* SKAH-*toh-lah* EH JAHL-*lah?*
Which box is yellow?

Quella.
KWELL-*lah.*
That one.

Questo è il mio libro;
KWESS-*toh* EH *eel* MEE-*oh* LEE-*broh;*
This is my book;

quello è il Suo libro;
KWELL-*loh* EH *eel* SOO-*oh* LEE-*broh;*
that is your book;

quello è il libro del signor Rossi;   quello è il suo libro.
KWELL-*loh* EH *eel* LEE-*broh del seen*-YOHR ROHS-*see;*   KWELL-*loh* EH *eel*
SOO-*oh* LEE-*broh.*
that one is Mr. Rossi's book;   that one is his book.

Questa è la mia penna;
KWESS-*tah* EH *lah* MEE-*ah* PEHN-*nah;*
This is my pen;

quella è la Sua penna;
KWELL-*lah* EH *lah* SOO-*ah* PEHN-*nah;*
that one is your pen;

quella è la penna della signora Barbirolli;
KWELL-*lah* EH *lah* PEHN-*nah* DEL-*lah seen*-YOH-*rah Bahr-bee*-ROHL-*lee;*
that one is Mrs. Barbirolli's pen;

quella è la sua penna.
KWELL-*lah* EH *lah* SOO-*ah* PEHN-*nah.*
that is her pen.

Che cosa è questo?
Keh KOH-*zah* EH KWESS-*toh?*
What is this?

È il mio libro.
EH *eel* MEE-*oh* LEE-*broh.*
It is my book.

È questo il guanto del signor Brazzi?
EH KWESS-*toh eel* GWAHN-*toh del
seen*-YOHR BRAH-*tsee?*
Is this Mr. Brazzi's glove?

Sì, è il suo guanto.
See, EH *eel* SOO-*oh* GWAHN-*toh.*
Yes, it is his glove.

È questo il mio libro?
EH KWESS-*toh eel* MEE-*oh* LEE-*broh?*
Is this my book?

Sì, è il Suo libro.
See, EH *eel* SOO-*oh* LEE-*broh.*
Yes, it is your book.

È questo il Suo vestito o la Sua camicia?
EH KWESS-*toh eel* SOO-*oh vehs*-TEE-*toh oh lah* SOO-*ah kah*-MEE-*chah?*
Is this your suit or your shirt?

Non è nè il mio vestito nè la mia camicia,
Noh-NEH NEH *eel* MEE-*oh vehs*-TEE-*toh* NEH *lah* MEE-*ah kah*-MEE-*chah*,
It is neither my suit nor my shirt,

è la mia giacca.
EH *lah* MEE-*ah* JAHK-*kah*.
it is my jacket.

DON'T FORGET! *Suo* (masculine) and *Sua* (feminine) means "your" when written with a capital *S*, but they express "his" or "her" when written with a small *s*. Ex: *Questo è il Suo fazzoletto*—"This is your handkerchief."; *Questo è il suo fazzoletto*—"This is his (or her) handkerchief." Of course the sound of *Suo* is the same in either case, yet, surprisingly enough, this similarity does not create confusion in the course of a conversation.

Questo signore è mio padre;
KWESS-*toh seen*-YOH-*reh* EH MEE-*oh* PAH-*dreh;*
This gentleman is my father;

quel giovane è mio fratello;
kwell JOH-*vah-neh* EH MEE-*oh frah*-TEL-*loh;*
that young man is my brother;

quel bambino è mio figlio.
kwell bahm-BEE-*noh* EH MEE-*oh* FEE-*l'yoh*.
that child is my son.

È Sua sorella questa signora?
EH SOO-*ah soh*-REHL-*lah* KWESS-*tah seen*-YOH-*rah?*
Is this lady your sister?

No, signore, è mia moglie.
Noh, seen-YOH-*reh,* EH MEE-*ah* MOH-*l'yeh*.
No, sir, she is my wife.

Questa signorina è mia sorella.
KWESS *tah seen-yoh*-REE-*nah* EH MEE-*ah soh*-REHL-*lah*.
This young lady is my sister.

Chi è quella signora?
Kee EH KWELL-*lah seen*-YOH-*rah?*
Who is that lady?

È mia madre.
EH MEE-*ah* MAH-*dreh*.
It is my mother.

NOTE to Student: *Mio*—"my", *Suo*—"your", *suo*—"his or her" and their corresponding feminine forms are always preceded by the articles *il* or *la* when indicating a possession. Ex: *Il mio libro*—"My book."; *Questo è il Suo cappello*—"This is your hat." The same adjectives are used without the articles whenever they indicate family relatives, but only in the singular form. Ex: *Questo signore è mio padre*—"This gentleman is my father."; *Quella signorina è Sua sorella?*—"Is that young lady your sister?"

Di chi è questo cappello?
Dee kee EH KWESS-*toh kahp*-PEL-*loh?*
Whose hat is this?

È del signor Vinci.
EH *dehl seen*-YOHR VEEN-*chee.*
It is Mr. Vinci's.

È della signora Masi.
EH DEHL-*lah seen*-YOH-*rah* MAH-*see.*
It is Mrs. Masi's.

È questo il Suo lapis?
EH KWESS-*toh eel* SOO-*oh* LAH-*peess?*
Is this your pencil?

No, signore.
Noh, seen-YOH-*reh.*
No, sir.

Qual'è il Suo lapis?
Kwahl-EH *eel* SOO-*oh* LAH-*peess?*
Which is your pencil?

Quello.
KWELL-*loh.*
That one.

È questa la mia penna?
EH KWESS-*tah lah* MEE-*ah* PEHN-*nah?*
Is this my pen?

No, signora.
Noh, seen-YOH-*rah.*
No, madam.

Qual'è la mia penna?
Kwahl-EH *lah* MEE-*ah* PEHN-*nah?*
Which is my pen?

È quella.
EH KWELL-*lah.*
That one is.

È questo il cappello del signor Pecora?
EH KWESS-*toh eel kahp*-PEL-*loh dehl seen*-YOHR PEH-*koh-rah?*
Is this Mr. Pecora's hat?

No, non è il suo cappello.
Noh, noh-NEH *eel* SOO-*oh kahp*-PEL-*loh.*
No, it is not his hat.

REMEMBER: *Quale è*—"which is" becomes *qual'è* because purity and simplicity of sounds is an important part of the Italian language. For the same reason *di il* and *di la*—"of the" become respectively *del* (masculine) and *della* (feminine).

Qual'è il cappello del signor Pecora?
*Kwahl-*EH *eel kahp-*PEL-*loh dehl seen-*YOHR PEH-*koh-rah?*
Which is Mr. Pecora's hat?

Quello.
KWELL-*loh.*
That one.

Qual'è il mio lapis?
*Kwahl-*EH *eel* MEE-*oh* LAH-*peess?*
Which is my pencil?

Questo.
KWESS-*toh.*
This one.

Qual'è il Suo guanto?
*Kwahl-*EH *eel* SOO-*oh* GWAHN-*toh?*
Which is your glove?

Quello.
KWELL-*loh.*
That one.

Qual'è il guanto della signorina Respighi?
*Kwahl-*EH *eel* GWAHN-*toh* DEHL-*lah*
    *seen-yoh-*REE-*nah Rehs-*PEE-*ggee?*
Which is Miss Respighi's glove?

È quello.
EH KWELL-*loh.*
It is that one.

Quale libro è rosso?
KWAH-*leh* LEE-*broh* EH ROHS-*soh?*
Which book is red?

Questo.
KWESS-*toh.*
This one.

È questo il libro rosso?
EH KWESS-*toh eel* LEE-*broh* ROHS-*soh?*
Is this the red book?

Sì, è questo.
See, EH KWESS-*toh.*
Yes, this is it.

Qual'è il libro blu (azzurro)?
*Kwahl-*EH *eel* LEE-*broh bloo (ah-*DZOOR-*roh)?*
Which is the blue book?

NOTE on "Blue": *Blu*—"blue" is used in Italian as much as *azzurro;* technically, *blu* is dark blue, *azzurro* is light blue (azure).

21	22	23
ventuno	**ventidue**	**ventitrè**
*vehn-*TOO-*noh*	*vehn-tee-*DOO-*eh*	*vehn-tee-*TREH

24	25
ventiquattro	**venticinque**
*vehn-tee-*KWAHT-*troh*	*vehn-tee-*CHEEN-*kweh*

THINKING IN ITALIAN

(Answers on page 282)

1. È nero il cappello del professore?
2. È grande il cappello del soldato?
3. Di che colore è il Suo cappello?
4. È il mio cappello verde?
5. È piccola la borsetta della signora Fibronia?
6. E la borsetta di Titina, è grande?
7. Questo lapis è blu, quello è verde È questo lapis blu?

8. È quel lapis grigio?
9. Di che colore è il Suo fazzoletto?
10. La Sua casa è grande o piccola?
11. È quello il suo libro?
12. Di che colore è il cappello del professore?
13. È lunga la gonnella della signora Fibronia?
14. È corta la gonnella di Titina?

Signora Fibronia

Titina

LEZIONE 7

Dov'è?

Doh-VEH?

Where is it?

Il libro è sopra la tavola.
Eel LEE-*broh* EH SOH-*prah lah* TAH-*voh-lah*.
The book is on the table.

Il libro è sulla tavola.
Eel LEE-*broh* EH SOOL-*lah*
TAH-*voh-lah*.
The book is on the table.

La scatola è sotto la tavola.
Lah SKAH-*toh-lah* EH SOHT-*toh lah* TAH-*voh-lah*.
The box is under the table.

Il cappello non è sul pavimento.
Eel kahp-PEL-*loh* noh-NEH *sool pah-vee*-MEHN-*toh*.
The hat is not on the floor.

NOTE to Student: *Sul,* masculine (formed by *su* and *il*) *sulla,* feminine (formed by *su* and *la*) meaning "on the", and *sopra,* meaning "on top" or "above" can be equally used.

Io sono il professore.
EE-*oh* SOH-*noh eel proh-fess-*SOH-*reh.*
I am the teacher.

Lei è lo studente.
Lay EH *loh stoo-*DEN-*teh.*
You are the student.

Io sono davanti alla porta.
EE-*oh* SOH-*noh dah-*VAHN-*tee* AHL-*lah* POHR-*tah.*
I am in front of the door.

Lei è dietro alla tavola.
Lay EH *d'*YEH-*troh* AHL-*lah* TAH-*voh-lah.*
You are behind the table.

Il signor Palmieri è italiano.
*Eel seen-*YOHR *Pahl-m'*YEH-*ree* EH
    *ee-tahl-*YAH-*noh.*
Mr. Palmieri is Italian.

Egli è fra me e Lei.
EHL-*yee* EH *frah meh eh Lay.*
He is between me and you.

Questa signora è italiana.
KWESS-*tah seen-*YOH-*rah* EH
    *ee-tahl-*YAH-*nah.*
This lady is Italian.

Essa è seduta.
ESS-*sah* EH *seh-*DOO-*tah.*
She is sitting.

Quella signorina è spagnola.
KWELL-*lah seen-yoh-*REE-*nah* EH *spahn-*YOH-*lah.*
That young lady is Spanish.

È in piedi.
EH *een p'*YEH-*dee.*
She is standing.

Dov'è il libro?
*Doh-*VEH *eel* LEE-*broh?*
Where is the book?

È sopra la tavola.
EH SOH-*prah lah* TAH-*voh-lah.*
It is on the table.

Dov'è la scatola?
*Doh-*VEH *lah* SKAH-*toh-lah?*
Where is the box?

La scatola è sotto la tavola.
Lah SKAH-*toh-lah* EH SOHT-*toh lah*
    TAH-*voh-lah.*
The box is under the table.

Chi sono io?
Kee SOH-*noh* EE-*oh?*
Who am I?

Lei è il professore.
Lay EH *eel proh-fess-*SOH-*reh.*
You are the teacher.

Dove sono io?
DOH-*veh* SOH-*noh* EE-*oh?*
Where am I?

Lei è davanti alla porta.
Lay EH *dah-*VAHN-*tee* AHL-*lah* POHR-*tah.*
You are in front of the door.

NOTE to Student: *Dov'è* is the combination of *dove,* "where" and *è,* "is".

Chi è Lei?
Kee EH *Lay?*
Who are you?

Io sono lo studente.
EE-*oh* SOH-*noh loh stoo-*DEN-*teh.*
I am the pupil.

Dov'è Lei?
*Doh-*VEH *Lay?*
Where are you?

Io sono dietro alla tavola.
EE-*oh* SOH-*noh d'*YEH-*troh* AHL-*lah* TAH-*voh-lah.*
I am behind the table.

Dov'è il signor Palmieri?
*Doh-*VEH *eel seen-*YOHR *Pahl-m'*YEH-*ree?*
Where is Mr. Palmieri?

Fra Lei e me.
Frah Lay eh meh.
Between you and me.

La porta è davanti a me.
Lah POHR-*tah* EH *dah-*VAHN-*tee*
ah meh.
The door is in front of me.

È davanti a Lei.
EH *dah-*VAHN-*tee ah Lay.*
It is in front of you.

La finestra è dietro a me.
*Lah fee-*NESS-*trah* EH *d'*YEH-*troh ah meh.*
The window is behind me.

Dov'è la finestra?
*Doh-*VEH *lah fee-*NESS-*trah?*
Where is the window?

Dietro a Lei.
*d'*YEH-*troh ah Lay.*
Behind you.

Bravo!
BRAH-*voh!*
Very good!

Grazie!
GRAHTS-*yeh!*
Thank you!

REMEMBER: *Alla* is formed by *a* ("of") and *la* ("the") and is used in conjunction with feminine names; *al* is the preposition to be used in front of masculine names, as we will see in the course of future lessons. You must have noticed, however, that in front of the pronouns only *a* ("of") is being used, the same as in English. Ex: *Il signor Berlitz è davanti alla finestra*—"Mr. Berlitz is in front of the window."; *La signora è davanti al muro*—"The lady is in front of the wall."; *La tavola è davanti a me*—"The table is in front of me."

Il cappello è sulla sedia.
*Eel kahp-*PEL-*loh* EH SOOL-*lah*
SEHD-*yah.*
The hat is on the chair.

Il lapis è sul cappello.
Eel LAH-*peess* EH *sool kahp-*PEL-*loh.*
The pencil is on the hat.

Dov'è il lapis?
*Doh-*VEH *eel* LAH-*peess?*
Where is the pencil?

È sul cappello.
EH *sool kahp-*PEL-*loh.*
It is on the hat.

Dov'è il cappello?
*Doh-*VEH *eel kahp·*PEL-*loh?*
Where is the hat?

La carta è sotto la scatola.
Lah KAHR-*tah* EH SOHT-*toh lah*
   SKAH-*toh-lah.*
The paper is under the box.

Dov'è la carta?
*Doh-*VEH *lah* KAHR-*tah?*
Where is the paper?

Dov'è la penna?
*Doh-*VEH *lah* PEHN-*nah?*
Where is the pen?

La penna è dentro la scatola.
Lah PEHN-*nah* EH DEHN-*troh lah* SKAH-*toh-lah.*
The pen is in the box.

>   **(La penna è nella scatola.)**
>   **(*Lah* PEHN-*nah* EH NEHL-*lah* SKAH-*toh-lah.*)**
>   (The pen is in the box.)

La camicia è dentro il cassetto.
*Lah kah-*MEE-*chah* EH DEHN-*troh eel kahs-*SET-*toh.*
The shirt is in the drawer.

>   **(La camicia è nel cassetto.)**
>   **(*Lah kah-*MEE-*chah* EH *nehl kahs-*SET· *toh.*)**
>   (The shirt is in the drawer.)

È sulla sedia.
EH SOOL-*lah* SEHD-*yah.*
It is on the chair.

La penna è sul libro.
Lah PEHN-*nah* EH *sool*
   LEE-*broh.*
The pen is on the book.

È sotto la scatola.
EH SOHT-*toh lah* SKAH-*toh-lah.*
It is under the box.

È sul libro. (È sopra il libro.)
(EH *sool* LEE-*broh.* (EH SOH-*prah eel* LEE-*broh.*)
It is on the book. (It is on top of the book.)

 NOTE ON CONTRACTIONS: *Nel,* masculine and *nella,* feminine are respectively the combined form of *in il* and *in la;* they both mean "in the". *Dentro* is "inside"; therefore: *Nel cassetto*—"In the drawer" or *dentro il cassetto*— "inside the drawer" express the same thought.

Dov'è la penna?
*Doh-*VEH *lah* PEHN-*nah?*
Where is the pen?

Dov'è la camicia?
*Doh-*VEH *lah kah-*MEE-*chah?*
Where is the shirt?

È nella scatola.
EH NEHL-*lah* SKAH-*toh-lah.*
It is in the box.

È nel cassetto.
EH *nehl kahs-*SET-*toh.*
It is in the drawer.

E la cravatta, è sotto il letto?
*Eh lah krah-*VAHT-*tah,* EH SOHT-*toh eel* LET-*toh?*
And the tie, is it under the bed?

No, signore, la cravatta è sopra il letto.
*Noh, seen-*YOH*-reh, lah krah-*VAHT*-tah* EH SOH-*prah eel* LET-*toh.*
No, sir, the tie is on the bed.

La parete è dietro a me;
*Lah pah-*REH*-teh* EH *d'*YEH-*troh
ah meh;*
The wall is behind me;

la tavola è davanti a me.
lah TAH-*voh-lah* EH *dah-*VAHN-*tee
ah meh.*
the table is in front of me.

Perciò, io sono fra la tavola e la parete.
*Pehr-*CHOH*, ee-oh* SOH-*noh frah lah* TAH-*voh-lah eh lah pah-*REH-*teh.*
Therefore, I am between the table and the wall.

È la tavola dietro a me?
EH *lah* TAH-*voh-lah d'*YEH-*troh
ah meh?*
Is the table behind me?

No, la tavola è davanti a Lei.
Noh, lah TAH-*voh-lah* EH *dah-*VAHN-*tee
ah Lay.*
No, the table is in front of you.

Che cosa è dietro a me?
Keh KOH-*zah* EH *d'*YEH-*troh ah meh?*
What is behind me?

La parete, signore.
*Lah pah-*REH-*teh, seen-*YOH-*reh.*
The wall, sir.

Dove sono io, allora?
DOH-*veh* SOH-*noh* EE-*oh, ahl-*LOH-*rah?*
Where am I, then?

Lei è fra la tavola e la parete.
Lay EH *frah lah* TAH-*voh-lah eh lah pah-*REH-*teh.*
You are between the table and the wall.

Dov'è il signor Palmieri?
*Doh-*VEH *eel seen-*YOHR *Pahl-m'*YEH-*ree?*
Where is Mr. Palmieri?

Egli è tra Lei e me.
EHL-*yee* EH *trah Lay eh meh.*
He is between you and me.

HELPFUL HINT: That *tra,* in the sentence: *Egli è tra Lei e me,* is not a misprint; it means "between", the same as *fra.*

Bravissimo! La Sua memoria è ottima.
*Brah-*VEES-*see-moh! Lah* SOO-*ah meh-*MOH-*r'yah* EH OHT-*tee-mah.*
Excellent! Your memory is very good.

Grazie, signore, Lei è molto buono.
GRAHTS-*yeh, seen-*YOH-*reh, Lay* EH MOHL-*toh b'*WOH-*noh.*
Thank you, sir, you are very kind.

Io sono in piedi davanti alla porta.
EE-*oh* SOH-*noh een p'*YEH-*dee dah-*VAHN-*tee* AHL-*lah* POHR-*tah.*
I am standing in front of the door.

Lei è seduto dietro alla tavola.
Lay EH *seh-*DOO-*toh d'*YEH-*troh* AHL-*lah* TAH-*voh-lah.*
You are sitting behind the table.

La signorina De Marco è seduta davanti alla finestra.
*Lah seen-yoh-*REE-*nah Deh* MAHR-*koh* EH *seh-*DOO-*tah dah-*VAHN-*tee*
    AHL-*lah fee-*NESS-*trah.*
Miss De Marco is sitting in front of the window.

Il signor Vergara è in piedi davanti alla parete.
*Eel seen-*YOHR *Vehr-*GAH-*rah* EH *een p'*YEH-*dee dah-*VAHN-*tee*
    AHL-*lah pah-*REH-*teh.*
Mr. Vergara is standing in front of the wall.

Dove sono io?	**Lei è davanti alla porta.**
DOH-*veh* SOH-*noh* EE-*oh?*	*Lay* EH *dah-*VAHN-*tee* AHL-*lah* POHR-*tah.*
Where am I?	You are in front of the door.

Sono io in piedi o seduto?	**Lei è in piedi.**
SOH-*noh* EE-*oh een p'*YEH-*dee oh seh-*DOO-*toh?*	*Lay* EH *een p'*YEH-*dee.*
Am I standing or sitting?	You are standing.

È Lei in questa stanza?	**Sì, signore.**
EH *Lay een* KWESS-*tah* STAHN-*tsah?*	*See, seen-*YOH-*reh.*
Are you in this room?	Yes, sir.

È Lei in piedi?
EH *Lay een p'*YEH-*dee?*
Are you standing?

No, io non sono in piedi, sono seduto.
Noh, EE-*oh nohn* SOH-*noh een p'*YEH-*dee,* SOH-*noh seh-*DOO-*toh.*
No, I am not standing, I am sitting.

È la signorina De Marco in piedi?
EH *lah seen-yoh-*REE-*nah Deh* MAHR-*koh een p'*YEH-*dee?*
Is Miss De Marco standing?

No, essa non è in piedi, ma seduta.
Noh, ESS-*sah noh-*NEH *een p'*YEH-*dee, mah seh-*DOO-*tah.*
No, she is not standing, but sitting.

È in piedi il signor Vergara?
EH *een p'*YEH-*dee eel seen-*YOHR *Vehr-*GAH-*rah?*
Is Mr. Vergara standing?

Sì, egli è in piedi davanti alla parete.
See, EHL-*yee* EH *een p'*YEH-*dee dah-*VAHN-*tee* AHL-*lah pah-*REH-*teh.*
Yes, he is standing in front of the wall.

È egli in questa stanza?
EH EHL-*yee een* KWESS-*tah*
STAHN-*tsah?*
Is he in this room?

Sì, egli è in questa stanza.
See, EHL-*yee* EH *een* KWESS-*tah*
STAHN-*tsah.*
Yes, he is in this room.

REMEMBER: *Parete* applies to indoor walls, such as the room divisions within a house. An outside wall is called: *muro.*

Roma è in Italia.
ROH-*mah* EH *een* Ee-TAHL-*yah.*
Rome is in Italy.

Parigi è in Francia.
*Pah-*REE-*jee* EH *een* FRAHNT-*chah.*
Paris is in France.

Vienna è in Austria.
*Vee-*EHN-*nah* EH *een* AOUS-*tree-ah.*
Vienna is in Austria.

Londra è in Inghilterra.
LOHN-*drah* EH *een* Een-ggeel-TEHR-*rah.*
London is in England.

È Napoli in Italia?
EH NAH-*poh-lee een* Ee-TAHL-*yah?*
Is Naples in Italy?

Sì, è in Italia.
See, EH *een* Ee-TAHL-*yah.*
Yes, it is in Italy.

È Londra in Francia?
EH LOHN-*drah een* FRAHNT-*chah?*
Is London in France?

No, Londra non è in Francia, ma in Inghilterra.
Noh, LOHN-*drah noh-*NEH *een* FRAHNT-*chah, mah een* Een-ggeel-TEHR-*rah.*
No, London is not in France, but in England.

Dov'è Parigi?
*Doh-*VEH *Pah-*REE-*jee?*
Where is Paris?

Parigi è in Francia.
*Pah-*REE-*jee* EH *een* FRAHNT-*chah.*
Paris is in France.

Dov'è Vienna?
*Doh-*VEH *Vee-*EHN-*nah?*
Where is Vienna?

In Austria.
Een AOUS-*tree-ah.*
In Austria.

È il signor Palmieri in questa stanza?
EH *eel seen-*YOHR *Pahl-m'*YEH-*ree een* KWESS-*tah* STAHN-*tsah?*
Is Mr. Palmieri in this room?

Sì, egli è qui.
See, EHL-*yee* EH *kwee.*
Yes, he is here.

Dov'è il mio cappello?
*Doh-*VEH *eel* MEE-*oh kahp-*PEL-*loh?*
Where is my hat?

È qui, sulla sedia.
EH *kwee,* SOOL-*lah* SEHD-*yah.*
It is here, on the chair.

Dov'è il libro?
*Doh-*VEH *eel* LEE-*broh?*
Where is the book?

È li, sulla tavola.
EH *lee,* SOOL-*lah* TAH-*voh-lah.*
It is there, on the table.

Dov'è la parete?
*Doh-*VEH *lah pah-*REH-*teh?*
Where is the wall?

È li, dietro a Lei.
EH *lee, d'*YEH-*troh ah Lay.*
It is there, behind you.

Dov'è la finestra?
*Doh-*VEH *lah fee-*NESS-*trah?*
Where is the window?

Dov'è la tavola?
*Doh-*VEH *lah* TAH-*voh-lah?*
Where is the table?

È qui, davanti a me.
EH *kwee, dah-*VAHN-*tee ah meh.*
It is here, in front of me.

Dov'è la porta?
*Doh-*VEH *lah* POHR-*tah?*
Where is the door?

È li, davanti a Lei.
EH *lee, dah-*VAHN-*tee ah Lay.*
It is there, in front of you.

È qui il signor Berlitz?
EH *kwee eel seen-*YOHR BEHR-*leets?*
Is Mr. Berlitz here?

No, egli non è qui,
Noh, EHL-*yee noh-*NEH *kwee,*
No, he is not here,

è in Italia.
EH *een Ee-*TAHL-*yah.*
he is in Italy.

26	27	28
ventisei	ventisette	ventotto
*vehn-tee-*SAY	*vehn-tee-*SET-*teh*	*vehn-*TOHT-*toh*

29	30
ventinove	trenta
*vehn-tee-*NOH-*veh*	TREHN-*tah*

NOTE to Student: *Italia, America, Roma, Francia, Vienna,* etc., being proper geographical names, begin with capital letters; but the adjectives and nouns deriving from such names will be written with a small first letter: *italiano, americano, romano, francese, viennese,* etc.; unless, of course, they are at the beginning of a sentence.

THINKING IN ITALIAN

(Answers on page 282)

1. Dov'è il libro?
2. È sotto la sedia il libro?
3. È la penna davanti alla tavola?
4. Dov'è la penna?
5. Dov'è la sedia?
6. Dov'è il professore?
7. È il professore sotto la tavola?
8. È il professore in piedi dietro alla tavola?
9. È Lei in piedi davanti alla porta?
10. È Lei seduto sulla sedia?
11. È la carta dentro il libro?
12. È la carta nella scatola?
13. Dov'è la scatola?
14. È la scatola sopra la tavola?
15. È la penna nella scatola?
16. È la chiave sotto la sedia?
17. Questo lapis è rosso, quel lapis è nero. Di che colore è quel lapis?
18. È nero quel lapis?
19. Di che colore è questo lapis?
20. È grande o piccolo questo libro?

LEZIONE 8

Che cosa fa il professore?
Keh KOH-*zah fah eel proh-fess-*SOH-*reh?*
What does the teacher do?

Il professore prende il libro.
*Eel proh-fess-*SOH-*reh* PREHN-*deh eel* LEE-*broh.*
The teacher takes the book.

Il professore mette il libro sulla sedia.
*Eel proh-fess-*SOH-*reh* MET-*teh eel* LEE-*broh* SOOL-*lah* SEHD-*yah.*
The teacher puts the book on the chair.

Il professore prende la riga.
*Eel proh-fess-*SOH-*reh* PREHN-*deh lah* REE-*gah.*
The teacher takes the ruler.

Egli mette la riga sotto la tavola.
EHL-*yee* MET-*teh lah* REE-*gah* SOHT-*toh lah* TAH-*voh-lah.*
He puts the ruler under the table.

Il professore apre il libro.
*Eel proh-fess-*SOH-*reh* AH-*preh eel* LEE-*broh.*
The teacher opens the book.

Egli chiude il libro.
EHL-*yee k'*YOO-*deh eel* LEE-*broh.*
He closes the book.

Il professore porta la sedia alla finestra.
*Eel proh-fess-*SOH-*reh* POHR-*tah lah* SEHD-*yah* AHL-*lah fee-*NESS-*trah.*
The teacher carries the chair to the window.

Prende il lapis il professore?
PREHN-*deh eel* LAH-*peess eel proh-fess-*SOH-*reh?*
Does the teacher take the pencil?

No, egli non prende il lapis,
Noh, EHL-*yee nohn* PREHN-*deh eel* LAH-*peess,*
No, he does not take the pencil,

> **prende il libro.**
> PREHN-*deh eel* LEE-*broh.*
> he takes the book.

Adesso, prende egli la scatola?
*Ah-*DEHS-*soh,* PREHN-*deh* EHL-*yee lah* SKAH-*toh-lah?*
Now, does he take the box?

No, egli non prende la scatola.
Noh, EHL-*yee nohn* PREHN-*deh lah* SKAH-*toh-lah.*
No, he does not take the box.

Mette la scatola sulla tavola il professore?
MET-*teh lah* SKAH-*toh-lah* SOOL-*lah* TAH-*voh-lah eel proh-fess-*SOH-*reh?*
Does the teacher put the box on the table?

Sì, egli mette la scatola sulla tavola.
See, EHL-*yee* MET-*teh lah* SKAH-*toh-lah* SOOL-*lah* TAH-*voh-lah.*
Yes, he puts the box on the table.

Mette egli la riga sulla sedia?
MET-*teh* EHL-*yee lah* REE-*gah* SOOL-*lah* SEHD-*yah?*
Does he put the ruler on the chair?

No, egli non mette la riga sulla sedia.
Noh, EHL-*yee nohn* MET-*teh lah* REE-*gah* SOOL-*lah* SEHD-*yah.*
No, he does not put the ruler on the chair.

Dove mette la riga il professore?
DOH-*veh* MET-*teh lah* REE-*gah eel proh-fess-*SOH-*reh?*
Where does the teacher put the ruler?

Egli mette la riga sotto la tavola.
EHL-yee MET-teh lah REE-gah SOHT-toh lah TAH-voh-lah.
He puts the ruler under the table.

Apre il libro il professore?
AH-preh eel LEE-broh eel proh-fess-SOH-reh?
Does the teacher open the book?

Sì, egli apre il libro.
See, EHL-yee AH-preh eel LEE-broh.
Yes, he opens the book.

Apre la porta il professore?
AH-preh lah POHR-tah eel proh-fess-SOH-reh?
Does the teacher open the door?

Sì, egli apre la porta.
See, EHL-yee AH-preh lah POHR-tah.
Yes, he opens the door.

Chiude egli la porta?
k'YOO-deh EHL-yee lah POHR-tah?
Does he close the door?

No, egli non chiude la porta.
Noh, EHL-yee nohn k'YOO-deh lah POHR-tah.
No, he does not close the door.

Porta la sedia nel corridoio il professore?
POHR-tah lah SEHD-yah nehl kohr-ree-DOY-oh eel proh-fess-SOH-reh?
Does the teacher carry the chair into the corridor?

No, egli non porta la sedia nel corridoio.
Noh, EHL-yee nohn POHR-tah lah SEHD-yah nehl kohr-ree-DOY-oh.
No, he does not carry the chair into the corridor.

Che cosa fa il professore?
Keh KOH-zah fah eel proh-fess-SOH-reh?
What does the teacher do?

Egli porta la sedia alla finestra.
EHL-yee POHR-tah lah SEHD-yah AHL-lah fee-NESS-trah.
He carries the chair to the window.

NOTE to Student: "To bring" and "to take" are translated in Italian by *portare* when referring to objects. The true meaning of *portare* is "to carry". Therefore, when referring to persons one must avoid the use of this verb unless one actually carries somebody.

REMEMBER: Do not confuse *porta,* verb, with *porta,* noun, meaning "door"; the noun is always accompanied by the article.

Il professore va alla porta.
*Eel proh-fess-*SOH*-reh vah* AHL-*lah* POHR-*tah.*
The teacher goes to the door.

Va alla finestra il professore?
Vah AHL-*lah fee-*NESS-*trah eel proh-fess-*SOH-*reh?*
Does the teacher go to the window?

No, egli non va alla finestra.
Noh, EHL-*yee nohn vah* AHL-*lah fee-*NESS-*trah.*
No, he does not go to the window.

Dove va?
DOH-*veh vah?*
Where does he go?

Egli va alla porta.
EHL-*yee vah* AHL-*lah* POHR-*tah.*
He goes to the door.

Che cosa fa il professore?
Keh KOH-*zah fah eel proh-fess-*SOH-*reh?*
What does the teacher do?

Va alla porta.
Vah AHL-*lah* POHR-*tah.*
He goes to the door.

Il professore viene davanti a Lei.
EEL *proh-fess-*SOH-*reh v'*YEH-*neh dah-*VAHN-*tee ah Lay.*
The teacher comes before you.

Viene davanti a Lei il professore?
*v'*YEH-*neh dah-*VAHN-*tee ah Lay eel proh-fess-*SOH-*reh?*
Does the teacher come before you?

Sì, egli viene davanti a me.
See, EHL-*yee v'*YEH-*neh dah-*VAHN-*tee ah meh.*
Yes, he comes before me.

Viene il professore in questa stanza?
*v'*YEH-*neh eel proh-fess-*SOH-*reh een* KWESS-*tah* STAHN-*tsah?*
Does the teacher come into this room?

Sì, egli viene in questa stanza.
See EHL-*yee v'*YEH-*neh een* KWESS-*tah* STAHN-*tsah.*
Yes, he comes into this room.

Il professore chiude la porta.
*Eel proh-fess-*SOH-*reh k'*YOO-*deh lah* POHR-*tah.*
The teacher closes the door.

Egli apre la finestra.
EHL-*yee* AH-*preh lah*
*fee-*NESS-*trah.*
He opens the window.

NOTE to Student: In the previous lesson you saw the word *alla* being used to express "of the": *Il professore è davanti alla porta*—"The teacher is in front of the door." In the present lesson it is demonstrated that *alla* also means "to the": *Il professore va alla porta*—"The teacher goes to the door."

Io sono il professore.
EE-*oh* SOH-*noh eel proh-fess*-SOH-*reh.*
I am the teacher.

Io prendo il libro.
EE-*oh* PREHN-*doh eel* LEE-*broh.*
I take the book.

Prenda il libro, signor Calvi.
PREHN-*dah eel* LEE-*broh, seen*-YOHR KAHL-*vee.*
Take the book, Mr. Calvi.

Lei prende il libro.
Lay PREHN-*deh eel* LEE-*broh.*
You take the book.

Egli prende il libro.
EHL-*yee* PREHN-*deh eel* LEE-*broh.*
He takes the book.

Io metto il libro sulla sedia.
EE-*oh* MET-*toh eel* LEE-*broh* SOOL-*lah* SEHD-*yah.*
I put the book on the chair.

Che cosa faccio io?
Keh KOH-*zah* FAHT-*choh* EE-*oh?*
What am I doing?

Signorina Costanzi, metta il libro sulla tavola.
Seen-yoh-REE-*nah Kohs*-TAHN-*tsee,* MET-*tah eel* LEE-*broh* SOOL-*lah* TAH-*voh-lah.*
Miss Costanzi, put the book on the table.

Che cosa fa Lei?
Keh KOH-*zah fah Lay?*
What are you doing?

Prende Lei il libro?
PREHN-*deh Lay eel* LEE-*broh?*
Do you take the book?

Sì, io prendo il libro.
See, EE-*oh* PREHN-*doh eel* LEE-*broh.*
Yes, I take the book.

Prendo io la scatola?
PREHN-*doh* EE-*oh lah* SKAH-*toh-lah?*
Do I take the box?

No, Lei non prende la scatola.
Noh, Lay nohn PREHN-*deh lah* SKAH-*toh-lah.*
No, you do not take the box.

Mette Lei il libro sulla sedia?
MET-*teh Lay eel* LEE-*broh* SOOL-*lah* SEHD-*yah?*
Do you put the book on the chair?

Sì, io metto il libro sulla sedia.
See, EE-*oh* MET-*toh eel* LEE-*broh* SOOL-*lah* SEHD-*yah.*
Yes, I put the book on the chair.

No, io non metto il libro sulla sedia.
Noh, EE-*oh nohn* MET-*toh eel* LEE-*broh* SOOL-*lah* SEHD-*yah.*
No, I do not put the book on the chair.

Metto io il denaro nella mia tasca?
MET-*toh* EE-*oh eel deh-*NAH-*roh* NEHL-*lah* MEE-*ah* TAHS-*kah?*
Do I put the money in my pocket?

No, Lei non mette il denaro nella Sua tasca.
Noh, Lay nohn MET-*teh eel deh-*NAH-*roh* NEHL-*lah* SOO-*ah* TAHS-*kah.*
No, you do not put the money in your pocket.

Che cosa faccio io? *Keh* KOH-*zah* FAHT-*choh* EE-*oh?* What am I doing?	**Lei prende il libro.** *Lay* PREHN-*deh eel* LEE-*broh.* You take the book.
Prenda la penna. PREHN-*dah lah* PEHN-*nah.* Take the pen.	**Prende Lei la penna?** PREHN-*deh Lay lah* PEHN-*nah?* Do you take the pen?

No, io non prendo la penna.
Noh, EE-*oh nohn* PREHN-*doh lah* PEHN-*nah.*
No, I do not take the pen.

Sì, io prendo la penna.
See, EE-*oh* PREHN-*doh lah* PEHN-*nah.*
Yes, I take the pen.

Prego, ripeta. PREH-*goh,* ree-PEH-*tah.* Please, repeat.	**Prendo la penna.** PREHN-*doh lah* PEHN-*nah.* Take the pen.	**Grazie.** GRAHTS-*yeh.* Thanks.

ATTENTION: You must have noticed that in many instances the pronoun subject does not appear in a sentence. The verb form indicates the subject, as you have been told in a previous lesson.

Che cosa faccio io? *Keh* KOH-*zah* FAHT-*choh* EE-*oh?* What am I doing?	**(Che faccio io?)** *(Keh* FAHT-*choh* EE-*oh?)* (What am I doing?)
Lei apre il libro. *Lay* AH-*preh eel* LEE-*broh.* You open the book.	**Apro io la finestra?** AH-*proh* EE-*oh lah fee-*NESS-*trah?* Do I open the window?

No, Lei non apre la finestra, ma il libro.
Noh, Lay nohn AH-*preh lah fee-*NESS-*trah, mah eel* LEE-*broh.*
No, you don't open the window, but the book.

Dove vado io?
DOH-*veh* VAH-*doh* EE-*oh?*
Where am I going?

Io vado verso la finestra.
EE-*oh* VAH-*doh* VEHR-*soh lah* fee-NESS-*trah.*
I am going to the window.

Vado io verso la porta?
VAH-*doh* EE-*oh* VEHR-*soh lah* POHR-*tah?*
Do I go to the door?

No, signore, Lei va verso la finestra.
*Noh, seen-*YOH-*reh, Lay vah* VEHR-*soh lah* fee-NESS-*trah.*
No, sir, you go to the window.

Vada verso la porta, signore.
VAH-*dah* VEHR-*soh lah* POHR-*tah, seen-*YOH-*reh.*
Go to the door, sir.

Va Lei verso la finestra?
Vah Lay VEHR-*soh lah* fee-NESS-*trah?*
Do you go to the window?

No, io non vado verso la finestra.
Noh, EE-*oh nohn* VAH-*doh* VEHR-*soh lah* fee-NESS-*trah.*
No, I am not going to the window.

Verso dove va Lei?
VEHR-*soh* DOH-*veh vah Lay?*
Towards where are you going?

Vado verso la porta.
VAH-*doh* VEHR-*soh lah* POHR-*tah.*
I go to the door.

Venga verso la tavola.
VEHN-*gah* VEHR-*soh lah* TAH-*voh-lah.*
Come to the table.

Viene Lei verso la sedia?
*v'*YEH-*neh Lay* VEHR-*soh lah* SEHD-*yah?*
Do you come to the chair?

No, io non vengo verso la sedia.
Noh, EE-*oh nohn* VEHN-*goh* VEHR-*soh lah* SEHD-*yah.*
No, I am not coming to the chair.

Che cosa fa Lei?
Keh KOH-*zah fah Lay?*
What are you doing?

Vengo verso la tavola.
VEHN-*goh* VEHR-*soh lah* TAH-*voh-lah.*
I am coming to the table.

Io vengo dal corridoio nella stanza.
EE-*oh* VEHN-*goh dahl kohr-ree-*DOY-*oh* NEHL-*lah* STAHN-*tsah.*
I come from the corridor into the room.

Vengo io verso Lei?
VEHN-*goh* EE-*oh* VEHR-*soh Lay?*
Do I come towards you?

No, signore, Lei non viene verso di me.
*Noh, seen-*YOH-*reh, Lay nohn v'*YEH-*neh*
VEHR-*soh dee meh.*
No, sir, you do not come towards me.

Verso chi vado io?
VEHR-*soh kee* VAH-*doh* EE-*oh?*
Towards whom do I go?

Lei va verso il signor Ratti.
Lay vah VEHR-*soh eel seen-*YOHR RAHT-*tee.*
You go towards Mr. Ratti.

Venga qui.
VEHN-*gah kwee.*
Come here.

Viene Lei davanti a me?
*v'*YEH-*neh Lay dah-*VAHN-*tee ah meh?*
Do you come before me?

Sì, io vengo davanti a Lei.
See, EE-*oh* VEHN-*goh dah-*VAHN-*tee ah Lay.*
Yes, I come in front of you.

Da dove viene Lei?
Dah DOH-*veh v'*YEH-*neh Lay?*
From where do you come?

Vengo dalla porta.
VEHN-*goh* DAHL-*lah* POHR-*tah.*
I come from the door.

Venga alla lavagna, signore.
VEHN-*gah* AHL-*lah lah-*VAHN-*yah, seen-*YOH-*reh.*
Come to the blackboard, sir.

Venga alla lavagna, signorina.
VEHN-*gah* AHL-*lah lah-*VAHN-*yah, seen-yoh-*REE-*nah.*
Come to the blackboard, miss.

Che cosa fa Lei?
Keh KOH-*zah fah Lay?*
What are you doing?

E che cosa fa la signorina?
Eh keh KOH-*zah fah lah seen-yoh-*REE-*nah?*
And what is the young lady doing?

Niente, signore!
*n'*YEHN-*teh, seen-*YOH-*reh!*
Nothing, sir!

Lei non capisce la mia domanda, non è vero?
*Lay nohn kah-*PEE-*sheh lah* MEE-*ah doh-*MAHN-
*dah, noh-*NEH VEH-*roh?*
You do not understand my question, do you?

No, signore, non capisco.
*Noh, seen-*YOH-*reh, nohn kah-*PEESS-*koh.*
No, sir, I do not understand it.

Male! Lei viene alla lavagna, e la signorina viene pure alla lavagna.
MAH-*leh! Lay v'*YEH-*neh* AHL-*lah lah-*VAHN-*yah, eh lah seen-yoh-*REE-*nah*
*v'*YEH-*neh* POO-*reh* AHL-*lah lah-*VAHN-*yah.*
Too bad! You come to the blackboard and the young lady also comes to the
blackboard.

Capisce adesso?
*Kah-*PEE-*sheh ah-*DEHS-*soh?*
Do you understand now?

Sì, signore, capisco.
*See, seen-*YOH-*reh, kah-*PEESS-*koh.*
Yes, sir, I understand.

Benone!
Very good!
*Beh-*NOH-*neh!*

Prenda il lapis, signore.
PREHN-*dah eel* LAH-*peess,*
*seen-*YOH-*reh.*
Take the pencil, sir.

Metta la carta sulla tavola.
MET-*tah lah* KAHR-*tah* SOOL-*lah*
TAH-*voh-lah.*
Put the paper on the table.

NOTE on the Imperative: When asking a person to do something you must use the imperative form of the verb instead of the indicative. Ex. *Lei va alla finestra*—"You go to the window." *Vada all finestra*—"Go to the window." The regular verbs form this imperative by adding *a* to the root (of verbs with infinitive ending in *ere* and *ire*) or adding *i* to the root (of verbs with infinitive ending in *are*). The sad truth is that in Italian, as in most languages, few of the most commonly used verbs are regular, so just watch the text and note the exceptions.

Prende Lei la penna?
PREHN-*deh Lay lah* PEHN-*nah?*
Do you take the pen?

No, io non la prendo.
Noh, EE-*oh nohn lah* PREHN-*doh.*
No, I do not take it.

Prende il lapis?
PREHN-*deh eel* LAH-*peess?*
Do you take the pencil?

Sì, lo prendo.
See, loh PREHN-*doh.*
Yes, I take it.

Mette Lei la carta sulla tavola?
MET-*teh Lay lah* KAHR-*tah* SOOL-*lah* TAH-*voh-lah?*
Do you put the paper on the table?

Sì, io la metto sulla tavola.
See, EE-*oh lah* MET-*toh* SOOL-*lah* TAH-*voh-lah.*
Yes, I put it on the table.

Prende Lei il cappello?
PREHN-*deh Lay eel kahp-*PEL-*loh?*
Do you take the hat?

No, io non lo prendo.
Noh, EE-*oh nohn loh* PREHN-*doh.*
No, I do not take it.

Prendo io il cappello?
PREHN-*doh* EE-*oh eel kahp-*PEL-*loh?*
Do I take the hat?

Sì, Lei lo prende.
See, Lay loh PREHN-*deh.*
Yes, you take it.

IMPORTANT NOTE: *Lo* (masculine) and *la* (feminine) used here as pronouns, mean "it" and they invariably precede the verb, (except in some cases when used with imperative form of verbs, but we will tell you more about it in future lessons). Ex: *Prendo io il cappello?*—"Do I take the hat?"; *Sì, Lei lo prende*—"Yes, you take it."; *Prende Lei la penna?*—"Do you take the pen?"; *Sì, io la prendo*—"Yes, I take it."

THINKING IN ITALIAN
(Answers on page 283)

1. Che cosa fa il professore?
2. Prende il libro il professore?
3. Mette egli il libro sulla tavola?
4. Prende egli la scatola?
5. È il professore in piedi o seduto?

6. Chiude la finestra il professore?
7. Che cosa fa il professore?
8. Apre egli la porta o la finestra?
9. Apre Lei la porta?
10. Apre la porta il professore?

11. Va a New York il professore?
12. Va egli a Parigi?
13. Dove va il professore?
14. È Roma grande o piccola?
15. Va Lei a Roma?
16. Chi va a Pisa, Lei o il professore?

LEZIONE 9

Contando
Kohn-TAHN-*doh*
Counting

1
Uno
ɔo-noh
One

5
cinque
CHEEN-*kweh*
five

9
nove
NOH-*veh*
nine

13
tredici
TREH-*dee-chee*
thirteen

2
due
DOO-*eh*
two

6
sei
say
six

10
dieci
*d'*YEH-*chee*
ten

14
quattordici
*kwaht-*TOHR-*dee-chee*
fourteen

3
tre
treh
three

7
sette
SET-*teh*
seven

11
undici
OON-*dee-chee*
eleven

15
quindici
KWEEN-*dee-chee*
fifteen

4
quattro
KWAHT-*troh*
four

8
otto
OHT-*toh*
eight

12
dodici
DOH-*dee-chee*
twelve
47

16
sedici
SEH-*dee-chee*
sixteen

17
diciassette
*dee-chahs-*SET*-teh*
seventeen

18
diciotto
*dee-*CHOT*-toh*
eighteen

19
diciannove
*dee-chahn-*NOH*-veh*
nineteen

20
venti
VEHN*-tee*
twenty

21
ventuno
*vehn-*TOO*-noh*
twenty-one

22
ventidue
*vehn-tee-*DOO*-eh*
twenty-two

23
ventitrè
*vehn-tee-*TREH
twenty-three

30
trenta
TREHN*-tah*
thirty

31
trentuno
*trehn-*TOO*-noh*
thirty-one

32
trentadue
*trehn-tah-*DOO*-eh*
thirty-two

33
trentatrè
*trehn-tah-*TREH
thirty-three

40
quaranta
*kwah-*RAHN*-tah*
forty

41
quarantuno
*kwah-rahn-*TOO*-noh*
forty-one

42
quarantadue
*kwah-rahn-tah-*DOO*-eh*
forty-two

50
cinquanta
*cheen-*KWAHN*-tah*
fifty

51
cinquantuno
*cheen-kwahn-*TOO*-noh*
fifty-one

52
cinquantadue
*cheen-kwahn-tah-*DOO*-eh*
fifty-two

60
sessanta
*sehs-*SAHN*-tah*
sixty

61
sessantuno
*sehs-sahn-*TOO*-noh*
sixty-one

62
sessantadue
*sehs-sahn-tah-*DOO*-eh*
sixty-two

70
settanta
*set-*TAHN*-tah*
seventy

71
settantuno
*set-tahn-*TOO*-noh*
seventy-one

72
settantadue
*set-tahn-tah-*DOO*-eh*
seventy-two

80
ottanta
*oht-*TAHN*-tah*
eighty

81
ottantuno
*oht-tahn-*TOO*-noh*
eighty-one

82
ottantadue
*oht-tahn-tah-*DOO*-eh*
eighty-two

90
novanta
*noh-*VAHN*-tah*
ninety

91
novantuno
*noh-vahn-*TOO*-noh*
ninety-one

92
novantadue
*noh-vahn-tah-*DOO*-eh*
ninety-two

100
cento
CHEHN*-toh*
one hundred

500
cinquecento
*cheen-kweh-*CHEHN*-toh*
five hundred

1000
mille
MEEL*-leh*
one thousand

365
trecentosessantacinque
*treh-*CHEHN*-toh-sehs-*SAHN*-tah-*CHEEN*-kweh*
three hundred sixty-five

2000
due mila
DOO*-eh* MEE*-lah*
two thousand

1950
millenovecentocinquanta.
MEEL*-leh-noh-veh-*CHEHN*-toh-cheen-*KWAHN*-tah.*
nineteen hundred fifty.

Contare:
*Kohn-*TAH*-reh:*
To count:

Io conto.
EE*-oh* KOHN*-toh.*
I count.

Lei conta.
Lay KOHN*-tah.*
You count.

Conti.
KOHN*-tee.*
Count.

Uno, due, tre, quattro .... ecc.
OO*-noh,* DOO*-eh, treh,* KWAHT*-troh ....* eht*-*CHEH*-teh-rah.*
One, two, three, four .... etc.

Lei conta da uno a quattro.
Lay KOHN*-tah dah* OO*-noh ah* KWAHT*-troh.*
You count from one to four.

Io conto da dieci a quindici:
EE*-oh* KOHN*-toh dah d'*YEH*-chee ah* KWEEN*-dee-chee:*
I count from ten to fifteen:

dieci
*d'*YEH*-chee*
ten

undici
OON*-dee-chee*
eleven

dodici
DOH*-dee-chee*
twelve

tredici
TREH*-dee-chee*
thirteen

quattordici
*kwaht-*TOHR*-dee-chee*
fourteen

quindici
KWEEN*-dee-chee*
fifteen

Che cosa faccio io?
Keh KOH*-zah* FAHT*-choh* EE*-oh?*
What do I do?

Lei conta.
Lay KOHN*-tah.*
You count.

Che cosa fa Lei?
Keh KOH*-zah fah Lay?*
What do you do?

Io conto.
EE*-oh* KOHN*-toh.*
I count.

Conti da venti a trenta.
KOHN*-tee dah* VEHN*-tee ah* TREHN*-tah.*
Count from twenty to thirty.

Da che numero conta Lei?
Dah keh NOO-*meh-roh* KOHN-*tah Lay?*
From what number do you count?

Fino a che numero conta il signore?
FEE-*noh ah keh* NOO-*meh-roh* KOHN-*tah eel seen-*YOH-*reh?*
Up to what number does the gentleman count?

Che numeri sono questi?
Keh NOO-*meh-ree* SOH-*noh* KWESS-*tee?*
What numbers are these?

3, 13, 30, 50, ecc.
Treh, TREH-*dee-chee,* TREHN-*tah,*
  *cheen-*KWAHN-*tah, eht-*CHEH-*teh-rah.*
Three, thirteen, thirty, fifty, etc.

NOTE to Student: In previous lessons you have seen the word *sono*—"I am", being applied to the first person singular: *Io sono italiano*—"I am Italian." In the above sentence. *Che numeri sono questi?*—"What numbers are these?" the same word is used for the third person plural. This coincidence occurs *only* in the case of the verb *essere,* "to be."

Un libro
Oon LEE-*broh*
One book

due libri
DOO-*eh* LEE-*bree*
two books

tre libri
treh LEE-*bree*
three books

una sedia
OO-*nah* SEHD-*yah*
one chair

due sedie
DOO-*eh* SEHD-*yeh*
two chairs

tre sedie
treh SEHD-*yeh*
three chairs

  2 più 2 fanno 4
  DOO-*eh p'*YOO DOO-*eh* FAHN-*noh* KWAHT-*troh.*
  Two and two make four.

Quanto fanno 3 più 5?
KWAHN-*toh* FAHN-*noh treh p'*YOO
  CHEEN-*kweh?*
How much do three and five make?

3 più 5 fanno 8.
*Treh p'*YOO CHEEN-*kweh* FAHN-*noh*
  OHT-*toh.*
Three and five make eight.

2 per 4 fanno 8.
DOO-*eh pehr* KWAHT-*troh* FAHN-*noh*
  OHT-*toh.*
Two times four make eight.

Quanto fanno 5 per 3?
KWAHN-*toh* FAHN-*noh* CHEEN-*kweh*
  pehr treh?
How much do five times three make?

  5 per 3 fanno quindici.
  CHEEN-*kweh pehr treh* FAHN-*noh* KWEEN-*dee-chee.*
  Five times three make fifteen.

  Questo giornale costa quindici lire.
  KWESS-*toh johr-*NAH-*leh* KOHS-*tah* KWEEN-*dee-chee* LEE-*reh.*
  This newspaper costs fifteen lire.

Il cappello costa 3000 lire.
*Eel kahp-*PEL*-loh* KOHS*-tah treh-*MEE*-lah* LEE*-reh.*
The hat costs 3000 lire.

Quanti libri vi sono sulla tavola?
KWAHN*-tee* LEE*-bree vee* SOH*-noh* SOOL*-lah* TAH*-vohlah?*
How many books are there on the table?

Sei.
Say.
Six.

Quanti lapis vi sono?
KWAHN*-tee* LAH*-peess vee* SOH*-noh?*
How many pencils are there?

Otto.
OHT*-toh.*
Eight.

Quante sedie vi sono in questa stanza?
KWAHN*-teh* SEHD*-yeh vee* SOH*-noh een* KWESS*-tah* STAHN*-tsah?*
How many chairs are there in this room?

Dieci.
*d'*YEH*-chee.*
Ten.

Quante finestre?
KWAHN*-teh fee-*NESS*-treh?*
How many windows?

Quante porte?
KWAHN*-teh* POHR*-teh?*
How many doors?

REMEMBER: *Quanti* and *quante*—"how many", are respectively the plural of *quanto* (masculine) and *quanta* (feminine) meaning: "how much". When the noun is plural the adjectives, and of course the predicate verbs, also become plural. As a general rule when an adjective ends with *o* or *e* in the singular it becomes *i* in the plural; if it ends with *a* it becomes *e*. You will learn the plural verb forms progressively in the course of future lessons.

Quanti chilometri vi sono da Roma a Firenze?
KWAHN*-tee kee-*LOH*-meh-tree vee* SOH*-noh dah* ROH*-mah ah Fee-*REHN*-tseh?*
How many kilometers are there from Rome to Florence?

Quanto costa questo libro?
KWAHN*-toh* KOHS*-tah* KWESS*-toh* LEE*-broh?*
How much does this book cost?

Costa 300 lire.
KOHS*-tah treh-*CHEHN*-toh* LEE*-reh.*
It costs 300 lire.

Quanto costa l'orologio?
KWAHN*-toh* KOHS*-tah loh-roh-*LOH*-joh?*
How much does the watch cost?

Costa 5000 lire.
KOHS*-tah* CHEEN*-kweh-*MEE*-lah* LEE*-reh.*
It costs 5000 lire.

THINKING IN ITALIAN
(Answers on page 283)

1. Signore, conti da uno a dieci. Che fa Lei?
2. Io conto: 1, 2, 3,...ecc. Che faccio io?
3. Che cosa fa il professore?
4. Quante sedie vi sono in questa stanza?
5. Vi è una tavola?
6. Quanti libri italiani vi sono sulla tavola?
7. Quanto fanno 6 più 5?
8. Fanno cinque 2 più 2?
9. Quanto fanno 7 per 3?
10. Fanno tredici 4 per 3?
11. Quanto costa un giornale americano?
12. Costa mille dollari questo libro?
13. Vale 300 lire un dollaro?
14. Vale un dollaro una lira?
15. Che numero è questo?

LEZIONE 10

Il corpo umano
Eel KOHR-*poh* oo-MAH-*noh*
The human body

La testa
Lah TESS-*tah*
The head

i capelli
*ee kah-*PEHL-*lee*
the hair

il naso
eel NAH-*zoh*
the nose

la bocca
lah BOHK-*kah*
the mouth

le spalle
leh SPAHL-*leh*
the shoulders

la lingua
lah LEEN-*gwah*
the tongue

un occhio
oon OCK-*k'yoh*
one eye

i due occhi
ee DOO-*eh* OCK-*kee*
the two eyes

la fronte
lah FROHN-*teh*
the forehead

il collo
eel KOLL-*loh*
the neck

una gamba
oo-nah GAHM-*bah*
one leg

le due gambe
leh DOO-*eh*
  GAHM-*beh*
the two legs

il dorso
eel DOHR-*soh*
the back.

il petto
eel PET-*toh*
the chest

un dito
oon DEE-*toh*
a finger

le dita
leh DEE-*tah*
the fingers

un orecchio
*oon oh-*REHK-*k'yoh*
one ear

i due orecchi
ee DOO-*eh*
   *oh-*REHK-*kee*
the two ears

un piede
*oon p'*YEH-*deh*
one foot

i due piedi
ee DOO-*eh p'*YEH-*dee*
the two feet

un braccio
oon BRAHT-*choh*
an arm

le due braccia
leh DOO-*eh*
   BRAHT-*chah*
the two arms

una mano
oo-nah MAH-*noh*
a hand

le due mani
leh DOO-*eh* MAH-*nee*
the two hands

il ginocchio
*eel jee-*NOCK-*k'yoh*
the knee

le ginocchia
*leh jee-*NOCK-*k'yah*
the knees

il dente
eel DEHN-*teh*
the tooth

i denti
ee DEHN-*tee*
the teeth

il labbro
eel LAHB-*broh*
the lip

le labbra
leh LAHB-*brah*
the lips

il braccio destro
eel BRAHT-*choh* DEHS-*troh*
the right arm

il braccio sinistro
eel BRAHT-*choh* see-NEES-*troh*
the left arm

la mano destra
lah MAH-*noh* DEHS-*trah*
the right hand

la mano sinistra
lah MAH-*noh* see-NEES-*trah*
the left hand

LOOK OUT! *Braccio, dito, ginocchio* and *labbro* are masculine nouns that become feminine in the plural. Do not let these exceptions bewilder you, for they are not very frequent in the Italian language. They exist, in the case of parts of the human body, to distinguish them from the masculine plural forms of the same words which apply to other things. Ex: *Le braccia umane.*—"Human arms." *I bracci del candeliere.*—"The arms of a chandelier."

Che cosa è questo?
Keh KOH-*zah* EH KWESS-*toh?*
What is this?

È il libro.
EH *eel* LEE-*broh.*
It is the book.

Sono i libri.
SOH-*noh ee* LEE-*bree.*
They are the books.

È la scatola.
EH *lah* SKAH-*toh-lah.*
It is the box.

Sono le scatole.
SOH-*noh leh* SKAH-*toh-leh.*
They are the boxes.

È il gesso.
EH *eel* JEHS-*soh.*
It is the chalk.

È del gesso.
EH *dehl* JEHS-*soh.*
It is some chalk.

È la carta.
EH *lah* KAHR-*tah*.
It is the paper.

È un libro.
EH *oon* LEE-*broh*.
It is a book.

Sono dei libri.
SOH-*noh day* LEE-*bree*.
These are some books.

È della carta.
EH DEHL-*lah* KAHR-*tah*.
It is some paper.

È una scatola.
EH OO-*nah* SKAH-*toh-lah*.
It is a box.

Sono delle scatole.
SOH-*noh* DEHL-*leh* SKAH-*toh-leh*.
These are some boxes.

REMEMBER: *Dei* and *delle* are the plural of *del* (masculine) and *della* (feminine) meaning "some". Ex: *Del gesso* —"some chalk", *dei libri*—"some books", *della carta*—"some paper", *delle scatole*—"some boxes".

Che cosa è questo?
Keh KOH-*zah* EH KWESS-*toh?*
What is this?

È il piede destro.
EH *eel p'*YEH-*deh* DEHS-*troh*.
It is the right foot.

Sono i piedi.
SOH-*noh ee p'*YEH-*dee*.
These are the feet.

Che cosa è?
Keh KOH-*zah* EH?
What is it?

La mano destra.
Lah MAH-*noh* DEHS-*trah*.
The right hand.

È la mano sinistra.
EH *lah* MAH-*noh* see-NEES-*trah*.
It is the left hand.

Sono le mani.
SOH-*noh leh* MAH-*nee*.
These are the hands.

Di che colore è questo libro?
Dee keh koh-LOH-*reh* EH KWESS-*toh* LEE-*broh?*
What color is this book?

È rosso.
EH ROHS-*soh*.
It is red.

Di che colore sono questi libri?
Dee keh koh-LOH-*reh* SOH-*noh* KWESS-*tee* LEE-*bree?*
What color are these books?

Sono rossi.
SOH-*noh* ROHS-*see*.
They are red.

Sono blu le penne?
SOH-*noh bloo leh* PEHN-*neh?*
Are the pens blue?

No, non sono blu.
Noh, nohn SOH-*noh bloo*.
No, they are not blue.

Di che colore è questa sedia?
Dee keh koh-LOH-*reh* EH KWESS-*tah* SEHD-*yah?*
What color is this chair?

È gialla.
EH JAHL-*lah*.
It is yellow.

Di che colore sono queste sedie?
Dee keh koh-LOH-*reh* SOH-*noh* KWESS-*teh* SEHD-*yeh?*
What color are these chairs?

Sono gialle.
SOH-*noh* JAHL-*leh*.
They are yellow.

Sono grigie queste scatole?
SOH-*noh* GREE-*jeh* KWESS-*teh* SKAH-*toh-leh?*
Are these boxes gray?

No, non sono grigie.
Noh, nohn SOH-*noh* GREE-*jeh.*
No, they are not gray.

Di che colore sono questi libri?
*Dee keh koh-*LOH-*reh* SOH-*noh* KWESS-*tee* LEE-*bree?*
What color are these books?

L'uno è rosso, l'altro è nero.
LOO-*noh* EH ROHS-*soh,* LAHL-*troh* EH NEH-*roh.*
One is red, the other is black.

Chi è questo signore?
Kee EH KWESS-*toh seen-*YOH-*reh?*
Who is this gentleman?

È il signor Manzoni.
EH *eel seen-*YOHR *Mahn-*TSOH-*nee.*
It is Mr. Manzoni.

Chi sono questi signori?
Kee SOH-*noh* KWESS-*tee seen-*YOH-*ree?*
Who are these gentlemen?

Sono i signori Manzoni e Cerutti.
SOH-*noh ee seen-*YOH-*ree Mahn-*TSOH-*nee eh Cheh-*ROOT-*tee.*
These are Mr. Manzoni and Mr. Cerutti.

Chi è questa signora?
Kee EH KWESS-*tah seen-*YOH-*rah?*
Who is this lady?

È la signora Petrucci.
EH *lah seen-*YOH-*rah Peh-*TROOT-*chee.*
It is Mrs. Petrucci.

Chi sono queste signore?
Kee SOH-*noh* KWESS-*teh seen-*YOH-*reh?*
Who are these ladies?

Sono le signore Petrucci e Barberini.
SOH-*noh leh seen-*YOH-*reh Peh-*TROOT-*chee eh Bahr-beh-*REE-*nee.*
They are Mrs. Petrucci and Mrs. Barberini.

Chi è questa signorina?
Kee EH KWESS-*tah seen-yoh-*REE-*nah?*
Who is this young lady?

È la signorina Galli.
EH *lah seen-yoh-*REE-*nah* GAHL-*lee.*
It is Miss Galli.

Chi sono queste signorine?
Kee SOH-*noh* KWESS-*teh seen-yoh-*REE-*neh?*
Who are these young ladies?

Sono le signorine Galli e Visconti.
SOH-*noh leh seen-yoh-*REE-*neh* GAHL-*lee eh Vees-*KOHN-*tee.*
They are Miss Galli and Miss Visconti.

È italiana Lei, signorina?
EH *ee-tahl-*YAH-*nah Lay, seen-yoh-*REE-*nah?*
Are you Italian, Miss?

Sì, signore, sono italiana.
*See, seen-*YOH*-reh,* SOH*-noh ee-tahl-*YAH*-nah.*
Yes, sir, I am Italian.

Signorine, sono italiane Loro?
*Seen-yoh-*REE*-neh,* SOH*-noh ee-tahl-*YAH*-neh* LOH*-roh?*
Young ladies, are you Italians?

Sì, signore, siamo italiane.
*See, seen-*YOH*-reh, s'*YAH*-moh ee-tahl-*YAH*-neh.*
Yes, sir, we are Italians.

Signore, sono inglesi Loro?
*Seen-*YOH*-reh,* SOH*-noh een-*GLEH*-zee* LOH*-roh?*
Ladies, are you English?

No, non siamo inglesi, siamo americane.
*Noh, nohn s'*YAH*-moh een-*GLEH*-zee, s'*YAH*-moh ah-meh-ree-*KAH*-neh.*
No, we are not English, we are Americans.

> **Questo è il mio cappello.**
> KWESS*-toh* EH *eel* MEE*-oh kahp-*PEL*-loh.*
> This is my hat.

> **Questi sono i miei guanti.**
> KWESS*-tee* SOH*-noh ee m'*YAY GWAHN*-tee.*
> These are my gloves.

> **Questa è la Sua cravatta.**
> KWESS*-tah* EH *lah* SOO*-ah krah-*VAHT*-tah.*
> This is your tie.

> **Queste sono le Sue scarpe.**
> KWESS*-teh* SOH*-noh leh* SOO*-eh* SKAHR*-peh.*
> These are your shoes.

Qual'è il mio cappello? — **Questo.**
*Kwahl-*EH *eel* MEE*-oh kahp-*PEL*-loh?* — KWESS*-toh.*
Which is my hat? — This one.

Quali sono i miei guanti? — **Questi.**
KWAH*-lee* SOH*-noh ee m'*YAY GWAHN*-tee?* — KWESS*-tee.*
Which are my gloves? — These.

Qual'è la Sua cravatta? — **Questa.**
*Kwahl-*EH *lah* SOO*-ah krah-*VAHT*-tah?* — KWESS*-tah.*
Which is your tie? — This one.

Quali sono le Sue penne? — **Queste.**
KWAH*-lee* SOH*-noh leh* SOO*-eh* PEHN*-neh?* — KWESS*-teh.*
Which are your pens? — These.

Di chi è questo cappello?
Dee kee EH KWESS-*toh kahp-*PEL-*loh?*
Whose hat is this?

È del signor Orsini.
EH *dehl seen-*YOHR *Ohr-*SEE-*nee.*
It is Mr. Orsini's.

Di chi sono questi cappelli?
Dee kee SOH-*noh* KWESS-*tee kahp-*PEL-*lee?*
Whose hats are these?

Sono degli allievi.
SOH-*noh* DEHL-*yee ahl-l'*YEH-*vee.*
They are the pupils'.

Quali sono i libri degli allievi?
KWAH-*lee* SOH-*noh ee* LEE-*bree* DEHL-*yee ahl-l'*YEH-*vee?*
Which are the pupils' books?

Sono quelli.
SOH-*noh* KWELL-*lee.*
Those are.

Quali sono le sedie delle signorine?
KWAH-*lee* SOH-*noh leh* SEHD-*yeh* DEHL-*leh
seen-yoh-*REE-*neh?*
Which are the chairs of the ladies?

Sono quelle.
SOH-*noh* KWELL-*leh.*
Those are.

Di chi è questa sedia?
Dee kee EH KWESS-*tah* SEHD-*yah?*
Whose chair is this?

È di Giovanni.
EH *dee Joh-*VAHN-*nee.*
It is John's.

Di chi sono queste sedie?
Dee kee SOH-*noh* KWESS-*teh* SEHD-*yeh?*
Whose chairs are these?

Sono dei signori Berlitz e La Guardia.
SOH-*noh day seen-*YOH-*ree* BEHR-*leets eh Lah* GWAHR-*d'yah.*
They are Messrs. Berlitz's and La Guardia's.

THINKING IN ITALIAN

(Answers on page 283)

1. Che cosa ha sotto il braccio il professore?
2. Vi è un giornale sotto il braccio sinistro del professore?
3. Vi è la pipa nella tasca del professore?
4. Dov'è la carta?
5. È sotto il piede destro del professore la riga?
6. Che cosa vi è nella mano destra del professore?
7. Vi sono dei lapis nella scatola?
8. Vi sono delle chiavi sulla tavola?
9. Dove sono i libri?
10. Vi sono dei quadri alla parete?
11. Vi sono due cani sotto la tavola?
12. Quanti libri vi sono sulla tavola?
13. Vi è denaro nella tasca del professore?
14. Vi è un cappello sulla sedia?

Io scrivo l'alfabeto

EE-*oh* SKREE-*voh lahl-fah-*BEH-*toh*

I write the alphabet

Il professore prende il gesso;
*Eel proh-fess-*SOH-*reh* PREHN-*deh eel* JEHS-*soh;*
The teacher takes the chalk;

egli scrive sulla lavagna.
EHL-*yee* SKREE-*veh* SOOL-*lah lah-*VAHN-*yah.*
he writes on the blackboard.

Egli scrive l'alfabeto.
EHL-*yee* SKREE-*veh lahl-fah-*BEH-*toh.*
He writes the alphabet.

Che cosa fa il professore?
Keh KOH-*zah fah eel proh-fess-*SOH-*reh?*
What does the teacher do?

Prende il gesso e scrive.
PREHN-*deh eel* JEHS-*soh eh* SKREE-*veh.*
He takes the chalk and writes.

Dove scrive?
DOH-*veh* SKREE-*veh?*
Where does he write?

Sulla lavagna.
SOOL-*lah lah-*VAHN-*yah.*
On the blackboard.

Che cosa scrive?
Keh KOH-*zah* SKREE-*veh?*
What does he write?

L'alfabeto.
*Lahl-fah-*BEH-*toh.*
The alphabet.

Chi scrive sulla lavagna?
Kee SKREE-*veh* SOOL-*lah lah-*VAHN-*yah?*
Who is writing on the blackboard?

Il professore.
*Eel proh-fess-*SOH-*reh.*
The teacher.

Prenda un lapis e della carta, signor Bonelli.
PREHN-*dah oon* LAH-*peess eh* DEHL-*lah* KAHR-*tah, seen-*YOHR *Boh-*NEL-*lee.*
Take a pencil and paper, Mr. Bonelli.

Scriva l'alfabeto.
SKREE-*vah lahl-fah-*BEH-*toh.*
Write the alphabet.

Lei scrive l'alfabeto sulla carta.
Lay SKREE-*veh lahl-fah-*BEH-*toh* SOOL-*lah* KAHR-*tah.*
You write the alphabet on the paper.

Prenda il gesso e scriva l'alfabeto sulla lavagna.
PREHN-*dah eel* JEHS-*soh eh* SKREE-*vah lahl-fah-*BEH-*toh* SOOL-*lah lah-*VAHN-*yah.*
Take the chalk and write the alphabet on the blackboard.

Io scrivo;
EE-*oh* SKREE-*voh;*
I write;

Lei scrive.
Lay SKREE-*veh.*
you write.

Io scrivo l'alfabeto.
EE-*oh* SKREE-*voh lahl-fah-*BEH-*toh.*
I write the alphabet.

Scrive Lei?
SKREE-*veh Lay?*
Do you write?

Che cosa scrive Lei?
Keh KOH-*zah* SKREE-*veh Lay?*
What do you write?

Io scrivo delle lettere.
EE-*oh* SKREE-*voh* DEHL-*leh* LET-*teh-reh.*
I write letters.

Chi è che scrive?
Kee EH *keh* SKREE-*veh?*
Who is writing?

Che cosa scrivo io?
Keh KOH-*zah* SKREE-*voh* EE-*oh?*
What do I write?

Prenda un libro e legga.
PREHN-*dah oon* LEE-*broh eh* LEG-*gah.*
Take a book and read.

Io leggo,
EE-*oh* LEG-*goh,*
I read,

Lei legge.
Lay LEH-*djeh.*
You read.

Che cosa fa Lei?
Keh KOH-*zah fah Lay?*
What are you doing?

Io leggo.
EE-*oh* LEG-*goh.*
I am reading.

Che faccio io?
Keh FAHT-*choh* EE-*oh?*
What am I doing?

Lei legge.
Lay LEH-*djeh.*
You are reading.

Io leggo l'alfabeto:
EE-*oh* LEG-*goh lahl-fah-*BEH-*toh:*
I read the alphabet:

A,	B,	C,	D,	ecc.
Ah,	*Bee,*	*Chee,*	*Dee,*	*eht-*CHEH-*teh-rah.*
A,	B,	C,	D,	etc.

Che cosa leggo?
Keh KOH-*zah* LEG-*goh?*
What am I reading?

Lei legge l'alfabeto.
Lay LEH-*djeh lahl-fah-*BEH-*toh.*
You are reading the alphabet.

Io scrivo dei numeri sulla lavagna.
EE-*oh* SKREE-*voh day* NOO-*meh-ree* SOOL-*lah lah-*VAHN-*yah.*
I write numbers on the blackboard.

Legga questi numeri.
LEG-*gah* KWESS-*tee* NOO-*meh-ree.*
Read these numbers.

Io scrivo le lettere A e B.
EE-*oh* SKREE-*voh leh* LET-*teh-reh Ah eh Bee.*
I write the letters A and B.

Ecco una lettera;
ECK-*koh* OO-*nah* LET-*teh-rah;*
Here is a letter;

ecco un'altra lettera.
ECK-*koh oo-*NAHL-*trah* LET-*teh-rah.*
here is another letter.

Scrivo delle lettere:
SKREE-*voh* DEHL-*leh* LET-*teh-reh:*
I am writing letters:

A,	B,	C,	D.
Ah,	*Bee,*	*Chee,*	*Dee.*
A,	B,	C,	D.

Che cosa è questa?
Keh KOH-*zah* EH KWESS-*tah?*
What is this?

È una lettera.
EH OO-*nah* LET-*teh-rah.*
It is a letter.

Che lettera è questa?
Keh LET-*teh-rah* EH KWESS-*tah?*
What letter is this?

La lettera A.
Lah LET-*teh-rah Ah.*
The letter A.

Ecco la lettera C.
ECK-*koh lah* LET-*teh-rah Chee.*
Here is the letter C.

Che lettere sono queste?
Keh LET-*teh-reh* SOH-*noh* KWESS-*teh?*
What letters are these?

Sono le lettere A e B.
SOH-*noh leh* LET-*teh-reh Ah eh Bee.*
They are the letters A and B.

Io scrivo delle parole.
EE-*oh* SKREE-*voh* DEHL-*leh pah-*ROH-*leh*
I am writing (some) words.

Io scrivo la parola "tavola".
EE-*oh* SKREE-*voh lah pah-*ROH-*lah* "TAH-*voh-lah".*
I write the word "table".

Legga questa parola.
LEG-*gah* KWESS-*tah pah-*ROH-*lah.*
Read this word.

Che cosa legge Lei?
Keh KOH-*zah* LEH-*djeh Lay?*
What are you reading?

Signore, legga questo libro.
*Seen-*YOH-*reh,* LEG-*gah* KWESS-*toh* LEE-*broh.*
Sir, read this book.

Signorina, legga alla lavagna.
*Seen-yoh-*REE-*nah,* LEG-*gah* AHL-*lah lah-*VAHN-*yah.*
Young lady, read from the blackboard.

Che fa Lei?
Keh fah Lay?
What are you doing?

Io leggo il libro.
EE-*oh* LEG-*goh eel* LEE-*broh.*
I am reading the book.

Che cosa fa essa?
Keh KOH-*zah fah* ESS-*sah?*
What does she do?

Legge alla lavagna.
LEH-*djeh* AHL-*lah lah-*VAHN-*yah.*
She reads from the blackboard.

HELPFUL HINT: *Che fa?* is accepted in place of *che cosa fa?* but the second expression is more precise.

Ecco un'altra parola: "muro".
ECK-*koh oo-*NAHL-*trah pah-*ROH-*lah:* "MOO-*roh".*
Here is another word: "wall".

Quante lettere vi sono nella parola "Italia"?
KWAHN-*teh* LET-*teh-reh vee* SOH-*noh* NEHL-*lah pah-*ROH-*lah* "Ee-*TAHL-yah"?*
How many letters are there in the word "Italia"?

Nella parola "Italia" vi sono sei lettere.
NEHL-*lah pah-*ROH-*lah* "Ee-*TAHL-yah" vee* SOH-*noh say* LET-*teh-reh.*
In the word "Italia" there are six letters.

Ecco una parola francese: "monsieur".
ECK-*koh oo-nah pah-*ROH-*lah frahn-*CHEH-*zeh:* "*muss-yuh".*
Here is a French word: "monsieur".

"Monsieur" è una parola francese.
"Muss-yuh" EH oo-*nah pah-*ROH-*lah frahn-*CHEH-*zeh.*
"Monsieur" is a French word.

"Mister" è una parola inglese.
"Mister" EH oo-*nah pah-*ROH-*lah een-*GLEH-*zeh.*
"Mister" is an English word.

"Signore" è una parola italiana.
*"Seen-*YOH-*reh"* EH oo-*nah pah-*ROH-*lah ee-tahl-*YAH-*nah.*
"Signore" is an Italian word.

"Herr" è una parola tedesca.
"Hehr" EH OO-*nah* pah-ROH-*lah* teh-DESS-*kah.*
"Herr" is a German word.

È questo un libro francese?
EH KWESS-*toh oon* LEE-*broh* frahn-CHEH-*zeh?*
Is this a French book?

No, signore, quel libro non è francese.
Noh, seen-YOH-*reh, kwell* LEE-*broh noh*-NEH frahn-CHEH-*zeh.*
No, sir, this book is not French.

È inglese?   No, signore, è italiano.
EH *een*-GLEH-*zeh?*   *Noh, seen*-YOH-*reh,* EH *ee-tahl*-YAH-*noh.*
Is it English?   No, sir, it is Italian.

Io recito l'alfabeto italiano:
EE-*oh* REH-*chee-toh lahl-fah*-BEH-*toh ee-tahl*-YAH-*noh:*
I recite the Italian alphabet:

A	B	C	D	E	F
Ah	*Bee*	*Chee*	*Dee*	EH	EH-*feh*

G	H	I	L	M	N
Jee	AH-*kah*	*Ee*	EHL-*leh*	EHM-*meh*	EHN-*neh*

O	P	Q	R	S	T
OH	*Pee*	*Koo*	EHR-*reh*	ESS-*seh*	*Tee*

U	V	Z
Oo	*Voo*	DZEH-*tah*

Che cosa fa il professore?
Keh KOH-*zah fah eel proh-fess*-SOH-*reh?*
What does the teacher do?

Egli recita l'alfabeto.
EHL-*yee* REH-*chee-tah lahl-fah*-BEH-*toh.*
He recites the alphabet.

Reciti l'alfabeto, signore.
REH-*chee-tee lahl-fah*-BEH-*toh, seen*-YOH-*reh.*
Recite the alphabet, sir.

Io scrivo una frase:
EE-*oh* SKREE-*voh* OO-*nah* FRAH-*zeh:*
I write a sentence:

"Il cappello è sulla sedia".
"Eel kahp-PEL-*loh* EH SOOL-*lah* SEHD-*yah".*
"The hat is on the chair".

Quante parole vi sono in questa frase?
*KWAHN-teh pah-*ROH*-leh vee* SOH*-noh een* KWESS*-tah* FRAH*-zeh?*
How many words are there in this sentence?

In questa frase vi sono cinque parole.
Een KWESS*-tah* FRAH*-zeh vee* SOH*-noh* CHEEN*-kweh pah-*ROH*-leh.*
In this sentence there are five words.

NOTE to Student: When you want to know how a word is spelled in Italian you ask how the word is written. Ex: *Come si scrive la parola "grazie"?*—"How is the word 'grazie' written?"

A Roma si parla italiano.
Ah ROH*-mah see* PAHR*-lah ee-tahl-*YAH*-noh.*
In Rome they speak Italian.

A Parigi si parla francese.
*Ah Pah-*REE*-jee see* PAHR*-lah frahn-*CHEH*-zeh.*
In Paris they speak French.

A Londra si parla inglese.
Ah LOHN*-drah see* PAHR*-lah een-*GLEH*-zeh.*
In London they speak English.

A Berlino si parla tedesco.
*Ah Behr-*LEE*-noh see* PAHR*-lah teh-*DESS*-koh.*
In Berlin they speak German.

A Madrid si parla spagnolo.
*Ah Mah-*DREED *see* PAHR*-lah spahn-*YOH*-loh.*
In Madrid they speak Spanish.

NOTE on Geography: When referring to a city, "to" and "in" are translated by *a.* Ex: "In Paris they speak French"— *A Parigi si parla francese.* "The professor goes to Rome" —*Il professore va a Roma.* But you must use *in* when referring to a country or a continent. Ex: "The professor goes to Italy"—*Il professore va in Italia.* "In France they speak French"— *In Francia si parla francese.* "Mr. Berlitz goes to Europe"—*Il signor Berlitz va in Europa.* Exception is made for those countries which in Italian are considered of masculine gender, in which case *al* and *nel* are used, meaning "to the" and "in the". Ex. "In Canada"—*Nel Canada;* "To Canada" —*Al Canada.* As you can see from the above examples the impersonal form of *parlare,* "to speak", is—*si parla.* The true meaning of the sentence *A Parigi si parla francese,* is: "In Paris French is spoken."

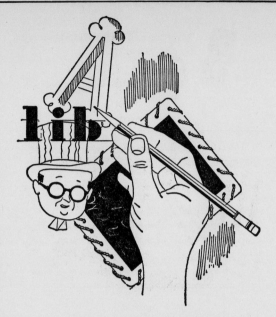

THINKING IN ITALIAN

(Answers on page 284)

1. Scriva la lettera A sulla carta. Che cosa fa Lei?
2. Io scrivo la parola "libertà". Che cosa scrivo io?
3. Il signor Cerutti scrive l'alfabeto sulla lavagna. Chi scrive l'alfabeto sulla lavagna?
4. Legga questa frase: "Io sono americano." Che fa Lei?
5. Quante lettere vi sono in questa frase?
6. Legge Lei questo libro?
7. Legge l'italiano il signor Berlitz?
8. Parla egli l'italiano?
9. Parla il russo il signor Galli?
10. Che parla Lei, l'inglese o l'italiano?
11. Parla lo spagnolo la signora Guasti?
12. È tedesca o francese la parola "gentleman"?
13. Io recito: A, B, C, D, ecc. Recito io l'alfabeto?
14. Recita Lei l'alfabeto russo?
15. Che alfabeto recita il professore d'italiano?
16. Che lingua si parla a New York?
17. Si parla italiano a Roma?
18. Si parla russo a Madrid?
19. Che lingua si parla a Berlino, lo spagnolo o l'italiano?

Dalla A alla Z
DAHL-*lah Ah* AHL-*lah* DZEH-*tah*
From A to Z

L'alfabeto italiano comincia con la lettera A
*Lahl-fah-*BEH-*toh ee-tahl-*YAH-*noh koh-*MEENT-*chah kohn lah* LET-*teh-rah Ah*
The Italian alphabet begins with the letter A

e finisce con la lettera Z.
*eh fee-*NEE-*sheh kohn lah* LET-*teh-rah* DZEH-*tah.*
and ends with the letter Z.

A è la prima lettera,	**B la seconda,**
Ah EH *lah* PREE-*mah* LET-*teh-rah,*	*Bee lah seh-*KOHN-*dah,*
A is the first letter,	B the second,
C è la terza,	**D è la quarta,**
Chee EH *lah* TEHR-*tsah,*	*Dee* EH *lah* KWAHR-*tah,*
C is the third,	D is the fourth,
E è la quinta,	**F la sesta,**
EH EH *lah* KWEEN-*tah.*	EH-*feh lah* SEHS-*tah,*
E is the fifth,	F the sixth,

G la settima,
Jee lah SET-*tee-mah*
G the seventh,

H la ottava,
AH-*kah lah* oht-TAH-*vah,*
H the eighth,

I la nona,
Ee lah NOH-*nah,*
I the ninth,

L la decima, ecc.
EHL-*leh lah* DEH-*chee-mah,* eht-CHEH-*teh-rah.*
L the tenth, etc.

Z è l'ultima lettera.
DZEH-*tah* EH LOOL-*tee-mah* LET-*teh-rah.*
Z is the last letter.

Quante lettere vi sono nell'alfabeto italiano?
KWAHN-*teh* LET-*teh-reh vee* SOH-*noh nehl-lahl-fah-*BEH-*toh ee-tahl-*YAH-*noh?*
How many letters are there in the Italian alphabet?

Nell'alfabeto italiano vi sono 21 lettere.
*Nehl-lahl-fah-*BEH-*toh ee-tahl-*YAH-*noh vee* SOH-*noh vehn-*TOO-*nah*
LET-*teh-reh.*
In the Italian alphabet there are twenty-one letters.

NOTE to Student: *J, K, X, Y, W,* do not really belong to the Italian alphabet, but they are used in foreign and scientific words. *J* was once part of the alphabet, but it is now replaced by *I. W* is used in Italian as the abbreviation for *Viva* or *Evviva,* meaning "Long live".
Ex: *W l'Italia!*—"Long live Italy!"

Quale è la lettera D, la terza o la quarta?
KWAH-*leh* EH *lah* LET-*teh-rah Dee, lah* TEHR-*tsah
oh lah* KWAHR-*tah?*
What letter is D, the third or the fourth?

È la quarta.
EH *lah* KWAHR-*tah.*
It is the fourth.

Con quale lettera comincia l'alfabeto italiano?
Kohn KWAH-*leh* LET-*teh-rah koh-*MEENT-*chah
lahl-fah-*BEH-*toh ee-tahl-*YAH-*noh?*
With what letter does the Italian alphabet begin?

Con la lettera A.
Kohn lah LET-*teh-rah Ah.*
With the letter A.

Con quale lettera finisce?
Kohn KWAH-*leh* LET-*teh-rah fee-*NEE-*sheh?*
With what letter does it end?

Con la lettera Z.
Kohn lah LET-*teh-rah* DZEH-*tah.*
With the letter Z.

A che pagina finisce la prima lezione di questo libro?
Ah keh PAH-*jee-nah fee-*NEE-*sheh lah* PREE-*mah leh-ts'*YOH-*neh dee* KWESS-*toh*
LEE-*broh?*
On what page does the first lesson of this book end?

La prima lezione di questo libro finisce a pagina 3.
Lah PREE-*mah leh-ts'*YOH-*neh dee* KWESS-*toh* LEE-*broh fee-*NEE-*sheh ah*
PAH-*jee-nah 3.*
The first lesson of this book ends on page 3.

Che pagina è questa?   **Questa è la pagina 69.**
Keh PAH-*jee-nah* EH KWESS-*tah?*   KWESS-*tah* EH *lah* PAH-*jee-nah 69.*
What page is this?   This is page 69.

A che pagina comincia la terza lezione?
Ah keh PAH-*jee-nah koh-*MEENT-*chah lah* TEHR-*tsah leh-ts'*YOH-*neh?*
On what page does the third lesson begin?

La terza lezione comincia a pagina 7.
Lah TEHR-*tsah leh-ts'*YOH-*neh koh-*MEENT-*chah ah* PAH-*jee-nah 7.*
The third lesson begins on page 7.

La lettera A è prima della lettera B;
Lah LET-*teh-rah Ah* EH PREE-*mah* DEHL-*lah* LET-*teh-rah Bee;*
The letter A is before the letter B;

la lettera C è dopo della lettera B.
lah LET-*teh-rah Chee* EH DOH-*poh* DEHL-*lah* LET-*teh-rah Bee.*
the letter C is after the letter B.

La lettera H è fra la lettera G e la lettera I.
Lah LET-*teh-rah* AH-*kah* EH *frah lah* LET-*teh-rah Jee eh lah* LET-*teh-rah Ec.*
The letter H is between the letter G and the letter I.

Dov'è la lettera H, prima o dopo della lettera G?
*Doh-*VEH *lah* LET-*teh-rah* AH-*kah,* PREE-*mah oh* DOH-*poh* DEHL-*lah*
LET-*teh-rah Jee?*
Where is the letter H, before or after the letter G?

Quale lettera vi è prima della lettera Z?
KWAH-*leh* LET-*teh-rah vee* EH PREE-*mah* DEHL-*lah* LET-*teh-rah* DZEH-*tah?*
Which letter is before the letter Z?

Quale lettera vi è dopo la lettera G?
KWAH-*leh* LET-*teh-rah vee* EH DOH-*poh lah* LET-*teh-rah Jee?*
Which letter is after the letter G?

Quale lettera vi è fra la M e la O?
KWAH-*leh* LET-*teh-rah vee* EH *frah lah* EHM-*meh eh lah* OH?
Which letter is between M and O?

Io faccio una domanda: "Chi è questo signore?"
EE-*oh* FAHT-*choh* OO-*nah doh-*MAHN-*dah: "Kee* EH KWESS-*toh seen-*YOH-*reh?"*
I ask a question: "Who is this gentleman?"

Risponda alla domanda, signora.
*Rees-*POHN-*dah* AHL-*lah doh-*MAHN-*dah,*
*seen-*YOH-*rah.*
Answer the question, madam.

È il signor Tonioni."
"EH *eel seen-*YOHR
*Toh-n'*YOH-*nee."*
"It is Mr. Tonioni."

Che cosa fa Lei?
Keh KOH-*zah fah Lay?*
What are you doing?

Rispondo alla domanda.
*Rees-*POHN-*doh* AHL-*lah doh-*MAHN-*dah.*
I am answering the question.

Faccia una domanda al signor Cerutti.
FAHT-*chah* OO-*nah doh-*MAHN-*dah ahl seen-*YOHR *Cheh-*ROOT-*tee.*
Ask Mr. Cerutti a question.

Chi fa la domanda?
*Kee fah lah doh-*MAHN-*dah?*
Who asks the question?

Io faccio la domanda.
EE-*oh* FAHT-*choh lah doh-*MAHN-*dah.*
I ask the question.

Signore, risponda alla domanda della signora.
*Seen-*YOH-*reh, rees-*POHN-*dah* AHL-*lah doh-*MAHN-*dah* DEHL-*lah seen-*YOH-*rah.*
Sir, answer the lady's question.

NOTE to Student: In Italian you don't answer "a question", but "to a question" or "to a letter". Ex: *Io rispondo alla Sua domanda.*—"I answer to your question."

Alla fine di una domanda si mette un punto interrogativo (?)
AHL-*lah* FEE-*neh dee* OO-*nah doh-*MAHN-*dah see* MET-*teh oon* POON-*toh*
*een-tehr-roh-gah-*TEE-*voh* (?)
At the end of a question we put a question mark (?)

Alla fine di una risposta, o di una frase, si mette un punto (.)
AHL-*lah* FEE-*neh dee* OO-*nah rees-*POHS-*tah, oh dee* OO-*nah* FRAH-*zeh, see*
MET-*teh oon* POON-*toh* (.)
At the end of an answer or a sentence, we put a period (.)

Ecco la virgola (,)
ECK-*koh lah* VEER-*goh-lah* (,)
Here is the comma (,)

Questo è l'accento (`)
KWESS-*toh* EH *l'aht-*CHEHN-*toh* (`)
This is the accent (`)

Ecco il punto esclamativo (!)
ECK-*koh eel* POON-*toh ess-klah-mah-*TEE-*voh* (!)
Here is the exclamation point (!)

Questa è la lineetta (-)
KWESS-*tah* EH *lah lee-neh-*EHT-*tah* (-)
This is the hyphen (-)

Ecco l'apostrofo (')
ECK-*koh lah-*POHS-*troh-foh* (')
Here is the apostrophe (')

THINKING IN ITALIAN

(Answers on page 284)

1. Chi scrive sulla lavagna?
2. Scrive la signora Fibronia?
3. Che giornale legge essa?
4. Che legge Titina?
5. Che parole scrive sulla lavagna il professore?
6. Scrive il professore con il lapis o con il gesso?
7. Scrive l'alfabeto il professore?
8. Legge la signora Fibronia un giornale italiano?
9. Parla italiano il professore?
10. Parla italiano il cane di Titina?
11. Legge Lei l'italiano?
12. Parla Lei l'inglese?
13. Parla il francese il signor Berlitz?
14. Parla l'inglese Titina?
15. È seduta o in piedi Titina?
16. Quante lettere vi sono nell'alfabeto italiano?
17. Quante lettere vi sono nell'alfabeto inglese?
18. Quante vocali vi sono nell'alfabeto italiano?

Che cosa abbiamo?
Keh KOH-*zah ahb-b'*YAH-*moh?*
What have we?

Prenda un libro, signor Betti.
PREHN-*dah oon* LEE-*broh, seen-*YOHR BET-*ee.*
Take a book, Mr. Betti.

Lei ha in mano un libro.
Lay AH *een* MAH-*noh oon* LEE-*broh.*
You have a book in your hand.

Io ho in mano due libri.
EE-*oh* OH *een* MAH-*noh* DOO-*eh* LEE-*bree.*
I have two books in my hand.

La signorina Corelli ha un cappello in testa.
*Lah seen-yoh-*REE-*nah Koh-*REHL-*lee* AH *oon kahp-*PEL-*loh een* TESS-*tah.*
Miss Corelli has a hat on her head.

Il signore non ha il cappello in testa.
*Eel seen-*YOH-*reh noh-*NAH *eel kahp-*PEL-*loh een* TESS-*tah.*
The gentleman hasn't his hat on his head.

Lei ha dei guanti.
Lay AH *day* GWAHN-*tee.*
You have gloves.

Io non ho guanti.
EE-*oh noh-*NOH GWAHN-*tee.*
I have no gloves.

Lei ha un vestito blu.
Lay AH *oon vehs-*TEE-*toh bloo.*
You have a blue dress.

Lei ha gli occhi azzurri.
Lay AH *l'yee* OCK-*kee ah-*DZOOR-*ree.*
You have blue eyes.

Io ho gli occhi bruni.
EE-*oh* OH *l'yee* OCK-*kee* BROO-*nee.*
I have brown eyes.

Lei ha un libro ed io ho un libro.
Lay AH *oon* LEE-*broh ehd* EE-*oh* OH *oon* LEE-*broh.*
You have a book and I have a book.

Noi abbiamo dei libri.
*Noy ahb-b'*YAH-*moh day* LEE-*bree.*
We have books.

Noi abbiamo delle penne.
*Noy ahb-b'*YAH-*moh* DEHL-*leh* PEHN-*neh.*
We have pens.

REMEMBER: In a note on page 2 we told you that the article *il* becomes *lo* in front of masculine nouns beginning with a vowel or the letter *z* or *s* followed by another consonant. The plural of *il* is *i,* but the plural of *lo* is *gli.*

Noi non abbiamo penne.
*Noy nohn ahb-b'*YAH-*moh* PEHN-*neh.*
We have no pens.

Gli allievi hanno dei libri.
*L'yee ahl-l'*YEH-*vee* AHN-*noh day* LEE-*bree.*
The pupils have books.

Gli allievi non hanno quaderni.
*L'yee ahl-l'*YEH-*vee noh-*NAHN-*noh kwah-*DEHR-*nee.*
The pupils have no notebooks.

I signori hanno i capelli corti.
*Ee seen-*YOH-*ree* AHN-*noh ee kah-*PEHL-*lee* KOHR-*tee.*
Gentlemen have short hair.

Le signore hanno i capelli lunghi.
*Leh seen-*YOH-*reh* AHN-*noh ee kah-*PEHL-*lee* LOON-*ggee.*
Ladies have long hair.

Io non ho un capello in testa.
EE-*oh noh*-NOH *oon kah*-PEHL-*loh een* TESS-*tah.*
I haven't a hair on my head.

Hanno il cappello in testa queste signore?
AHN-*noh eel kahp*-PEL-*loh een* TESS-*tah* KWESS-*teh seen*-YOH-*reh?*
Have those ladies their hats on?

Sì, esse hanno il cappello in testa.
See, EHS-*seh* AHN-*noh eel kahp*-PEL-*loh een* TESS-*tah.*
Yes, they have their hats on.

I signori non hanno il cappello in testa.
Ee seen-YOH-*ree noh*-NAHN-*noh eel kahp*-PEL-*loh een* TESS-*tah.*
Gentlemen have no hats on (their) head.

Ha Lei un libro? AH *Lay oon* LEE-*broh?* Have you a book?	**Sì, io ho un libro.** *See,* EE-*oh* OH *oon* LEE-*broh.* Yes, I have a book.
No, io non ho un libro. *Noh,* EE-*oh noh*-NOH *oon* LEE-*broh.* No, I have no book.	**Ho io un lapis?** OH EE-*oh oon* LAH-*peess?* Have I a pencil?

Ha capelli in testa la signorina?
AH *kah*-PEHL-*lee een* TESS-*tah lah seen-yoh-REE-nah?*
Has the young lady hair on her head?

Sì, essa ha capelli in testa.
See, ESS-*sah* AH *kah*-PEHL-*lee een* TESS-*tah.*
Yes, she has hair on her head.

Ha Lei un cappello in testa?
AH *Lay oon kahp*-PEL-*loh een* TESS-*tah?*
Have you a hat on (your) head?

No, io non ho un cappello in testa.
Noh, EE-*oh noh*-NOH *oon kahp*-PEL-*loh een* TESS-*tah.*
No, I have no hat on (my) head.

REMEMBER: The words *capello*—"hair" and *cappello*—"hat" can easily lead to mix-ups due to the close similarity of their sound. Be sure then to pronounce the one *p* in *capello* VERY LIGHTLY and don't be afraid of being too heavy on the two *p's* in *cappello.*

Ha un vestito blu la signora?
AH *oon vehs*-TEE-*toh bloo lah seen*-YOH-*rah?*
Has the lady a blue dress?

No, il vestito della signora è bianco.
Noh, eel vehs-TEE-toh DEHL-*lah seen-*YOH-*rah* EH *b'*YAHN-*koh.*
No, the lady's dress is white.

Ha Lei gli occhi neri?
AH *Lay l'yee* OCK-*kee* NEH-*ree?*
Have you dark eyes?

No, io ho gli occhi azzurri.
Noh, EE-*oh* OH *l'yee* OCK-*kee ah-*DZOOR-*ree.*
No, I have blue eyes.

Che cosa ha Lei in mano?	**Un libro, signore.**
Keh KOH-*zah* AH *Lay een* MAH-*noh?*	*Oon* LEE-*broh, seen-*YOH-*reh.*
What have you in (your) hand?	A book, sir.

Che cosa ha in testa questo signore?
Keh KOH-*zah* AH *een* TESS-*tah* KWESS-*toh seen-*YOH-*reh?*
What has this gentleman on (his) head?

Egli ha il cappello in testa.
EHL-*yee* AH *eel kahp-*PEL-*loh een* TESS-*tah.*
He has the hat on (his) head.

Abbiamo noi dei guanti?	**Io sì, ma non Lei.**
*Ahb-b'*YAH-*moh noy day* GWAHN-*tee?*	EE-*oh see, mah nohn Lay.*
Have we gloves?	I have, but you (have) not.

Abbiamo noi delle scarpe?	**Certamente!**
*Ahb-b'*YAH-*moh noy* DEHL-*leh* SKAHR-*peh?*	*Chehr-tah-*MEHN-*teh!*
Have we shoes?	Certainly!

Hanno il cappello in testa i signori?
AHN-*noh eel kahp-*PEL-*loh een* TESS-*tah ee seen-*YOH-*ree?*
Have the gentlemen the hat on (their) head?

No, i signori non hanno il cappello in testa.
*Noh, ee seen-*YOH-*ree noh-*NAHN-*noh eel kahp-*PEL-*loh een* TESS-*tah.*
No, the gentlemen have no hat on (their) head.

Hanno i capelli corti i signori?	**Naturalmente!**
AHN-*noh ee kah-*PEHL-*lee* KOHR-*tee ee seen-*YOH-*ree?*	*Nah-too-rahl-*MEHN-*teh!*
Have the gentlemen short hair?	Naturally!

Hanno i capelli lunghi le signore?
AHN-*noh ee kah-*PEHL-*lee* LOON-*ggee leh seen-*YOH-*reh?*
Have the ladies long hair?

Sì, esse hanno i capelli lunghi.
See, EHS-*seh* AHN-*noh ee kah-*PEHL-*lee* LOON-*ggee.*
Yes, they have long hair.

Lei ha due penne.
Lay AH DOO-*eh* PEHN-*neh.*
You have two pens.

Io ho cinque penne.
EE-*oh* OH CHEEN-*kweh* PEHN-*neh.*
I have five pens.

Gli allievi non hanno i loro libri.
*L'yee ahl-l'*YEH-*vee* noh-NAHN-*noh ee* LOH-*roh* LEE-*bree.*
The pupils haven't their books.

Quante penne ha Lei?
KWAHN-*teh* PEHN-*neh* AH *Lay?*
How many pens have you?

Io ho due penne.
EE-*oh* OH DOO-*eh* PEHN-*neh.*
I have two pens.

Quante dita abbiamo?
KWAHN-*teh* DEE-*tah ahb-b'*YAH-*moh?*
How many fingers have we?

Noi abbiamo dieci dita.
*Noy ahb-b'*YAH-*moh d'*YEH-*chee* DEE-*tah.*
We have ten fingers.

Quante mani abbiamo?
KWAHN-*teh* MAH-*nee ahb-b'*YAH-*moh?*
How many hands have we?

Due.
DOO-*eh.*
Two.

Quanti libri hanno gli allievi?
KWAHN-*tee* LEE-*bree* AHN-*noh l'yee
ahl-l'*YEH-*vee?*
How many books have the pupils?

Essi non hanno libri.
EHS-*see* noh-NAHN-*noh* LEE-*bree.*
They have no books.

Il mio cappello è bruno.
Eel MEE-*oh kahp-*PEL-*loh* EH BROO-*noh.*
My hat is brown.

Il Suo cappello è nero.
Eel SOO-*oh kahp-*PEL-*loh* EH NEH-*roh.*
Your hat is black.

La mia cravatta è nera.
Lah MEE-*ah krah-*VAHT-*tah* EH
NEH-*rah.*
My tie is black.

La Sua cravatta è grigia.
Lah SOO-*ah krah-*VAHT-*tah* EH
GREE-*jah.*
Your tie is gray.

È bruno il mio cappello?
EH BROO-*noh eel* MEE-*oh kahp-*PEL-*loh?*
Is my hat brown?

Sì, signore, il Suo cappello è bruno.
*See, seen-*YOH-*reh, eel* SOO-*oh kahp-*PEL-*loh* EH BROO-*noh.*
Yes, sir, your hat is brown.

È nera la mia cravatta?
EH NEH-*rah lah* MEE-*ah krah-*VAHT-*tah?*
Is my tie black?

Sì, signore, la Sua cravatta è nera.
*See, seen-*YOH-*reh, lah* SOO-*ah krah-*VAHT-*tah* EH NEH-*rah.*
Yes, sir, your tie is black.

È questo il guanto del signor Collodi?
EH KWESS-*toh eel* GWAHN-*toh dehl seen-*YOHR *Kohl-*LOH-*dee?*
Is this Mr. Collodi's glove?

Sissignore, è il suo guanto.
*Sees-seen-*YOH-*reh,* EH *eel* SOO-*oh* GWAHN-*toh.*
Yes sir, it is his glove.

È questa la cravatta del signor Collodi?
EH KWESS-*tah lah krah-*VAHT-*tah dehl seen-*YOHR *Kohl-*LOH-*dee?*
Is this Mr. Collodi's tie?

Nossignore, non è la sua cravatta, è il suo fazzoletto.
*Noks-seen-*YOH-*reh, noh-*NEH *lah* SOO-*ah krah-*VAHT-*tah,* EH *eel* SOO-*oh*
*fah-tsoh-*LET-*toh.*
No sir, it is not his tie, it is his handkerchief.

 NOTE: Instead of *sì, signore* and *no, signore* one can say: *Sissignore* and *nossignore;* but in social conversation it is preferable to use the two words as a sign of unaffected courtesy. The second form is used more by a pupil talking to a teacher, or the employee to the employer, or the servant to his master. It is, in other words, the unwritten regulation form of respect. This form is also used in the case where one wants to put more emphasis in affirming or denying something. Ex: *È l'Italia veramente bella?* —*Sissignore, e come!*—"Is Italy really beautiful?—Yes sir, and how!"

È questo il cappello della signora Collodi?
EH KWESS-*toh eel kahp-*PEL-*loh* DEHL-*lah seen-*YOH-*rah Kohl-*LOH-*dee?*
Is this Mrs. Collodi's hat?

Sì, signore, è il suo cappello.
*See, seen-*YOH-*reh,* EH *eel* SOO-*oh kahp-*PEL-*loh.*
Yes, sir, it is her hat.

È questo il fazzoletto della signorina Fabbri?
EH KWESS-*toh eel fah-tsoh-*LET-*toh* DEHL-*lah seen-yoh-*REE-*nah* FAHB-*bree?*
Is this Miss Fabbri's handkerchief?

No, signore, non è il suo fazzoletto.
*Noh, seen-*YOH-*reh, noh-*NEH *eel* SOO-*oh fah-tsoh-*LET-*toh.*
No, sir, it is not her handkerchief.

È rosso il Suo vestito?
EH ROHS-*soh eel* SOO-*oh vehs-*TEE-*toh?*
Is your dress red?

Nossignore, il mio vestito è grigio.
*Nohs-seen-*YOH-*reh, eel* MEE-*oh vehs-*TEE-*toh* EH GREE-*joh.*
No sir, my dress is gray.

Chi è il nostro professore?
Kee EH *eel* NOHS-*troh proh-fess-*SOH-*reh?*
Who is our teacher?

È il signor Berlitz.
EH *eel seen-*YOHR BEHR-*leets.*
It is Mr. Berlitz.

THINKING IN ITALIAN
(Answers on page 284)

1. Ha Lei un libro?
2. Ha degli allievi il professore Berlitz?
3. Ho io due occhi?
4. Quante dita ha Lei?
5. Hanno i capelli lunghi o corti i signori?
6. Ha Lei dei libri italiani?
7. Di che colore sono i Suoi occhi?
8. I miei occhi sono verdi; sono essi dello stesso colore dei Suoi?
9. Hanno i loro libri gli allievi?
10. Mette il professore Berlitz la sua cravatta prima della camicia?
11. Mette egli le sue calze prima o dopo le sue scarpe?
12. Scrive bene la Sua penna?
13. È più grande la mia mano destra della mia mano sinistra?

LEZIONE 14

Che cosa facciamo noi?
Keh KOH-*zah faht-*CHAH-*moh noy?*
What do we do?

Prenda un libro.
PREHN-*dah oon* LEE-*broh.*
Take a book.

Io prendo un libro.
EE-*oh* PREHN-*doh oon* LEE-*broh.*
I take a book.

Che cosa fa Lei?
Keh KOH-*zah fah Lay?*
What do you do?

Che cosa faccio io?
Keh KOH-*zah* FAHT-*choh* EE-*oh?*
What do I do?

Che facciamo noi?
*Keh faht-*CHAH-*moh noy?*
What do we do?

Lei prende un libro.
Lay PREHN-*deh oon* LEE-*broh.*
You take a book.

Noi prendiamo un libro.
*Noy prehn-d'*YAH-*moh oon* LEE-*broh.*
We take a book.

Io prendo un libro.
EE-*oh* PREHN-*doh oon* LEE-*broh.*
I take a book.

Lei prende un libro.
Lay PREHN-*deh oon* LEE-*broh.*
You take a book.

Noi prendiamo un libro.
*Noy prehn-d'*YAH-*moh oon* LEE-*broh.*
We take a book.

79

Che cosa fa il signor Cerutti?
Keh KOH-*zah fah eel seen-*YOHR *Cheh-*ROOT-*tee?*
What does Mr. Cerutti do?

Il signor Cerutti prende il suo cappello.
*Eel seen-*YOHR *Cheh-*ROOT-*tee* PREHN-*deh eel* SOO-*oh kahp-*PEL-*loh.*
Mr. Cerutti takes his hat.

Che cosa fanno gli allievi?
Keh KOH-*zah* FAHN-*noh l'yee ahl-l'*YEH-*vee?*
What do the students do?

Gli allievi prendono i loro cappelli.
*L'yee ahl-l'*YEH-*vee* PREHN-*doh-noh ee* LOH-*roh kahp-*PEL-*lee.*
The students take their hats.

Io metto il mio libro sulla tavola.
EE-*oh* MET-*toh eel* MEE-*oh* LEE-*broh* SOOL-*lah* TAH-*voh-lah.*
I put my book on the table.

Che cosa faccio io?
Keh KOH-*zah* FAHT-*choh* EE-*oh?*
What do I do?

Lei mette il Suo libro sulla tavola.
Lay MET-*teh eel* SOO-*oh* LEE-*broh* SOOL-*lah*
TAH-*voh-lah.*
You put your book on the table.

Che cosa fa Lei?
Keh KOH-*zah fah Lay?*
What do you do?

Io metto il mio libro sulla tavola.
EE-*oh* MET-*toh eel* MEE-*oh* LEE-*broh* SOOL-*lah*
TAH-*voh-lah.*
I put my book on the table.

Noi mettiamo i nostri libri sulla tavola.
Noy MET-*t'yah-moh ee* NOHS-*tree* LEE-*bree* SOOL-*lah* TAH-*voh-lah.*
We put our books on the table.

Apra il Suo libro.
AH-*prah eel* SOO-*oh* LEE-*broh.*
Open your book.

Che cosa fa Lei?
Keh KOH-*zah fah Lay?*
What do you do?

Io apro il mio libro.
EE-*oh* AH-*proh eel* MEE-*oh* LEE-*broh.*
I open my book.

Che cosa facciamo?
Keh KOH-*zah faht-*CHAH-*moh?*
What do we do?

Noi apriamo i nostri libri.
*Noy ah-pr'*YAH-*moh ee* NOHS-*tree* LEE-*bree.*
We open our books.

Il signor Goldoni apre il suo libro.
*Eel seen-*YOHR *Gohl-*DOH-*nee* AH-*preh eel* SOO-*oh* LEE-*broh.*
Mr. Goldoni opens his book.

Che cosa fa egli?
Keh KOH-*zah fah* EHL-*yee?*
What does he do?

Egli apre il suo libro.
EHL-*yee* AH-*preh eel* SOO-*oh*
LEE-*broh.*
He opens his book.

Gli allievi aprono i loro libri.
*L'yee ahl-l'*YEH-*vee* AH-*proh-noh ee* LOH-*roh*
LEE-*bree.*
The students open their books.

Che cosa fanno essi?
Keh KOH-*zah* FAHN-*noh* EHS-*see?*
What do they do?

Essi aprono i loro libri.
EHS-*see* AH-*proh-noh ee* LOH-*roh* LEE-*bree.*
They open their books.

Noi chiudiamo la finestra.
*Noy k'yoo-d'*YAH-*moh lah fee-*NESS-*trah.*
We close the window.

Che facciamo noi?
*Keh faht-*CHAH-*moh noy?*
What do we do?

Gli allievi chiudono i loro libri.
*L'yee ahl-l'*YEH-*vee k'*YOO-*doh-noh ee* LOH-*roh* LEE-*bree.*
The students close their books.

Che fanno?
Keh FAHN-*noh?*
What do they do?

Chiudono i loro libri.
*k'*YOO-*doh-noh ee* LOH-*roh* LEE-*bree.*
They shut their books.

io scrivo,	**Lei scrive,**	**noi scriviamo.**
EE-*oh* SKREE-*voh,*	*Lay* SKREE-*veh,*	*noy skree-v'*YAH-*moh.*
I write,	you write,	we write.

Che cosa facciamo noi?
Keh KOH-*zah faht-*CHAH-*moh noy?*
What do we do?

Noi scriviamo.
*Noy skree-v'*YAH-*moh.*
We write.

Scrive Lei sulla carta?
SKREE-*veh Lay* SOOL-*lah* KAHR-*tah?*
Do you write on the paper?

Sì, scrivo sulla carta.
See, SKREE-*voh* SOOL-*lah* KAHR-*tah.*
Yes, I write on the paper.

Scrivo io sulla lavagna?
SKREE-*voh* EE-*oh* SOOL-*lah lah-*VAHN-*yah?*
Do I write on the blackboard?

Sì, signore, Lei scrive sulla lavagna.
*See, seen-*YOH-*reh, Lay* SKREE-*veh* SOOL-*lah lah-*VAHN-*yah.*
Yes, sir, you write on the blackboard.

Un signore scrive,
*Oon seen-*YOH-*reh* SKREE-*veh,*
One gentleman writes,

due signori scrivono.
DOO-*eh seen-*YOH-*ree* SKREE-*voh-noh.*
two gentlemen write.

Dove scrivono gli allievi?
DOH-*veh* SKREE-*voh-noh l'yee*
*ahl-l'*YEH-*vee?*
Where do the students write?

Essi scrivono sulla carta.
EHS-*see* SKREE-*voh-noh*
SOOL-*lah* KAHR-*tah.*
They write on the paper.

Io leggo un libro.
EE-*oh* LEG-*goh oon* LEE-*broh.*
I read a book.

Lei legge le parole sulla lavagna.
Lay LEH-*djeh leh pah*-ROH-*leh* SOOL-*lah
lah*-VAHN-*yah.*
You read the words on the blackboard

Noi leggiamo.
Noy leh-DJAH-*moh.*
We read.

Un signore legge,
Oon seen-YOH-*reh* LEH-*djeh,*
One gentleman reads,

due signori leggono.
DOO-*eh seen*-YOH-*ree* LEG-*goh-noh.*
two gentlemen read.

Che cosa fa il professore?
Keh KOH-*zah fah eel proh-fess*-SOH-*reh?*
What does the teacher do?

Egli legge.
EHL-*yee* LEH-*djeh.*
He reads.

Che cosa fanno gli allievi?
Keh KOH-*zah* FAHN-*noh l'yee ahl-l'*YEH-*vee?*
What do the students do?

Essi leggono il giornale.
EHS-*see* LEG-*goh-noh eel johr*-NAH-*leh.*
They read the newspaper.

Io vado a teatro.
EE-*oh* VAH-*doh ah teh*-AH-*troh.*
I go to the theatre.

Lei va a teatro.
Lay vah ah teh-AH-*troh.*
You go to the theatre.

Noi andiamo a teatro.
*Noy ahn-d'*YAH-*moh ah teh*-AH-*troh.*
We go to the theatre.

Il signor Barberini va in chiesa.
Eel seen-YOHR *Bahr-beh*-REE-*nee vah een k'*YEH-*zah.*
Mr. Barberini goes to church.

Elisa e Paolo vanno a scuola.
Eh-LEE-*zah eh* PAH-*oh-loh* VAHN-*noh ah sk'*WOH-*lah.*
Elisa and Paul go to school.

Va Lei a teatro?
Vah Lay ah teh-AH-*troh?*
Do you go to the theatre?

No, non vado a teatro, ma al cinema.
Noh, nohn VAH-*doh ah teh*-AH-*troh, mah ahl* CHEE-*neh-mah.*
No, I do not go to the theatre, but to the movies.

Dove va il signor Cerutti?
DOH-*veh vah eel seen*-YOHR *Cheh*-ROOT-*tee?*
Where does Mr. Cerutti go?

Va in chiesa.
*Vah een k'*YEH-*zah.*
He goes to church.

Dove vanno Elisa e Paolo?
DOH-*veh* VAHN-*noh Eh*-LEE-*zah eh* PAH-*oh-loh?*
Where do Elisa and Paul go?

Vanno a scuola.
VAHN-*noh ah sk'*WOH-*lah.*
They go to school.

Va al negozio la signora Volpi?
Vah ahl neh-GOH-*ts'yoh lah seen*-YOH-*rah*
VOHL-*pee?*
Does Mrs. Volpi go to the store?

Sì, va al negozio.
See, vah ahl neh-GOH-*ts'yoh.*
Yes, she goes to the store.

Va alla banca il signor Collodi?
Vah AHL-*lah* BAHN-*kah eel seen*-YOHR *Kohl*-LOH-*dee?*
Does Mr. Collodi go to the bank?

No, non va alla banca, ma al ristorante.
Noh, nohn vah AHL-*lah* BAHN-*kah, mah ahl rees-toh*-RAHN-*teh.*
No, he doesn't go to the bank, but to the restaurant.

Noi veniamo qui.
*Noy veh-n'*YAM-*moh kwee.*
We come here.

Il professore viene alla scuola Berlitz.
Eel proh-fess-SOH-*reh v'*YEH-*neh* AHL-*lah*
*sk'*WOH-*lah* BEHR-*leets.*
The teacher comes to the Berlitz school.

Gli allievi vengono alla scuola Berlitz.
*L'yee ahl-l'*YEH-*vee* VEHN-*goh-noh* AHL-*lah sk'*WOH-*lah* BEHR-*leets.*
The students come to the Berlitz school.

Chi viene qui?
*Kee v'*YEH-*neh kwee?*
Who comes here?

Noi veniamo qui.
*Noy veh-n'*YAH-*moh kwee.*
We come here.

Il signor Berlitz e gli allievi vengono in classe.
Eel seen-YOHR BEHR-*leets eh l'yee ahl-l'*YEH-*vee* VEHN-*goh-noh een* KLAHS-*seh.*
Mr. Berlitz and the students come to class.

 **NOTE to Student:** The first person plural of the Italian verbs, in all indicative tenses, invariably ends with *-iamo.* Ex: *Noi prendiamo, noi facciamo, noi mettiamo, noi apriamo, noi chiudiamo,* etc. The third person plural, also in all indicative tenses, always ends with *-no.* Ex: *Essi* (or *loro*) *prendono, fanno, mettono, aprono, chiudono,* etc.

THINKING IN ITALIAN
(Answers on page 285)

1. Vanno al cinema le signore?
2. Hanno esse il cappello in testa in chiesa?
3. Andiamo noi alla scuola Berlitz?
4. Dove mettono i signori i loro guanti?
5. Aprono gli allievi i loro libri in classe?
6. Chiudiamo noi la porta?
7. Apriamo noi la finestra della classe?
8. Scrivono i professori sulla lavagna?
9. Scriviamo noi delle parole italiane?
10. Mettiamo noi i nostri libri sulla tavola dopo la lezione?
11. Vengono gli allievi a scuola?
12. Leggono essi i loro libri?
13. Leggiamo noi il giornale in classe?
14. Prendiamo noi le sedie della scuola?
15. Scrive Lei i Suoi compiti dopo la lezione?

LEZIONE 15

Chi ha più danaro?
Kee AH *p'*YOO *dah-*NAH*-roh?*
Who has more money?

Lei ha un libro.
Lay AH *oon* LEE*-broh.*
You have a book.

Io ho più libri di Lei.
EE*-oh* OH *p'*YOO LEE*-bree dee Lay.*
I have more books than you.

Io ho tre libri.
EE*-oh* OH *treh* LEE*-bree.*
I have three books.

Lei ha dieci lire.
Lay AH *d'*YEH*-chee* LEE*-reh.*
You have ten lire.

Il signor Grandi ha cinque lire.
Eel seen*-*YOHR GRAHN*-dee* AH CHEEN*-kweh* LEE*-reh.*
Mr. Grandi has five lire.

Lei ha più danaro del signor Grandi.
Lay AH *p'*YOO *dah-*NAH*-roh dehl* seen*-*YOHR GRAHN*-dee.*
You have more money than Mr. Grandi.

Il signor Grandi ha meno danaro di Lei.
*Eel seen-*YOHR GRAHN-*dee* AH MEH-*noh dah-*NAH-*roh dee Lay.*
Mr. Grandi has less money than you.

Io ho quattro guanti.
EE-*oh* OH KWAHT-*troh* GWAHN-*tee.*
I have four gloves.

Lei ha due guanti.
Lay AH DOO-*eh* GWAHN-*tee.*
You have two gloves.

Ho io più guanti di Lei?
OH EE-*oh* p'YOO GWAHN-*tee dee Lay?*
Have I more gloves than you?

Sì, Lei ha più guanti di me.
See, Lay AH p'YOO GWAHN-*tee dee meh.*
Yes, you have more gloves than I.

Ha Lei meno guanti di me?
AH *Lay* MEH-*noh* GWAHN-*tee dee meh?*
Have you fewer gloves than I?

Sì, io ho meno guanti di Lei.
See, EE-*oh* OH MEH-*noh* GWAHN-*tee dee Lay.*
Yes, I have fewer gloves than you.

Lei ha cento lire.
Lay AH CHEHN-*toh* LEE-*reh*
You have a hundred lire.

Io ho cinquanta lire.
EE-*oh* OH *cheen-*KWAHN-*tah* LEE-*reh.*
I have fifty lire.

Quanto danaro ha Lei?
KWAHN-*toh dah-*NAH-*roh* AH *Lay?*
How much money have you?

Io ho cento lire.
EE-*oh* OH CHEHN-*toh* LEE-*reh.*
I have hundred lire.

 **NOTE on Money:** Often you will see the word *danaro* spelled *denaro.* Both forms are widely used.

Quanto danaro ho io?
KWAHN-*toh dah-*NAH-*roh* OH EE-*oh?*
How much money have I?

Lei ha cinquanta lire.
Lay AH *cheen-*KWAHN-*tah* LEE-*reh.*
You have fifty lire.

Ha Lei più danaro di me?
AH *Lay* p'YOO *dah-*NAH-*roh dee meh?*
Have you more money than I?

Sì, io ho più danaro di Lei.
See, EE-*oh* OH p'YOO *dah-*NAH-*roh dee Lay.*
Yes, I have more money than you.

Ho io piu danaro di Lei?
OH EE-*oh p'*YOO *dah-*NAH*-roh dee Lay?*
Have I more money than you?

No, Lei ha meno danaro di me.
Noh, Lay AH MEH-*noh dah-*NAH*-roh dee meh.*
No, you have less money than I.

Chi ha più danaro, Lei o io?
Kee AH *p'*YOO *dah-*NAH*-roh, Lay oh* EE-*oh?*
Who has more money, you or I?

Io ho più danaro di Lei.
EE-*oh* OH *p'*YOO *dah-*NAH*-roh dee Lay.*
I have more money than you.

Il libro grosso ha trecento pagine.
Eel LEE-*broh* GROHS-*soh* AH *treh-*CHEHN*-toh* PAH-*jee-neh.*
The big book has 300 pages.

Il libro piccolo ha cinquanta pagine.
Eel LEE-*broh* PEEK-*koh-loh* AH *cheen-*KWAHN*-tah* PAH-*jee-neh.*
The small book has 50 pages.

Quale libro ha più pagine?
KWAH-*leh* LEE-*broh* AH *p'*YOO PAH-*jee-neh?*
Which book has more pages?

Il libro grosso ha più pagine.
Eel LEE-*broh* GROHS-*soh* AH *p'*YOO PAH-*jee-neh.*
The big book has more pages.

NOTE to Student: When a qualitative adjective is the very essential factor of a sentence it is preferable that it follow the noun instead of preceding it. If we say, for instance: *Questo è un piccolo libro*—"this is a small book", we mean to indicate that "this is a book"; the fact that this book is small is rather secondary. But when we say: *Il libro piccolo ha cinquanta pagine*—"the small book has fifty pages", we intend to make it very definite that it is "the SMALL book" that has fifty pages.

Io ho venti lire.
EE-*oh* OH VEHN-*tee* LEE-*reh.*
I have twenty lire.

Lei ha trenta lire.
Lay AH TREHN-*tah* LEE-*reh.*
You have thirty lire.

Il signor Grandi ha venti lire.
*Eel seen-*YOHR GRAHN-*dee* AH VEHN-*tee* LEE-*reh.*
Mr. Grandi has twenty lire.

Io ho meno danaro di Lei,
EE-oh OH MEH-*noh dah-*NAH-*roh dee Lay,*
I have less money than you,

ma io ho tanto danaro quanto il signor Grandi.
mah EE-*oh* OH TAHN-*toh dah-*NAH-*roh* KWAHN-*toh eel seen-*YOHR GRAHN-*dee.*
but I have as much money as Mr. Grandi.

Ho io tanto danaro quanto Lei?
OH EE-*oh* TAHN-*toh dah-*NAH-*roh* KWAHN-*toh Lay?*
Have I as much money as you?

No, Lei non ha tanto danaro quanto me.
*Noh, Lay noh-*NAH TAHN-*toh dah-*NAH-*roh* KWAHN-*toh meh.*
No, you do not have so much money as I.

Ha Lei più danaro di me?
AH *Lay p'*YOO *dah-*NAH-*roh dee me?*
Have you more money than I?

Sì, io ho più danaro di Lei.
See, EE-*oh* OH *p'*YOO *dah-*NAH-*roh dee Lay.*
Yes, I have more money than you.

Ho io tanto danaro quanto il signor Grandi?
OH EE-*oh* TAHN-*toh dah-*NAH-*roh* KWAHN-*toh eel seen-*YOHR GRAHN-*dee?*
Have I as much money as Mr. Grandi?

Sì, Lei ha tanto danaro quanto il signor Grandi.
See, Lay AH TAHN-*toh dah-*NAH-*roh* KWAHN-*toh eel seen-*YOHR GRAHN-*dee.*
Yes, you have as much money as Mr. Grandi.

Vi sono molti allievi in questa classe?
Vee SOH-*noh* MOHL-*tee ahl-l'*YEH-*vee een* KWESS-*tah* KLAHS-*seh?*
Are there many students in this class?

No, in questa classe non vi sono molti allievi.
Noh, een KWESS-*tah* KLAHS-*seh nohn vee* SOH-*noh* MOHL-*tee ahl-l'*YEH-*vee.*
No, in this class there are not many students.

Ha Lei molto danaro in tasca?
AH *Lay* MOHL-*toh dah-*NAH-*roh een* TAHS-*kah?*
Have you much money in your pocket?

Ha il signor Berlitz molti capelli?
AH *eel seen-*YOHR BEHR-*leets* MOHL-*tee kah-*PEHL-*lee?*
Has Mr. Berlitz much hair?

THINKING IN ITALIAN

(Answers on page 285)

1. Quanto danaro ha Titina?
2. Ha ella tanto danaro quanto il professore?
3. Chi ha più danaro, il professore o la signora Fibronia?
4. Ha il professore dei lapis dietro l'orecchio?
5. Ha egli più lapis di Titina?
6. Ha Titina meno libri del maestro?
7. Chi ha più libri?
8. Chi ha meno danaro?
9. Ha molto danaro Titina?
10. Ha il professore pochi libri?
11. Legge Lei molte parole italiane?
12. Vi sono molte pagine in questo libro?
13. Ha il "New York Times" tante pagine quante questo libro?
14. Chi ha più libri, Lei o il professore?

Gli oggetti nella stanza
*L'yee oh-*DJET-*tee* NEHL-*lah* STAHN-*tsah*
The objects in the room

Io ho una scatola di fiammiferi.
EE-*oh* OH OO-*nah* SKAH-*toh-lah dee* f'yahm-MEE-*feh-ree.*
I have a box of matches.

Io metto dei fiammiferi sulla tavola,
EE-*oh* MET-*toh day* f'yahm-MEE-*feh-ree* SOOL-*lah* TAH-*voh-lah,*
I put some matches on the table,

ed io metto dei fiammiferi sulla sedia.
ehd EE-*oh* MET-*toh day* f'yahm-MEE-*feh-ree* SOOL-*lah* SEHD-*yah.*
and I put some matches on the chair.

Che cosa metto sulla tavola?
Keh KOH-*zah* MET-*toh* SOOL-*lah* TAH-*voh-lah?*
What do I put on the table?

Lei mette dei fiammiferi sulla tavola.
Lay MET-*teh day* f'yahm-MEE-*feh-ree* SOOL-*lah* TAH-*voh-lah.*
You put some matches on the table.

Che cosa è questa?
Keh KOH-*zah* EH KWESS-*tah?*
What is this?

90

È una scatola di fiammiferi.
EH OO-*nah* SKAH-*toh-lah dee f'yahm*-MEE-*feh-ree.*
It is a box of matches.

Che cosa è questa?
Keh KOH-*zah* EH KWESS-*tah?*
What is this?

È una scatola di penne.
EH OO-*nah* SKAH-*toh-lah dee* PEHN-*neh.*
It is a box of pens.

Che cosa è questa?
Keh KOH-*zah* EH KWESS-*tah?*
What is this?

È una penna.
EH OO-*nah* PEHN-*nah.*
It is a pen.

Che cosa sono queste?
Keh KOH-*zah* SOH-*noh* KWESS-*teh?*
What are these?

Sono delle penne.
SOH-*noh* DEHL-*leh* PEHN-*neh.*
They are pens.

Che cosa sono queste?
Keh KOH-*zah* SOH-*noh* KWESS-*teh?*
What are these?

Sono le penne.
SOH-*noh leh* PEHN-*neh.*
They are the pens.

Vi sono dei libri sulla tavola e dei libri sulla sedia.
Vee SOH-*noh day* LEE-*bree* SOOL-*lah* TAH-*voh-lah eh day* LEE-*bree* SOOL-*lah*
    SEHD-*yah.*
There are some books on the table and some books on the chair.

> **I libri rossi sono sulla tavola**
> *Ee* LEE-*bree* ROHS-*see* SOH-*noh* SOOL-*lah* TAH-*voh-lah*
> The red books are on the table

> **ed i libri neri sono sulla sedia.**
> *ehd ee* LEE-*bree* NEH-*ree* SOH-*noh* SOOL-*lah* SEHD-*yah.*
> and the black books are on the chair.

NOTE: The conjunction *e* often becomes *ed* when followed by a word that begins with a vowel.

Sulla tavola vi è un pacchetto di sigarette.
SOOL-*lah* TAH-*voh-lah vee* EH *oon pahk*-KEHT-*toh dee see-gah*-RET-*teh.*
There is a package of cigarettes on the table.

> **Nel pacchetto vi sono delle sigarette.**
> *Nehl pahk*-KEHT-*toh vee* SOH-*noh* DEHL-*leh see-gah*-RET-*teh.*
> There are cigarettes in the package.

> **Di che colore sono queste sedie?**
> *Dee keh koh*-LOH-*reh* SOH-*noh* KWESS-*teh* SEHD-*yeh?*
> What color are these chairs?

L'una è bruna e l'altra è nera.
LOO-*nah* EH BROO-*nah eh* LAHL-*trah* EH NEH-*rah*.
One is brown and the other is black.

Sono le due sedie del medesimo colore?
SOH-*noh leh* DOO-*eh* SEHD-*yeh dehl* meh-DEH-*zee-moh* koh-LOH-*reh?*
Are the two chairs of the same color?

> No, sono di colore differente.
> *Noh,* SOH-*noh dee* koh-LOH-*reh* deef-*feh*-REHN-*teh*.
> No, they are of different colors.

Quale differenza vi è fra queste due sedie?
KWAH-*leh* deef-*feh*-REHN-*tsah vee* EH *frah* KWESS-*teh* DOO-*eh* SEHD-*yeh?*
What difference is there between these two chairs?

> L'una è bruna e l'altra è nera.
> LOO-*nah* EH BROO-*nah eh* LAHL-*trah* EH NEH-*rah*.
> One is brown and the other is black.

NOTE to Student: *L'una è bruna e l'altra è nera,* literally translated would be: "The one is brown and the other is black."

Sono del medesimo colore questi libri?
SOH-*noh dehl* meh-DEH-*zee-moh* koh-LOH-*reh* KWESS-*tee* LEE-*bree?*
Are these books of the same color?

Sì, questi libri sono del medesimo colore.
See, KWESS-*tee* LEE-*bree* SOH-*noh dehl* meh-DEH-*zee-moh* koh-LOH-*reh*.
Yes, these books are of the same color.

Ha Lei tanti libri quanti ne ho io?
AH *Lay* TAHN-*tee* LEE-*bree* KWAHN-*tee neh* OH EE-*oh?*
Have you as many books as I?

No, io non ho tanti libri quanti ne ha Lei.
Noh, EE-*oh* noh-NOH TAHN-*tee* LEE-*bree* KWAHN-*tee neh* AH *Lay*.
No, I have not so many books as you.

DON'T FORGET! In previous lessons we have used the word *nè* (with the accent on the *è*) as a negative meaning "neither" and "nor"; Ex: *Nè questo nè quello*—"Neither this nor that." The same word, but without the accent, acquires the meaning of "of it" or "of them". Ex: *Ha Lei tanti libri quanti ne ho io?* The actual meaning is: "Have you as many books as I?" But a word by word translation would be: "Have you as many books as, of them, have I?" Therefore the word *ne* in a sentence stands as a repetition of the subject.

THINKING IN ITALIAN

(Answers on page 285)

1. Vi sono dei cappelli sulla sedia?
2. Che cosa vi è nella tasca del professore?
3. Che cosa vi è nella scatola?
4. Di che colore è il fazzoletto del professore?
5. Vi è una scatola di penne sulla sedia?
6. Vi sono dei cappelli sulla tavola?
7. Dov'è il pacchetto di sigarette?
8. Vi sono delle sigarette nella tasca del professore?
9. Ha il professore una sigaretta fra le labbra?
10. Vi è un cappello sulla testa del professore?
11. Vi sono delle sigarette sulla tavola?
12. Sono sulla tavola le sigarette?
13. Vi sono dei cappelli sul pavimento?
14. Dove sono i cappelli?

Che cosa vi è sulla tavola?

Keh KOH-*zah vee* EH SOOL-*lah* TAH-*voh-lah?*

What is there on the table?

Sulla tavola vi sono dei libri, della carta ed una scatola.
SOOL-*lah* TAH-*voh-lah vee* SOH-*noh day* LEE-*bree,* DEHL-*lah* KAHR-*tah ehd*
OO-*nah* SKAH-*toh-lah.*
On the table there are some books, some paper and a box.

Nella mia tasca vi è (c'è) un fazzoletto.
NEHL-*lah* MEE-*ah* TAHS-*kah vee* EH (CHEH) *oon* ʃ*ah-tsoh-*LET-*toh.*
In my pocket there is a handkerchief.

Nella scatola vi sono delle penne.
NEHL-*lah* SKAH-*toh-lah vee* SOH-*noh* DEHL-*leh* PEHN-*neh.*
In the box there are some pens.

Che cosa vi è sulla tavola?
Keh KOH-*zah vee* EH SOOL-*lah* TAH-*voh-lah?*
What is there on the table?

Sulla tavola vi sono dei lapis e dei libri.
SOOL-*lah* TAH-*voh-lah vee* SOH-*noh day* LAH-*peess eh day* LEE-*bree.*
On the table there are some pencils and some books.

Che cosa c'è nella mia tasca?
Keh KOH-*zah* CHEH NEHL-*lah* MEE-*ah* TAHS-*kah?*
What is in my pocket?

Nella Sua tasca c'è un fazzoletto.
NEHL-*lah* SOO-*ah* TAHS-*kah* CHEH *oon fah-tsoh-*LET-*toh.*
In your pocket there is a handkerchief.

E nella scatola?
Eh NEHL-*lah* SKAH-*toh-lah?*
And in the box?

Vi sono delle penne.
Vee SOH-*noh* DEHL-*leh* PEHN-*neh.*
There are some pens.

Nella mia mano destra c'è un lapis.
NEHL-*lah* MEE-*ah* MAH-*noh* DEHS-*trah* CHEH *oon* LAH-*peess.*
In my right hand there is a pencil.

Nella mia mano sinistra non c'è nulla.
NEHL-*lah* MEE-*ah* MAH-*noh* see-NEES-*trah nohn* CHEH NOOL-*lah.*
In my left hand there is nothing.

Che cosa c'è nella mia mano sinistra?
Keh KOH-*zah* CHEH NEHL-*lah* MEE-*ah* MAH-*noh*
see-NEES-*trah?*
What is there in my left hand?

Non c'è nulla.
Nohn CHEH NOOL-*lah.*
There is nothing.

Che cosa c'è nella mia mano destra?
Keh KOH-*zah* CHEH NEHL-*lah* MEE-*ah* MAH-*noh*
DEHS-*trah?*
What is there in my right hand?

C'è un lapis.
CHEH *oon* LAH-*peess.*
There is a pencil.

Che cosa c'è nella piccola scatola?
Keh KOH-*zah* CHEH NEHL-*lah* PEEK-*koh-lah* SKAH-*toh-lah?*
What is in the small box?

Vi sono delle penne.
Vee SOH-*noh* DEHL-*leh* PEHN-*neh.*
There are some pens.

E che cosa c'è nella grande scatola?
Eh keh KOH-*zah* CHEH NEHL-*lah* GRAHN-*deh* SKAH-*toh-lah?*
And what is in the big box?

Non c'è nulla.
Nohn CHEH NOOL-*lah.*
There is nothing.

Sulla sedia non c'è nulla.
SOOL-*lah* SEHD-*yah nohn* CHEH NOOL-*lah.*
There is nothing on the chair.

NOTE: *C'è*, which is an abbreviation of *ci è*, can be used in place of *vi è* or *v'è*, meaning "there is". Likewise, in the plural, two forms are current: *vi sono* or *ci sono*—"there are".

C'è qualche cosa sulla tavola.
CHEH KWAHL-*keh* KOH-*zah* SOOL-*lah* TAH-*voh-lah*.
There is something on the table.

C'è qualche cosa nella mia mano destra?
CHEH KWAHL-*keh* KOH-*zah* NEHL-*lah* MEE-*ah* MAH-*noh* DEHS-*trah?*
Is there something in my right hand?

Non c'è nulla nella mia mano sinistra.
Nohn CHEH NOOL-*lah* NEHL-*lah* MEE-*ah* MAH-*noh* see-NEES-*trah.*
There is nothing in my left hand.

Vi è qualche cosa sulla tavola?
Vee EH KWAHL-*keh* KOH-*zah* SOOL-*lah* TAH-*voh-lah?*
Is there anything on the table?

Sì, vi è qualche cosa sulla tavola.
See, vee EH KWAHL-*keh* KOH-*zah* SOOL-*lah* TAH-*voh-lah.*
Yes, there is something on the table.

C'è qualche cosa sulla sedia?   No, non c'è nulla.
CHEH KWAHL-*keh* KOH-*zah* SOOL-*lah* SEHD-*yah?*   *Noh, nohn* CHEH NOOL-*lah.*
Is there something on the chair?   No, there is nothing.

Chi è davanti a questa tavola?   È Carlo.
Kee EH *dah*-VAHN-*tee ah* KWESS-*tah* TAH-*voh-lah?*   EH KAHR-*loh.*
Who is in front of this table?   It is Carlo.

Chi è dietro a questa tavola?
Kee EH *d'*YEH-*troh ah* KWESS-*tah* TAH-*voh-lah?*
Who is in back of this table?

È la signorina Bracco.
EH *lah seen-yoh*-REE-*nah* BRAHK-*koh.*
It is Miss Bracco.

Chi è davanti alla finestra?   Non c'è nessuno.
Kee EH *dah*-VAHN-*tee* AHL-*lah fee*-NESS-*trah?*   *Nohn* CHEH *nehs*-SOO-*noh.*
Who is in front of the window?   No one.

Non c'è nessuno sulla sedia gialla,
Nohn CHEH *nehs*-SOO-*noh* SOOL-*lah* SEHD-*yah* JAHL-*lah,*
There is no one on the yellow chair,

ma c'è qualcuno sulla sedia bruna.
mah CHEH *kwahl*-KOO-*noh* SOOL-*lah* SEHD-*yah* BROO-*nah.*
but there is someone on the brown chair.

C'è qualcuno dietro alla tavola.
CHEH *kwahl*-KOO-*noh d'*YEH-*troh* AHL-*lah* TAH-*voh-lah.*
There is someone in back of the table.

Non c'è nessuno davanti alla tavola.
Nohn CHEH *nehs-*SOO-*noh dah-*VAHN-*tee* AHL-*lah* TAH-*voh-lah.*
There is no one in front of the table.

Vi è qualcuno dietro alla tavola?
Vee EH *kwahl-*KOO-*noh d'*YEH-*troh* AHL-*lah* TAH-*voh-lah?*
Is there someone in back of the table?

Sì, v'è qualcuno dietro alla tavola.
See VEH *kwahl-*KOO-*noh d'*YEH-*troh* AHL-*lah* TAH-*voh-lah.*
Yes, there is someone in back of the table.

Lei è davanti alla finestra.	Davanti a che cosa è Lei?
Lay EH *dah-*VAHN-*tee* AHL-*lah*	*Dah-*VAHN-*tee ah keh* KOH-*zah* EH *Lay?*
*fee-*NESS-*trah.*	What are you in front of?
You are in front of the window.	

NOTE to Student: *Nessuno* means "nobody" or "no one",
but when used in a negative sentence it also means "anybody".

Io sono davanti alla finestra.	Lei è accanto al signor Ratti.
EE-*oh* SOH-*noh dah-*VAHN-*tee* AHL-*lah*	*Lay* EH *ahk-*KAHN-*toh ahl seen-*YOHR
*fee-*NESS-*trah.*	RAHT-*tee.*
I am in front of the window.	You are beside Mr. Ratti.

Accanto a chi è Lei?	Io sono accanto al signor Ratti.
*Ahk-*KAHN-*toh ah kee* EH *Lay?*	EE-*oh* SOH-*noh ahk-*KAHN-*toh ahl*
Beside whom are you?	*seen-*YOHR RAHT-*tee.*
	I am beside Mr. Ratti.

Accanto a che è Lei?
*Ahk-*KAHN-*toh ah keh* EH *Lay?*
Beside what are you?

Io sono accanto alla tavola.
EE-*oh* SOH-*noh ahk-*KAHN-*toh* AHL-*lah* TAH-*voh-lah.*
I am beside the table.

Chi è alla destra del signor Galli?
Kee EH AHL-*lah* DEHS-*trah dehl seen-*YOHR GAHL-*lee?*
Who is on Mr. Galli's right?

Sono io, signore.
SOH-*noh* EE-*oh, seen-*YOH-*reh.*
I am, sir.

Chi è alla sua sinistra?	Nessuno.
Kee EH AHL-*lah* SOO-*ah see-*NEES-*trah?*	*Nehs-*SOO-*noh.*
Who is on his left?	No one.

THINKING IN ITALIAN

(Answers on page 286)

1. Ha una sigaretta in mano il professore?
2. Che cosa è nella mano sinistra della signora Fibronia?
3. Ha Titina qualche cosa nella sua mano destra?
4. Che cosa c'è nella sua mano sinistra?
5. C'è qualcuno alla sinistra del professore?
6. Dov'è Titina?
7. È il libro nella mano destra della signora Fibronia?
8. Chi è seduto sulla sedia?
9. Vi è qualche cosa sulla tavola?
10. Che cosa c'è sotto il braccio sinistro del professore?
11. Chi è alla sua destra?
12. Che cosa c'è sotto la sedia?
13. Vi è qualcuno alla destra di Titina?
14. Chi è alla sua sinistra?
15. Vi è qualcuno dietro alla tavola?
16. Ha un cappello in testa il professore?
17. Che cosa ha sulla testa il professore?

LEZIONE 18

Entri!
EHN-*tree!*
Come in!

Io entro nella stanza.
EE-*oh* EHN-*troh* NEHL-*lah* STAHN-*tsah.*
I come into the room.

Prendo una sedia.
PREHN-*doh* OO-*nah* SEHD-*yah.*
I take a chair.

Io mi siedo.
EE-*oh mee s'*YEH-*doh.*
I sit down.

Io mi alzo.
EE-*oh mee* AHL-*tsoh.*
I get up.

Io esco dalla stanza.
EE-*oh* EHS-*koh* DAHL-*lah* STAHN-*tsah.*
I go out of the room.

Signor Cuccio, esca dalla stanza, prego.
*Seen-*YOHR KOOT-*choh,* EHS-*kah* DAHL-*lah* STAHN-*tsah,* PREH-*goh.*
Mr. Cuccio, go out of the room, please.

Lei esce dalla stanza.
Lay EH-*sheh* DAHL-*lah* STAHN-*tsah.*
You go out of the room.

NOTE to Student: *Io entro, io esco* actually mean: "I get in", "I get out". That is why *esco* is followed by *dal* (masculine) or *dalla* (feminine) meaning "of the" or "from the", and *entro* is followed by *nel* (masculine) or *nella* (feminine) meaning "in the". Ex: *Io esco dalla stanza,* literally means "I get out of the room." *Io entro nella stanza* means "I get into the room."

Signor Cuccio, si alza ed esce Lei dalla stanza?
*Seen-*YOHR KOOT-*choh, see* AHL-*tsah ehd* EH-*sheh Lay* DAHL-*lah* STAHN-*tsah?*
Mr. Cuccio, do you get up and go out of the room?

Sì, io mi alzo ed esco dalla stanza.
See, EE-*oh mee* AHL-*tsoh ehd* EHS-*koh* DAHL-*lah* STAHN-*tsah.*
Yes, I get up and go out of the room.

Egli si alza ed esce dalla stanza.
EHL-*yee see* AHL-*tsah ehd* EH-*sheh* DAHL-*lah* STAHN-*tsah.*
He gets up and goes out of the room.

Entri, per piacere.
EHN-*tree, pehr p'yah-*CHEH-*reh.*
Come in, please.

Che cosa fa Lei?
Keh KOH-*zah fah Lay?*
What do you do?

Io entro nella stanza.
EE-*oh* EHN-*troh* NEHL-*lah* STAHN-*tsah.*
I come into the room.

Si sieda.
*See s'*YEH-*dah.*
Sit down.

Che fa Lei?
Keh fah Lay?
What do you do?

Mi siedo.
*Mee s'*YEH-*doh.*
I sit down.

Si alzi, per favore.
See AHL-*tsee, pehr fah-*VOH-*reh.*
Get up, please.

Cosa fa Lei?
KOH-*zah fah Lay?*
What do you do?

(Io) mi alzo.
(EE-*oh) mee* AHL-*tsoh.*
I get up.

Io mi alzo ed esco dalla stanza.
EE-*oh mee* AHL-*tsoh ehd* EHS-*koh* DAHL-*lah* STAHN-*tsah.*
I get up and go out of the room.

Che faccio io?
Keh FAHT-*choh* EE-*oh?*
What do I do?

Lei si alza ed esce dalla stanza.
Lay see AHL-*tsah ehd* EH-*sheh* DAHL-*lah* STAHN-*tsah.*
You get up and go out of the room.

Lei entra.
Lay EHN-trah.
You come in.

Lei si siede.
Lay see s'YEH-deh.
You sit down.

NOTE to Student: "What do you do?" can be translated by: *Che cosa fa Lei?—Che fa Lei?—Cosa fa Lei?* Does this choice puzzle you? Here is the explanation: *Che* and *cosa* have the same meaning, "what"; therefore, either *che fa Lei?* or *cosa fa Lei?* mean: "What do you do?" But *cosa* also means "thing", "matter", "business"; thus, the full meaning of *che cosa fa Lei?* is: "What matter do you do?"

Entriamo noi nella classe prima della lezione?
Ehn-tr'YAH-moh noy NEHL-lah KLAHS-seh PREE-mah DEHL-lah leh-ts'YOH-neh?
Do we come into the class before the lesson?

Sì, noi entriamo nella classe prima della lezione.
See, noy ehn-tr'YAH-moh NEHL-lah KLAHS-seh PREE-mah DEHL-lah leh-ts'YOH-neh.
Yes, we come into the class before the lesson.

Ci sediamo sulle sedie?
Chee seh-d'YAH-moh SOOL-leh SEHD-yeh?
Do we sit on the chairs?

Sì, noi ci sediamo sulle sedie.
See, noy chee seh-d'YAH-moh SOOL-leh SEHD-yeh.
Yes, we sit on the chairs.

Usciamo noi dalla classe dopo la lezione?
Oo-sh'YAH-moh noy DAHL-lah KLAHS-seh DOH-poh lah leh-ts'YOH-neh?
Do we go out of the class after the lesson?

Sì, noi usciamo dalla classe dopo la lezione.
See, noy oo-sh'YAH-moh DAHL-lah KLAHS-seh DOH-poh lah leh-ts'YOH-neh.
Yes, we go out of the class after the lesson.

Il signor Cuccio e Lei entrano nella classe e si siedono.
Eel seen-YOHR KOOT-choh eh Lay EHN-trah-noh NEHL-lah KLAHS-seh eh see s'YEH-doh-noh.
Mr. Cuccio and you come into the class and sit down.

Prego, signori, entrino.
PREH-goh, seen-YOH-ree, EHN-tree-noh.
Please, gentlemen, come in.

Che cosa fanno Loro?
Keh KOH-zah FAHN-noh LOH-roh?
What do you do?

Noi entriamo nella classe.
Noy ehn-tr'YAH-moh NEHL-lah KLAHS-seh.
We come into the class.

Si siedano davanti a me.
See s'YEH-dah-noh dah-VAHN-tee ah meh.
Sit down in front of me.

Che cosa fanno Loro?
Keh KOH-*zah* FAHN-*noh* LOH-*roh?*
What do you do?

Noi entriamo e ci sediamo davanti a Lei.
*Noy ehn-tr'*YAH-*moh eh chee seh-d'*YAH-*moh dah-*VAHN-*tee ah Lay.*
We come in and sit down in front of you.

Si alzino, signori.
See AHL-*tsee-noh, seen-*YOH-*ree.*
Get up, gentlemen.

Che fanno Loro?
Keh FAHN-*noh* LOH-*roh?*
What do you do?

Noi ci alziamo.
*Noy chee ahl-ts'*YAH-*moh.*
We get up.

Escano, signori.
EHS-*kah-noh, seen-*YOH-*ree.*
Go out, gentlemen.

Che fanno Loro?
Keh FAHN-*noh* LOH-*roh?*
What do you do?

Noi usciamo dalla classe.
*Noy oo-sh'*YAH-*moh* DAHL-*lah* KLAHS-*seh.*
We go out of the class.

Entrano gli allievi?
EHN-*trah-noh l'yee ahl-l'*YEH-*vee?*
Do the students come in?

Sì, (essi) entrano.
See, (EHS-*see)* EHN-*trah-noh.*
Yes, they come in.

Si siedono essi?
*See s'*YEH-*doh-noh* EHS-*see?*
Do they sit down?

Sì, si siedono.
*See, see s'*YEH-*doh-noh.*
Yes, they sit down.

Si alzano gli alunni?
See AHL-*tsah-noh l'yee ah-*LOON-*nee?*
Do the students get up?

Sì, si alzano.
See, see AHL-*tsah-noh.*
Yes, they get up.

Escono essi?
EHS-*koh-noh* EHS-*see?*
Do they go out?

Sì, essi escono.
See, EHS-*see* EHS-*koh-noh.*
Yes, they go out.

 DON'T FORGET: *Alzarsi*—"to get up" and *sedersi*—"to sit down" are reflexive verbs meaning "to get oneself up" and "to sit oneself down." In Italian one must say: *Io mi alzo*—"I get myself up", or *Io mi siedo*—"I sit myself down." This explains the reason for the accent on the *ì* in *sì*, meaning "yes"; it is to distinguish the affirmative *sì* from the reflective *si.*

Si alzi, signore.
See AHL-*tsee, seen-*YOH-*reh.*
Get up, sir.

Che fa Lei?
Keh fah Lay?
What do you do?

Mi alzo.
Mee AHL-*tsoh.*
I get up.

Si sieda, prego.
*See s'*YEH-*dah,* PREH-*goh.*
Sit down, please.

Che cosa fa Lei?
Keh KOH-*zah fah Lay?*
What do you do?

Io mi siedo.
EE-*oh mee s'*YEH-*doh.*
I sit down.

Esca.
EHS-*kah.*
Go out.

Che cosa fa Lei?
Keh KOH-*zah fah Lay?*
What do you do?

Io esco.
EE-*oh* EHS-*koh.*
I go out.

Si alzino, signori.
See AHL-*tsee-noh, seen-*YOH-*ree.*
Get up, gentlemen.

Che cosa fanno Loro?
Keh KOH-*zah* FAHN-*noh* LOH-*roh?*
What do you do?

(Noi) ci alziamo.
*(Noy) chee ahl-ts'*YAH-*moh.*
We get up.

Si siedano.
*See s'*YEH-*dah-noh.*
Sit down.

Che cosa fanno Loro?
Keh KOH-*zah* FAHN-*noh* LOH-*roh?*
What do you do?

Ci sediamo.
*Chee seh-d'*YAH-*moh.*
We sit down.

Escano, signori.
EHS-*kah-noh, seen-*YOH-*ree.*
Go out, gentlemen.

Che fanno Loro?
Keh FAHN-*noh* LOH-*roh?*
What do you do?

Noi usciamo.
*Noy oo-sh'*YAH-*moh.*
We go out.

Alziamoci.
*Ahl-ts'*YAH-*moh-chee.*
Let's get up.

Che cosa facciamo?
Keh KOH-*zah faht-*CHAH-*moh?*
What do we do?

Ci alziamo.
*Chee ahl-ts'*YAH-*moh.*
We get up.

Sediamoci.
*Seh-d'*YAH-*moh-chee.*
Let's sit down.

Usciamo.
*Oo-sh'*YAH-*moh.*
Let's go out.

Entriamo.
*Ehn-tr'*YAH-*moh.*
Let's go in.

Che cosa facciamo noi?
Keh KOH-*zah faht-*CHAH-*moh noy?*
What do we do?

Noi ci sediamo, usciamo, entriamo.
*Noy chee seh-d'*YAH-*moh, oo-sh'*YAH-*moh, ehn-tr'*YAH-*moh.*
We sit down, go out, come in.

REMEMBER: By affixing *ci* to the reflexive verbs you form the first person plural of the imperative. Ex: *Ci alziamo,* "we get up" (indicative), becomes *alziamoci,* "Let's get up."

Il professore   Giuseppe   Sofia   Gina   Arturo

THINKING IN ITALIAN

(Answers on page 286)

1. Chi esce dalla stanza?
2. È seduta Sofia?
3. Si siede Arturo?
4. Chi si alza?
5. Entra Arturo nella stanza?
6. Entra Gina?
7. Esce dalla stanza Arturo?
8. Esce dalla stanza il professore?
9. Sono Gina ed Arturo in piedi?
10. Che cosa fa Arturo?
11. È seduto il professore?
12. Si alza Lei dopo la lezione?
13. Si siede Lei sulla sedia?
14. Mi siedo io sulla sedia o sulla tavola?
15. Escono gli allievi dopo la lezione?
16. Ci sediamo noi al cinema?
17. Si siede Lei in chiesa?

Io Le do un libro
EE-*oh Leh doh oon* LEE-*broh*
I give you a book

Io Le do il libro.
EE-*oh Leh doh eel* LEE-*broh.*
I give you the book.

Lei mi dà il libro.
Lay mee dah eel LEE-*broh.*
You give me the book.

Per piacere, mi dia il lapis.
*Pehr p'yah-*CHEH-*reh, mee* DEE-*ah eel* LAH-*peess.*
Give me the pencil, please.

Che cosa fa Lei?
Keh KOH-*zah fah Lay?*
What do you do?

Che cosa faccio?
Keh KOH-*zah* FAHT-*choh?*
What do I do?

Io Le do il lapis.
EE-*oh Leh doh eel* LAH-*peess.*
I give you the pencil.

Io do della carta al signor Mascherini.
EE-*oh doh* DEHL-*lah* KAHR-*tah ahl seen-*YOHR *Mahs-keh-*REE-*nee.*
I give some paper to Mr. Mascherini.

Che cosa do io al signor Mascherini?
Keh KOH-*zah doh* EE-*oh ahl seen*-YOHR *Mahs-keh-*REE-*nee?*
What do I give to Mr. Mascherini?

Lei gli dà della carta.
Lay l'yee dah DEHL-*lah* KAHR-*tah.*
You give him some paper.

Dia il Suo libro alla signorina.
DEE-*ah eel* SOO-*oh* LEE-*broh* AHL-*lah seen-yoh-*REE-*nah.*
Give your book to the young lady.

Che cosa dà Lei alla signorina?
Keh KOH-*zah dah Lay* AHL-*lah seen-yoh-*REE-*nah?*
What do you give to the young lady?

Io le do il mio libro.
EE-*oh leh doh eel* MEE-*oh* LEE-*broh.*
I give her my book.

Signore, io do Loro delle lezioni d'italiano.
*Seen-*YOH-*reh,* EE-*oh doh* LOH-*roh* DEHL-*leh leh-ts'*YOH-*neh dee-tahl-*YAH-*noh.*
Ladies, I give you Italian lessons.

Che cosa do Loro io?
Keh KOH-*zah doh* LOH-*roh* EE-*oh?*
What do I give you?

Lei ci dà delle lezioni.
Lay chee dah DEHL-*leh leh-ts'*YOH-*nee.*
You give us lessons.

Il professore dà dei compiti agli allievi.
*Eel proh-fess-*SOH-*reh dah day* KOHM-*pee-tee* AHL-*yee ahl-l'*YEH-*vee.*
The teacher gives some exercises to the students.

Che cosa dà il professore agli allievi?
Keh KOH-*zah dah eel proh-fess-*SOH-*reh* AHL-*yee ahl-l'*YEH-*vee?*
What does the teacher give to the students?

Egli dà loro dei compiti.
EHL-*yee dah* LOH-*roh day* KOHM-*pee-tee.*
He gives them some exercises.

Io Le do un lapis.
EE-*oh Leh doh oon* LAH-*peess.*
I give you a pencil.

Io Le do qualche cosa.
EE-*oh Leh doh* KWAHL-*keh* KOH-*zah.*
I give you something.

Io Le parlo.
EE-*oh Leh* PAHR-*loh.*
I speak to you.

Io Le dico qualche cosa.
EE-*oh Leh* DEE-*koh* KWAHL-*keh* KOH-*zah.*
I tell you something.

Lei mi parla.
Lay mee PAHR-*lah.*
You speak to me.

Lei mi dice qualche cosa.
Lay mee DEE-*cheh* KWAHL-*keh* KOH-*zah.*
You tell me something.

Il signor Berlitz ci parla.
*Eel seen-*YOHR BEHR-*leets chee* PAHR-*lah.*
Mr. Berlitz speaks to us.

Egli ci dice qualche cosa.
EHL-*yee chee* DEE-*cheh* KWAHL-*keh* KOH-*zah.*
He tells us something.

Noi parliamo al signor Berlitz.
*Noy pahr-l'*YAH-*moh ahl seen-*YOHR
BEHR-*leets.*
We speak to Mr. Berlitz.

Noi gli diciamo qualche cosa.
*Noy l'yee dee-ch'*YAH-*moh* KWAHL-*keh*
KOH-*zah.*
We tell him something.

REMEMBER: *Le* and *gli* in front of nouns are the plural forms of the articles *la* and *lo,* but in front of verbs *le* means "to you" and "to her", and *gli* means "to him". *Ci* stands for "to us".

Il signor Berlitz parla agli allievi.
*Eel seen-*YOHR BEHR-*leets* PAHR-*lah* AHL-*yee ahl-l'*YEH-*vee.*
Mr. Berlitz speaks to the students.

Egli dice loro qualche cosa.
EHL-*yee* DEE-*cheh* LOH-*roh* KWAHL-*keh* KOH-*zah.*
He tells them something.

Gli allievi parlano al signor Berlitz.
*L'yee ahl-l'*YEH-*vee* PAHR-*lah-noh ahl seen-*YOHR BEHR-*leets.*
The students speak to Mr. Berlitz.

Essi gli dicono qualche cosa.
EHS-*see l'yee* DEE-*koh-noh* KWAHL-*keh* KOH-*zah.*
They tell him something.

Io Le parlo.
EE-*oh Leh* PAHR-*loh.*
I speak to you.

Io Le dico il mio nome.
EE-*oh Leh* DEE-*koh eel* MEE-*oh* NOH-*mel.*
I tell you my name.

Che cosa Le dico?
Keh KOH-*zah Leh* DEE-*koh?*
What do I tell you?

Lei mi dice il Suo nome.
Lay mee DEE-*cheh eel* SOO-*oh* NOH-*meh.*
You tell me your name.

Mi dica il Suo nome, per piacere.
Mee DEE-*kah eel* SOO-*oh* NOH-*meh, pehr p'yah-*CHEH-*reh.*
Tell me your name, please.

Mi dica che cosa c'è sulla tavola.
Mee DEE-*kah keh* KOH-*zah* CHEH SOOL-*lah* TAH-*voh-lah.*
Tell me what is on the table.

Signora, dica il Suo nome al signor Berlitz.
*Seen-*YOH-*rah,* DEE-*kah eel* SOO-*oh* NOH-*meh ahl seen-*YOHR BEHR-*leets.*
Madam, tell Mr. Berlitz your name.

Che cosa dice Lei al signor Berlitz?
Keh KOH-*zah* DEE-*cheh Lay ahl seen-*YOHR BEHR-*leets?*
What do you tell Mr. Berlitz?

Io gli dico il mio nome.
EE-*oh l'yee* DEE-*koh eel* MEE-*oh* NOH-*meh.*
I tell him my name.

Signor Berlitz, che cosa Le dice questa signora?
*Seen-*YOHR BEHR-*leets, keh* KOH-*zah Leh* DEE-*cheh* KWESS-*tah seen-*YOH-*rah?*
Mr. Berlitz, what does this lady say to you?

Essa mi dice il suo nome.
ESS-*sah mee* DEE-*cheh eel* SOO-*oh* NOH-*meh.*
She tells me her name.

Che cosa dice Lei?	**Non dico nulla.**
Keh KOH-*zah* DEE-*cheh Lay?*	*Nohn* DEE-*koh* NOOL-*lah.*
What do you say?	I say nothing.

Io do qualche cosa al signor Berlitz.
EE-*oh doh* KWAHL-*keh* KOH-*zah ahl seen-*YOHR BEHR-*leets.*
I give something to Mr. Berlitz.

Io gli do qualche cosa.	**Io Le do qualche cosa.**
EE-*oh l'yee doh* KWAHL-*keh* KOH-*zah.*	EE-*oh Leh doh* KWAHL-*keh* KOH-*zah.*
I give him something.	I give you something.

Io do il libro al signor Berlitz.	**Io glielo do.**
EE-*oh doh eel* LEE-*broh ahl seen-*YOHR BEHR-*leets.*	EE-*oh l'yee-*EH-*loh doh.*
I give the book to Mr. Berlitz.	I give it to him.

Lei mi dà il libro blu.	**Lei me lo dà.**
Lay mee dah eel LEE-*broh bloo.*	*Lay meh loh dah.*
You give me the blue book.	You give it to me.

Ci dà qualche cosa il signor Berlitz?
Chee dah KWAHL-*keh* KOH-*zah eel seen-*YOHR BEHR-*leets?*
Does Mr. Berlitz give us something?

Sì, signore, ci dà qualche cosa.
*See, seen-*YOH-*reh, chee dah* KWAHL-*keh* KOH-*zah.*
Yes, sir, he gives us something.

Ci dà il libro il signor Berlitz?	**Ce lo dà.**
Chee dah eel LEE-*broh eel seen-*YOHR BEHR-*leets?*	*Cheh loh dah.*
Does Mr. Berlitz give us the book?	He gives it to us.

Ci dà la scatola?
Chee dah lah SKAH-*toh-lah?*
Does he give us the box?

No, non ce la dà.
Noh, nohn cheh lah dah.
No, he does not give it to us.

Io le do la mia cravatta.
EE-*oh Leh doh lah* MEE-*ah krah-*VAHT-*tah.*
I give you my tie.

Io gliela do.
EE-*oh l'yee-*EH-*lah doh.*
I give it to you.

Io Le do i miei libri.
EE-*oh Leh doh ee m'*YAY *LEE-bree.*
I give you my books.

Io glieli do.
EE-*oh l'yee-*EH-*lee doh.*
I give them to you.

Mi dà Lei qualche cosa?
Mee dah Lay KWAHL-*keh* KOH-*zah?*
Do you give something to me?

No, signore, non Le do niente.
*Noh, seen-*YOH-*reh, nohn Leh doh n'*YEHN-*teh.*
No, sir, I do not give anything to you.

Mi dà Lei il Suo libro?
Mee dah Lay eel SOO-*oh* LEE-*broh?*
Do you give me your book?

No, signore, non glielo do.
*Noh, seen-*YOH-*reh, nohn l'yee-*EH-*loh doh.*
No sir, I do not give it to you.

NOTE to Student: When two pronoun objects are used together, *Le, le* and *gli* have the form of *glie.* Note the following cases: "I give it to him"—*Io glielo do.* "He tells it to you"—*Egli glielo dice.* In the same way, the indirect objects *mi* and *ci,* become *me* and *ce* when followed by a direct object pronoun. "She tells it to me"—*Essa me lo dice.* "They send them to us"—*Essi ce li mandano.* Note that *me* and *ce* are written separ-ately and not joined as in the case of *glie.*

Il professore dice "buon giorno" agli allievi.
*Eel proh-fess-*SOH-*reh* DEE-*cheh "b'*WOHN JOHR-*noh"* AHL-*yee ahl-l'*YEH-*vee.*
The teacher says "good morning" to the students.

Che cosa dice il professore dopo la lezione?
Keh KOH-*zah* DEE-*cheh eel proh-fess-*SOH-*reh* DOH-*poh lah leh-ts'*YOH-*neh?*
What does the teacher say after the lesson?

Il professore dice "a rivederci".
*Eel proh-fess-*SOH-*reh* DEE-*cheh "ah-ree-veh-*DEHR-*chee".*
The teacher says "good bye".

Gli allievi dicono "a rivederla".
*L'yee ahl-l'*YEH-*vee* DEE-*koh-noh "ah-ree-veh-*DEHR-*lah".*
The students say "good bye".

Grazie, signore.

THINKING IN ITALIAN
(Answers on page 286)

1. Dà il professore un libro alla signora Fibronia?
2. Che cosa dà il professore a Titina?
3. Che cosa fa la signora Fibronia?
4. Titina e la signora Fibronia danno un cappello al professore?
5. Chi parla a Titina?
6. Che cosa le dice il professore?
7. Dice qualche cosa a Fido la signora Fibronia?
8. Gli dà essa qualche cosa?
9. Che cosa dice Fido?
10. Parlano gli allievi al professore durante la lezione?
11. Gli dicono essi "buon giorno" prima della lezione?
12. Che cosa dice loro il professore dopo la lezione?
13. Mi dica che cosa c'è nella mano sinistra della signora Fibronia?
14. Che cosa mi dice?
15. Che cosa dice al professore la signora Fibronia?

LEZIONE 20

Con che cosa camminiamo?
Kohn keh KOH-*zah kahm-mee-n'*YAH-*moh?*
With what do we walk?

Che cosa facciamo col lapis? (con il lapis?)
Keh KOH-*zah faht-ch'*YAH-*moh kohl* LAH-*peess?* (*kohn eel* LAH-*peess?*)
What do we do with the pencil?

Col lapis scriviamo.
Kohl LAH-*peess skree-v'*YAH-*moh.*
We write with the pencil.

Con la penna? (Colla penna?)
Kohn lah PEHN-*nah?* (KOHL-*lah* PEHN-*nah?*)
With the pen?

Con la penna scriviamo.
Kohn lah PEHN-*nah skree-v'*YAH-*moh.*
We write with the pen.

Col coltello? (Con il coltello?)
*Kohl kohl-*TEHL-*loh?* (*Kohn eel kohl-*TEHL-*loh?*)
With the knife?

Col coltello tagliamo.
*Kohl kohl-*TEHL-*loh tahl-l'*YAH-*moh.*
We cut with the knife.

Con le mani? (Colle mani?)
Kohn leh MAH-*nee?* (KOHL-*leh* MAH-*nee?*)
With the hands?

Con le mani prendiamo.
Kohn leh MAH-*nee prehn-d'*YAH-*moh.*
We take with our hands.

Con i piedi? (Coi piedi?)
*Kohn ee p'*YEH-*dee?* (*Koy p'*YEH-*dee?*)
With the feet?

Con i piedi camminiamo.
*Kohn ee p'*YEH-*dee kahm-mee-n'*YAH-*moh.*
We walk with our feet.

 NOTE to Student: "With the" is translated either by:

REGULAR FORM		COMBINED FORM
Con il Con lo	} Masculine singular	Col Collo (regular form preferred)
Con i Con gli	} Masculine plural	Coi Cogli (regular form preferred)
Con la	Feminine singular	Colla (regular form preferred)
Con le	Feminine plural	Colle (regular form preferred)

Con che cosa scriviamo?
Kohn keh KOH-*zah skree-v'*YAH-*moh?*
With what do we write?

Scriviamo col lapis o con la penna.
*Skree-v'*YAH-*moh kohl* LAH-*peess oh kohn lah* PEHN-*nah.*
We write with the pencil or with the pen.

Con gli occhi vediamo. (Cogli occhi vediamo.)
Kohn l'yee OCK-*kee veh-d'*YAH-*moh.* (KOHL-*yee* OCK-*kee veh-d'*YAH-*moh.*)
We see with our eyes.

Con gli orecchi sentiamo.
*Kohn l'yee oh-*REHK*-kee sehn-t'*YAH*-moh.*
We hear with our ears.

REMEMBER: In Italian "you walk with the feet", "you see with the eyes" etc. It isn't necessary to specify that you are using *your own feet* to walk or *your own eyes* to see. The Italians take that for granted.

Io chiudo gli occhi,
EE-*oh k'*YOO-*doh l'yee* OCK-*kee,*
I shut my eyes,

io non vedo.
EE-*oh nohn* VEH-*doh.*
I don't see.

Io apro gli occhi,
EE-*oh* AH-*proh l'yee* OCK-*kee,*
I open my eyes,

io vedo.
EE-*oh* VEH-*doh.*
I see.

Lei è davanti a me,
Lay EH *dah-*VAHN*-tee ah meh,*
You are in front of me,

io La vedo.
EE-*oh Lah* VEH-*doh.*
I see you.

Il signor Delbosco non è qui,
*Eel seen-*YOHR *Dehl-*BOHS*-koh
noh-*NEH *kwee,*
Mr. Delbosco is not here,

io non vedo il signor Delbosco.
EE-*oh nohn* VEH-*doh eel seen-*YOHR
*Dehl-*BOHS*-koh.*
I do not see Mr. Delbosco.

È la tavola davanti a Lei?
EH *lah* TAH-*voh-lah dah-*VAHN*-tee ah Lay?*
Is the table in front of you?

Vede Lei la tavola?
VEH-*deh Lay lah* TAH-*voh-lah?*
Do you see the table?

È la finestra dietro a Lei?
EH *lah fee-*NESS*-trah d'*YEH*-troh ah Lay?*
Is the window behind you?

Vede Lei la finestra?
VEH-*deh Lay lah fee-*NESS*-trah?*
Do you see the window?

Chiuda gli occhi.
*k'*YOO-*dah l'yee* OCK-*kee.*
Close your eyes.

Vede Lei?
VEH-*deh Lay?*
Do you see?

Che cosa vede sulla tavola?
Keh KOH-*zah* VEH-*deh* SOOL-*lah* TAH-*voh-lah?*
What do you see on the table?

Io vedo un libro.
EE-*oh* VEH-*doh oon* LEE-*broh.*
I see a book.

Chi vede Lei qui?
Kee VEH-*deh Lay kwee?*
Whom do you see here?

Vedo il signor Ratti.
VEH-*doh eel seen-*YOHR RAHT-*tee.*
I see Mr. Ratti.

Io parlo,
EE-*oh* PAHR-*loh,*
I speak,

Io batto sulla tavola.
EE-*oh* BAHT-*toh* SOOL-*lah* TAH-*voh-lah.*
I knock on the table.

Io sento battere sulla tavola.
EE-*oh* SEHN-*toh* BAHT-*teh-reh* SOOL-*lah* TAH-*voh-lah.*
I hear knocking on the table.

Sente Lei il rumore della strada?
SEHN-*teh Lay eel* roo-MOH-*reh* DEHL-*lah* STRAH-*dah?*
Do you hear the noise from the street?

Sentiamo noi le automobili nella strada?
*Sehn-t'*YAH-*moh noy leh* aou-toh-MOH-*bee-lee* NEHL-*lah* STRAH-*dah?*
Do we hear the automobiles in the street?

Sì, noi le sentiamo.
*See, noy leh sehn-t'*YAH-*moh.*
Yes, we hear them.

Sentono Loro parlare il professore?
SEHN-*toh-noh* LOH-*roh* pahr-LAH-*reh eel* proh-fess-SOH-*reh?*
Do you hear the teacher speak?

Sì, noi lo sentiamo parlare.
*See, noy loh sehn-t'*YAH-*moh* pahr-LAH-*reh.*
Yes, we hear him speak.

Sentono gli alunni parlare il professore?
SEHN-*toh-noh l'yee* ah-LOON-*nee* pahr-LAH-*reh eel* proh-fess-SOH-*reh?*
Do the students hear the teacher speak?

Sì, essi lo sentono parlare.
See, EHS-*see loh* SEHN-*toh-noh* pahr-LAH-*reh.*
Yes, they hear him speak.

Lei mi sente parlare.
Lay mee SEHN-*teh* pahr-LAH-*reh.*
you hear me speak.

Che cosa sente Lei?
Keh KOH-*zah* SEHN-*teh Lay?*
What do you hear?

IMPORTANT NOTE: When a double verb construction is used, as in "they hear him speak"—*essi lo sentono parlare,* the second verb is put in the infinitive. Also notice "I see him coming"—*io lo vedo venire.*

Che cosa sente Lei sulla radio?
Keh KOH-*zah* SEHN-*teh Lay* SOOL-*lah* RAH-*d'yoh?*
What do you hear on the radio?

Io sento della musica.
EE-*oh* SEHN-*toh* DEHL-*lah* MOO-*zee-kah*.
I hear music.

Che cosa vede Lei nella strada?
Keh KOH-*zah* VEH-*deh Lay* NEHL-*lah* STRAH-*dah?*
What do you see in the street?

Io vedo delle automobili e molte persone.
EE-*oh* VEH-*doh* DEHL-*leh aou-toh-*MOH-*bee-lee eh* MOHL-*teh pehr-*SOH-*neh*.
I see automobiles and many persons.

Col naso odoriamo, sentiamo l'odore.
Kohl NAH-*zoh oh-doh-r'*YAH-*moh, sehn-t'*YAH-*moh loh-*DOH-*reh*.
We smell with the nose, we smell odors.

Sente Lei l'odore dei fiori?
SEHN-*teh Lay loh-*DOH-*reh day f'*YOH-*ree?*
Do you smell the odor of the flowers?

Sì, io sento.	**Io non lo sento.**
See, loh SEHN-*toh.*	EE-*oh nohn loh* SEHN-*toh.*
Yes, I smell it.	I don't smell it.

REMEMBER: *Sentire* (infinitive) means two things, "to hear" and "to feel". Ex: *Io sento un rumore*—"I hear a noise"; *io sento un dolore*—"I feel a pain."

I fiori hanno buon odore.
*Ee f'*YOH-*ree* AHN-*noh b'*WOHN *oh-*DOH-*reh*.
Flowers have a good odor.

L'inchiostro non ha buon odore, ha cattivo odore.
*Leen-k'*YOHS-*troh noh-*NAH *b'*WOHN *oh-*DOH-*reh,* AH *kaht-*TEE-*voh oh-*DOH-*reh*.
Ink hasn't a good odor, it has a bad odor.

Il gas ha cattivo odore.
Eel gahs AH *kaht-*TEE-*voh oh-*DOH-*reh*.
Gas has a bad odor.

WATCH OUT! Don't confuse forms of the verb *odorare*—"to smell" with the noun *odore*—"odor".

Ecco dei fiori: una rosa, una violetta, un tulipano, un garofano,
ECK-*koh day f'*YOH-*ree:* OO-*nah* ROH-*zah,* OO-*nah* vee-oh-LET-*tah,*
*oon too-lee-*PAH-*noh, oon gah-*ROH-*fah-noh,*
Here are some flowers: a rose, a violet, a tulip, a carnation,

una mammola.	**Ha buon odore la rosa?**
OO-*nah* MAHM-*moh-lah.*	AH *b'*WOHN *oh-*DOH-*reh lah* ROH-*zah?*
a pansy.	Has the rose a good odor?
Sì, la rosa ha buon odore.	**Ha buon odore il gas?**
See, lah ROH-*zah* AH *b'*WOHN *oh-*DOH-*reh.*	AH *b'*WOHN *oh-*DOH-*reh eel gahs?*
Yes, the rose has a good odor.	Has gas a good odor?

Colla bocca mangiamo e beviamo.
KOHL-*lah* BOHK-*kah mahn-*JAH-*moh eh beh-v'*YAH-*moh.*
With our mouth we eat and drink.

**Noi mangiamo del pane, della carne, del pesce, dei vegetali,
della frutta.**
*Noy mahn-*JAH-*moh dehl* PAH-*neh,* DEHL-*lah* KAHR-*neh, dehl* PEH-*sheh,
day veh-jeh-*TAH-*lee,* DEHL-*lah* FROOT-*tah.*
We eat bread, meat, fish, vegetables, fruit.

Alcuni vegetali: i fagioli, i piselli, i cavoli, le patate, le carote,
*Ahl-*KOO-*nee veh-jeh-*TAH-*lee: ee fah-*JOH-*lee, ee pee-*SEHL-*lee, ee* KAH-*voh-lee,
leh pah-*TAH-*teh, leh kah-*ROH-*teh,*
Some vegetables: beans, peas, cabbage, potatoes, carrots,

i fagiolini, i cavolifiori, gli asparagi, il riso, le cipolle.
*ee fah-joh-*LEE-*nee, ee* KAH-*voh-lee-f'*YOH-*ree, l'yee ahs-*PAH-*rah-jee, eel*
REE-*zoh, leh chee-*POHL-*leh.*
stringbeans, cauliflower, asparagus, rice, onions.

Frutta: la mela, la pera, la pesca, l'uva, la fragola, la prugna.
FROOT-*tah: lah* MEH-*lah, lah* PEH-*rah, lah* PESS-*kah,* LOO-*vah,
lah* FRAH-*goh-lah, lah* PROO-*n'yah.*
Fruit, the apple, the pear, the peach, the grape, the strawberry, the plum.

Carne: il rosbiffe, la bistecca, la costoletta di maiale,
KAHR-*neh: eel rohs-*BEEF-*feh, lah bees-*TEHK-*kah, lah kohs-toh-*LET-*tah dee
migh-*YAH-*leh,*
Meat: roastbeef, steak, pork chop,

la costoletta di agnello, il pollo.
*lah kohs-toh-*LET-*tah dee ah-n'*YEHL-*loh, eel* POHL-*loh.*
lamb chop, chicken.

Beviamo dell'acqua, del vino, della birra, del tè, del latte, del caffè.
*Beh-v'*YAH-*moh dehl-*LAHK-*kwah, dehl* VEE-*noh,* DEHL-*lah* BEER-*rah, dehl* TEH,
dehl LAHT-*teh, dehl kahf-*FEH.
We drink water, wine, beer, tea, milk, coffee.

THINKING IN ITALIAN
(Answers on page 287)

1. Con che cosa odora la cipolla il professore?
2. Ha buon odore la cipolla?
3. Ha buon odore la rosa?
4. Odora una rosa o una cipolla la signora Fibronia?
5. Vede Lei le cose dietro a Lei?
6. Vediamo noi le cose davanti a noi?
7. Sentiamo noi qualcuno battere sulla tavola?
8. Sente Lei parlare il Presidente degli Stati Uniti?
9. Mangiamo noi del pane?
10. Vediamo noi il film al cinema?
11. Mettiamo noi dello zucchero nel caffè?
12. Mangiano del pane bianco gli americani?
13. Bevono molto vino gl'italiani?
14. Mettiamo noi dello zucchero sulla carne?
15. Mette Lei del latte nel tè?
16. Con che cosa tagliamo noi la carne?
17. Mangiamo noi i piselli col coltello?
18. Scrive Lei con un lapis o una penna?
19. Beviamo noi col naso?
20. Con che cosa beviamo?

LEZIONE 21

Con che cosa mangiamo?
Kohn keh KOH-*zah mahn-*JAH-*moh?*
With what do we eat?

Con che cosa mangiamo la minestra?
Kohn keh KOH-*zah mahn-*JAH-*moh lah mee-*NESS-*trah?*
With what do we eat soup?

Mangiamo la minestra col cucchiaio.
*Mahn-*JAH-*moh lah mee-*NESS-*trah kohl kook-k'*YIGH-*yoh.*
We eat soup with a spoon.

Con che cosa tagliamo la carne?
Kohn keh KOH-*zah tahl-l'*YAH-*moh lah* KAHR-*neh?*
With what do we cut meat?

Tagliamo la carne col coltello.
*Tahl-l'*YAH-*moh lah* KAHR-*neh kohl kohl-*TEHL-*loh.*
We cut meat with a knife.

Con che cosa mangiamo la carne?
Kohn keh KOH-*zah mahn-*JAH-*moh lah* KAHR-*neh?*
With what do we eat meat?

Mangiamo la carne colla forchetta.
*Mahn-*JAH-*moh lah* KAHR-*neh* KOHL-*lah fohr-*KEHT-*tah.*
We eat meat with a fork.

Ecco un piatto.
ECK-*koh oon p'*YAHT-*toh.*
Here is a plate.

Dove mettiamo la carne?
DOH-*veh meht-t'*YAH-*moh lah* KAHR-*neh?*
Where do we put the meat?

Noi mettiamo la carne nel piatto.
*Noy meht-t'*YAH-*moh lah* KAHR-*neh nehl p'*YAHT-*toh.*
We put the meat on the plate.

Il bicchiere, la tazza.
*Eel beek-k'*YEH-*reh, lah* TAHT-*tsah.*
The glass, the cup.

Con che cosa beviamo il vino?
Kohn keh KOH-*zah beh-v'*YAH-*moh
   eel* VEE-*noh?*
In what do we drink wine?

Beviamo il vino col bicchiere.
*Beh-v'*YAH-*moh eel* VEE-*noh kohl
   beek-k'*YEH-*reh.*
We drink wine in a glass.

Con che cosa beviamo il tè?
Kohn keh KOH-*zah beh-v'*YAH-*moh
   eel* TEH?
In what do we drink tea?

Beviamo il tè colla tazza.
*Beh-v'*YAH-*moh eel* TEH KOHL-*lah
   * TAHT-*tsah.*
We drink tea in a cup.

Il pane è buono da mangiare.
Eel PAH-*neh* EH *b'*WOH-*noh dah mahn-*JAH-*reh.*
Bread is good to eat.

La carta non è buona da mangiare.
Lah KAHR-*tah noh-*NEH *b'*WOH-*nah dah mahn-*JAH-*reh.*
Paper is not good to eat.

È cattiva.
EH *kaht-*TEE-*vah.*
It is bad.

L'acqua è buona da bere.
LAHK-*kwah* EH *b'*WOH-*nah dah* BEH-*reh.*
Water is good to drink.

L'inchiostro non è buono da bere.
*Leen-k'*YOHS-*troh noh-*NEH *b'*WOH-*noh dah* BEH-*reh.*
Ink is not good to drink.

È cattivo.
EH *kaht-*TEE-*voh.*
It is bad.

Questo lapis non scrive; non è buono, è cattivo.
KWESS-*toh* LAH-*peess nohn* SKREE-*veh; noh-*NEH *b'*WOH-*noh,
   * EH *kaht-*TEE-*voh.*
This pencil doesn't write; it isn't good, it is bad.

Il mio coltello non taglia, è cattivo.
Eel MEE-*oh kohl-*TEHL-*loh nohn* TAHL-*l'yah,* EH *kaht-*TEE-*voh.*
My knife doesn't cut, it is bad.

Questa penna è rotta, è cattiva.
KWESS-*tah* PEHN-*nah* EH ROHT-*tah,* EH *kaht*-TEE-*vah.*
This pen is broken, it is bad.

Scrive male.
SKREE-*veh* MAH-*leh.*
It writes badly.

L'altra penna è buona, scrive molto bene.
LAHL-*trah* PEHN-*nah* EH *b'*WOH-*nah,* SKREE-*veh* MOHL-*toh* BEH-*neh.*
The other pen is good, it writes very well.

La rosa ha buon odore.
Lah ROH-*zah* AH *b'*WOHN
   oh-DOH-*reh.*
The rose has a good odor.

L'odore della rosa è gradevole.
Loh-DOH-*reh* DEHL-*lah* ROH-*zah*
   EH *grah*-DEH-*voh-leh.*
The odor of the rose is pleasant.

L'inchiostro ha cattivo odore.
*Leen-k'*YOHS-*troh* AH *kaht*-TEE-*voh oh*-DOH-*reh.*
Ink has a bad odor.

L'odore dell'inchiostro è sgradevole.
Loh-DOH-*reh dehl-leen-k'*YOHS-*troh* EH *sgrah*-DEH-*voh-leh.*
The odor of ink is unpleasant.

È gradevole l'odore del gas?
EH *grah*-DEH-*voh-leh loh*-DOH-*reh dehl gahs?*
Is the odor of gas pleasant?

No, non è gradevole, ma sgradevole.
Noh, noh-NEH *grah*-DEH-*voh-leh, mah sgrah*-DEH-*voh-leĥ.*
No, it is not pleasant, but unpleasant.

Le fragole hanno buon odore e piacevole gusto.
Leh FRAH-*goh-leh* AHN-*noh b'*WOHN *oh*-DOH-*reh eh p'yah*-CHEH-*voh-leh*
   GOOS-*toh.*
Strawberries have a good odor and a pleasant taste.

Le fragole mi piacciono.
Leh FRAH-*goh-leh mee p'*YAH-*choh-noh.*
I like strawberries.

Le piace l'odore del gas?
*Leh p'*YAH-*cheh loh*-DOH-*reh*
   dehl gahs?
Do you like the smell of gas?

No, non mi piace, mi dispiace.
*Noh, nohn mee p'*YAH-*cheh,*
   *mee dees-p'*YAH-*cheh.*
No, I don't like it, it displeases me.

IMPORTANT NOTE: To translate "to like", use the verb *piacere* intransitively. When you say *mi piace,* you are really saying, "it pleases me". Ex: "She likes champagne"—*Lo sciampagna le piace.* But if the subject of the verb is plural, the verb becomes plural. Ex: "I like beans"—*I fagioli mi piacciono.* A verb in the infinitive form can also be used with *piacere.* Ex: "Do you like to dance the tango?"—*Le piace ballare il tango?*

Il gusto del caffè con zucchero mi piace.
Eel GOOS-*toh dehl kahf*-FEH *kohn* TSOOK-*keh-roh mee p'*YAH-*cheh.*
I like the taste of coffee with sugar.

Il caffè senza zucchero mi dispiace.
Eel kahf-FEH SEHN-*tsah* TSOOK-*keh-roh mee dees-p'*YAH-*cheh.*
I don't like coffee without sugar.

Un buon odore Le piace.
*Oon b'*WOHN *oh-*DOH-*reh Leh*
*p'*YAH-*cheh.*
You like a good smell.

Un cattivo odore Le dispiace.
Oon kaht-TEE-*voh oh-*DOH-*reh*
*Leh dees-p'*YAH-*cheh.*
You don't like a bad smell.

 CONVERSATIONAL HINT: *Dispiace* means not only "dislike" but is also used to express the conversational formula "I regret" or "I am sorry". Ex: *Mi dispiace non potere venire con Lei.*—"I regret not to be able to come with you.", *Mi dispiace sentire che Sua moglie non sta bene.* —"I am sorry to hear that your wife doesn't feel well."

Le cose che si vedono con piacere sono belle.
Leh KOH-*zeh keh see* VEH-*doh-noh kohn p'yah-*CHEH-*reh* SOH-*noh* BELL-*leh.*
Things which are pleasant to see are beautiful.

La statua di Venere è bella;
Lah STAH-*too-ah dee* VEH-*neh-reh* EH BELL-*lah;*
The statue of Venus is beautiful;

Venezia è bella.
*Veh-*NEH-*ts'yah* EH BELL-*lah.*
Venice is beautiful.

Nei musei vi sono belle statue e bei quadri.
*Nay moo-*ZEH-*ee vee* SOH-*noh* BELL-*leh* STAH-*too-eh eh bay* KWAH-*dree.*
There are beautiful statues and beautiful pictures in the museums.

Le cose che non si vedono con piacere sono brutte.
Leh KOH-*zeh keh nohn see* VEH-*doh-noh kohn p'yah-*CHFH-*reh*
SOH-*noh* BROOT-*teh.*
Things that are not pleasant to see are ugly.

Il ragno è brutto.
Eel RAHN-*yoh* EH BROOT-*toh.*
The spider is ugly.

La scimmia non è bella, è brutta.
Lah SHEEM-*m'yah noh-*NEH BELL-*lah,* EH BROOT-*tah.*
The ape is not beautiful, it is ugly.

Il cavallo è bello.
*Eel kah-*VAHL-*loh* EH BELL-*loh.*
The horse is beautiful.

Il cammello è brutto.
*Eel kahm-*MEHL-*loh* EH BROOT-*toh.*
The camel is ugly.

THINKING IN ITALIAN

(Answers on page 287)

1. Con che cosa tagliamo la carne?
2. Mangiamo la carne col cucchiaio?
3. Che cosa mangiamo col cucchiaio?
4. Le piace l'odore della rosa?
5. Le piace l'odore del formaggio?
6. Il caffè con zucchero Le piace?
7. Le piace la minestra con lo zucchero?
8. Le piace l'odore del cavolo?
9. Le piace il sapore della fragola?
10. Le piace il formaggio?
11. Le piace il tè senza zucchero?
12. Le piace la birra?

13. Piacciono i fiori alle signorine?
14. Le piace parlare italiano?
15. È bella la statua di Venere?
16. Sono belli i vestiti di Schiaparelli?
17. Sono belli i suoi cappelli?
18. È bella la mia cravatta?
19. È bello o brutto il gufo?
20. È bello il pavone?

21. È bella la lingua italiana?
22. Le piace di sentirla?

LEZIONE 22

Non ne ho—ne prendo
Nohn neh OH—*neh* PREHN-*doh*
I have none—I take some

Mangia Lei della carne?
MAHN-*jah Lay* DEHL-*lah* KAHR-*neh?*
Do you eat meat?

Sì, io mangio della carne.
See, EE-*oh* MAHN-*joh* DEHL-*lah* KAHR-*neh.*
Yes, I eat meat.

No, non mangio carne.
Noh, nohn MAHN-*joh* KAHR-*neh.*
No, I don't eat meat.

Sì, ne mangio.
See, neh MAHN-*joh.*
Yes, I eat some.

No, non ne mangio.
Noh, nohn neh MAHN-*joh.*
No, I don't eat any.

Beve Lei del vino?
BEH-*veh Lay dehl* VEE-*noh?*
Do you drink wine?

Sì, bevo del vino.
See, BEH-*voh dehl* VEE-*noh.*
Yes, I drink wine.

No, non bevo vino.
Noh, nohn BEH-*voh* VEE-*noh.*
No, I don't drink wine.

Sì, ne bevo.
See, neh BEH-*voh.*
Yes, I drink some.

No, non ne bevo.
Noh, nohn neh BEH-*voh.*
No, I don't drink any.

NOTE ON *NE: Ne* is one of those very important little words you must understand and use to speak natural Italian. Look at the various ways it is used in the text. It means "some", "of it", "of them" or, with a negative "none" or "any".

Ex: "I have little *of it*."—Io *ne* ho poco.
"I have *some*."—Io *ne* ho.
"I have five *of them*."—Io *ne* ho cinque.
"Have you *any?*"—*Ne* ha?
"No, I have *none*."—No, non *ne* ho.

Mangia della carne questo signore?
MAHN-*jah* DEHL-*lah* KAHR-*neh* KWESS-*toh* seen-YOH-*reh?*
Does this gentleman eat meat?

Sì, egli mangia carne.
See, EHL-*yee* MAHN-*jah* KAHR-*neh.*
Yes, he eats meat.

Sì, ne mangia.
See, neh MAHN-*jah.*
Yes, he eats some.

No, egli non mangia carne.
Noh, EHL-*yee nohn* MAHN-*jah* KAHR-*neh.*
No, he doesn't eat meat.

No, non ne mangia.
Noh, nohn neh MAHN-*jah.*
No, he doesn't eat any.

Il signor Barberini beve limonata?
*Eel seen-*YOHR *Bahr-beh-*REE-*nee* BEH-*veh lee-moh-*NAH-*tah?*
Does Mr. Barberini drink limonade?

Sì, egli beve limonata.
See, EHL-*yee* BEH-*veh lee-moh-*NAH-*tah.*
Yes, he drinks limonade.

Sì, egli ne beve.
See, EHL-*yee neh* BEH-*veh.*
Yes, he drinks some.

Non, egli non beve limonata.
Nohn, EHL-*yee nohn* BEH-*veh*
*lee-moh-*NAH-*tah.*
No, he doesn't drink limonade.

No, egli non ne beve.
Noh, EHL-*yee nohn neh* BEH-*veh.*
No, he doesn't drink any.

Mangiamo noi delle mele?
*Mahn-*JAH-*moh noy* DEHL-*leh* MEH-*leh?*
Do we eat apples?

Sì, noi mangiamo mele.
*See, noy mahn-*JAH-*moh* MEH-*leh.*
Yes, we eat apples.

Sì, noi ne mangiamo.
*See, noy neh mahn-*JAH-*moh.*
Yes, we eat some.

No, noi non mangiamo mele.
*Noh, noy nohn mahn-*JAH-*moh* MEH-*leh.*
No, we do not eat apples.

No, non ne mangiamo.
*Noh, nohn neh mahn-*JAH-*moh.*
No, we do not eat any.

Io ho un lapis.
EE-*oh* OH *oon* LAH-*peess.*
I have a pencil.

Lei ha due lapis.
Lay AH DOO-*eh* LAH-*peess.*
You have two pencils.

Noi abbiamo tre penne.
*Noy ahb-b'*YAH-*moh treh* PEHN-*neh.*
We have three pens.

Loro hanno molti libri.
LOH-*roh* AHN-*noh* MOHL-*tee* LEE-*bree*
They have many books.

Io ho molte mele.
EE-*oh* OH MOHL-*teh* MEH-*leh.*
I have many apples.

Nino ha libri.
NEE-*noh* AH LEE-*bree.*
Nino has books.

Io non ho libri.
EE-*oh noh*-NOH LEE-*bree.*
I haven't any books.

Egli non ha danaro.
EHL-*yee noh*-NAH *dah*-NAH-*roh.*
He hasn't any money.

Ne ho uno.
Neh OH OO-*noh.*
I have one.

Ne ha due.
Neh AH DOO-*eh.*
You have two.

Ne abbiamo tre.
*Neh ahb-b'*YAH-*moh treh.*
We have three.

Ne hanno molti.
Neh AHN-*noh* MOHL-*tee.*
They have many.

Ne ho molte.
Neh OH MOHL-*teh.*
I have many of them.

Ne ha.
Neh AH.
He has some.

Non ne ho.
Nohn neh OH.
I haven't any.

Non ne ha.
Nohn neh AH.
He hasn't any.

THINKING IN ITALIAN
(Answers on page 287)

(Try substituting *ne* for the nouns in your answers to the questions below. Answer each both affirmatively and negatively.)

1. Mangia Titina del pane?

2. Beve il professore del vino?

3. Mangia la signora Fibronia della carne?

4. Beve Lei del latte?

5. Bevo io della limonata?

6. Questi signori mangiano delle mele?

7. Bevono loro dell'acqua?

8. Prendono loro del caffè?

9. Beve Lei del vino?

10. Prendono loro del latte?

11. Scrive Lei delle lettere?

12. Il suo professore legge dei libri inglesi?

13. Ha Lei dei fiammiferi?

14. Beve Lei dell'acqua?

15. Beve Lei del caffè con latte?

16. Quante dita abbiamo?

17. Ha Lei molto danaro?

18. Ha molti capelli il signor Berlitz?

19. Ha Lei poco danaro?

20. Abbiamo noi molti compiti?

21. Scrive Lei molte lettere?

22. Legge Lei molti libri?

LEZIONE 23

Io non posso vedere
EE-*oh nohn* POHS-*soh veh*-DEH-*reh*
I cannot see

Io tocco la tavola, la sedia, il libro, ecc.
EE-*oh* TOHK-*koh lah* TAH-*voh-lah, lah* SEHD-*yah, eel* LEE-*broh,*
eht-CHEH-*teh-rah.*
I touch the table, the chair, the book, etc.

Tocchi la tavola.	**Lei tocca la tavola.**
TOHK-*kee lah* TAH-*voh-lah.*	*Lay* TOHK-*kah lah* TAH-*voh-lah.*
Touch the table.	You touch the table.
Che cosa fa Lei?	**Io tocco la tavola.**
Keh KOH-*zah fah Lay?*	EE-*oh* TOHK-*koh lah* TAH-*voh-lah.*
What do you do?	I touch the table.

Tocchi il libro, la sedia, la tavola.
TOHK-*kee eel* LEE-*broh, lah* SEHD-*yah, lah* TAH-*voh-lah.*
Touch the book, the chair, the table.

Tocchi il soffitto.
TOHK-*kee eel sohf*-FEET-*toh.*
Touch the ceiling.

Lei non può toccare il soffitto.
*Lay nohn p'*WOH *tohk*-KAH-*reh eel
sohf*-FEET-*toh.*
You cannot touch the ceiling.

Io non posso toccare il soffitto.
EE-*oh nohn* POHS-*soh tohk*-KAH-*reh eel sohf*-FEET-*toh.*
I cannot touch the ceiling.

Il signore non può toccare il soffitto.
Eel seen-YOH-*reh nohn p'*WOH *tohk*-KAH-*reh eel sohf*-FEET-*toh.*
The gentleman cannot touch the ceiling.

Lei può toccare la tavola.
*Lay p'*WOH *tohk*-KAH-*reh lah* TAH-*voh-lah.*
You can touch the table.

Io posso toccare la sedia.
EE-*oh* POHS-*soh tohk*-KAH-*reh lah* SEHD-*yah.*
I can touch the chair.

Il signor Danieli può toccare il libro.
Eel seen-YOHR *Dah-n'*YEH-*lee p'*WOH *tohk*-KAH-*reh eel* LEE-*broh.*
Mr. Danieli can touch the book.

Può Lei toccare la tavola?
*p'*WOH *Lay tohk*-KAH-*reh lah* TAH-*voh-lah?*
Can you touch the table?

Sì, posso toccarla.
See, POHS-*soh tohk*-KAHR-*iah.*
Yes, I can touch it.

Posso io toccare il soffitto?
POHS-*soh* EE-*oh tohk*-KAH-*reh eel sohf*-FEET-*toh?*
Can I touch the ceiling?

No, non può toccarlo.
*Noh, nohn p'*WOH *tohk*-KAHR-*loh.*
No, you cannot touch it.

Può la signora toccare la sedia?
*p'*WOH *lah seen*-YOH-*rah tohk*-KAH-*reh lah* SEHD-*yah?*
Can the lady touch the chair?

Sì, può toccarla.
*See, p'*WOH *tohk*-KAHR-*lah.*
Yes, she can touch it.

Io non posso uscire.
EE-*oh nohn* POHS-*soh* oo-SHEE-*reh.*
I cannot go out.

La porta è chiusa.
Lah POHR-*tah* EH *k'*YOO-*zah.*
The door is closed.

La porta è aperta.
Lah POHR-*tah* EH *ah*-PEHR-*tah.*
The door is open.

Io posso uscire.
EE-*oh* POHS-*soh* oo-SHEE-*reh.*
I can go out.

Io ho un lapis.
EE-*oh* OH *oon* LAH-*peess*.
I have a pencil.

Io posso scrivere.
EE-*oh* POHS-*soh* SKREE-*veh-reh*.
I can write.

Il signor Gatti non ha il lapis, non può scrivere.
*Eel seen-*YOHR GAHT-*tee noh-*NAH *eel* LAH-*peess, nohn p'*WOH SKREE-*veh-reh*.
Mr. Gatti has no pencil, he cannot write.

Il soffitto è alto.
*Eel sohf-*FEET-*toh* EH AHL-*toh*.
The ceiling is high.

Io non lo posso toccare.
EE-*oh nohn loh* POHS-*soh tohk-*KAH-*reh*.
I cannot touch it.

La lampada è bassa.
Lah LAHM-*pah-dah* EH BAHS-*sah*.
The lamp is low.

Io posso toccarla.
EE-*oh* POHS-*soh tohk-*KAHR-*lah*.
I can touch it.

IMPORTANT NOTE: *Lo* and *la,* at the end of a verb, are the equivalent of "it", "him" and "her". Ex: "Can you touch the book?" *Può Lei toccare il libro?;* "Yes I can touch it."—*Sì, io posso toccarlo.* "Can you touch the professor?"— *Può Lei toccare il professore?"*; "Yes, I can touch him."— *Sì, posso toccarlo.* "Can the professor touch the table?"—*Può il professore toccare la tavola?;* "Yes, he can touch it."—*Sì, egli può toccarla.* "Can I see the lady?"—*Posso io vedere la signora?;* "Yes, you can see her."—*Sì, Lei può vederla.*

Io chiudo gli occhi.
EE-*oh k'*YOO-*doh l'yee* OCK-*kee*.
I close my eyes.

Non posso vedere.
Nohn POHS-*soh veh-*DEH-*reh*.
I cannot see.

Il signore ha un coltello, egli può tagliare la carta.
*Eel seen-*YOH-*reh* AH *oon kohl-*TEHL-*loh,* EHL-*yee p'*WOH *tahl-l'*YAH-*reh
lah* KAHR-*tah*.
The gentleman has a knife, he can cut the paper.

Io non ho un coltello, non posso tagliare la carta.
EE-*oh noh-*NOH *oon kohl-*TEHL-*loh, nohn* POHS-*soh tahl-l'*YAH-*reh
lah* KAHR-*tah*.
I have no knife, I cannot cut the paper.

Il signor Berlitz porta gli occhiali,
*Eel seen-*YOHR BEHR-*leets* POHR-*tah l'yee ock-k'*YAH-*lee,*
Mr. Berlitz wears glasses,

egli può vedere con i suoi occhiali.
EHL-*yee p'*WOH *veh-*DEH-*reh kohn ee s'*WOY *ock-k'*YAH-*lee*
He can see with his glasses.

Egli non può vedere senza occhiali.
EHL-*yee nohn p'*WOH *veh-*DEH-*reh* SEHN-*tsah ock-k'*YAH-*lee.*
He cannot see without glasses.

Posso io toccare il soffitto?
POHS-*soh* EE-*oh tohk-*KAH-*reh eel sohf-*FEET-*toh?*
Can I touch the ceiling?

No, Lei non può toccare il soffitto.
*Noh, Lay nohn p'*WOH *tohk-*KAH-*reh eel sohf-*FEET-*toh.*
No, you cannot touch the ceiling.

Posso io toccare la lampada? POHS-*soh* EE-*oh tohk-*KAH-*reh* *lah* LAHM-*pah-dah?* Can I touch the lamp?	**Sì, Lei la può toccare.** *See, Lay lah p'*WOH *tohk-*KAH-*reh.* Yes, you can touch it.
Può Lei contare i miei capelli? *p'*WOH *Lay kohn-*TAH-*reh ee* *m'*YAY *kah-*PEHL-*lee?* Can you count my hair?	**No, non posso contarli.** *Noh, nohn* POHS-*soh kohn-*TAHR-*lee.* No, I cannot count them.
Può Lei contare i miei libri? *p'*WOH *Lay kohn-*TAH-*reh ee* *m'*YAY LEE-*bree?* Can you count my books?	**Sì, io posso contarli.** *See,* EE-*oh* POHS-*soh kohn-*TAHR-*lee.* Yes, I can count them.

Li conti. *Lee* KOHN-*tee.* Count them.	**Ve ne sono dieci.** *Veh neh* SOH-*noh d'*YEH-*chee.* There are ten (of them).

Possiamo noi rompere la chiave?
*Pohs-s'*YAH-*moh noy* ROHM-*peh-reh*
   *lah k'*YAH-*veh?*
Can we break the key?
	No, noi non possiamo romperla.
	*Noh, noy nohn pohs-s'*YAH-*moh*
	   ROHM-*pehr-lah.*
	No, we cannot break it.

Possiamo noi rompere il fiammifero?
*Pohs-s'*YAH-*moh noy* ROHM-*peh-reh eel f'yahm-*MEE-*feh-roh?*
Can we break the match?

Sì, possiamo romperlo.
*See, pohs-s'*YAH-*moh* ROHM-*pehr-loh.*
Yes, we can break it.

REMEMBER: *Posso—può—possiamo—possono—*is the present of the verb *potere,* which means "can", "may", "to be able", "to have the power".

THINKING IN ITALIAN
(Answers on page 288)

1. Titina tocca Fido?
2. Può essa toccare la mano destra del professore?
3. Può il professore toccare il cappello di Titina?
4. Lo tocca egli?
5. È bassa la lampada?
6. Può il professore toccarla?
7. Che cosa tocca il professore?
8. Porta occhiali il professore?
9. Può egli vedere senza gli occhiali?
10. La porta è aperta; può egli uscire dalla stanza?
11. Io non ho nè penna nè lapis: posso scrivere?
12. Possiamo noi vedere le cose dietro a noi?
13. Possono gli allievi toccare il soffitto?
14. Può Lei rompere un fiammifero?
15. Può Lei rompere la chiave della porta?
16. Può Lei toccare il Suo libro?

LEZIONE 24

Senza occhiali non posso vedere
SEHN-*tsah ock-k'*YAH-*lee nohn* POHS-*soh*
*veh-*DEH-*reh*
Without glasses I cannot see

Io non posso tagliare la carta, non ho forbici.
EE-*oh nohn* POHS-*soh tahl-l'*YAH-*reh lah* KAHR-*tah,*
*noh-*NOH FOHR-*bee-chee.*
I cannot cut the paper, I have no scissors.

Io non posso tagliare la carta, perchè non ho forbici.
EE-*oh nohn* POHS-*soh tahl-l'*YAH-*reh lah* KAHR-*tah, pehr-*KEH
*noh-*NOH FOHR-*bee-chee.*
I cannot cut the paper, because I have no scissors.

Posso tagliare la carta?   **No, Lei non può tagliarla.**
POHS-*soh tahl-l'*YAH-*reh lah*   *Noh, Lay nohn p'*WOH *tahl-l'*YAHR-*lah.*
   KAHR-*tah?*   No, you cannot cut it.
Can I cut the paper?

Perchè?   **Perchè non ha forbici.**
*Pehr-*KEH**?**   *Pehr-*KEH *noh-*NAH FOHR-*bee-chee.*
Why?   Because you have no scissors.

La porta è chiusa.
Lah POHR-*tah* EH *k'*YOO-*zah.*
The door is closed.

Perchè non può uscire?
*Pehr-*KEH *nohn p'*WOH *oo-*SHEE-*reh?*
Why can't you go out?

Questa scatola è piccola.
KWESS-*tah* SKAH-*toh-lah* EH
PEEK-*koh-lah.*
This box is small.

Lei non può uscire.
*Lay nohn p'*WOH *oo-*SHEE-*reh.*
You cannot go out.

Perchè la porta è chiusa.
*Pehr-*KEH *lah* POHR-*tah* EH *k'*YOO-*zah.*
Because the door is closed.

Questo libro è grande.
KWESS-*toh* LEE-*broh* EH
GRAHN-*deh.*
This book is large.

Non possiamo mettere il libro nella scatola.
*Nohn pohs-s'*YAH-*moh* MEHT-*teh-reh eel* LEE-*broh* NEHL-*lah*
SKAH-*toh-lah.*
We cannot put the book in the box.

Perchè non possiamo mettere il libro nella scatola?
*Pehr-*KEH *nohn pohs-s'*YAH-*moh* MEHT-*teh-reh eel* LEE-*broh* NEHL-*lah*
SKAH-*toh-lah?*
Why can't we put the book in the box?

Perchè il libro è grande e la scatola è piccola.
*Pehr-*KEH *eel* LEE-*broh* EH GRAHN-*deh eh lah* SKAH-*toh-lah*
EH PEEK-*koh-lah.*
Because the book is large and the box is small.

Chiuda gli occhi.
*k'*YOO-*dah l'yee* OCK-*kee.*
Close your eyes.

Perchè non può vedere?
*Pehr-*KEH *nohn p'*WOH *veh-*DEH-*reh?*
Why can't you see?

Lei non può vedere.
*Lay nohn p'*WOH *veh-*DEH-*reh.*
You cannot see.

Perchè chiudo gli occhi.
*Pehr-*KEH *k'*YOO-*doh l'yee* OCK-*kee.*
Because I close my eyes.

Il signor Berlitz non è qui.
*Eel seen-*YOHR BEHR-*leets noh-*NEH *kwee.*
Mr. Berlitz is not here.

Perchè gli allievi non possono vedere il signor Berlitz?
*Pehr-*KEH *l'yee ahl-l'*YEH-*vee nohn* POHS-*soh-noh veh-*DEH-*reh*
*eel seen-*YOHR BEHR-*leets?*
Why can the students not see Mr. Berlitz?

Perchè non è qui.
*Pehr-*KEH *noh-*NEH *kwee.*
Because he is not here.

Io prendo il Suo libro.
EE-oh PREHN-*doh eel* SOO-*oh* LEE-*broh.*
I take your book.

No, non posso.
Noh, nohn POHS-*soh.*
No, I cannot.

Perchè non ho libro.
*Pehr-*KEH *noh-*NOH LEE-*broh.*
Because I have no book.

Il signor Berlitz non ha i suoi occhiali.
*Eel seen-*YOHR BEHR-*leets noh-*NAH *ee s'*WOY *ock-k'*YAH-*lee.*
Mr. Berlitz hasn't his glasses.

Può egli vedere senza occhiali?
*p'*WOH EHL-*yee veh-*DEH-*reh* SEHN-*tsah ock-k'*YAH-*lee?*
Can he see without glasses?

No, non può.
*Noh, nohn p'*WOH.
No, he cannot.

Perchè non può vedere?
*Pehr-*KEH *nohn p'*WOH *veh-*DEH-*reh?*
Why isn't he able to see?

Perchè non ha i suoi occhiali.
*Pehr-*KEH *noh-*NAH *ee s'*WOY *ock-k'*YAH-*lee.*
Because he hasn't his glasses.

La porta è aperta.
Lah POHR-*tah* EH *ah-*PEHR-*tah.*
The door is open.

Può Lei uscire?
*p'*WOH *Lay oo-*SHEE-*reh?*
Can you go out?

Sì, posso uscire.
See, POHS-*soh oo-*SHEE-*reh.*
Yes, I can go out.

Perchè non esce?
*Pehr-*KEH *nohn* EH-*sheh?*
Why don't you go out?

Perchè non voglio.
*Pehr-*KEH *nohn* VOHL-*l'yoh.*
Because I don't want to.

Lei non esce, perchè non vuole.
Lay nohn EH-*sheh, pehr-*KEH *nohn v'*WOH-*leh.*
You don't go out because you don't want to.

Può Lei leggere?
*p'*WOH *Lay* LEH-*djeh-reh?*
Can you read?

Perchè non può?
*Pehr-*KEH *nohn p'*WOH?
Why can't you?

NOTE to Student: *Volere* means "to wish" or "to want" and takes the infinitive as does *potere* in the preceding lesson. It can also be used as an invitation. Ex: *Vuole andare al cinema?*—"Do you wish to go to the movies?" *Vuole Lei della cioccolata?*—"Do you wish some chocolate?"

Può Lei stracciare il Suo libro?
*p'*WOH *Lay straht-*CHAH-*reh eel* SOO-*oh* LEE-*broh?*
Can you tear your book?

Perchè non lo straccia?
*Pehr-*KEH *nohn loh* STRAHT-*chah?*
Why don't you tear it?

Perchè non voglio.
*Pehr-*KEH *nohn* VOHL-*l'yoh.*
Because I don't want to.

Lei non lo straccia perchè non vuole.
Lay nohn loh STRAHT-*chah pehr-*KEH *nohn v'*WOH-*leh.*
You don't tear it because you don't want to.

Io posso rompere il mio orologio, ma io non voglio romperlo.
EE-*oh* POHS-*soh* ROHM-*peh-reh eel* MEE-*oh oh-roh-*LOH-*joh, mah* EE-*oh nohn*
VOHL-*l'yoh* ROHM-*pehr-loh.*
I can break my watch, but I don't want to break it.

Io posso stracciare il mio vestito, ma non voglio stracciarlo.
EE-*oh* POHS-*soh straht-*CHAH-*reh eel* MEE-*oh vehs-*TEE-*toh, mah nohn*
VOHL-*l'yoh straht-*CHAHR-*loh.*
I can tear my suit, but I don't want to tear it.

Il professore può scrivere sul muro, ma egli non vuole scrivere sul muro.
*Eel proh-fess-*SOH-*reh p'*WOH SKREE-*veh-reh sool* MOO-*roh, mah* EHL-*yee nohn*
*v'*WOH-*leh* SKREE-*veh-reh sool* MOO-*roh.*
The teacher can write on the wall, but he doesn't want to write on the
wall.

Perchè non usciamo?
*Pehr-*KEH *nohn oo-sh'*YAH-*moh?*
Why do we not go out?

Perchè non vogliamo uscire.
*Pehr-*KEH *nohn vohl-l'*YAH-*moh oo-*SHEE-*reh.*
Because we don't want to go out.

Gli allievi possono stracciare i loro libri, ma non vogliono.
*L'yee ahl-l'*YEH-*vee* POHS-*soh-noh straht-*CHAH-*reh ee* LOH-*roh* LEE-*bree,*
mah nohn VOHL-*l'yoh-noh.*
The students can tear their books, but they don't want to.

Essi possono rompere la finestra con un bastone.
EHS-*see* POHS-*soh-noh* ROHM-*peh-reh lah fee-*NESS-*trah kohn oon*
*bahs-*TOH-*neh.*
They can break the window with a stick.

Perchè non la rompono?
*Pehr-*KEH *nohn lah* ROHM-*poh-noh?*
Why don't they break it?

Perchè non vogliono romperla.
*Pehr-*KEH *nohn* VOHL-*l'yoh-noh* ROHM-*pehr-lah.*
Because they don't want to break it.

 SAME WORD, TWO MEANINGS: *Perchè* means both
"why" and "because"; the inflection of the voice makes it
easy to distinguish one from the other.

THINKING IN ITALIAN
(Answers on page 288)

1. Può Lei uscire?
2. Vuole Lei uscire?
3. Può Lei rompere la finestra?
4. Vuole Lei rompere la finestra?
5. Vuole Lei parlare italiano qui?
6. Vuole Lei parlare inglese?
7. Che cosa vuole leggere, il libro o il giornale?
8. Vuole mangiare qualche cosa?
9. Vuole bere qualche cosa?
10. Che cosa vuole bere?
11. Possiamo uscire se la porta non è aperta?
12. Possiamo mangiare la minestra se non abbiamo un cucchiaio?
13. Può Lei tagliare la carne se non ha un coltello?
14. Perchè non rompe il Suo orologio?
15. Perchè gli allievi non stracciano i loro libri?
16. Possono gli allievi rompere la finestra con una palla?

LEZIONE 25

Che cosa devo fare per uscire?
Keh KOH-*zah* DEH-*voh* FAH-*reh pehr oo*-SHEE-*reh?*
What must I do to go out?

La porta è chiusa; la porta è aperta.
Lah POHR-*tah* EH *k'*YOO-*zah; la* POHR-*tah* EH *ah*-PEHR-*tah.*
The door is closed; the door is open.

La porta è chiusa; non possiamo uscire.
Lah POHR-*tah* EH *k'*YOO-*zah; nohn pohs-s'*YAH-*moh oo*-SHEE-*reh.*
The door is closed; we cannot go out.

Se la porta è aperta possiamo uscire.
Seh lah POHR-*tah* EH *ah*-PEHR-*tah pohs-s'*YAH-*moh oo*-SHEE-*reh.*
If the door is open, we can go out.

Se chiudiamo gli occhi non possiamo vedere.
*Seh k'yoo-d'*YAH-*moh l'yee* OCK-*kee nohn pohs-s'*YAH-*moh veh*-DEH-*re.*
If we close our eyes, we cannot see.

Se non ho gesso non posso scrivere sulla lavagna.
Seh noh-NOH JEHS-*soh nohn* POHS-*soh* SKREE-*veh-reh* SOOL-*lah lah*-VAHN-*yah.*
If I have no chalk, I cannot write on the blackboard.

Se non abbiamo nè lapis nè penne non possiamo scrivere.
*Seh nohn ahb-b'*YAH-*moh* NEH LAH-*peess* NEH PEHN-*neh nohn*
*pohs-s'*YAH-*moh* SKREE-*veh-reh.*
If we have neither pencils nor pens, we cannot write.

Io posso toccare l'orologio salendo (se salgo) sulla sedia.
EE-*oh* POHS-*soh tohk*-KAH-*reh loh-roh*-LOH-*joh sah*-LEHN-*doh (seh* SAHL-*goh)*
SOOL-*lah* SEHD-*yah.*
I can touch the clock by climbing (if I climb) on the chair.

Se non salgo sulla sedia non posso toccare l'orologio.
Seh nohn SAHL-*goh* SOOL-*lah* SEHD-*yah nohn* POHS-*soh tohk*-KAH-*reh*
loh-roh-LOH-*joh.*
If I don't climb on the chair, I cannot touch the clock.

Aprendo la porta possiamo uscire dalla stanza.
*Ah-*PREHN-*doh lah* POHR-*tah pohs-s'*YAH-*moh oo*-SHEE-*reh* DAHL-*lah*
STAHN-*tsah.*
By opening the door we can go out of the room.

Se non l'apriamo non possiamo uscire.
*Seh nohn lah-pr'*YAH-*moh nohn pohs-s'*YAH-*moh oo*-SHEE-*reh.*
If we don't open it, we cannot go out.

Venendo a scuola Lei può parlare l'italiano.
*Veh-*NEHN-*doh ah sk'*WOH-*lah Lay p'*WOH *pahr*-LAH-*reh lee-tahl*-YAH-*noh.*
By coming to school you can speak Italian.

Prendendo lezioni d'italiano Lei può parlarlo.
*Prehn-*DEHN-*doh leh-ts'*YOH-*nee dee-tahl*-YAH-*noh Lay p'*WOH *pahr*-LAHR-*loh.*
By taking Italian lessons, you can speak it.

Senza studiare Lei non può parlare la lingua.
SEHN-*tsah stoo-d'*YAH-*reh Lay nohn p'*WOH *pahr*-LAH-*reh lah* LEEN-*gwah.*
Without studying, you cannot speak the language.

NOTE: *Prendendo* is the present participle of *prendere.*
It is formed by adding *endo* to the root of the verb.
Prendendo means "taking", "by taking", "in taking", etc.,
but if used after *senza* (without), the verb must be put in
the infinitive. The 1st conjugation forms the present participle by adding *ando* to the root, while the 2nd and 3rd add *endo*. Ex:
studiando, mangiando, scrivendo, etc. Usually the present tense of a verb
corresponds to both the English present and present progressive. Ex: *Leggo*
—"I read" also "I am reading." But you can also use the verb *stare* with

the present participle to give the exact meaning of "I am reading" (at this moment). *Stare* can be used with the present participle of all verbs. Ex: *Sto camminando*—"I am walking." *Stiamo arrivando*—"We are arriving." *Stanno parlando*—"They are talking."

La porta è chiusa.	**Lei vuole uscire.**
Lah POHR-*tah* EH *k'*YOO-*zah.*	*Lay v'*WOH-*leh* oo-SHEE-*reh.*
The door is closed.	You want to go out.

Lei non può uscire se non apre la porta.
*Lay nohn p'*WOH *oo-*SHEE-*reh seh nohn* AH-*preh lah* POHR-*tah.*
You cannot go out if you don't open the door.

Lei deve aprire la porta per uscire.
Lay DEH-*veh ah-*PREE-*reh lah* POHR-*tah pehr oo-*SHEE-*reh.*
You must open the door to go out.

Noi non possiamo vedere se non apriamo gli occhi;
*Noy nohn pohs-s'*YAH-*moh veh-*DEH-*reh seh nohn ah-pr'*YAH-*moh
l'yee* OCK-*kee;*
We cannot see if we do not open our eyes;

noi dobbiamo aprire gli occhi per vedere.
*noy dohb-b'*YAH-*moh ah-*PREE-*reh l'yee* OCK-*kee pehr veh-*DEH-*reh.*
we must open our eyes to see.

Per scrivere sulla lavagna devo prendere il gesso.
Pehr SKREE-*veh-reh* SOOL-*lah lah-*VAHN-*yah* DEH-*voh* PREHN-*deh-reh
eel* JEHS-*soh.*
To write on the blackboard, I must take the chalk.

Per mangiare la minestra devo avere un cucchiaio.
*Pehr mahn-*JAH-*reh lah mee-*NEHS-*trah* DEH-*voh ah-*VEH-*reh oon
kook-k'*YIGH-*yoh.*
To eat soup, I must have a spoon.

Per mangiare la carne dobbiamo avere un coltello ed una forchetta.
*Pehr mahn-*JAH-*reh lah* KAHR-*neh dohb-b'*YAH-*moh ah-*VEH-*reh oon
kohl-*TEHL-*loh ehd* oo-*nah fohr-*KEHT-*tah.*
To eat meat we must have a knife and a fork.

Che cosa dobbiamo fare per uscire?
Keh KOH-*zah dohb-b'*YAH-*moh* FAH-*reh pehr oo-*SHEE-*reh?*
What must we do in order to go out?

Dobbiamo aprire la porta.
*Dohb-b'*YAH-*moh ah-*PREE-*reh lah* POHR-*tah.*
We must open the door.

Che cosa dobbiamo fare per vedere?
Keh KOH-*zah dobbiamo fare per vedere?*
Keh KOH-*zah dohb-b'*YAH-*moh* FAH-*reh pehr veh-*DEH-*reh?*
What must we do to see?

Dobbiamo aprire gli occhi.
*Dohb-b'*YAH-*moh ah-*PREE-*reh l'yee* OCK-*kee.*
We must open our eyes.

Che cosa devo avere per scrivere sulla lavagna?
Keh KOH-*zah* DEH-*voh ah-*VEH-*reh pehr* SKREE-*veh-reh* SOOL-*lah lah-*VAHN-*vah?*
What must I have to write on the blackboard?

Lei deve avere il gesso.
Lay DEH-*veh ah-*VEH-*reh eel* JEHS-*soh.*
You must have chalk.

Che cosa dobbiamo avere per tagliare la carne?
Keh KOH-*zah dohb-b'*YAH-*moh ah-*VEH-*reh pehr tahl-l'*YAH-*reh lah* KAHR-*neh?*
What must we have to cut meat?

Dobbiamo avere un coltello.
*Dohb-b'*YAH-*moh ah-*VEH-*reh oon kohl-*TEHL-*loh.*
We must have a knife.

Che cosa deve Lei fare per parlare?
Keh KOH-*zah* DEH-*veh Lay* FAH-*reh pehr pahr-*LAH-*reh?*
What must you do to speak?

Io devo aprire la bocca.
EE-*oh* DEH-*voh ah-*PREE-*reh lah* BOHK-*kah.*
I must open my mouth.

Il libro del signor Monti è chiuso.
Eel LEE-*broh dehl seen-*YOHR MOHN-*tee* EH *k'*YOO-*zoh.*
Mr. Monti's book is closed.

Può egli leggere?	**No, egli non può leggere.**
*p'*WOH EHL-*yee* LEH-*djeh-reh?*	*Noh,* EHL-*yee nohn p'*WOH LEH-*djeh-reh.*
Can he read?	No, he can't read.

Che cosa deve fare se vuole leggere?
Keh KOH-*zah* DEH-*veh* FAH-*reh seh v'*WOH-*leh* LEH-*djeh-reh?*
What must he do if he wants to read?

Deve aprire il suo libro.
DEH-*veh ah-*PREE-*reh eel* SOO-*oh* LEE-*broh.*
He must open his book.

ATTENTION: *Devo (debbo), deve, dobbiamo, devono (debbono)* are the present indicative forms of *dovere* meaning *"must"*. Ex: *Io devo (debbo) aprire la bocca per parlare.* —"I must open the mouth in order to speak."

NOTICE that *per*—"for", in this case takes the place of "in order to". *Dovere* also means "to owe" when not followed by another verb. Ex: *Egli mi deve mille lire.*—"He owes me 1000 lire."

Gli allievi non hanno nè lapis nè carta.
*L'yee ahl-l'*YEH-*vee noh-*NAHN-*noh* NEH LAH-*peess* NEH KAHR-*tah.*
The pupils have neither pencil nor paper.

Possono scrivere?	**No, non possono.**	**Perchè?**
POHS-*soh-noh* SKREE-*veh-reh?*	*Noh, nohn* POHS-*soh-noh.*	*Pehr-*KEH?
Can they write?	No, they can't.	Why?

Perchè non hanno nè carta nè lapis.
*Pehr-*KEH *noh-*NAHN-*noh* NEH KAHR-*tah* NEH LAH-*peess.*
Because they have neither paper nor pencil.

Essi non possono scrivere senza carta e senza lapis.
EHS-*see nohn* POHS-*soh-noh* SKREE-*veh-reh* SEHN-*tsah* KAHR-*tah eh* SEHN-*tsah*
  LAH-*peess.*
They can't write without paper and without (a) pencil.

Che cosa devono avere se vogliono scrivere?
Keh KOH-*zah* DEH-*voh-noh ah-*VEH-*reh seh* VOHL-*l'yoh-noh* SKREE-*veh-reh?*
What must they have if they want to write?

Debbono avere carta e lapis.
DEHB-*boh-noh ah-*VEH-*reh* KAHR-*tah eh* LAH-*peess.*
They must have paper and pencil.

Per viaggiare si deve avere danaro.
*Pehr vee-ah-*DJAH-*reh see* DEH-*veh ah-*VEH-*reh dah-*NAH-*roh.*
To travel one must have money.

Per viaggiare, questo signore deve avere danaro.
*Pehr vee-ah-*DJAH-*reh,* KWESS-*toh seen-*YOH-*reh* DEH-*veh ah-*VEH-*reh*
  *dah-*NAH-*roh.*
To travel this gentleman needs money.

Per andare all'opera questi signori devono avere biglietti.
*Pehr ahn-*DAH-*reh ahl-*LOH-*peh-rah* KWESS-*tee seen-*YOH-*ree* DEH-*voh-noh*
  *ah-*VEH-*reh beel-*YET-*tee.*
To go to the opera these gentlemen must have tickets.

REMEMBER: Certain verbs in Italian, regardless of their tense or mood, require the infinitive form for any verb which immediately follows them.

Ex: *Posso leggere italiano.*—"I can read Italian."
Deve lavorare domani.—"He must work tomorrow."
Essa vuole studiare inglese.—"She wants to study English."

THINKING IN ITALIAN

(Answers on page 289)

1. Titina vuole mangiar la mela?
2. Può essa toccarla?
3. Dà il professore la mela a Titina?
4. Perchè egli non la dà a Titina?
5. Vuole egli darla a Titina?
6. Si deve aprire la porta per uscire?
7. Se vogliamo vedere, dobbiamo aprire gli occhi?
8. Si deve aver danaro per viaggiare?
9. Che cosa dobbiamo avere per scrivere?
10. Che cosa deve fare Lei se la porta è chiusa e vuole uscire?
11. Può il signor Berlitz leggere senza occhiali?
12. Che cosa deve egli avere per leggere?
13. Che cosa dobbiamo avere per andare all'opera?
14. Può Lei mangiare la minestra con un coltello?
15. Che cosa deve avere per mangiare la minestra?
16. Si deve avere una forchetta per mangiare la minestra?
17. Deve Lei rompere il Suo orologio?
18. Devo io andare al cinema?

Che ora è?

Keh OH-*rah* EH?

What time is it?

Ecco un orologio da tasca,

ECK-*koh oon oh-roh-*LOH-*joh dah* TAHS-*kah,*

Here is a pocket watch,

ecco un orologio da muro.

ECK-*koh oon oh-roh-*LOH-*joh dah* MOO-*roh.*

here is a wall clock.

L'orologio da muro è più grande dell'orologio da tasca.

*Loh-roh-*LOH-*joh dah* MOO-*roh* EH *p'*YOO GRAHN-*deh dehl-loh-roh-*LOH-*joh
dah* TAHS-*kah.*

The wall clock is larger than the pocket watch.

Noi appendiamo l'orologio alla parete o lo mettiamo sul caminetto.
*Noy ahp-pehn-d'*YAH-*moh loh-roh-*LOH-*joh* AHL-*lah pah-*REH-*teh oh loh meht-t'*YAH-*moh sool kah-mee-*NET-*toh.*
We hang the clock on the wall or put it on the mantelpiece.

L'orologio da tasca lo portiamo in tasca.
*Loh-roh-*LOH-*joh dah* TAHS-*kah loh pohr-t'*YAH-*moh een* TAHS-*kah.*
We carry the pocket watch in the pocket.

Ecco un orologio da polso.
ECK-*koh oon oh-roh-*LOH-*joh dah* POHL-*soh.*
Here is a wrist watch.

E questa è una sveglia.
Eh KWESS-*tah* EH OO-*nah* SVEHL-*l'yah.*
And this is an alarm clock.

Un orologio è di legno, di marmo o di bronzo.
*Oon oh-roh-*LOH-*joh* EH *dee* LEHN-*yoh, dee* MAHR-*moh, oh dee* BROHN-*dzoh.*
A clock is of wood, of marble, or of bronze.

Un orologio da tasca, o da polso, è d'oro, d'argento,
*Oon oh-roh-*LOH-*joh dah* TAHS-*kah, oh dah* POHL-*soh,* EH DOH-*roh, dahr-*JEHN-*toh,*
A pocket watch or a wrist watch is of gold, silver,

di nickelio o d'acciaio inossidabile.
*dee neek-*KEH-*l'yoh, oh daht-*CHIGH-*yoh ee-nohs-see-*DAH-*bee-leh.*
nickel, or stainless steel.

Una sveglia è pure di metallo, e si usa per svegliarci.
Oo-nah SVEHL-*l'yah* EH POO-*reh dee meh-*TAHL-*loh, eh see* OO-*zah pehr svehl-l'*YAHR-*chee.*
An alarm clock is also of metal, and is used to wake us up.

Un'ora contiene sessanta minuti.
*Oo-*NOH-*rah kohn-t'*YEH-*neh sehs-*SAHN-*tah mee-*NOO-*tee.*
An hour contains sixty minutes.

Un minuto contiene sessanta secondi.
*Oon mee-*NOO-*toh kohn-t'*YEH-*neh sehs-*SAHN-*tah seh-*KOHN-*dee.*
A minute contains sixty seconds.

Sul quadrante dell'orologio vi sono due lancette.
*Sool kwah-*DRAHN-*teh dehl-loh-roh-*LOH-*joh vee* SOH-*noh* DOO-*eh lahn-*CHEHT-*teh.*
On the face of the clock there are two hands.

La lancetta lunga segna i minuti.
*Lah lahn-*CHEHT-*tah* LOON-*gah* SEHN-*yah ee mee-*NOO-*tee.*
The long hand points out the minutes.

La lancetta corta segna le ore.
*Lah lahn-*CHEHT*-tah* KOHR*-tah* SEHN*-yah leh* OH*-reh.*
The short hand points out the hours.

Sul quadrante dell'orologio vi sono cifre arabe o numeri romani.
*Sool kwah-*DRAHN*-teh dehl-loh-roh-*LOH*-joh vee* SOH*-noh* CHEE*-freh ah-*RAH*-beh*
oh NOO*-meh-ree roh-*MAH*-nee.*
On the face of the watch there are arabic numbers or roman numbers.

Ventiquattro ore fanno un giorno.
*Vehn-tee-*KWAHT*-troh* OH*-reh* FAHN*-noh oon* JOHR*-noh.*
Twenty-four hours make a day.

È l'una,	**sono le due,**	**sono le tre, ecc**
EH LOO*-nah,*	SOH*-noh leh* DOO*-eh,*	SOH*-noh leh treh,* EHT*-*CHEH*-teh-rah.*
It is one o'clock,	two o'clock,	three o'clock, etc.

Sono le quattro e un quarto,
SOH*-noh leh* KWAHT*-troh eh oon* KWAHR*-toh,*
It is a quarter past four,

sono le quattro e mezzo,
SOH*-noh leh* KWAHT*-troh eh* MEH*-dzoh,*
it is half-past four,

le cinque.	**Sono le cinque e cinque,**
leh CHEEN*-kweh.*	SOH*-noh leh* CHEEN*-kweh eh* CHEEN*-kweh,*
five o'clock.	It is five past five,

le cinque e dieci,	**le cinque e venti,**
leh CHEEN*-kweh eh d'*YEH*-chee,*	*leh* CHEEN*-kweh eh* VEHN*-tee,*
ten past five,	twenty past five,

le cinque e venti cinque.
leh CHEEN*-kweh eh* VEHN*-tee* CHEEN*-kweh.*
five twenty-five.

Sono le sei meno venti,
SOH*-noh leh say* MEH*-noh* VEHN*-tee,*
It is twenty to six,

le sei meno dieci,	**le sei meno cinque.**
leh say MEH*-noh d'*YEH*-chee,*	*leh say* MEH*-noh* CHEEN*-kweh.*
ten to six,	five to six.

HOW TO TELL TIME: In telling the time in Italian you first mention the nearest whole hour and then the minutes to be added or subtracted. Ex: "5:20" will be: *Le cinque e venti.*—"Five and twenty."; *Le sei meno venti.*—"Twenty of six." On the half hour you can say: *Le cinque e trenta*—"five and thirty" or *le cinque e mezza*—"five and a half." When time is mentioned in an official form, the minutes are always added to the last whole hour. Ex: "7:15" or "7:56" will be: *Le sette e quindici* or *le sette e cinquantasei*. You will also find that from 1 P.M. to midnight the hours are listed as 13 to 24. For instance, "4:50 P.M." on Italian timetables will be marked: *16:50* and midnight will be *Le ventiquattro*.

In un'ora ci sono sessanta minuti,
*Een oo-*NOH-*rah chee* SOH-*noh sehs-*SAHN-*tah mee-*NOO-*tee,*
In an hour there are sixty minutes,

in una mezz'ora trenta,
een OO-*nah meh-*DZOH-*rah* TREHN-*tah,*
thirty minutes in a half-hour,

in un quarto d'ora ve ne sono quindici.
een oon KWAHR-*toh* DOH-*rah veh neh* SOH-*noh* KWEEN-*dee-chee.*
and in a quarter hour there are fifteen.

Quanti minuti vi sono in un'ora?
KWAHN-*tee mee-*NOO-*tee vee* SOH-*noh een oo-*NOH-*rah?*
How many minutes are there in an hour?

Quanti ve ne sono in una mezz'ora?
KWAHN-*tee veh neh* SOH-*noh een* OO-*nah meh-*DZOH-*rah?*
How many are there in a half-hour?

Quanti in un quarto d'ora?
KWAHN-*tee een oon* KWAHR-*toh* DOH-*rah?*
How many in a quarter hour?

Lei viene a scuola alle undici, e se ne va a mezzogiorno.
*Lay v'*YEH-*neh ah sk'woh-lah* AHL-*leh* OON-*dee-chee, eh seh neh vah ah meh-dzoh-*JOHR-*noh.*
You come to school at eleven, and you leave at noon.

Fa colazione all'una.
*Fah koh-lah-ts'*YOH-*neh ahl-*LOO-*nah.*
You have lunch at one.

A che ora viene a scuola?
Ah keh OH-*rah v'*YEH-*neh ah sk'woh-lah?*
At what time do you come to school?

Io vengo alle undici.
EE-*oh* VEHN-*goh* AHL-*leh* OON-*dee-chee.*
I come at eleven.

A che ora se ne va?
Ah keh OH-*rah seh neh vah?*
At what time do you leave (there)?

Io me ne vado a mezzogiorno.
ᴇᴇ-oh meh neh ᴠᴀʜ-*doh ah meh-dzoh-*ᴊᴏʜʀ-*noh.*
I leave (there) at noon.

A che ora fa colazione?
Ah keh ᴏʜ-*rah fah koh-lah-ts'*ʏᴏʜ-*neh?*
At what time do you have lunch?

Al tocco.
Ahl ᴛᴏᴄᴋ-*koh.*
At one.

NOTE to Student: *Il tocco* is 1 ᴘ.ᴍ. or ᴀ.ᴍ. The word *tocco* is the name given to the sound of a bell.

Appeso alla parete di questa stanza c'è un orologio che non va.
*Ahp-*ᴘᴇʜ-*soh* ᴀʜʟ-*lah pah-*ʀᴇʜ-*teh dee* ᴋᴡᴇꜱꜱ-*tah* ꜱᴛᴀʜɴ-*tsah* ᴄʜᴇʜ *oon oh-roh-*ʟᴏʜ-*joh keh nohn vah.*
Hanging on the wall of this room there is a clock which is not going.

Bisogna caricarlo.
*Bee-*ᴢᴏʜɴ-*yah kah-ree-*ᴋᴀʜʀ-*loh.*
One must wind it up.

Io lo carico.
ᴇᴇ-*oh lo* ᴋᴀʜ-*ree-koh.*
I wind it up.

Io lo metto all'ora precisa: le undici e un quarto.
ᴇᴇ-*oh loh* ᴍᴇʜᴛ-*toh ahl-*ʟᴏʜ-*rah preh-*ᴄʜᴇᴇ-*zah: leh* ᴏᴏɴ-*dee-chee eh oon* ᴋᴡᴀʜʀ-*toh.*
I set it at the exact time: a quarter past eleven.

Il mio orologio non va più bene.
Eel ᴍᴇᴇ-*oh oh-roh-*ʟᴏʜ-*joh nohn vah p'*ʏᴏᴏ ʙᴇʜ-*neh.*
My watch doesn't run well any more.

Vado dall'orologiaio.
ᴠᴀʜ-*doh dahl-loh-roh-loh-*ᴊɪɢʜ-*yoh.*
I go to the watchmaker's.

L'orologiaio l'esamina.
*Loh-roh-loh-*ᴊɪɢʜ-*yoh leh-*ᴢᴀʜ-*mee-nah.*
The watchmaker examines it.

Bisogna cambiare la molla.
*Bee-*ᴢᴏʜɴ-*yah kahm-b'*ʏᴀʜ-*reh lah* ᴍᴏʜʟ-*lah.*
He must change the spring.

Il Suo orologio va molto bene.
Eel ꜱᴏᴏ-*oh oh-roh-*ʟᴏʜ-*joh vah* ᴍᴏʜʟ-*toh* ʙᴇʜ-*neh.*
Your watch runs very well.

Non è nè avanti nè indietro.
*Noh-*ɴᴇʜ ɴᴇʜ *ah-*ᴠᴀʜɴ-*tee* ɴᴇʜ *een-d'*ʏᴇʜ-*troh.*
It is neither fast nor slow.

REMEMBER: In Italian the watch or clock, is "ahead" or "behind" to indicate that it is "fast" or "slow".

Che ora è, signorina Volpi?
Keh OH-*rah* EH, *seen-yoh-*REE-*nah* VOHL-*pee?*
What time is it, Miss Volpi?

Sono le dodici meno un quarto.
SOH-*noh leh* DOH-*dee-chee* MEH-*noh oon* KWAHR-*toh.*
It is a quarter to twelve.

La Sua lezione dura un'ora,
Lah SOO-*ah leh-ts'*YOH-*neh* DOO-*rah oo-*NOH-*rah,*
Your lesson lasts one hour,

perchè comincia alle undici è finisce a mezzogiorno.
*pehr-*KEH *koh-*MEENT-*chah* AHL-*leh* OON-*dee-chee eh fee-*NEE-*sheh ah*
*meh-dzoh-*JOHR-*noh.*
because it starts at eleven and finishes at noon.

L'orologio da tasca è più grande dell'orologio da polso.
*Loh-roh-*LOH-*joh dah* TAHS-*kah* EH *p'*YOO GRAHN-*deh dehl-loh-roh-*LOH-*joh*
dah POHL-*soh.*
The pocket watch is bigger than the wrist watch.

NOTE to Student: In Italian you can say either: *Che ora è?* or *che ore sono?* But in answering one must always use the plural "sono", except when it is one o'clock, in which case you will say: *È l'una.*

La giacchetta è più lunga del gilè.
*Lah jahk-*KEHT-*tah* EH *p'*YOO LOON-*gah dehl jee-*LEH.
The jacket is longer than the vest.

Roma non è così grande come Parigi, ma è più grande di Venezia.
ROH-*mah noh-*NEH *koh-*ZEE GRAHN-*deh* KOH-*meh Pah-*REE-*jee, mah* EH *p'*YOO
GRAHN-*deh dee Veh-*NEH-*ts'yah.*
Rome is not so big as Paris, but it is bigger than Venice.

La rosa ha buon odore.
Lah ROH-*zah* AH *b'*WOHN *oh-*DOH-*reh.*
The rose has a good odor.

Essa ha un odore migliore del garofano.
ESS-*sah* AH *oon oh*-DOH-*reh meel-l'*YOH-*reh dehl gah*-ROH-*fah-noh.*
It has a better odor than the carnation.

La frutta fresca è più buona di quella conservata.
Lah FROOT-*tah* FREHS-*kah* EH *p'*YOO *b'*WOH-*nah dee* KWELL-*lah
kohn-sehr-*VAH-*tah.*
Fresh fruit is better than preserved.

La frutta acerba non è così buona come quella matura.
Lah FROOT-*tah ah*-CHEHR-*bah noh*-NEH *koh*-ZEE *b'*WOH-*nah* KOH-*meh*
KWELL-*lah mah*-TOO-*rah.*
Green fruit is not so good as ripe.

È la pesca più buona della mela?
EH *lah* PESS-*kah p'*YOO *b'*WOH-*nah* DEHL-*lah* MEH-*lah?*
Is the peach better than the apple?

Lei è più alto di me.	**È buono il caffè nero?**
Lay EH *p'*YOO AHL-*toh dee meh.*	EH *b'*WOH-*noh eel kahf*-FEH NEH-*roh?*
You are taller than I.	Is black coffee good?

È il caffè con zucchero più buono del caffè senza zucchero?
EH *eel kahf*-FEH *kohn* TSOOK-*keh-roh p'*YOO *b'*WOH-*noh dehl kahf*-FEH
SEHN-*tsah* TSOO-*keh-roh?*
Is coffee with sugar better than coffee without sugar?

La sua penna è buona, essa scrive bene.
LAH SOO-*ah* PEHN-*nah* EH *b'*WOH-*nah,* ESS-*sah* SKREE-*veh* BEH-*neh.*
Your pen is good, it writes well.

La mia penna è cattiva, scrive male.
Lah MEE-*ah* PEHN-*nah* EH *kaht*-TEE-*vah,* SKREE-*veh* MAH-*leh.*
My pen is bad, it writes badly.

La Sua pronuncia è buona, Lei pronuncia bene.
Lah SOO-*ah proh*-NOONT-*chah* EH *b'*WOH-*nah, Lay proh*-NOONT-*chah* BEH-*neh.*
Your pronunciation is good, you pronounce well.

La pronuncia del signor Volpi non è buona, egli pronuncia male.
Lah proh-NOONT-*chah dehl seen*-YOHR VOHL-*pee noh*-NEH *b'*WOH-*nah,* EHL-*yee
proh*-NOONT-*chah* MAH-*leh.*
Mr. Volpi's pronunciation is not good: he pronounces badly.

Taglia bene questo coltello?
TAHL-*l'yah* BEH-*neh* KWESS-*toh kohl*-TEHL-*loh?*
Does this knife cut well?

No, questo coltello non taglia bene, taglia male.
Noh, KWESS-*toh kohl*-TEHL-*loh nohn* TAHL-*l'yah* BEH-*neh,* TAHL-*l'yah* MAH-*leh.*
No, this knife does not cut well; it cuts badly.

Lei parla bene l'italiano, ma parla l'inglese meglio dell'italiano.
Lay PAHR-*lah* BEH-*neh lee-tahl-*YAH-*noh, mah* PAHR-*lah leen-*GLEH-*zeh*
MEHL-*yoh dehl-lee-tahl-*YAH-*noh.*
You speak Italian well but you speak English better than Italian.

Parla Lei l'italiano così bene come l'inglese?
PAHR-*lah Lay lee-tahl-*YAH-*noh koh-*ZEE BEH-*neh* KOH-*meh leen-*GLEH-*zeh?*
Do you speak Italian as well as English?

No, io non parlo l'italiano così bene come l'inglese.
Noh, EE-*oh nohn* PAHR-*loh lee-tahl-*YAH-*noh koh-*ZEE BEH-*neh* KOH-*meh*
*leen-*GLEH-*zeh.*
No, I do not speak Italian as well as English.

Io parlo l'inglese meglio dell'italiano.
EE-*oh* PAHR-*loh leen-*GLEH-*zeh* MEHL-*yoh dehl-lee-tahl-*YAH-*noh.*
I speak English better than Italian.

Il signor Berlitz porta occhiali; Lei non ne porta.
*Eel seen-*YOHR BEHR-*leets* POHR-*tah ock-k'*YAH-*lee; Lay nohn neh* POHR-*tah.*
Mr. Berlitz wears glasses; you do not wear any.

Vede Lei meglio del signor Berlitz?
VEH-*deh Lay* MEHL-*yoh dehl seen-*YOHR BEHR-*leets?*
Do you see better than Mr. Berlitz?

Sì, io vedo meglio del signor Berlitz.
See, EE-*oh* VEH-*doh* MEHL-*yoh dehl seen-*YOHR BEHK-*leets.*
Yes, I see better than Mr. Berlitz.

IMPORTANT NOTE: The formation of the comparative and the superlative of adjectives in Italian is rather simple. Just remember that *più* means "more", and *il più* means "the most". When we say: *Piccolo, più piccolo, il più piccolo,* we are actually saying: "Small", "more small", "the most small", meaning, of course: "Small", "smaller", "the smallest".

THINKING IN ITALIAN

(Answers on page 289)

1. Vi sono degli orologi in questa stanza?   2. Dove sono gli orologi?

3. Ha Lei un orologio da tasca o da polso?

4. Dove mette l'orologio da tasca?   5. Di che metallo è il Suo orologio?

6. Segna i secondi il Suo orologio?   7. Quante ore fanno un giorno?

8. Quanti secondi vi sono in un minuto?   9. È avanti il Suo orologio?

10. Di che cosa è fatta questa tavola?   11. È questa sedia pure di legno?

12. È la tavola più grande della sedia?

13. È il quadro più lungo della parete?

14. È la finestra così grande come la porta?

15. È la giacchetta più lunga del mio gilè?

16. È la pesca più buona della mela?

17. Pronuncia Lei bene il francese?   18. Sono buoni i Suoi occhi?

19. Vede Lei bene?   20. Vede bene senza occhiali il signor Berlitz?

21. Vede egli meglio cogli occhiali?

LEZIONE 27

In che stagione siamo?
*Een keh stah-*JOH-*neh s'*YAH-*moh?*
In what season are we?

Ecco un calendario.
ECK-*koh oon kah-lehn-*DAH-*r'yoh.*
Here is a calendar.

Esso contiene i trecento sessanta cinque giorni che formano un anno.
EHS-*soh kohn-t'*YEH-*neh ee treh-*CHEHN-*toh sehs-*SAHN-*tah* CHEEN-*kweh*
JOHR-*nee keh* FOHR-*mah-noh oon* AHN-*noh.*
It contains the three hundred and sixty-five days that form a year.

L'anno si divide in dodici mesi ed in cinquantadue settimane.
LAHN-*noh see dee-*VEE-*deh een* DOH-*dee-chee* MEH-*zee ehd een*
*cheen-*KWAHN-*tah-*DOO-*eh set-tee-*MAH-*neh.*
The year is divided into twelve months and fifty-two weeks.

Una settimana si compone di sette giorni che si chiamano:
OO-*nah set-tee-*MAH-*nah see kohm-*POH-*neh dee* SET-*teh* JOHR-*nee keh see*
*k'*YAH-*mah-noh:*
A week is composed of seven days which are called:

152

lunedì, martedì, mercoledì, giovedì, venerdì, sabato, domenica.
*loo-neh-*DEE, *mahr-teh-*DEE, *mehr-koh-leh-*DEE, *joh-veh-*DEE, *veh-nehr-*DEE,
SAH-*bah-toh,* doh-MEH-*nee-kah.*
Monday, Tuesday, Wednesday, Thursday, Friday, Saturday, Sunday.

Durante cinque o sei giorni della settimana noi lavoriamo.
*Doo-*RAHN-*teh* CHEEN-*kweh oh say* JOHR-*nee* DEH-*lah set-tee-*MAH-*nah noy
lah-voh-r'*YAH-*moh.*
During five or six days of the week, we work.

Il settimo giorno, la domenica, non lavoriamo:
Eel SET-*tee-moh* JOHR-*noh, lah doh-*MEH-*nee-kah, nohn lah-voh-r'*YAH-*moh:*
The seventh day, Sunday, we do not work;

è un giorno di riposo.
EH *oon* JOHR-*noh dee ree-*POH-*zoh.*
it is a day of rest.

NOTE on the Passive: The construction *si forma* and *si compone* can be translated as "is formed" and "is composed". Ex: "The week is composed of seven days"—*La settimana si compone di sette giorni.*

I mesi si chiamano: gennaio, febbraio, marzo, aprile,
Ee MEH-*zee see k'*YAH-*mah-noh: jehn-*NIGH-*yoh, fehb-*BRIGH-*yoh,* MAHR-*tsoh,
ah-*PREE-*leh,*
The months are named: January, February, March, April,

maggio, giugno, luglio, agosto, settembre, ottobre,
MAH-*djoh,* JOON-*n'yoh,* LOOL-*l'yoh, ah-*GOHS-*toh, set-*TEHM-*breh, oht-*TOH-*breh,*
May, June, July, August, September, October,

novembre, dicembre.
*noh-*VEHM-*breh, dee-*CHEHM-*breh.*
November, December.

Alcuni di questi mesi hanno trentuno giorni,
*Ahl-*KOO-*nee dee* KWESS-*tee* MEH-*zee* AHN-*noh trehn-*TOO-*noh* JOHR-*nee,*
Some of these months have 31 days,

altri ne hanno trenta; solo febbraio ne ha ventotto.
AHL-*tree neh* AHN-*noh* TREHN-*tah;* SOH-*loh fehb-*BRIGH-*yoh neh* AH
*vehn-*TOHT-*toh.*
others have only 30; only February has 28.

Ogni quattro anni il mese di febbraio ha ventinove giorni,
OH-*n'yee* KWAHT-*troh* AHN-*nee eel* MEH-*zeh dee fehb-*BRIGH-*yoh* AH
*vehn-tee-*NOH-*veh* JOHR-*nee,*
Every four years the month of February has 29 days,

ed allora l'anno si chiama bisestile.
ehd ahl-LOH-rah LAHN-*noh see k'*YAH-*mah bee-*SEHS-*tee-leh.*
and then the year is called leap year.

L'anno si divide in quattro stagioni:
LAHN-*noh see dee-*VEE-*deh een* KWAHT-*troh stah-*JOH-*nee:*
The year is divided into four seasons:

la primavera, l'estate, l'autunno, l'inverno.
*lah pree-mah-*VEH-*rah, lehs-*TAH-*teh, laou-*TOON-*noh, leen-*VEHR-*noh.*
spring, summer, autumn, winter.

Marzo, aprile e maggio sono i mesi di primavera.
MAHR-*tsoh, ah-*PREE-*leh eh* MAH-*djoh* SOH-*noh ee* MEH-*zee dee*
*pree-mah-*VEH-*rah.*
March, April and May are the spring months.

Giugno, luglio e agosto sono i mesi d'estate.
JOON-*n'yoh,* LOOL-*l'yoh eh ah-*GOHS-*toh* SOH-*noh ee* MEH-*zee dehs-*TAH-*teh.*
June, July and August are the summer months.

Settembre, ottobre e novembre sono i mesi d'autunno.
*Set-*TEHM-*bre, oht-*TOH-*breh eh noh-*VEHM-*breh* SOH-*noh ee* MEH-*zee*
*daou-*TOON-*noh.*
September, October and November are the autumn months.

Dicembre, gennaio e febbraio sono i mesi d'inverno.
*Dee-*CHEM-*breh, jehn-*NIGH-*yoh eh fehb-*BRIGH-*yoh* SOH-*noh ee* MEH-*zee*
*deen-*VEHR-*noh.*
December, January and February are the winter months.

D'estate andiamo in campagna o alla spiaggia per nuotare.
*Dehs-*TAH-*teh ahn-d'*YAH-*moh een kahm-*PAHN-*n'yah oh* AHL-*lah sp'*YAH-*djah*
*pehr n'woh-*TAH-*reh.*
In summer we go to the country or to the beach to swim.

D'inverno non andiamo alla spiaggia, restiamo in città.
*Deen-*VEHR-*noh nohn ahn-d'*YAH-*moh* AHL-*lah sp'*YAH-*djah, rehs-t'*YAH-*moh*
*een cheet-*TAH.
In winter we do not go to the beach; we remain in the city.

In primavera vediamo molti bei fiori.
*Een pree-mah-*VEH-*rah veh-d'*YAH-*moh* MOHL-*tee bay f'*YOH-*ree.*
In spring we see many beautiful flowers.

In autunno le foglie cadono dagli alberi.
*Een aou-*TOON-*noh leh* FOH-*l'yeh* KAH-*doh-noh* DAHL-*yee* AHL-*beh-ree.*
In autumn the leaves fall from the trees.

In che mese siamo?
Een keh MEH-*zeh s'*YAH-*moh?*
In what month are we?

Siamo in settembre.
*s'*YAH-*moh een set-*TEHM-*breh.*
We are in September.

Quanti ne abbiamo del mese oggi?
KWAHN-*tee neh ahb-b'*YAH-*moh dehl* MEH-*zeh* OH-*djee?*
What day of the month is it today?

Oggi è il quindici.
OH-*djee* EH *eel* KWEEN-*dee-chee.*
Today is the fifteenth.

Che giorno è oggi?
Keh JOHR-*noh* EH OH-*djee?*
What day is today?

Oggi è giovedì.
OH-*djee* EH *joh-veh-*DEE.
Today is Thursday.

Questo è il mese di settembre.
KWESS-*toh* EH *eel* MEH-*zeh dee set-*TEHM-*breh.*
This is the month of September.

Il mese scorso era il mese di agosto.
Eel MEH-*zeh* SKOHR-*soh* EH-*rah eel* MEH-*zeh dee ah-*GOHS-*toh.*
Last month was the month of August.

Il mese venturo sarà ottobre.
Eel MEH-*zeh vehn-*TOO-*roh sah-*RAH *oht-*TOH-*breh.*
Next month will be October.

Oggi è giovedì.
OH-*djee* EH *joh-veh-*DEE.
Today is Thursday.

Ieri era mercoledì.
YEH-*ree* EH-*rah mehr-koh-leh-*DEE.
Yesterday was Wednesday.

Domani sarà venerdì.
*Doh-*MAH-*nee sah-*RAH *veh-nehr-*DEE.
Tomorrow will be Friday.

Oggi è il quindici.
OH-*djee* EH *eel* KWEEN-*dee-chee.*
Today is the fifteenth.

Ieri era il quattordici.
YEH-*ree* EH-*rah eel kwaht-*TOHR-*dee-chee.*
Yesterday was the fourteenth.

Domani sarà il sedici.
*Doh-*MAH-*nee sah-*RAH *eel* SEH-*dee-chee.*
Tomorrow will be the sixteenth.

NOTE to Student: *Era*—"was" and *sarà*—"will be", are past and future forms of the verb *essere*—"to be". Don't worry about them now. There are several variations of these forms, but you will learn them gradually in future lessons.

Se si vuole sapere la data si guarda nel calendario.
*Seh see v'*WOH-*leh sah-*PEH-*reh lah* DAH-*tah see* GWAHR-*dah nehl
kah-lehn-*DAH-*r'yoh.*
If you wish to know the date you look at the calendar.

THINKING IN ITALIAN

(Answers on page 289)

1. Quanti giorni vi sono in una settimana?
2. Di quanti giorni si compone una settimana?
3. Quando comincia l'anno?
4. Quando finisce?
5. Qual'è il primo, il terzo, il quinto mese dell'anno?
6. Quali sono i sette giorni della settimana?
7. Come si chiama l'ultimo giorno della settimana?
8. Che giorno della settimana è oggi?
9. Era ieri domenica?
10. In quale giorno va Lei in chiesa?
11. Sarà venerdì il quindici?
12. Che giorno del mese è oggi?
13. Che giorno sarà lunedì prossimo?
14. Che giorno era lunedì scorso?
15. Sarà domani la fine del mese?
16. Che ora è adesso?
17. Durante quanti giorni lavoriamo?
18. Lavora Lei la domenica?

LEZIONE 28

Il giorno e la notte
Eel JOHR-*noh eh lah* NOHT-*teh*
Day and night

Le ventiquattro ore si dividono in due parti:
*Leh vehn-tee-*KWAHT-*troh* OH-*reh see dee-*VEE-*doh-noh een* DOO-*eh* PAHR-*tee:*
The twenty-four hours are divided into two parts:

le ore del giorno e le ore della notte.
leh OH-*reh dehl* JOHR-*noh eh leh* OH-*reh* DEHL-*lah* NOHT-*teh.*
the hours of the day and the hours of the night.

Durante il giorno è chiaro e noi possiamo vedere,
*Doo-*RAHN-*teh eel* JOHR-*noh* EH *k'*YAH-*roh eh noy pohs-s'*YAH-*moh*
    *veh-*DEH-*reh,*
During the day it is light and we can see,

ma durante la notte è buio
*mah doo-*RAHN-*teh lah* NOHT-*teh* EH BOO-*yoh*
but during the night it is dark

e dobbiamo accendere la luce se vogliamo vedere.
*eh dohb-b'*YAH-*moh aht-*CHEHN-*deh-reh lah* LOO-*cheh seh vohl-l'*YAH-*moh*
    *veh-*DEH-*reh.*
and we must turn on the light if we want to see.

In questa stanza non è abbastanza chiaro;
Een KWESS-*tah* STAHN-*tsah* noh-NEH *ahb-bahs-*TAHN-*tsah* k'YAH-*roh;*
In this room it isn't light enough;

accenda la luce, La prego.
*aht-*CHEHN-*dah lah* LOO-*cheh, Lah* PREH-*goh.*
turn on the light, please.

Ora la luce elettrica rischiara la stanza.
OH-*rah lah* LOO-*cheh eh-*LET-*tree-kah rees-k'*YAH-*rah lah* STAHN-*tsah.*
Now the electric light lights up the room.

Non tocchi la lampadina perchè, pure non avendo fiamma, può bruciare.
Nohn TOCK-*kee lah lahm-pah-*DEE-*nah pehr-*KEH, POO-*reh nohn ah-*VEHN-*doh*
*f'*YAHM-*mah, p'*WOH *broo-*CHAH-*reh.*
Don't touch the light bulb because, although it has no flame, it can burn.

Noi accendiamo la sigaretta con un fiammifero.
*Noy aht-chehn-d'*YAH-*moh lah see-gah-*RET-*tah kohn oon f'yahm-*MEE-*feh-roh.*
We light the cigarette with a match.

Noi non abbiamo bisogno di fiammiferi per accendere la luce.
*Noy nohn ahb-b'*YAH-*moh bee-*ZOHN-*yoh dee f'yahm-*MEE-*feh-ree pehr*
*aht-*CHEHN-*deh-reh lah* LOO-*cheh.*
We do not need matches to turn on the light.

C'è ora abbastanza luce in questa stanza?
CHEH OH-*rah ahb-bahs-*TAHN-*tsah* LOO-*cheh een* KWESS-*tah* STAHN-*tsah?*
Is there enough light in the room now?

Sì, signore, ora c'è abbastanza luce.
*See, seen-*YOH-*reh,* OH-*rah* CHEH *ahb-bahs-*TAHN-*tsah* LOO-*cheh.*
Yes, sir, there is enough light now.

Può Lei vederci bene?
*p'*WOH *Lay veh-*DEHR-*chee* BEH-*neh?*
Can you see us well?

Generalmente durante il giorno non usiamo luce elettrica.
*Jeh-neh-rahl-*MEHN-*teh doo-*RAHN-*teh eel* JOHR-*noh nohn oo-z'*YAH-*mok*
LOO-*cheh eh-*LET-*tree-kah.*
Generally during the day we do not use electric light.

Spenga la luce, La prego.
SPEHN-*gah lah* LOO-*cheh, Lah* PREH-*goh.*
Turn the light off, please.

Che cosa fa Lei?	Io spengo la luce.
Keh KOH-*zah fah Ley?*	EE-*oh* SPEHN-*goh lah* LOO-*cheh.*
What do you do?	I turn the light off.

Spengo io la luce?
SPEHN-*goh* EE-*oh lah* LOO-*cheh?*
Do I turn the light off?

No, signore, Lei non spegne la luce.
Noh, seen-YOH-*reh, Lay nohn* SPEHN-*yeh lah* LOO-*cheh.*
No, sir, you do not turn the light off.

È la luce accesa o spenta ora?
EH *lah* LOO-*cheh aht*-CHEH-*zah oh* SPEHN-*tah* OH-*rah?*
Is the light on or off now?

Ora la luce è spenta.
OH-*rah lah* LOO-*cheh* EH SPEHN-*tah.*
The light is off now.

REMEMBER: Here are two words, which, though spelled alike, have different meanings.
Ora—"now"—"this moment"
Ora—"hour", "o'clock".

Quando accende Lei la luce?
KWAHN-*doh aht*-CHEHN-*deh Lay lah* LOO-*cheh?*
When do you turn the light on?

Io accendo la luce quando è scuro.
EE-*oh aht*-CHEHN-*doh lah* LOO-*cheh* KWAHN-*doh* EH SKOO-*roh.*
I turn on the light when it is dark.

Il professore accende un fiammifero.
Eel proh-fess-SOH-*reh aht*-CHEHN-*deh oon f'yahm*-MEE-*feh-roh.*
The teacher lights a match.

Il professore si brucia.
Eel proh-fess-SOH-*reh see* BROO-*chah.*
The teacher burns himself.

La luce del giorno viene dal sole che è nel cielo.
Lah LOO-*cheh dehl* JOHR-*noh v'*YEH-*neh dahl* SOH-*leh keh* EH *nehl ch'*YEH-*loh.*
The light of the day comes from the sun which is in the sky.

Guardi dalla finestra.
GWAHR-*dee* DAHL-*lah fee*-NESS-*trah.*
Look out of the window.

Vede Lei il cielo azzurro sopra di noi?
VEH-*deh Lay eel ch'*YEH-*loh ah*-DZOOR-*roh* SOH-*prah dee noy?*
Do you see the blue sky above us?

Di notte il sole non è visibile, non possiamo vederlo;
Dee NOHT-*teh eel* SOH-*leh noh*-NEH *vee*-ZEE-*bee-leh, nohn pohs-s'*YAH-*moh veh*-DEHR-*loh;*
At night the sun is not visible, we can not see it;

ma possiamo vedere la luna e le stelle.
*mah pohs-s'*YAH-*moh veh*-DEH-*reh lah* LOO-*nah eh leh* STEHL-*leh.*
but we can see the moon and the stars.

Le stelle sono innumerevoli, non si possono contare.
Leh STEHL-*leh* SOH-*noh een-noo-meh*-REH-*voh-lee, nohn see* POHS-*soh-noh kohn*-TAH-*reh.*
The stars are innumerable, they cannot be counted.

 NOTE: *Non si possono contare*—"They cannot be counted", is another typical example in which the *si* makes the verb form passive.

La prima parte del giorno si chiama mattina,
Lah PREE-*mah* PAHR-*teh dehl* JOHR-*noh see k'*YAH-*mah maht*-TEE-*nah,*
The first part of the day is called morning,

e la seconda parte si chiama sera.
eh lah seh-KOHN-*dah* PAHR-*teh see k'*YAH-*mah* SEH-*rah.*
and the second part is called evening.

La mattina il sole si leva, ed a sera tramonta.
Lah maht-TEE-*nah eel* SOH-*leh see* LEH-*vah, ehd ah* SEH-*rah trah*-MOHN-*tah.*
In the morning the sun rises and in the evening it sets.

La parte dalla quale il sole si leva si chiama Levante o Est,
Lah PAHR-*teh* DAHL-*lah* KWAH-*leh eel* SOH-*leh see* LEH-*vah see k'*YAH-*mah Leh*-VAHN-*teh oh Esst,*
The region where the sun rises is called east,

e la parte dove tramonta si chiama Ponente o Ovest.
eh lah PAHR-*teh* DOH-*veh trah*-MOHN-*tah see k'*YAH-*mah Poh*-NEHN-*teh oh* OH-*vesst.*
and the region where it sets is called west.

Ecco i quattro punti cardinali:
ECK-*koh ee* KWAHT-*troh* POON-*tee kahr-dee*-NAH-*lee:*
Here are the four cardinal points:

Levante o Est, Ponente o Ovest,
Leh-VAHN-*teh oh Esst, Poh*-NEHN-*teh oh* OH-*vesst.*
East, West,

Settentrione o Nord e Mezzogiorno o Sud.
*Set-tehn-tr'*YOH*-neh oh Nord eh Meh-dzoh-*JOHR*-noh oh Sood.*
North and South.

In estate il sole si leva presto,
*Een ehs-*TAH*-teh eel* SOH*-leh see* LEH*-vah* PREHS*-toh,*
In the summer the sun rises early,

alle quattro o le cinque, ed i giorni sono lunghi;
AHL*-leh* KWAHT*-troh oh leh* CHEEN*-kweh, ehd ee* JOHR*-nee* SOH*-noh*
    LOON*-ggee;*
at 4 or 5, and the days are long;

ma in inverno il sole si leva tardi, ed i giorni sono corti.
*mah een een-*VEHR*-noh eel* SOH*-leh see* LEH*-vah* TAHR*-dee, ehd ee* JOHR*-nee*
    SOH*-noh* KOHR*-tee.*
but in winter the sun rises late, and the days are short.

NOTE to Student: *Est, Ovest, Nord* and *Sud* are to all in-
tents and purposes used interchangeably with *Levante,*
Ponente, Settentrione and *Mezzogiorno* respectively. Ex:
"The sun rises in the east"—*Il sole si leva a Levante* or *Il*
sole si leva a Est. Mezzogiorno also means "noon".

La notte, quando abbiamo sonno, andiamo a letto e dormiamo.
Lah NOHT*-teh,* KWAHN*-doh ahb-b'*YAH*-moh* SOHN*-noh, ahn-d'*YAH*-moh ah*
    LET*-toh eh dohr-m'*YAH*-moh.*
At night, when we are sleepy, we go to bed and sleep.

La mattina ci alziamo, ci bagniamo,
*Lah maht-*TEE*-nah chee ahl-ts'*YAH*-moh, chee bahn-n'*YAH*-moh,*
In the morning we get up, we bathe,

ci radiamo, ci pettiniamo, ci vestiamo e facciamo colazione.
*chee rah-d'*YAH*-moh, chee pet-tee-n'*YAH*-moh, chee vehs-t'*YAH*-moh eh*
*faht-*CHAH*-moh koh-lah-ts'*YOH*-neh.*
we shave, we comb our hair, we dress, and we have breakfast.

NOTE on Reflexive Verbs: The majority of verbs describing actions or thoughts which reflect on one's person, such
as to wash oneself, to dress oneself, to shave oneself, etc.,
are reflexive. Ex: *Vestirsi*—"to dress", *bagnarsi*—"to bathe",
radersi—"to shave", *pettinarsi*—"to comb one's hair", *alzarsi*
—"to get up" and many others you will encounter.

THINKING IN ITALIAN

(Answers on page 290)

1. Come si dividono le ventiquattro ore del giorno?
2. Quando è chiaro?
3. È buio ora?
4. Da dove viene la luce del giorno?
5. Dov'è il sole?
6. Che cosa illumina questa stanza di notte?
7. Che cosa accendiamo noi la notte per poter vedere?
8. Che cosa si vede nel cielo durante la notte?
9. Da dove si leva il sole?
10. A che ora si leva il sole nel mese di marzo?
11. In quale stagione sono lunghi i giorni?
12. Le notti sono più lunghe dei giorni in estate?
13. In quale stagione sono lunghe le notti?
14. Quando accendiamo noi la luce?
15. A che ora va Lei a letto generalmente?
16. A che ora si alza?
17. A che ora fa colazione Lei?
18. A che ora comincia a lavorare?
19. Fino a che ora lavora Lei?
20. Le piace lavorare? (Bugiardo! ...)

Che tempo fa?
Keh TEHM-*poh fah?*
How is the weather?

Quando il cielo è grigio, è coperto di nuvole.
KWAHN-*doh eel ch'*YEH-*loh* EH GREE-*joh,* EH *koh-*PEHR-*toh dee* NOO-*voh-leh.*
When the sky is gray, it is covered with clouds.

Di che colore è il cielo?
*Dee keh koh-*LOH-*reh* EH *eel ch'*YEH-*loh?*
What color is the sky?

È grigio.
EH GREE-*joh.*
It is gray.

Di che cosa è coperto il cielo?
Dee keh KOH-*zah* EH *koh-*PEHR-*toh eel ch'*YEH-*loh?*
With what is the sky covered?

È coperto di nuvole.
EH *koh-*PEHR-*toh dee* NOO-*voh-leh.*
It is covered with clouds.

Di che colore sono le nuvole?
*Dee keh koh-*LOH-*reh* SOH-*noh leh* NOO-*voh-leh?*
What color are the clouds?

Sono grigie.
SOH-*noh* GREE-*jeh.*
They are gray.

La pioggia cade.
*Lah p'*YOH-*djah* KAH-*deh.*
The rain falls.

D'inverno cade la neve.
*Deen-*VEHR-*noh* KAH-*deh lah* NEH-*veh.*
In winter snow falls.

Nevica.
NEH-*vee-kah.*
It snows.

La neve è bianca.
Lah NEH-*veh* EH *b'*YAHN-*kah.*
The snow is white.

Il cielo è sereno.
*Eel ch'*YEH-*loh* EH *seh-*REH-*noh.*
The sky is clear.

Splende il sole.
SPLEHN-*deh eel* SOH-*leh.*
The sun is shining.

Fa bel tempo.
Fah bell TEHM-*poh.*
It is good weather.

IMPORTANT WORD! *Fa* is from the verb *fare,* which has several meanings, the most important being: "to do", "to make", "to cause", "to be". Therefore, when we say: *Fa bel tempo* we are applying the meaning "to be".

Piove.
*p'*YOH-*veh.*
It is raining.

Nevica.
NEH-*vee-kah.*
It is snowing.

Fa brutto tempo.
Fah BROOT-*toh* TEHM-*poh.*
It is bad weather.

Quando piove noi apriamo l'ombrello.
KWAHN-*doh p'*YOH-*veh noy ah-pr'*YAH-*moh lohm-*BREHL-*loh.*
When it rains, we open the umbrella.

Di che colore è il cielo quando piove?
*Dee keh koh-*LOH-*reh* EH *eel ch'*YEH-*loh* KWAHN-*doh p'*YOH-*veh?*
What color is the sky when it rains?

È grigio.
EH GREE-*joh.*
It is gray.

Piove spesso in aprile?
*p'*YOH-*veh* SPEHS-*soh een ah-*PREE-*leh?*
Does it rain frequently in April?

Sì, in aprile piove spesso.
*See, een ah-*PREE-*leh p'*YOH-*veh* SPEHS-*soh.*
Yes, in April it rains frequently.

Nevica d'estate?
NEH-*vee-kah dehs-*TAH-*teh?*
Does it snow in summer?

No, in estate non nevica mai.
*Noh, een ehs-*TAH-*teh nohn* NEH-*vee-kah migh.*
No, in summer it never snows.

Nevica d'inverno?
NEH-*vee-kah deen-*VEHR-*noh?*
Does it snow in winter?

Sì, d'inverno nevica spesso.
*See, deen-*VEHR-*noh* NEH-*vee-kah* SPEHS-*soh.*
Yes, in winter it snows often.

Di che cosa sono coperte le case e le strade quando nevica?
Dee keh KOH-*zah* SOH-*noh koh-*PEHR-*teh leh* KAH-*zeh eh leh* STRAH-*deh*
    KWAHN-*doh* NEH-*vee-kah?*
With what are the houses and streets covered when it snows?

Quando nevica sono coperte di neve.
KWAHN-*doh* NEH-*vee-kah* SOH-*noh* koh-PEHR-*teh dee* NEH-*veh.*
When it snows, they are covered with snow.

Quando usciamo nella pioggia senza ombrello,
KWAHN-*doh* oo-sh'YAH-*moh* NEHL-*lah* p'YOH-*djah* SEHN-*tsah* ohm-BREHL-*loh,*
When we go out in the rain without an umbrella

o senza impermeabile, ci bagniamo.
oh SEHN-*tsah* eem-pehr-meh-AH-*bee-leh, chee bahn-n'*YAH-*moh.*
or without a rain coat, we get wet.

Allora dobbiamo toglierci i vestiti bagnati e indossare vestiti asciutti.
*Ahl-*LOH-*rah* dohb-b'YAH-*moh* TOHL-*l'yehr-chee ee* vehs-TEE-*tee bahn-n'*YAH-
tee eh een-dohs-SAH-*reh* vehs-TEE-*tee* ah-SHOOT-*tee.*
Then we must take off our wet clothes and put on dry clothes.

Se non ci togliamo i vestiti bagnati, possiamo raffreddarci.
*Seh nohn chee tohl-l'*YAH-*moh ee* vehs-TEE-*tee bahn-n'*YAH-*tee,* pohs-s'YAH-
moh rahf-frehd-DAHR-*chee.*
If we don't take off our wet clothes we can catch cold.

DO NOT CONFUSE: *Raffreddare* means "to make cold"
or "to cool", but *raffreddarsi* (reflexive) means 'to catch
cold"; such is the case expressed in the sentence: *Se non ci
togliamo i vestiti bagnati possiamo raffreddarci.*—"If we
don't take off our wet clothes we can catch cold."

Fa bel tempo oggi?
Fah bell TEHM-*poh* OH-*djee?*
Is it good weather today?

Sì, fa bel tempo.
See, fah bell TEHM-*poh.*
Yes, it is good weather.

No, non fa bel tempo.
Noh, nohn fah bell TEHM-*poh.*
No, it is not good weather.

Fa brutto tempo.
Fah BROOT-*toh* TEHM-*poh.*
It is bad weather.

Esce Lei quando fa brutto tempo?
EH-*sheh Lay* KWAHN-*doh fah* BROOT-*toh* TEHM-*poh?*
Do you go out when it is bad weather?

No, io non esco quando fa brutto tempo.
Noh, EE-*oh nohn* EHS-*koh* KWAHN-*doh fah* BROOT-*toh* TEHM-*poh.*
No, I don't go out when it is bad weather.

D'estate mettiamo dei vestiti leggieri.
*Dehs-*TAH-*teh* meht-t'YAH-*moh day* vehs-TEE-*tee leh-*DJEH-*ree.*
In summer we put on light clothes.

D'inverno ne mettiamo dei pesanti.
*Deen-*VEHR*-noh neh meht-t'*YAH*-moh day peh-*SAHN*-tee.*
In winter we put on heavy ones.

In estate apriamo le finestre e le porte.
*Een ehs-*TAH*-teh ah-pr'*YAH*-moh leh fee-*NESS*-treh eh leh* POHR*-teh.*
In summer we open the windows and doors.

In inverno ci sediamo accanto al termosifone.
*Een een-*VEHR*-noh chee seh-d'*YAH*-moh ahk-*KAHN*-toh ahl*
*tehr-moh-see-*FOH*-neh.*
In winter we sit near the radiator.

D'estate fa caldo.	**D'inverno fa freddo.**
*Dehs-*TAH*-teh fah* KAHL*-doh.*	*Deen-*VEHR*-noh fah* FREHD*-doh.*
In summer it is warm.	In winter it is cold.

Lei porta il soprabito d'inverno?
Lay POHR*-tah eel soh-*PRAH*-bee-toh deen-*VEHR*-noh?*
Do you wear an overcoat in winter?

Sì, d'inverno io porto il soprabito.
*See, deen-*VEHR*-noh* EE*-oh* POHR*-toh eel soh-*PRAH*-bee-toh.*
Yes, in winter I wear an overcoat.

Fa caldo in agosto?
Fah KAHL*-doh een ah-*GOHS*-toh?*
Is it warm in August?

Sì, in agosto fa molto caldo.
*See, een ah-*GOHS*-toh fah* MOHL*-toh* KAHL*-doh.*
Yes, in August it is very warm.

Fa caldo nel centro dell'Africa?
Fah KAHL*-doh nehl* CHEHN*-troh dehl-*LAH*-free-kah?*
Is it warm in the center of Africa?

Sì, vi fa molto caldo.
See, vee fah MOHL*-toh* KAHL*-doh.*
Yes, it is very warm there.

Fa freddo al Polo Nord?	**Sì, vi fa molto freddo.**
Fah FREHD*-doh ahl* POH*-loh Nord?*	*See, vee fah* MOHL*-toh* FREHD*-doh.*
Is it cold at the North Pole?	Yes, it is very cold there.

Se indossiamo vestiti pesanti, abbiamo caldo.
*Seh een-dohs-s'*YAH*-moh vehs-*TEE*-tee peh-*SAHN*-tee, ahb-b'*YAH*-moh*
KAHL*-doh.*
If we wear heavy clothes, we are warm.

Se d'inverno usciamo senza soprabito, abbiamo freddo.
*Seh deen-*VEHR*-noh oo-sh'*YAH*-moh* SEHN*-tsah soh-*PRAH*-bee-toh,*
*ahb-b'*YAH*-moh* FREHD*-doh.*
If in winter we go out without an overcoat, we are cold.

Si ha caldo quando si cammina al sole in estate?
See AH KAHL-*doh* KWAHN-*doh see kahm*-MEE-*nah ahl* SOH-*leh een ehs*-TAH-*teh?*
Does one feel warm when one walks in the sun in summer?

Sì, si ha caldo quando si cammina al sole in estate.
See, see AH KAHL-*doh* KWAHN-*doh see kahm*-MEE-*nah ahl* SOH-*leh een*
ehs-TAH-*teh.*
Yes, one is very warm if one walks in the sun in summer.

Abbiamo freddo quando si aprono le finestre d'inverno?
*Ahb-b'*YAH-*moh* FREHD-*doh* KWAHN-*doh see* AH-*proh-noh leh fee*-NESS-*treh*
deen-VEHR-*noh?*
Are we cold when the windows are opened in winter?

Sì, abbiamo freddo se si aprono le finestre d'inverno.
*See, ahb-b'*YAH-*moh* FREHD-*doh seh see* AH-*proh-noh leh fee*-NESS-*treh*
deen-VEHR-*noh.*
Yes, we are cold if the windows are opened in winter.

In casa fa caldo.	**In istrada fa freddo.**
Een KAH-*zah fah* KAHL-*doh.*	*Een ees*-TRAH-*dah fah* FREHD-*doh.*
In the house it is warm.	In the street it is cold.

NOTE to Student: Whenever the preposition *in* precedes a word beginning with *s*, followed by another consonant, an *i* may be added in front of the word, for euphony. Ex: *Strada*—"street", becomes *istrada* in the sentence: *In istrada fa freddo.*—"In the street it is cold."

Una persona ha caldo.	**Un oggetto è caldo.**
oo-*nah pehr*-SOH-*nah* AH KAHL-*doh.*	*Oon oh*-DJET-*toh* EH KAHL-*doh.*
A person is warm.	An object is warm.
Una persona ha freddo.	**Un oggetto è freddo.**
oo-*nah pehr*-SOH-*nah* AH FREHD-*doh.*	*Oon oh*-DJET-*toh* EH FREHD-*doh.*
A person is cold.	An object is cold.

EXPRESSIONS TO REMEMBER:

"I am cold"—*Ho freddo.*
"I am hot"—*Ho caldo.*
"I am thirsty"—*Ho sete.*
"I am hungry"—*Ho fame.*
"I am sleepy"—*Ho sonno.*

BUT

"The beer is cold"—*La birra è fredda.*
"The coffee is hot"—*Il caffè è caldo.*
"My hands are cold"—*Le mie mani sono fredde.*
"My forehead is hot"—*La mia fronte è calda.*

Quando il termosifone è molto caldo Lei non può toccarlo.
KWAHN-*doh eel tehr-moh-see-*FOH-*neh* EH MOHL-*toh* KAHL-*doh Lay nohn*
*p'*WOH *tohk-*KAHR-*loh.*
When the radiator is very hot, you cannot touch it.

Se la minestra è fredda non è buona.
*Seh lah mee-*NEHS-*trah* EH FREHD-*dah noh-*NEH *b'*WOH-*nah.*
If the soup is cold, it isn't good.

Se il caffè è troppo caldo non lo può bere.
*Seh eel kahf-*FEH EH TROHP-*poh* KAHL-*doh, nohn lo p'*WOH BEH-*reh.*
If the coffee is too hot, you cannot drink it.

Le piace il caffè freddo?
*Leh p'*YAH-*cheh eel kahf-*FEH FREHD-*doh?*
Do you like cold coffee?

No, signore, il caffè freddo non mi piace.
*Noh, seen-*YOH-*reh, eel kahf-*FEH FREHD-*doh nohn mee p'*YAH-*cheh.*
No, sir, I don't like cold coffee.

Tocchi il termosifone.	**È caldo o freddo?**
TOCK-*kee eel tehr-moh-see-*FOH-*neh.*	EH KAHL-*doh oh* FREHD-*doh?*
Touch the radiator.	Is it hot or cold?

È caldo.	**Lei ha caldo o freddo ora?**
EH KAHL-*doh.*	*Lay* AH KAHL-*doh oh* FREHD-*doh* OH-*rah?*
It is hot.	Are you hot or cold now?

Non ho nè caldo nè freddo, sto bene.
*Noh-*NOH NEH KAHL-*doh* NEH FREHD-*doh, stoh* BEH-*neh.*
I am neither hot nor cold, I am comfortable.

Fa caldo o freddo in questa stanza?
Fah KAHL-*doh oh* FREHD-*doh een* KWESS-*tah* STAHN-*tsah?*
Is it hot or cold in this room?

Non fa nè caldo nè freddo, si sta bene.
Nohn fah NEH KAHL-*doh* NEH FREHD-*doh, see stah* BEH-*neh.*
It is neither hot nor cold, one is comfortable.

REMEMBER: Among its various meanings *stare* also expresses the state of being in a definite condition. *Io sto bene*—"I am well" means that your health condition is definitely good. *In questa stanza si sta bene*—"In this room one is comfortable."

Al Polo Nord fa tanto freddo quanto al Polo Sud.
Ahl POH-*loh Nord fah* TAHN-*toh* FREHD-*doh* KWAHN-*toh ahl* POH-*loh Sood.*
At the North Pole it is as cold as at the South Pole.

Fa sempre freddo, non fa mai caldo.
Fah SEHM-*preh* FREHD-*doh, nohn fah migh* KAHL-*doh.*
It is always cold, it is never hot.

A New York fa freddo d'inverno e fa caldo d'estate.
Ah New York fah FREHD-*doh deen-*VEHR-*noh eh fah* KAHL-*doh dehs-*TAH-*teh.*
In New York it is cold in winter and it is warm in summer.

Talvolta fa freddo, talvolta fa caldo.
*Tahl-*VOHL-*tah fah* FREHD-*doh, tahl-*VOHL-*tah fah* KAHL-*doh.*
Sometimes it is cold, sometimes it is hot.

A Roma d'inverno alle volte nevica, ma d'estate non nevica mai.
Ah ROH-*mah deen-*VEHR-*noh* AHL-*leh* VOHL-*teh* NEH-*vee-kah, mah
dehs-*TAH-*teh nohn* NEH-*vee-kah migh.*
In Rome it sometimes snows in winter but in summer it never snows.

Nevica qualche volta in marzo?
NEH-*vee-kah* KWAHL-*keh* VOHL-*tah een* MAHR-*tsoh?*
Does it sometimes snow in March?

Sì, alle volte nevica.
See, AHL-*leh* VOHL-*teh* NEH-*vee-kah.*
Yes, it sometimes snows.

Nevica qualche volta in agosto?
NEH-*vee-kah* KWAHL-*keh* VOHL-*tah een ah-*GOHS-*toh?*
Does it sometimes snow in August?

No, in agosto non nevica mai.
*Noh, een ah-*GOHS-*toh nohn* NEH-*vee-kah migh.*
No, in August it never snows.

 DON'T FORGET: *Mai* means "never" when used alone, as an answer. It means "ever" when used in a sentence, but, again it becomes "never" if it follows a verb which is preceded by the negative *non*. In the following group of sentences you will find the three cases clearly illustrated. Ex: "Do you ever go to the theatre?"—*Va Lei mai a teatro?* "Never!"—*Mai!* "I never go to the theatre."—*Io non vado mai a teatro.* Notice that the negative *non* precedes the verb *vado*, which is followed by the adverb *mai*.

A Londra piove spesso.
Ah LOHN-*drah p'*YOH-*veh* SPEHS-*soh.*
In London it rains often.

A Napoli piove raramente.
Ah NAH-*poh-lee p'*YOH-*veh rah-rah-*MEHN-*teh.*
In Naples it rains rarely.

Generalmente fa bel tempo.
*Jeh-neh-rahl-*MEHN-*teh fah bell* TEHM-*poh.*
Generally it is good weather.

THINKING IN ITALIAN
(Answers on page 290)

1. Di che colore è il cielo quando fa brutto tempo?
2. Di che cosa è coperto il cielo?   3. Piove adesso?
4. Che cosa cade dal cielo in inverno?
5. Le piace camminare per le strade quando piove?
6. Che cosa porta Lei in mano quando piove?
7. Che tempo fa oggi?   8. Esce Lei quando fa cattivo tempo?
9. Fa freddo al Polo Nord?   10. In quali mesi nevica?
11. Nevica spesso in febbraio?   12. Nevica spesso in aprile?
13. Da dove viene la pioggia?   14. È piacevole camminare quando piove?
15. In quali mesi porta Lei dei vestiti pesanti?
16. Che tempo fa generalmente a Napoli?
17. Dove si siede Lei per scaldarsi?   18. Quando splende il sole?

LEZIONE 30

Che cosa ho fatto ieri?
Keh KOH-*zah* OH FAHT-*toh* YEH-*ree?*
What did I do yesterday?

CARLO: **Che cosa ha fatto Lei ieri, Luigi?**
KAHR-*loh:* *Keh* KOH-*zah* AH FAHT-*toh* Lay YEH-*ree,* Loo-EE-*jee?*
CHARLES: What did you do yesterday, Luigi?

LUIGI: **Ieri ho fatto colazione alle undici,**
Loo-EE-*jee:* YEH-*ree* OH FAHT-*toh* koh-lah-ts'YOH-*neh* AHL-*leh* OON-*dee-chee,*
LOUIS: Yesterday I had lunch at 11,

ho bevuto un bicchiere d'acqua, e dopo avere
OH *beh-*VOO-*toh* oon *beek-k'*YEH-*reh* DAHK-*kwah,* eh DOH-*poh* ah-VEH-*reh*
I drank a glass of water, and after having

mangiato una costoletta d'agnello
*mahn-*JAH-*toh* OO-*nah* kohs-toh-LET-*tah* dah-n'YEHL-*loh*
eaten a lamb chop

ho preso una tazza di caffè.
OH PREH-*zoh* OO-*nah* TAH-*tsah* dee kahf-FEH.
I drank a cup of coffee.

171

Poi ho cominciato il mio lavoro:
Poy OH *koh-meent-*CHAH-*toh eel* MEE-*oh lah-*VOH-*roh:*
Afterward I began my work:

ho letto tutte le mie lettere, alle quali ho risposto,
OH LET-*toh* TOOT-*teh leh* MEE-*eh* LET-*teh-reh,* AHL-*leh* KWAH-*lee* OH
*rees-*POHS-*toh,*
I read all my letters, which I answered,

ed ho pregato il mio amico di metterle alla posta.
ehd OH *preh-*GAH-*toh eel* MEE-*oh ah-*MEE-*koh dee* MEHT-*tehr-leh*
AHL-*lah* POHS-*tah.*
and asked my friend to take them to the post office.

 NOTE ON THE PAST TENSE: "To have"—*avere,* is used to help form the past tense of other verbs, and for this reason is called an auxiliary verb. The formation of this tense is, in Italian, a little more complex than it is in English, but this should not discourage the student; the rational progression of these lessons will introduce the various forms in a simple, easy-to-learn way.

In this lesson you are introduced to the *passato prossimo*—"recent past". If the action you wish to describe has just occurred, or it occurred recently, up to a few months ago, in Italian you will say that "it has occurred" and not "it occurred". Therefore, if you wish to say that this morning, yesterday, or even three months ago you "wrote some letters", you will say in Italian: *Io ho scritto delle lettere*—"I have written some letters". Similarly: *Lei ha scritto ieri una lettera al signor Berlitz.*—"You have written, yesterday, a letter to Mr. Berlitz."; *Noi abbiamo studiato molto l'inverno scorso.* —"We have studied a lot last winter." In other words, the past participle of the verb describing the action is preceded by the auxiliary "to have" in the present tense.

CARLO: **Che cosa ha fatto a mezzogiorno?**
Keh KOH-*zah* AH FAHT-*toh ah meh-dzoh-*JOHR-*noh?*
What did you do at noon?

LUIGI: **A mezzogiorno il mio professore mi ha dato una lezione.**
*Ah meh-dzoh-*JOHR-*noh eel* MEE-*oh proh-fess-*SOH-*reh mee* AH DAH-*toh*
*oo-nah leh-ts'*YOH-*neh.*
At noon my teacher gave me a lesson.

Egli ha ricevuto un nuovo romanzo e me l'ha portato.
EHL-*yee* AH *ree-cheh-*VOO-*toh oon n'*WOH-*voh roh-*MAHN-*tsoh eh meh*
LAH *pohr-*TAH-*toh.*
He received a new novel and brought it to me.

Egli ha letto alcune pagine ad alta voce.
EHL-*yee* AH LET-*toh ahl*-KOO-*neh* PAH-*jee-neh ahd* AHL-*tah* VOH-*cheh.*
He read some pages aloud.

Poi mi ha fatto delle domande e io ho risposto.
Poy mee AH FAHT-*toh* DEHL-*leh doh*-MAHN-*deh eh* EE-*oh* OH
rees-POHS-*toh.*
Afterwards he asked me some questions and I replied.

Egli ha corretto i difetti della mia pronuncia,
EHL-*yee* AH *kohr*-RET-*toh ee dee*-FET-*tee* DEHL-*lah* MEE-*ah*
proh-NOON-*chah,*
He corrected the errors in my pronunciation,

mi ha fatto scrivere dei compiti e, all'una, se n'è andato.
mee AH FAHT-*toh* SKREE-*veh-reh day* KOHM-*pee-tee eh, ahl*-LOO-*nah,*
seh NEH *ahn*-DAH-*toh.*
had me write some exercises and, at one, he left.

EXPRESSION to Remember: When *fare* is used with another verb it conveys the sense of having something done. In the above lesson, you saw the expression: *Mi ha fatto scrivere dei compiti.* This means "He had me write exercises" or "He made me write exercises".

CARLO: **E nel pomeriggio?**
Eh nehl poh-meh-REE-*djoh?*
And in the afternoon?

LUIGI: **Alle due Edoardo mi ha fatto visita,**
AHL-*leh* DOO-*eh Eh-doh*-AHR-*doh mee* AH FAHT-*toh* VEE-*zee-tah,*
At two Edward visited me,

noi abbiamo passato insieme il pomeriggio.
*noy ahb-b'*YAH-*moh pahs*-SAH-*toh een-s'*YEH-*meh eel poh-meh*-REE-*djoh.*
we spent the afternoon together.

Abbiamo avuto una lunga conversazione.
*Ahb-b'*YAH-*moh ah*-VOO-*toh* OO-*nah* LOON-*gah kohn-vehr-sah-ts'*YOH-*neh.*
We had a long conversation.

Abbiamo parlato lungamente di Lei e,
*Ahb-b'*YAH-*moh pahr*-LAH-*toh loon-gah*-MEHN-*teh dee Lay eh,*
We spoke a long time about you and,

più tardi, abbiamo fatto una passeggiata nel parco,
*p'*YOO TAHR-*dee, ahb-b'*YAH-*moh* FAHT-*toh* OO-*nah pahs-seh*-DJAHT-*tah*
nehl PAHR-*koh,*
later, we took a walk in the park,

dove abbiamo incontrato Augusto.
DOH-*veh ahb-b'*YAH-*moh een-kohn-*TRAH-*toh Aou-*GOOS-*toh.*
where we met August.

Abbiamo cenato insieme alle sette.
*Ahb-b'*YAH-*moh cheh-*NAH-*toh een-s'*YEH-*meh* AHL-*leh* SET-*teh.*
We ate together at seven.

Abbiamo voluto mangiare nel giardino,
*Ahb-b'*YAH-*moh voh-*LOO-*toh mahn-*JAH-*reh nehl jahr-*DEE-*noh,*
We wanted to eat in the garden,

ma abbiamo dovuto cambiare i nostri piani
*mah ahb-b'*YAH-*moh doh-*VOO-*toh kahm-b'*YAH-*reh ee* NOHS-*tree p'*YAH-
nee
but had to change our plans

e rientrare nella sala da pranzo.
*eh ree-ehn-*TRAH-*reh* NEHL-*lah* SAH-*lah dah* PRAHN-*tsoh.*
and return to the dining room.

CARLO: Non ha fatto troppo caldo nella sala da pranzo?
*Noh-*NAH FAHT-*toh* TROHP-*poh* KAHL-*doh* NEHL-*lah* SAH-*lah dah*
PRAHN-*tsoh?*
Wasn't it too hot in the dining room?

LUIGI: No, noi abbiamo aperto le porte e non ha fatto troppo caldo.
*Noh, noy ahb-b'*YAH-*moh ah-*PEHR-*toh leh* POHR-*teh eh noh-*NAH
FAHT-*toh* TROHP-*poh* KAHL-*doh.*
No, we opened the doors and it wasn't too hot.

NOTE to Student: It is easy to transform adjectives into adverbs; simply make the adjective feminine and add the suffix -*mente.* Ex: *Largo—largamente; lungo—lungamente; vero—veramente.* Adjectives ending with *e* do not change in the feminine, therefore: *Dolce* will be *dolcemente; grande—grandemente,* etc. Exceptions: All adjectives terminating in -*le,* lose the final *e* before applying the suffix. Ex: *Gentile—*"kind", *gentilmente; crudele—*"cruel", *crudelmente;* etc.

CARLO: Il cattivo tempo ha durato molto tempo?
*Eel kaht-*TEE-*voh* TEHM-*poh* AH *doo-*RAH-*toh* MOHL-*toh* TEHM-*poh?*
Did the bad weather last a long time?

LUIGI: No, dopo un'ora ha cessato di
Noh, DOH-*poh oo-*NOH-*rah* AH *chehs-*SAH-*toh dee*
No, after an hour it stopped

piovere e ha fatto bel tempo tutta la serata.
*p'*YOH-*veh-reh eh* AH FAHT-*toh bell* TEHM-*poh* TOOT-*tah lah seh-*RAH-*tah.*
raining and it was good weather all evening.

CARLO: Ha visto Lei Andrea o ha ricevuto una lettera da lui?
AH VEES-*toh* Lay *Ahn*-DREH-*ah* oh AH *ree-cheh*-VOO-*toh* OO-*nah*
LET-*teh-rah* dah LOO-*ee?*
Have you seen Andrew, or have you received a letter from him?

LUIGI: Non lo ho visto ma ho ricevuto da lui una cartolina stamattina.
Nohn loh OH VEES-*toh mah* OH *ree-cheh*-VOO-*toh dah* LOO-*ee* OO-*nah*
kahr-toh-LEE-*nah stah-maht*-TEE-*nah.*
I haven't seen him but I received a card from him this morning.

CARLO: Le ha parlato di me?
Leh AH *pahr*-LAH-*toh dee meh?*
Did he speak to you about me?

LUIGI: Sì, mi ha scritto che non ha potuto vederla
See, mee AH SKREET-*toh keh noh*-NAH *poh*-TOO-*toh veh*-DEHR-*lah*
Yes, he wrote me that he couldn't see you

perchè il signor e la signora Berlitz
pehr-KEH *eel seen*-YOHR *eh lah seen*-YOH-*rah* BEHR-*leets*
because Mr. and Mrs. Berlitz

hanno passato la settimana da lui.
AHN-*noh pahs*-SAH-*toh lah set-tee*-MAH-*nah dah* LOO-*ee.*
spent the week with him.

Il signor Berlitz e lui hanno lavorato molto.
Eel seen-YOHR BEHR-*leets eh* LOO-*ee* AHN-*noh lah-voh*-RAH-*toh* MOHL-*toh.*
Mr. Berlitz and he worked a great deal.

Hanno scritto un libro nuovo.
AHN-*noh* SKREET-*toh oon* LEE-*broh n'*WOH-*voh.*
They wrote a new book.

CARLO: Ha sentito parlare del viaggio del signor
AH *sehn*-TEE-*toh pahr*-LAH-*reh dehl vee*-AH-*djoh dehl seen*-YOHR
Have you heard about Mr. and

e della signora Berlitz a Capri?
eh DEHL-*lah seen*-YOH-*rah* BEHR-*leets ah* KAH-*pree?*
Mrs. Berlitz' trip to Capri?

LUIGI: Sì, ho sentito che hanno fatto un bel viaggio.
See, OH *sehn*-TEE-*toh keh* AHN-*noh* FAHT-*toh oon bell vee*-AH-*djoh.*
Yes, I heard that they had a fine trip.

Prima di partire, hanno domandato
PREE-*mah dee pahr*-TEE-*reh,* AHN-*noh doh-mahn*-DAH-*toh*
Before they left, they asked

a Roberto di accompagnarli,
*ah Roh-*BEHR-*toh dee ahk-kohm-pahn-*YAHR-*lee,*
Robert to accompany them

ma egli non ha potuto.
mah EHL-*yee noh-*NAH *poh-*TOO-*toh.*
but he could not go.

Ha letto Lei i libri?
AH LET-*toh Lay ee* LEE-*bree?*
Have you read the books?

Sì, io ho letto i libri.
See, EE-*oh* OH LET-*toh ee* LEE-*bree.*
Yes, I have read the books.

Sì, io li ho letti.
See, EE-*oh lee* OH LET-*tee.*
Yes, I have read them.

THINKING IN ITALIAN

(Answers on page 291)

1. A che ora ha fatto colazione ieri?
2. Ha bevuto vino ieri a mezzogiorno?
3. A che ora ha cenato ieri sera?
4. Ha mangiato qualche cosa stamattina?
5. Ha Lei ricevuto delle lettere ieri l'altro?
6. Ha letto Lei "I promessi Sposi" del Manzoni?
7. Dove ha Lei messo il Suo ombrello?
8. Ha Lei fatto una passeggiata stamattina?
9. Che tempo ha fatto ieri?
10. Ha scritto una lettera?
11. Ha letto il giornale?
12. Ha visto il signor Berlitz la settimana scorsa?
13. Ha visto il sindaco La Guardia nel 1945?
14. Le ho scritto una cartolina il mese scorso?
15. Ha avuto una lezione ieri?
16. Abbiamo avuto una lezione lunedì scorso?
17. Ha Lei sentito cantare Gigli?
18. Che tempo ha fatto ieri?
19. Di che cosa abbiamo parlato la settimana scorsa?
20. L'ho visto ieri?
21. Che cosa ho detto stamattina quando ho salutato?
22. Ha visto Roma?

La signora è uscita!
*Lah seen-*YOH*-rah* EH *oo-*SHEE*-tah!*
Madam has left!

GIULIA:	È già stato in Italia, signore?
JOO-*l'yah:*	EH JAH STAH-*toh een* Ee-TAHL-*yah, seen-*YOH-*reh?*
JULIA:	Have you already been in Italy, sir?
ROBERTO:	Oh, sì, signora.
*Roh-*BEHR-*toh:*	OH, *see, seen-*YOH-*rah.*
ROBERT:	Yes indeed, madam.

Prima di sposarmi ho passato
PREE-*mah dee spoh-*SAHR-*mee* OH *pahs-*SAH-*toh*
Before getting married I spent

parecchi anni in Italia.
*pah-*RECK-*kee* AHN-*nee een* Ee-TAHL-*yah.*
a few years in Italy.

VERY, VERY IMPORTANT! In the last lesson you saw *avere*—"to have" being used in the formation of the *passato prossimo* of other verbs. But *essere* is also used, in the same way. No doubt you must be worried about when to use *avere* and when to use *essere*. It will be very simple, if you read carefully and try to remember the following rule: When the action described by the verb applies to "somebody" or "some thing", the auxiliary *avere* is invariably used. Ex: "I ate"; you will not eat somebody, but you can certainly eat something; therefore, in Italian you must say: *Io ho mangiato*. Again: "I saw"; can you "see" something or somebody? The answer is: Yes. Then, in Italian you will say: *Io ho veduto*. Take now the verb *arrivare*—"to arrive". Can you arrive something or somebody? It doesn't make sense, does it? Well then; in this case you must use *essere*, and say: *Io sono arrivato*—"I arrived." The technical way to say this is: for transitive verbs, use *avere*; for intransitive verbs, use *essere*.

E Lei vi è mai stata?
Eh Lay vee EH *migh* STAH-*tah?*
And have you ever been there?

GIULIA: **Oh sì! Ci siamo andate nel 1938.**
OH *see! Chee s'*YAH-*moh ahn-*DAH-*teh nehl* MEEL-*noh-veh-*CHEHN-*toh-trehn-*TOHT-*toh.*
Oh yes! We went there in 1938.

Siamo partite, mia madre ed io, da New York sul Vulcania.
*s'*YAH-*moh pahr-*TEE-*teh,* MEE-*ah* MAH-*dreh ehd* EE-*oh, dah New York sool Vool-*KAH-*n'yah.*
We left, my mother and I, from New York on the Vulcania.

Siamo arrivate a Napoli ed abbiamo preso il treno per Roma.
*s'*YAH-*moh ahr-ree-*VAH-*teh ah* NAH-*poh-lee ehd ahb-b'*YAH-*moh* PREH-*zoh eel* TREH-*noh pehr* ROH-*mah.*
We arrived at Naples and took the train to Rome.

ROBERTO: **A che albergo è scesa?**
*Ah keh ahl-*BEHR-*goh* EH SHEH-*zah?*
At what hotel did you stay?

EXPRESSION to Remember: The word *scesa*, in the sentence *a che albergo è scesa,* is from the verb *scendere,* which means "to come down" or "to step down". The expression originates from the fact that in the old days one had to step down from a stage-coach, when one wanted to stop at an hotel. *Quando vado a Venezia io scendo all'Albergo Danieli.*—"When I go to Venice I stop at the Hotel Danieli."

GIULIA: **All'Excelsior. Ci siamo divertite molto durante**
*Ahl-lehs-*CHEHL-*s'yohr. Chee s'*YAH-*moh dee-vehr-*TEE-*teh* MOHL-*toh doo-*
RAHN-*teh*
At the Excelsior. We had a fine time during

tutto il nostro soggiorno.
TOOT-*toh eel* NOHS-*troh soh-*DJOHR-*noh.*
our entire stay.

Poi siamo ritornate in America sul Saturnia.
*Poy s'*YAH-*moh ree-tohr-*NAH-*teh een Ah-*MEH-*ree-kah sool*
*Sah-*TOOR-*n'yah.*
Afterwards we returned to America on the Saturnia.

ROBERTO: **Allora, signora, Lei è partita**
*Ahl-*LOH-*rah, seen-*YOH-*rah, Lay* EH *pahr-*TEE-*tah*
Then, madam, you left

dall'Italia un anno prima della guerra?
*dahl-lee-*TAHL-*yah oon* AHN-*noh* PREE-*mah* DEHL-*lah* GWEHR-*rah?*
Italy a year before the war?

GIULIA: **Per fortuna!**
*Pehr fohr-*TOO-*nah!*
Thank heavens!

E Lei, signore, è mai ritornato in Italia dopo la guerra?
*Eh Lay, seen-*YOH-*reh,* EH *migh ree-tohr-*NAH-*toh een Ee-*TAHL-*yah*
DOH-*poh lah* GWEHR-*rah?*
And you, sir, did you ever return to Italy after the war?

ROBERTO: **Purtroppo, no.**
*Poor-*TROHP-*poh, noh.*
Unfortunately, no.

Ma un mio amico vi è andato poco tempo fa
Mah oon MEE-*oh ah-*MEE-*koh vee* EH *ahn-*DAH-*toh* POH-*koh*
TEHM-*poh fah*
But a friend of mine went there a short time ago;

e ne è ritornato la settimana scorsa.
eh neh EH *ree-tohr-*NAH-*toh lah set-tee-*MAH-*nah* SKOHR-*sah.*
and came back from there last week.

Mi ha raccontato molto di Roma,
Mee AH *rahk-kohn-*TAH-*toh* MOHL-*toh dee* ROH-*mah,*
He told me a great deal about Rome,

che non ha perduto nulla della sua bellezza.
*keh noh-*NAH *pehr-*DOO-*toh* NOOL-*lah* DEHL-*lah* SOO-*ah behl-*LEH-*tsah.*
which has lost nothing of its beauty.

Adesso voglio andarvi anch'io.
Ah-DEHS-soh VOHL-*l'yoh ahn-*DAHR-*vee ahn-*KEE-*oh.*
Now I want to go there too.

Ora è molto facile d'andarvi in aeroplano.
OH-*rah* EH MOHL-*toh* FAH-*chee-leh dahn-*DAHR-*vee een*
*ah-eh-roh-*PLAH-*noh.*
Now it is very easy to go there by plane.

NOTE: Among its various meanings, *ne* also stands for "from it" or "from there". *Ne è ritornato la settimana scorsa,* actually means: "From there he returned last week."

GIULIA: **Anch'io ho l'intenzione di far**
*Ahn-*KEE-*oh* OH *leen-tehn-ts'*YOH-*neh dee fahr*
I too intend to make

la traversata in aeroplano.
*lah trah-vehr-*SAH-*tah een ah-eh-roh-*PLAH-*noh.*
the trip by plane.

Ma mia madre ha paura degli aeroplani.
Mah MEE-*ah* MAH-*dreh* AH *pah-oo-rah* DEHL-*yee ah-eh-roh-*PLAH-*nee.*
But my mother is afraid of aeroplanes.

Non vi è ancora salita.
Nohn vee EH *ahn-*KOH-*rah sah-*LEE-*tah.*
She has not yet gone up.

REMEMBER the Declension of the Past Participle: When a past participle is conjugated with the auxiliary *essere* it must always agree with the object, in number and gender. Ex: *Il libro è letto*—"the book is read"; *i libri sono letti*—"the books are read". *La signorina è seduta*—"the young lady is sitting"; *le signorine sono sedute*—"the young ladies are seated". When conjugated with the auxiliary *avere* the past participle does not change. Ex: *Io ho letto i libri*—"I have read the books". *Ho veduto le signore*—"I have seen the ladies". But whenever the object in the sentence is substituted by the pronouns *lo, la, li, le, ne,* the past participle must agree with the pronoun, in number and gender. Ex: *Il libro l'ho letto*—"the book: I have read it". *I libri, li ho letti*—"the books: I have read them". *La signora, l'ho veduta*—"the lady: I have seen her". *Le signore, le ho vedute*—"The ladies: I have seen them".

THINKING IN ITALIAN

(Answers on page 291)

1. Si è coricato nell'amaca il professore?
2. Chi ha bevuto una limonata?
3. Si è tolta la giacchetta?   4. Dove l'ha messa?
5. Ha egli letto il suo giornale?   6. Si è addormentato?
7. Quando è andato al cinematografo?
8. È andato al teatro ieri sera?   9. È uscito di casa domenica scorsa?
10. È rimasto in casa lunedì scorso?
11. La signora Bianchi è partita per l'Europa?
12. In quale mese è partita?   13. In quale mese è arrivata?
14. Fino a che mese è rimasta in Europa?
15. A che ora è uscito di casa ieri matina?
16. Quando è ritornato a casa?
17. È andato a Londra l'anno scorso?
18. È venuto qualcuno a vederla ieri mattina?
19. Sono uscito io alla stessa ora in cui e uscito Lei?
20. È Lei caduto quando è uscito dall'ascensore?
21. È stato Lei all'esposizione mondiale di Parigi nel 1938?
22. Quante volte è salito sul Vesuvio?
23. In quale giorno è arrivato a Genova il Vulcania?
24. Quando è partito da New York?
25. È spesso salito in aeroplano?

LEZIONE 32

Che cosa faremo domani?
Keh KOH-*zah fah*-REH-*moh doh*-MAH-*nee?*
What shall we do tomorrow?

GIORGIO:	**È molto occupato oggi?**
JOHR-*joh:*	EH MOHL-*toh ohk-koo*-PAH-*toh* OH-*djee?*
GEORGE:	Are you very busy today?

FRANCESCO:	**No, oggi non ho nulla da fare,**
Frahn-CHESS·*koh:*	*Noh,* OH-*djee noh*-NOH NOOL-*lah dah* FAH-*reh,*
FRANCIS:	No, today I haven't anything to do,

ma domani avrò da lavorare.
mah doh-MAH-*nee ah*-VROH *dah lah-voh*-RAH-*reh.*
but tomorrow I must work.

Sarò occupato tutto il giorno.
Sah-ROH *ohk-koo*-PAH-*toh* TOOT-*toh eel* JOHR-*noh.*
I shall be busy all day.

 NOTE on Future: It is easy to recognize the future tense of the Italian verbs by the endings: *rò, rà, remo* and *ranno.* Ex: *Sarò sarà, saremo, saranno. Parlerò,* etc.

183

GIORGIO: **Che cosa avrà da fare?**
Keh KOH-*zah ah-*VRAH *dah* FAH-*reh?*
What will you have to do?

FRANCESCO: **Mi alzerò di buon'ora, alle otto di mattina.**
*Mee ahl-tseh-*ROH *dee b'woh-*NOH-*rah,* AHL-*leh* OHT-*toh
dee maht-*TEE-*nah.*
I shall get up early, at eight in the morning.

Prenderò una lezione.
*Prehn-deh-*ROH OO-*nah leh-ts'*YOH-*neh.*
I shall take a lesson.

Poi scriverò gli esercizi,
*Poy skree-veh-*ROH *l'yee eh-zehr-*CHEE-*tsee,*
Then I shall write exercises,

e leggerò qualche pagina d'un libro
*eh leh-djeh-*ROH KWAHL-*keh* PAH-*jee-nah doon* LEE-*broh*
and I shall read a few pages of a book

che mi ha dato il mio professore.
keh mee AH DAH-*toh eel* MEE-*oh proh-fess-*SOH-*reh.*
that my teacher gave me.

GIORGIO: **Ma che cosa farà Lei dopo?**
Mah keh KOH-*zah fah-*RAH *Lay* DOH-*poh?*
But what will you do later?

Starà in casa?
*Stah-*RAH *een* KAH-*zah?*
Will you stay at home?

Non pranzerà con noi?
*Nohn prahn-tseh-*RAH *kohn noy?*
Won't you eat with us?

FRANCESCO: **Sì, pranzerò con Loro.**
*See, prahn-tseh-*ROH *kohn* LOH-*roh.*
Yes, I shall eat with you.

Verrò a mezzogiorno.
*Vehr-*ROH *ah meh-dzoh-*JOHR-*noh.*
I shall come at noon.

Dopo pranzo andrò dal pittore Guasti.
DOH-*poh* PRAHN-*tsoh ahn-*DROH *dahl peet-*TOH-*reh* GWAHS-*tee.*
After lunch I shall go to Guasti, the painter.

Se Lei viene con me vedrà il nuovo quadro
*Seh Lay v'*YEH-*neh kohn meh veh-*DRAH *eel n'*WOH-*voh* KWAH-*droh*
If you come with me, you will see the new painting

che ha incominciato.
keh AH *een-koh-meent-*CHAH-*toh.*
he has begun.

Poi potrà venire con me, andremo al teatro...
*Poy poh-*TRAH *veh-*NEE-*reh kohn meh, ahn-*DREH-*moh ahl teh-*AH-*troh* ..
Afterwards you can come with me, we shall go to the theatre...

GIORGIO: **Io non potrò andare alla mattinata.**
EE-*oh nohn poh-*TROH *ahn-*DAH-*reh* AHL-*lah maht-tee-*NAH-*tah.*
I shall not be able to go to the matinee.

Vi andremo la sera, se vuole.
*Vee ahn-*DREH-*moh lah* SEH-*rah, seh v'*WOH-*leh.*
We shall go in the evening, if you like.

Possiamo riservare i posti,
*Pohs-s'*YAH-*moh ree-zehr-*VAH-*reh ee* POHS-*tee,*
We can reserve seats,

e ceneremo insieme.
*eh cheh-neh-*REH-*moh een-s'*YEH-*meh.*
and we shall eat together.

Durante gl'intermezzi usciremo
*Doo-*RAHN-*teh l'yeen-tehr-*MEH-*dzee oo-shee-*REH-*moh*
During the intermissions we shall go out

e prenderemo un po' d'aria.
*eh prehn-deh-*REH-*moh oon* POH DAH-*r'yah.*
and take a bit of air.

Dopo la rappresentazione ritorneremo
DOH-*poh lah rahp-preh-zehn-tah-ts'*YOH-*neh ree-tohr-neh-*REH-*moh*
After the show we shall return

a casa e faremo una cenetta.
ah KAH-*zah eh fah-*REH-*moh* OO-*nah cheh-*NEHT-*tah.*
home and have supper.

Passeremo una bella serata insieme.
*Pahs-seh-*REH-*moh* OO-*nah* BELL-*lah seh-*RAH-*tah een-s'*YEH-*meh.*
We shall spend a fine evening together.

FRANCESCO: **Mi dispiace, ma non potrò venire con Lei,**
*Mee dees-p'*YAH-*cheh, mah nohn poh-*TROH *veh-*NEE-*reh kohn Lay,*
I am sorry, but I shall not be able to come with you

perchè il signor Conti verrà
*pehr-*KEH *eel seen-*YOHR KOHN-*tee vehr-*RAH
because Mr. Conti is coming

a passare la serata in casa mia.
ah pahs-SAH-reh lah seh-RAH-tah een KAH-zah MEE-ah.
to spend the evening. at my home.

GIORGIO: Ebbene, gli scriverà due parole.
Ehb-BEH-neh, l'yee skree-veh-RAH DOO-eh pah-ROH-leh.
Well then, you will write him a line.

 AN ITALIAN IDIOM: "To write a line or a few words" is translated by: *Scrivere due parole*—"to write two words."

Egli riceverà la Sua lettera domattina.
EHL-yee ree-cheh-veh-RAH lah SOO-ah LET-teh-rah doh-maht-TEE-nah.
He will receive your letter tomorrow morning.

Gli dirà che venga posdomani.
L'yee dee-RAH keh VEHN-gah pohs-doh-MAH-nee.
You can tell him to come the day after tomorrow.

FRANCESCO: Ma egli non verrà solo, condurrà sua moglie.
Mah EHL-yee nohn vehr-RAH SOH-loh, kohn-door-RAH SOO-ah MOH-l'yeh.
But he is not coming alone, he is bringing his wife.

Preferisco andare al teatro qualche altra volta.
Preh-feh-REES-koh ahn-DAH-reh ahl teh-AH-troh KWAHL-keh AHL-trah VOHL-tah.
I prefer to go to the theatre some other time.

GIORGIO: Va bene, vi andremo posdomani, se vuole.
Vah BEH-neh, vee ahn-DREH-moh pohs-doh-MAH-nee, seh v'WOH-leh.
All right, we can go the day after tomorrow, if you wish.

Mi dica, il signor e la signora Baratti
Mee DEE-kah, eel seen-YOHR eh lah seen-YOH-rah Bah-RAHT tee
Tell me, will Mr. and Mrs. Baratti

resteranno in città durante l'estate?
rehs-teh-RAHN-noh een cheet-TAH doo-RAHN-teh lehs-TAH-teh?
remain in town during the summer?

FRANCESCO: No, passeranno un mese in campagna
Noh, pahs-seh-RAHN-noh oon MEH-zeh een kahm-PAHN-yah
No, they will spend a month in the country

e ritorneranno in autunno.
eh ree-tohr-neh-RAHN-noh een aou-TOON-noh.
and will return in autumn.

Sarò io una stella del cinema un jorno.

Che cosa mangeremo stasera in casa della Signora Fibronia?

Verrà a cena in tempo il professore?

THINKING IN ITALIAN

(Answers on page 292)

1. Dove andrà il profesore stasera?
2. Sarà la Signora Fibronia in casa stasera?
3. Avrà Lei una lezione d'italiano domani?
4. Sarà Lei in casa stasera?
5. Che cosa farà stasera?
6. Potrà accompagnarmi all'opera stasera?
7. Potremo uscire durante gl'intermezzi?
8. Vi andremo in automobile?
9. A che ora partiremo?
10. Rimarrà in casa dopo pranzo?
11. La vedrò stasera?
12. Che cosa faremo domani?
13. Leggerà Lei il giornale domattina?
14. Scriverà Lei delle lettere stasera?
15. Mangerà Lei carne stasera?
16. Berrà Lei del vino?
17. Verrà Lei qui domani?
18. Andrà Lei in Italia l'anno venturo?
19. La vedrò domani?
20. Che libro leggeremo alla prossima lezione?
21. Parleremo italiano alla prossima lezione?
22. Usciremo dopo la lezione?
23. Avrà Lei dei biglietti per l'opera stasera?

LEZIONE 33

Gli animali
*L'yee ah-nee-*MAH*-lee*
The animals

Il cavallo, la vacca e il cane sono animali domestici.
*Eel kah-*VAHL*-loh, lah* VAHK*-kah eh eel* KAH*-neh* SOH*-noh ah-nee-*MAH*-lee*
    *doh-*MESS*-tee-chee.*
The horse, the cow and the dog are domestic animals.

Ecco qui un leone, una tigre, un elefante, un lupo.
ECK*-koh kwee oon leh-*OH*-neh,* OO*-nah* TEE*-greh, oon eh-leh-*FAHN*-teh,*
    oon LOO*-poh.*
Here is a lion, a tiger, an elephant, a wolf.

Sono animali selvatici.
SOH*-noh ah-nee-*MAH*-lee sel-*VAH*-tee-chee.*
They are wild animals.

Gli animali domestici fanno dei lavori per l'uomo.
*L'yee ah-nee-*MAH*-lee doh-*MESS*-tee-chee* FAHN*-noh day lah-*VOH*-ree*
    *pehr loo-*OH*-moh.*
The domestic animals work for man.

188

Il cane guarda la casa.
Eel KAH-*neh* GWAHR-*dah lah* KAH-*zah.*
The dog watches the house.

Il gatto caccia i topi.
Eel GAHT-*toh* KAHT-*chah ee* TOH-*pee.*
The cat hunts mice.

Il cavallo tira la carrozza.
*Eel kah-*VAHL-*loh* TEE-*rah lah kahr-*ROH-*tsah.*
The horse pulls the wagon.

E la vacca ci dà il latte.
Eh lah VAHK-*kah chee* DAH *eel* LAHT-*teh.*
And the cow gives us milk.

Ma gli animali selvatici vivono nella selva e sono pericolosi.
*Mah l'yee ah-nee-*MAH-*lee sel-*VAH-*tee-chee* VEE-*voh-noh* NEHL-*lah* SEL-*vah
eh* SOH-*noh peh-ree-koh-*LOH-*zee.*
But the wild animals live in the jungle and are dangerous.

Il cavallo ha quattro gambe, è un quadrupede.
*Eel kah-*VAHL-*loh* AH KWAHT-*troh* GAHM-*beh,* EH *oon kwah-*DROO-*peh-deh.*
The horse has four legs, it is a quadruped.

La tigre ha quattro zampe.
Lah TEE-*greh* AH KWAHT-*troh* DZAHM-*peh.*
The tiger has four paws.

È pure un quadrupede.
EH POO-*reh oon kwah-*DROO-*peh-deh.*
It is also a quadruped.

I quadrupedi corrono, camminano e saltano.
*Ee kwah-*DROO-*peh-dee* KOHR-*roh-noh, kahm-*MEE-*nah-noh eh* SAHL-*tah-noh,*
Quadrupeds run, walk and jump.

L'aquila, il passero, il gallo e la gallina sono uccelli.
LAH-*kwee-lah, eel* PAHS-*seh-roh, eel* GAHL-*loh eh lah gahl-*LEE-*nah
soh-*noh *oot-*CHEHL-*lee.*
The eagle, the sparrow, the rooster and the hen are birds.

Gli uccelli hanno due zampe per camminare e due ali per volare.
*L'yee oot-*CHEHL-*lee* AHN-*noh* DOO-*eh* DZAHM-*peh pehr kahm-mee-*NAH-*reh
eh* DOO-*eh* AH-*lee pehr voh-*LAH-*reh.*
Birds have two legs to walk (with) and two wings to fly (with).

Gli animali camminano o corrono sulla terra.
*L'yee ah-nee-*MAH-*lee kahm-*MEE-*nah-noh oh* KOHR-*roh-noh* SOOL-*lah
TEHR-*rah.*
Animals walk and run on the ground.

Gli uccelli volano nell'aria.
*L'yee oot-*CHEHL-*lee* VOH-*lah-noh nehl-*LAH-*r'yah.*
Birds fly in the air.

La nostra testa è coperta di capelli,
Lah NOHS-*trah* TESS-*tah* EH *koh-*PEHR-*tah dee kah-*PEHL-*lee.*
Our head is covered with hair.

Il corpo degli animali è coperto di peli.
Eel KOHR-*poh* DEHL-*yee ah-nee-*MAH-*lee* EH *koh-*PEHR-*toh dee* PEH-*lee.*
The body of animals is covered with fur.

Il corpo degli uccelli è coperto di piume.
Eel KOHR-*poh* DEHL-*yee oot-*CHEHL-*lee* EH *koh-*PEHR-*toh dee p'*YOO-*meh*
Birds' bodies are covered with feathers.

I pesci stanno nell'acqua.
Ee PEH-*shee* STAHN-*noh nehl-*LAHK-*kwah.*
Fish stay in the water.

Essi non hanno nè zampe nè ali.
EHS-*see noh-*NAHN-*noh* NEH DZAHM-*peh* NEH AH-*lee.*
They have neither legs nor wings.

Essi hanno pinne e si muovono nuotando.
EHS-*see* AHN-*noh* PEEN-*neh eh see m'*WOH-*voh-noh n'woh-*TAHN-*doh.*
They have fins and move by swimming.

 NOTE to Student: The formation of the present participle is, in Italian, as simple as it is in English; you simply substitute the ending of the infinitive with *ando,* if the verb ends with *are* (1st conjugation), or with *endo,* if the verb ends with *ere* (2nd conjugation) or *ire* (3rd conjugation). Ex: *Mangi-are*—"to eat", becomes *mangi-ando*—"eating"; *scriv-ere*—"to write", becomes *scriv-endo*—"writing"; *sent-ire*—"to hear" or "to feel", becomes *sent-endo*—"hearing" or "feeling", etc. There are a few exceptions. but they need not worry you at this point.

Il loro corpo è coperto di scaglie.
Eel LOH-*roh* KOHR-*poh* EH *koh-*PEHR-*toh dee* SKAHL-*l'yeh.*
Their body is covered with scales.

Il pescecane è il pesce più pericoloso, perchè è molto feroce.
*Eel peh-sheh-*KAH-*neh* EH *eel* PEH-*sheh p'*YOO *peh-ree-koh-*LOH-*zoh, pehr-*KEH
EH MOHL-*toh feh-*ROH-*cheh.*
The shark is the most dangerous fish, because it is very ferocious.

Vi sono molti pescecani nel Mediterraneo.
Vee SOH-*noh* MOHL-*tee peh-sheh-*KAH-*nee nehl Meh-dee-tehr-*RAH-*neh-oh.*
There are many sharks in the Mediterranean.

Se Lei vede un pescecane dove vi sono delle
Seh Lay VEH-*deh oon peh-sheh-*KAH-*neh* DOH-*veh vee* SOH-*noh* DEHL-*leh*
If you see a shark where there are

persone che nuotano, deve dare l'allarme.
*pehr-*SOH-*neh keh n'*WOH-*tah-noh,* DEH-*veh* DAH-*reh lahl-*LAHR-*meh.*
people swimming, you must give the alarm.

Lei grida: Attenti al pescecane!
Lay GREE-*dah: Aht-*TEN-*tee ahl peh-sheh-*KAH-*neh!*
You cry: Look out for the shark!

IMPORTANT NOTE: Here are some exclamations you must learn by heart because you won't have time to consult your dictionary if you need to use them!

Help!—*Aiuto!*   Watch out!—*Attenzione!*
Stop thief!—*Al ladro!*   Police!—*Polizia!*
Stop!—*Ferma!*   Run!—*Scappa!*
Hurrah!—*Evviva!*   To your health!—*Salute!*
                I love you!—*Io L'amo!*

Il serpente è un rettile e non ha zampe; striscia sulla terra.
*Eel sehr-*PEHN-*teh* EH *oon* REHT-*tee-leh eh noh-*NAH DZAHM-*peh;* STREE-*shah*
SOOL-*lah* TEHR-*rah.*
The snake is a reptile and has no legs; it crawls on the ground.

La rana è un anfibio; essa può vivere nell'acqua e sulla terra.
Lah RAH-*nah* EH *oon ahn-*FEE-*bee-oh;* ESS-*sah p'*WOH VEE-*veh-reh*
*nehl-*LAH-*kwah eh* SOOL-*lah* TEHR-*rah.*
The frog is an amphibian; he can live in the water and on the ground.

In Italia ed in Francia le zampe di rana
*Een Ee-*TAHL-*yah ehd een* FRAHNT-*chah leh* DZAHM-*peh dee* RAH-*nah*
In Italy and in France frogs' legs

sono considerate un piatto prelibato.
SOH-*noh kohn-see-deh-*RAH-*teh oon p'*YAHT-*toh preh-lee-*BAH-*toh.*
are considered a favorite dish.

Sono deliziose.
SOH-*noh deh-lee-ts'*YOH-*zeh.*
They are delicious.

Fra gli insetti vi sono le farfalle, le mosche e le zanzare.
*Frah l'yee een-*SET*-tee vee* SOH*-noh leh jahr-*FAHL*-leh, leh* MOHS*-keh
eh leh dzahn-*DZAH*-reh.*
Among the insects there are butterflies, flies and mosquitoes.

L'ape, che produce il miele, ed il baco da seta,
LAH*-peh, keh proh-*DOO*-cheh eel m'*YEH*-leh, ehd eel* BAH*-koh dah* SEH*-tah,*
The bee, which produces honey, and the silk worm,

che ci dà la seta, sono utili.
keh chee dah lah SEH*-tah,* SOH*-noh* OO*-tee-lee.*
which produces silk, are useful.

La mosca e la zanzara sono inutili e spiacevoli.
Lah MOHS*-kah eh lah dzahn-*DZAH*-rah* SOH*-noh ee-*NOO*-tee-lee
eh sp'yah-*CHEH*-voh-lee.*
The fly and the mosquito are useless and unpleasant.

Non producono nulla, ma, al contrario, sono dannosi.
*Nohn proh-*DOO*-koh-noh* NOOL*-lah, mah, ahl kohn-*TRAH*-r'yoh,* SOH*-noh
dahn-*NOH*-zee.*
They don't produce anything, but on the contrary, are harmful.

Gli animali mangiano, bevono e respirano perchè vivono.
*L'yee ah-nee-*MAH*-lee* MAHN*-djah-noh,* BEH*-voh-noh eh rehs-*PEE*-rah-noh
pehr-*KEH VEE*-voh-noh.*
Animals eat, drink and breathe because they live.

Se un animale non respira, non può vivere.
*Seh oon ah-nee-*MAH*-leh nohn rehs-*PEE*-rah, nohn p'*WOH VEE*-veh-reh.*
If an animal does not breathe, it cannot live.

L'uomo e quasi tutti gli animali (la maggior parte degli animali)
*Loo-*OH*-moh eh* KWAH*-zee* TOOT*-tee l'yee ah-nee-*MAH*-lee (lah mah-*DJOHR
PAHR*-teh* DEHL*-yee ah-nee-*MAH*-lee)*
Men and almost all animals (the majority of animals)

hanno cinque sensi per vedere, udire,
AHN*-noh* CHEEN*-kweh* SEHN*-see pehr veh-*DEH*-reh, oo-*DEE*-reh,*
have five senses to see, hear,

odorare, sentire il gusto, ed il tatto.
*oh-doh-*RAH*-reh, sehn-*TEE*-reh eel* GOOS*-toh, ehd eel* TAHT*-toh.*
smell, taste and touch.

Noi vediamo con gli occhi.
*Noy veh-d'*YAH*-moh kohn l'yee* OCK*-kee.*
We see with our eyes.

Gli occhi sono gli organi della vista.
L'yee OCK-*kee* SOH-*noh l'yee* OHR-*gah-nee* DEHL-*lah* VEES-*tah.*
The eyes are the organs of sight.

Noi udiamo con gli orecchi.
*Noy oo-d'*YAH-*moh kohn l'yee oh-*REHK-*kee.*
We hear with our ears.

Gli orecchi sono gli organi dell'udito.
*L'yee oh-*REHK-*kee* SOH-*noh l'yee* OHR-*gah-nee dehl-loo-*DEE-*toh.*
The ears are the organs of hearing.

Noi odoriamo col naso.
*Noy oh-doh-r'*YAH-*moh kohl* NAH-*zoh.*
We smell with the nose.

Il naso è l'organo dell'odorato.
Eel NAH-*zoh* EH LOHR-*gah-noh dehl-loh-doh-*RAH-*toh.*
The nose is the organ of smell.

Con la lingua e col palato noi sentiamo il
Kohn lah LEEN-*gwah eh kohl pah-*LAH-*toh noy sehn-t'*YAH-*moh eel*
With the tongue and with the palate we taste

gusto dei cibi e delle bevande.
GOOS-*toh day* CHEE-*bee eh* DEHL-*leh beh-*VAHN-*deh.*
food and drink.

La lingua ed il palato sono gli organi del gusto.
Lah LEEN-*gwah ehd eel pah-*LAH-*toh* SOH-*noh l'yee* OHR-*gah-nee*
   dehl GOOS-*toh.*
The tongue and the palate are the organs of taste.

Il tatto è diffuso su tutto il corpo.
Eel TAHT-*toh* EH *deef-*FOO-*zoh soo* TOOT-*toh eel* KOHR-*poh.*
Touch is distributed throughout the whole body.

La vista ci mostra il colore, la forma,
Lah VEES-*tah chee* MOSS-*trah eel koh-*LOH-*reh, lah* FOHR-*mah,*
Sight shows us the color, the form,

le dimensioni, il posto e la posizione degli oggetti.
*leh dee-mehn-s'*YOH-*nee, eel* POHS-*toh eh lah poh-zee-ts'*YOH-*neh*
   DEHL-*yee oh-d*JET-*tee.*
the dimensions, the location and the position of objects.

Con l'udito percepiamo i suoni ed i rumori.
*Kohn loo-*DEE-*toh pehr-cheh-p'*YAH-*moh ee soo-*OH-*nee ehd ee roo-*MOH-*ree.*
Through hearing, we perceive sounds and noises.

Mediante il tatto sentiamo il freddo del ghiaccio,
*Meh-d'*YAHN-*teh eel* TAHT-*toh sehn-t'*YAH-*moh eel* FREHD-*doh*
*dehl g'*YAHT-*choh,*
Through touch we feel the coldness of ice,

il calore del termosifone, il dolore quando ci bruciamo.
*eel kah-*LOH-*reh dehl tehr-moh-zee-*FOH-*neh, eel doh-*LOH-*reh* KWAHN-*doh*
*chee broo-ch'*YAH-*moh.*
the heat of the radiator, and pain when we burn ourselves.

Inoltre, mediante il tatto percepiamo
*Ee-*NOHL-*treh, meh-d'*YAHN-*teh eel* TAHT-*toh pehr-cheh-p'*YAH-*moh*
Moreover, through the touch we perceive

se un oggetto è molle o duro.
*seh oon oh-*DJET-*toh* EH MOHL-*leh oh* DOO-*roh.*
if an object is soft or hard.

Noi respiriamo l'aria.
*Noy rehs-pee-r'*YAH-*moh* LAH-*r'yah.*
We breathe air.

Respiriamo coi polmoni.
*Rehs-pee-r'*YAH-*moh koy pohl-*MOH-*nee.*
We breathe with the lungs.

I polmoni sono gli organi della respirazione.
*Ee pohl-*MOH-*nee* SOH-*noh l'yee* OHR-*gah-nee* DEHL-*lah*
*rehs-pee-rah-ts'*YOH-*neh.*
The lungs are the organs of breathing.

I polmoni sono nel petto.
*Ee pohl-*MOH-*nee* SOH-*noh nehl* PET-*toh.*
The lungs are in the chest.

Noi mangiamo con la bocca.
*Noy mahn-*JAH-*moh kohn lah* BOHK-*kah.*
We eat with the mouth.

Prendiamo il cibo, ci nutriamo.
*Prehn-d'*YAH-*moh eel* CHEE-*boh, chee noo-tr'*YAH-*moh.*
We take food, we feed ourselves.

Il nutrimento discende nello stomaco.
*Eel noo-tree-*MEHN-*toh dee-*SHEHN-*deh* NEHL-*loh* STOH-*mah-koh.*
The food goes down into the stomach.

Lo stomaco digerisce il nutrimento.
Loh STOH-*mah-koh dee-jeh-*REE-*sheh eel noo-tree-*MEHN-*toh.*
The stomach digests the food.

Se mi taglio, dalla ferita esce un liquido rosso: è il sangue.
Seh mee TAHL-*l'yoh,* DAHL-*lah feh-*REE-*tah* EH-*sheh oon* LEE-*kwee-doh*
ROHS-*soh:* EH *eel* SAHN-*gweh.*
If I cut myself, a red liquid flows out of the wound; it is blood.

Il sangue circola per tutto il corpo.
Eel SAHN-*gweh* CHEER-*koh-lah pehr* TOOT-*toh eel* KOHR-*poh.*
Blood circulates through the whole body.

È il cuore che fa circolare il sangue.
EH *eel k'*WOH-*reh keh fah cheer-koh-*LAH-*reh eel* SAHN-*gweh.*
It is the heart that makes the blood circulate.

Il cuore è nel petto.
*Eel k'*WOH-*reh* EH *nehl* PET-*toh.*
The heart is in the chest.

Se si digerisce bene, se si respira bene,
*Seh see dee-jeh-*REE-*sheh* BEH-*neh, seh see rehs-*PEE-*rah* BEH-*neh,*
If one digests well, if one breathes well,

e se la circolazione del sangue è buona,
*eh seh lah cheer-koh-lah-ts'*YOH-*neh dehl* SAHN-*gweh* EH *b'*WOH-*nah,*
and if the circulation of the blood is good,

si ha buona salute, si sta bene.
see AH *b'*WOH-*nah sah-*LOO-*teh, see stah* BEH-*neh.*
one is in good health, one is well.

Se si digerisce male, se la respirazione
*Seh see dee-jeh-*REE-*sheh* MAH-*leh, seh lah rehs-pee-rah-ts'*YOH-*neh*
If one digests badly, if the respiration

o la circolazione del sangue non sono regolari,
*oh lah cheer-koh-lah-ts'*YOH-*neh dehl* SAHN-*gweh nohn* SOH-*noh*
*reh-goh-*LAH-*ree,*
or the circulation of the blood are not regular,

si è ammalati.
see EH *ahm-mah-*LAH-*tee.*
one is ill.

Allora bisogna chiamare il medico.
*Ahl-*LOH-*rah bee-*ZOHN-*yah k'yah-*MAH-*reh eel* MEH-*dee-koh.*
Then one needs to call a doctor.

THINKING IN ITALIAN

(Answers on page 292)

1. Che cosa devono fare gli animali per vivere?
2. Di che abbiamo bisogno per vivere?
3. Quali sono i cinque sensi?
4. Come si chiamano i principali animali domestici?
5. Quali sono gli organi della digestione e della respirazione?
6. Dove stanno i pesci?   7. Come si muove il serpente?
8. Cammina la rana?   9. Appartiene a Lei questo libro?
10. Perchè l'ape è un insetto utile?
11. Nomini i principali animali domestici e selvatici.
12. Quante zampe ha il cane?   13. Quante zampe ha un uccello?
14. Che cosa fanno gli animali colle zampe?
15. Che cosa fanno gli uccelli colle ali?
16. Dove volano gli uccelli?   17. Nuota il pesce nel mare?
18. Possiamo noi vivere senza mangiare e senza respirare?
19. Con che cosa respiriamo?   20. Dove sono i polmoni?
21. Di che colore è il sangue? 22. Che cosa fa circolare il sangue?
23. Dov'è il cuore?   24. Sta bene di salute?
25. Se si mangia troppo, si digerisce facilmente?

LEZIONE 34

L'uomo e le sue emozioni
*Loo-*OH*-moh eh leh* SOO*-eh eh-moh-ts'*YOH*-nee*
Man and his emotions

L'uomo è simile agli animali:
*Loo-*OH*-moh* EH SEE*-mee-leh* AHL*-yee ah-nee-*MAH*-lee:*
Man resembles the animals:

deve mangiare, bere e respirare.
DEH*-veh mahn-*JAH*-reh,* BEH*-reh eh rehs-pee-*RAH*-reh.*
he must eat, drink and breathe.

Ma l'uomo si distingue dagli animali
*Mah loo-*OH*-moh see dees-*TEEN*-gweh* DAHL*-yee ah-nee-*MAH*-lee*
But man distinguishes himself from the animals

perchè parla e perchè pensa.
*pehr-*KEH PAHR*-lah eh pehr-*KEH PEN*-sah.*
because he speaks and because he thinks.

Pensiamo col cervello, che è nella testa.
*Pen-s'*YAH*-moh kohl chehr-*VEHL*-loh keh* EH NEHL*-lah* TESS*-tah.*
We think with the brain, which is in the head.

Il cervello è l'organo del pensiero.
*Eel chehr-*VEHL*-loh* EH LOHR*-gah-noh dehl pen-s'*YEH*-roh.*
The brain is the organ of thought.

In quali cose siamo simili agli animali?
Een KWAH*-lee* KOH*-zeh s'*YAH*-moh* SEE*-mee-lee* AHL*-yee ah-nee-*MAH*-lee?*
In what ways are we similar to the animals?

Come essi noi abbiamo bisogno di mangiare, di bere e di respirare.
KOH*-meh* EHS*-see noy ahb-b'*YAH*-moh bee-*ZOHN*-yoh dee mahn-*JAH*-reh,
dee* BEH*-reh eh dee rehs-pee-*RAH*-reh.*
Like them we must eat, drink and breathe.

Che cosa è che distingue grandemente l'uomo dagli animali?
Keh KOH*-zah* EH *keh dees-*TEEN*-gweh grahn-deh-*MEHN*-teh loo-oh-moh
DAHL*-yee ah-nee-*MAH*-lee?*
What is it that distinguishes man greatly from the animals?

La parola ed il pensiero.
*Lah pah-*ROH*-lah ehd eel pen-s'*YEH*-roh.*
Speech and thought.

Noi pensiamo a cose presenti o assenti.
*Noy pen-s'*YAH*-moh ah* KOH*-zeh preh-*ZEHN*-tee oh ahs-*SEHN*-tee.*
We think of things (both) present and absent.

EXPRESSIONS TO REMEMBER: *Pensare a...* "to think of" (to direct one's thought to). Ex: *Io penso a Lei*—"I am thinking of you." *Pensare di*—"to think of" (to have an opinion about). Ex: *Che pensa Lei del libro Berlitz?*—"What do you think of the Berlitz book?"

Nel cervello noi abbiamo delle immagini, chiamate idee.
*Nehl chehr-*VEHL*-loh noy ahb-b'*YAH*-moh* DEHL*-leh eem-*MAH*-jee-nee,
k'yah-*MAH*-teh ee-*DEH*-eh.*
In our brain we have images called ideas.

NOTE on Pronunciation: Remember to sound each "e" separately in the word *idee.*

Noi parliamo per comunicare le nostre idee ad altre persone.
*Noy pahr-l'*YAH*-moh pehr koh-moo-nee-*KAH*-reh leh* NOHS*-treh ee-*DEH*-eh
ahd* AHL*-treh pehr-*SOH*-neh.*
We speak to communicate our ideas to other persons.

Noi possiamo pensare a cose e persone presenti od assenti.
Noy pohs-s'YAH-moh pen-SAH-reh ah KOH-zeh eh pehr-SOH-neh preh-ZEHN-tee ohd ahs-SEHN-tee.
We are able to think of present or absent things and persons.

Ora Lei pensa alla Sua lezione.
OH-rah Lay PEN-sah AHL-lah SOO-ah leh-ts'YOH-neh.
Now you are thinking of your lesson.

Se pensa ad altra cosa, non mi può comprendere.
Seh PEN-sah ahd AHL-trah KOH-zah, nohn mee p'WOH kohm-PREHN-deh-reh.
If you are thinking of something else, you are not able to understand me.

Spesso Lei pensa alla Sua lezione quando è a casa Sua.
SPEHS-soh Lay PEN-sah AHL-lah SOO-ah leh-ts'YOH-neh KWAHN-doh EH ah KAH-zah SOO-ah.
Often you think of your lesson when you are at home.

Che cosa fa Lei adesso?
Keh KOH-zah fah Lay ah-DEHS-soh?
What are you doing now?

Lei impara l'italiano.
Lay eem-PAH-rah lee-tahl-YAH-noh.
You are learning Italian.

Il professore insegna.
Eel proh-fess-SOH-reh een-SEHN-n'yah.
The teacher teaches.

L'allievo impara.
Lahl-l'YEH-voh eem-PAH-rah.
The pupil learns.

Ora Lei impara l'italiano.
OH-rah Lay eem-PAH-rah lee-tahl-YAH-noh.
Now you are learning Italian.

L'anno scorso ha imparato il francese.
LAHN-noh SKOHR-soh AH eem-pah-RAH-toh eel frahn-CHEH-zeh.
Last year you learned French.

Due anni fa ha imparato il tedesco.
DOO-eh AHN-nee fah AH eem-pah-RAH-toh eel teh-DESS-koh.
Two years ago you learned German.

EXPRESSION TO REMEMBER: The literal translation of *due anni fa* is: "It makes two years." Therefore *fa* has the meaning of "ago".

Quando abbiamo imparato bene una cosa, la sappiamo.
KWAHN-doh ahb-b'YAH-moh eem-pah-RAH-toh BEH-neh OO-nah KOH-zah, lah sahp-p'YAH-moh.
When we have learned something well, we know it.

Lei sa contare, Lei sa scrivere perchè l'ha imparato.
Lay SAH *kohn*-TAH-*reh, Lay* SAH SKREE-*veh-reh pehr-*KEH LAH
*eem-pah-*RAH-*toh.*
You know how to count, you know how to write because you have
learned it.

Lei sa che io ho un orologio, perchè l'ha veduto.
Lay SAH *keh* EE-*oh* OH *oon oh-roh-*LOH-*joh, pehr-*KEH LAH *veh-*DOO-*toh.*
You know that I have a watch, because you have seen it.

Lei ha imparato molte parole italiane ma ne ha dimenticate alcune.
Lay AH *eem-pah-*RAH-*toh* MOHL-*teh pah-*ROH-*leh ee-tahl-*YAH-*neh mah neh*
AH *dee-mehn-tee-*KAH-*teh ahl-*KOO-*neh.*
You have learned many Italian words but you have forgotten some of
them.

IMPORTANT NOTE: *Conoscere* means "to be ac-
quainted" with somebody or something. *Sapere* means "to
know how" or "to know of." Ex: *Conosce Lei il signor de
Luca?*—"Do you know Mr. De Luca?" *Conosce Lei molte
opere italiane?*—"Do you know many Italian operas?" *Sa
Lei cantare?*—"Do you know how to sing?" *Io so che Lei ha una bella voce.*
—"I know that you have a beautiful voice."

Nell'uomo le sensazioni e le emozioni sono
*Nehl-loo-*OH-*moh leh sehn-sah-ts'*YOH-*nee eh leh eh-moh-ts'*YOH-*nee* SOH-*noh*
In man, the sensations and emotions are

più sviluppate che negli animali.
*p'*YOO *svee-loop-*PAH-*teh keh* NEHL-*yee ah-nee-*MAH-*lee.*
more (highly) developed than in the animals.

Gli animali amano generalmente i loro piccoli,
*L'yee ah-nee-*MAH-*lee* AH-*mah-noh jeh-neh-rahl-*MEHN-*teh ee* LOH-*roh*
PEEK-*koh-lee,*
The animals usually love their young ones,

ma l'amore di nostra madre per noi è molto più forte.
*mah lah-*MOH-*reh dee* NOHS-*trah* MAH-*dreh pehr noy* EH MOHL-*toh p'*YOO
FOHR-*teh.*
but the love of our mother for us is much stronger.

Ci piace vedere un bel quadro.
*Chee p'*YAH-*cheh veh-*DEH-*reh oon bell* KWAH-*droh.*
We like to see a nice picture.

Ci piace la bellezza; al contrario, non ci piace la bruttezza.
Chee p'YAH-cheh lah behl-LEH-tsah; ahl kohn-TRAH-r'yoh, nohn chee p'YAH-cheh lah broot-TEH-tsah.
We like beauty; on the contrary, we do not like ugliness.

Sentiamo della ripugnanza a toccare delle cose sporche.
Sehn-t'YAH-moh DEHL-lah ree-poon-n'YAHN-tsah ah tohk-KAH-reh DEHL-leh KOH-zeh SPOHR-keh.
We feel repugnance on touching dirty things.

La paura è un'altra emozione.
Lah pah-OO-rah EH oo-NAHL-trah eh-moh-ts'YOH-neh.
Fear is another emotion.

I piccoli animali hanno paura dei grandi.
Ee PEEK-koh-lee ah-nee-MAH-lee AHN-noh pah-OO-rah day GRAHN-dee.
Small animals have fear of large ones.

I bambini temono il buio.
Ee bahm-BEE-nee TEH-moh-noh eel BOO-yoh.
Children fear darkness.

Temono le fanciulle i ragni, i serpenti ed i topi?
TEH-moh-noh leh fahnt-CHOOL-leh ee RAHN-n'yee, ee sehr-PEHN-tee ehd ee TOH-pee?
Do young girls fear frogs, snakes and mice?

Sì, ne hanno paura.
See, neh AHN-noh pah-OO-rah.
Yes, they fear them.

REMEMBER: The *ne* in *ne hanno paura* means "of it" or "of them".

Chi non ha paura, è coraggioso.
Kee noh-NAH pah-OO-rah, EH koh-rah-DJOH-zoh.
(He) who has no fear is courageous.

Lei prova piacere vedendo o udendo delle cose piacevoli.
Lay PROH-vah p'yah-CHEH-reh veh-DEHN-doh oh oo-DEHN-doh DEHL-leh KOH-zeh p'yah-CHEH-voh-lee.
You like to see and to hear pleasant things.

Se Lei vede una bella commedia o sente della
Seh Lay VEH-deh oo-nah BELL-lah kohm-MEH-d'yah oh SEHN-teh DEHL-lah
If you see a beautiful play or hear

buona musica prova piacere.
b'woh-nah MOO-*zee-kah* PROH-*vah* *p'yah*-CHEH-*reh*.
good music you like it.

Quando il Suo professore Le dice che il Suo
KWAHN-*doh eel* SOO-*oh proh-fess*-SOH-*reh Leh* DEE-*cheh keh eel* SOO-*oh*
When your teacher tells you that your

esercizio è fatto bene, ne è contento.
eh-zehr-CHEE-*ts'yoh* EH FAHT-*toh* BEH-*neh, neh* EH *kohn*-TEHN-*toh*.
exercise is well done, you are happy about it.

Le piace.
*Leh p'*YAH-*cheh*.
You are pleased.

Siamo malcontenti quando il rumore ci impedisce di dormire.
*s'*YAH-*moh mahl-kohn*-TEHN-*tee* KWAHN-*doh eel roo*-MOH-*reh chee*
 eem-peh-DEE-*sheh dee dohr*-MEE-*reh*.
We are annoyed when noise prevents us from sleeping.

Ci dispiace quando dobbiamo aspettare a lungo
*Chee dees-p'*YAH-*cheh* KWAHN-*doh dohb-b'*YAH-*moh ahs-pet*-TAH-*reh ah*
 LOON-*goh*
We are displeased when we have to wait a long time

per un posto al cinematografo.
pehr oon POHS-*toh ahl chee-neh-mah*-TOH-*grah-foh*.
for a seat at the movies.

Quando i bambini sono malcontenti, piangono.
KWAHN-*doh ee bahm*-BEE-*neh* SOH-*noh mahl-kohn*-TEHN-*tee, p'*YAHN-*goh-noh*.
When small children are annoyed, they cry.

 EXPRESSION to Remember: *A lungo* means "for a long time". Ex: *Ho aspettato a lungo una Sua lettera.*—"I have been waiting for a letter from you for a long time." *A lungo andare*—"In the long run".

Ma gli adulti mostrano il loro malcontento in altro modo.
Mah l'yee ah-DOOL-*tee* MOSS-*trah-noh eel* LOH-*roh mahl-kohn*-TEN-*toh een*
 AHL-*troh* MOH-*doh*.
But adults show their annoyance in other ways.

Tuttavia è meglio ridere che arrabbiarsi o esser tristi.
Toot-tah-VEE-*ah* EH MEH-*l'yoh* REE-*deh-reh keh ahr-rahb-b'*YAHR-*see oh*
 EHS-*sehr* TREES-*tee*.
In any case it is better to laugh than to get angry or to be sad.

THINKING IN ITALIAN

(Answers on page 293)

1. Perchè il professore è contento?
2. È felice Titina? 3. Perchè piange?
4. È triste la signora Fibronia? 5. Perchè è triste?
6. È l'uomo superiore agli animali in tutte le cose?
7. Si può parlare correttamente senza pensare?
8. Ho freddo quando mi siedo presso il termosifone?
9. Che cosa impara Lei adesso?
10. Ha imparato la musica l'anno scorso? 11. Ha imparato a ballare?
12. Sa Lei il nome del Presidente degli Stati Uniti?
13. So io quante stelle vi sono in cielo?
14. Sappiamo noi che tempo farà la prossima settimana?
15. Sa il maestro la distanza fra Roma e Napoli?
16. Ha Lei imparato il tedesco? 17. Lo sa ancora?
18. Lo ha dimenticato? 19. Ha Lei buona memoria?
20. Si dimentica presto quando non si ha buona memoria?
21. Conosce l'opera Tosca? 22. Sa chi ha scritto l'opera?
23. Desidera Lei avere molto danaro?
24. È contento quando vede che fa bel tempo?
25. È contento di lasciar la città in estate?
26. Ha Lei conosciuto il signor Berlitz nel 1878?

LEZIONE 35

Quando si viaggia
KWAHN-*doh see vee*-AH-*djah*
When one travels

L'Italia è un paese.
Lee-TAHL-*yah* EH *oon pah*-EH-*zeh.*
Italy is a country.

Ecco alcuni dei paesi d'Europa:
ECK-*koh ahl*-KOO-*neh day pah*-EH-*zee deh-oo*-ROH-*pah*:
Here are some of the countries of Europe:

la Francia	**l'Inghilterra**	**la Russia**
lah FRAHNT-*chah*	*leen-ggeel*-TEHR-*rah*	*lah* ROOS-*s'yah*
France	England	Russia
la Svizzera	**la Germania**	**la Spagna**
lah SVEE-*tseh-rah*	*lah Jehr*-MAH-*n'yah*	*lah* SPAHN-*yah*
Switzerland	Germany	Spain

GEOGRAPHICAL NOTE: Watch out for the gender of countries. Ex: *La Spagna*—"Spain", *il Portogallo*—"Portugal". *Ho veduto la Spagna ed il Portogallo.* "I have seen Spain and Portugal". But: *Vado in Italia*—"I go to Italy"; *vado in Francia*—"I go to France". But: *Nella Francia meridionale.*—"In southern France."

Gli Stati Uniti sono nell'America settentrionale.
L'yee STAH-*tee Oo-*NEE-*tee* SOH-*noh nehl-lah-*MEH-*ree-kah set-ten-tree-oh-*NAH-*leh.*
The United States are in North America.

La Cina ed il Giappone sono in Asia.
Lah CHEE-*nah ehd eel Jahp-*POH-*neh* SOH-*noh een* AH-*z'yah.*
China and Japan are in Asia.

Le più grandi città del mondo sono:
*Leh p'*YOO GRAHN-*dee cheet-*TAH *dehl* MOHN-*doh* SOH-*noh:*
The largest cities in the world are:

Roma	**Londra**	**New York**	**Parigi**
ROH-*mah*	LOHN-*drah*	*New York*	*Pah-*REE-*jee*
Rome	London	New York	Paris
Berlino	**Mosca**	**Shanghai**	**ecc.**
*Behr-*LEE-*noh*	MOHS-*kah*	SHAHN-*ggigh*	*eht-*CHEH-*teh-rah.*
Berlin	Moscow	Shanghai	etc.

Quando andiamo da una città ad un'altra
KWAHN-*doh ahn-d'*YAH-*moh dah* OO-*nah cheet-*TAH *ahd oo-*NAHL-*trah*
When we go from one city to another

o da un paese ad un altro noi viaggiamo.
*oh dah oon pah-*EH-*zeh ahd oo-*NAHL-*troh noy vee-ah-*DJAH-*moh.*
or from one country to another, we travel.

Per viaggiare per terra ci serviamo del treno
*Pehr vee-ah-*DJAH-*reh pehr* TEHR-*rah chee sehr-v'*YAH-*moh dehl* TREH-*noh*
To travel by land, we use the train

o di automobili.
*oh dee aou-toh-*MOH-*bee-lee.*
or the autombile.

Per i viaggi per mare ci imbarchiamo su di una nave.
*Pehr ee vee-*AH-*djee pehr* MAH-*reh chee eem-bahr-k'*YAH-*moh soo dee* OO-*nah* NAH-*veh.*
To travel by sea we embark on a ship.

Se il luogo dove andiamo è lontano, a volte prendiamo l'aereo.
*Seh eel loo-*OH-*goh* DOH-*veh ahn-d'*YAH-*moh* EH *lohn-*TAH-*noh, ah* VOHL-*teh
prehn-d'*YAH-*moh lah-*EH-*reh-oh.*
If the place to which we are going is far away, we occasionally take the
airplane.

**Se è molto vicino, possiamo andarci in un automobile, o prendiamo il
treno.**
Seh EH MOHL-*toh vee-*CHEE-*noh, pohs-s'*YAH-*moh ahn-*DAHR-*chee een oon
aou-toh-*MOH-*bee-leh, oh prehn-d'*YAH-*moh eel* TREH-*noh.*
If it is quite nearby, we can drive in a car or we take the train.

Prima di partire dobbiamo fare i nostri bagagli.
PREE-*mah dee pahr-*TEE-*reh dohb-b'*YAH-*moh* FAH-*reh ee* NOHS-*tree
bah-*GAH-*l'yee.*
Before leaving we must prepare our luggage.

Noi mettiamo nelle valigie tutto ciò che
*Noy meht-t'*YAH-*moh* NEHL-*leh vah-lee-jeh* TOOT-*toh* CHOH *keh*
We put in the bags everything we shall

adopereremo durante il nostro viaggio:
*ah-doh-peh-reh-*REH-*moh doo-*RAHN-*teh eel* NOHS-*troh vee-*AH-*djoh:*
use during our trip:

vestiti, calze, camice, articoli di toeletta,
*vehs-*TEE-*tee,* KAHL-*tseh, kah-*MEE-*cheh, ahr-*TEE-*koh-lee dee toh-eh-*LET-*tah,*
clothes, shoes, shirts, toilet articles,

biancheria e molte altre cose.
*b'yahn-keh-*REE-*ah eh* MOHL-*teh* AHL-*treh* KOH-*zeh.*
linen and many other things.

Poi prendiamo un taxi e vi facciamo caricare i bagagli.
*Poy prehn-d'*YAH-*moh oon tahs-*SEE *eh vee faht-*CH'YAH-*moh kah-ree-*KAH-*reh
ee bah-*GAH-*l'yee.*
Then we take a taxi and have our luggage brought down.

Noi diciamo all'autista: alla stazione!
*Noy dee-ch'*YAH-*moh ahl-laou-*TEES-*tah:* AHL-*lah stah-ts'*YOH-*neh!*
We tell the driver: to the station!

Faccia presto, per favore.
FAHT-*chah* PRESS-*toh, pehr fah-*VOH-*reh.*
Hurry up, please.

Arrivati alla stazione, andiamo allo sportello per prendere il biglietto.
*Ahr-ree-*VAH-*tee* AHL-*lah stah-ts'*YOH-*neh, ahn-d'*YAH-*moh* AHL-*loh
spohr-*TEHL-*loh pehr* PREHN-*deh-reh eel bee-l'*YET-*toh.*
When we arrive at the station we go to the ticket window to buy the ticket.

CONSTRUCTION to Remember: The past participle *arrivati* as used above can include the sense "when", "after" or "once we have arrived." Ex: *Sbarcato nel nuovo mondo Colombo issò la bandiera spagnola.*—"When Columbus landed in the new world he raised the Spanish flag."

Diciamo all'impiegato: due biglietti di prima classe
*Dee-ch'*YAH-*moh ahl-leem-p'yeh-*GAH-*toh:* DOO-*eh bee-l'*YET-*tee dee* PREE-*mah* KLAHS-*seh*
We tell the clerk: two tickets first class

d'andata e ritorno per Roma.
*dahn-*DAH-*tah eh ree-*TOHR-*noh pehr* ROH-*mah.*
round trip for Rome.

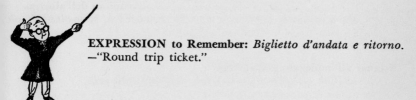

EXPRESSION to Remember: *Biglietto d'andata e ritorno.* —"Round trip ticket."

Il facchino porta i nostri bagagli alla vettura.
*Eel fahk-*KEE-*noh* POHR-*tah ee* NOHS-*tree bah-*GAH-*l'yee* AHL-*lah veht-*TOO-*rah*
The porter brings our luggage to the (railroad) car.

Lei gli domanda: Quant'è?
*Lay l'yee doh-*MAHN-*dah: Kwahn-*TEH?
You ask him: How much is it?

Alcune espressioni delle quali avrà bisogno durante
*Ahl-*KOO-*neh ehs-prehs-s'*YOH-*nee* DEHL-*leh* KWAH-*lee ah-*VRAH *bee-*ZOHN-*yoh doo-*RAHN-*teh*
Some expressions which you will need during

il viaggio: È occupato questo posto d'angolo?
*eel vee-*AH-*djoh:* EH *ohk-koo-*PAH-*toh* KWESS-*toh* POHS-*toh* DAHN-*goh-loh?*
the trip (are): Is this corner seat taken?

Quando arriveremo a Firenze?
KWAHN-*doh ahr-ree-veh-*REH-*moh ah Fee-*REHN-*dzeh?*
When do we arrive in Florence?

Quanti minuti di fermata abbiamo a Bologna?
KWAHN-*tee mee-*NOO-*tee dee fehr-*MAH-*tah ahb-b'*YAH-*moh ah Boh-*LOH-*n'yah?*
How many minutes do we stop in Bologna?

In quante ore si va a Milano?
Een KWAHN-*tee* OH-*reh see* VAH *ah* Mee-LAH-*noh?*
How many hours does it take to go to Milan?

EXPRESSION to Remember: *Avere bisogno*—"to need".
Ex: *Io ho bisogno di cinque dollari.*—"I need five dollars."

Arrivati a destinazione domandiamo il nome d'un buon albergo
*Ahr-ree-*VAH-*tee ah dehs-tee-nah-ts'*YOH-*neh doh-mahn-d'*YAH-*moh eel*
NOH-*meh doon b'*WOHN *ahl-*BEHR-*goh*
When we arrive at our destination we ask the name of a good hotel

e vi andiamo con un automobile pubblica o con l'omnibus dell'albergo.
*eh vee ahn-d'*YAH-*moh kohn oon aou-toh-*MOH-*bee-leh* POOB-*blee-kah oh*
kohn LOHM-*nee-booss dehl-lahl-*BEHR-*goh.*
and we go there by taxi or by the hotel bus.

Diciamo all'impiegato dell'albergo:
*Dee-ch'*YAH-*moh ahl-leem-p'yeh-*GAH-*toh dehl-lahl-*BEHR-*goh:*
We say to the employee of the hotel:

Ha una camera con bagno?
AH OO-*nah* KAH-*meh-rah kohn* BAHN-*n'yoh?*
Have you a room with bath?

Resterò una settimana.
*Rehs-teh-*ROH OO-*nah set-tee-*MAH-*nah.*
I shall be staying a week.

E il prezzo?
Eh eel PREHT-*tsoh?*
And the price?

Quando si smarrisce in una città che non conosce,
KWAHN-*doh see smah-*REE-*sheh een* OO-*nah cheet-*TAH *keh nohn koh-*NOH-*sheh,*
When you lose your way in a city which you do not know,

deve domandare ad una guardia:
DEH-*veh doh-mahn-*DAH-*reh ahd* OO-*nah* GWAHR-*d'yah:*
you must ask a policeman:

Mi dica per favore, qual'è la via per andare all'albergo Danieli?
Mee DEE-*kah pehr fah-*VOH-*reh, kwahl-*LEH *lah* VEE-*ah pehr ahn-*DAH-*reh*
*ahl-lahl-*BEHR-*goh Dah-n'*YEH-*lee?*
Please tell me the way to (go to) the Hotel Danieli?

Se Lei non capisce quello che la guardia Le risponde,
*Seh Lay nohn kah-*PEE-*sheh* KWELL-*loh keh lah* GWAHR-*d'yah Leh*
*rees-*POHN-*deh,*
If you do not understand what the policeman tells you,

Lei deve dire: La prego, parli più adagio,
Lay DEH-*veh* DEE-*reh: Lah* PREH-*goh,* PAHR-*lee p'*YOO *ah-*DAH-*joh,*
you must reply: Please, speak more slowly,

io non capisco bene l'italiano.
EE-*oh nohn kah-*PEES-*koh* BEH-*neh lee-tahl-*YAH-*noh.*
I do not understand Italian well.

In una grande città vi sono dei negozi.
Een OO-*nah* GRAHN-*deh cheet-*TAH *vee* SOH-*noh day neh-*GOH-*tsee.*
In a big city there are shops.

I libri si vendono in una libreria.
Ee LEE-*bree see* VEHN-*doh-noh een* OO-*nah lee-breh-*REE-*ah.*
Books are sold in a book shop.

REMEMBER: *Si vendono* has the construction of "sell
themselves" but actually means "are sold".

La carne si vende in una macelleria
Lah KAHR-*neh see* VEHN-*deh een* OO-*nah mah-chehl-leh-*REE-*ah*
Meat is sold at the butcher's

e le medicine nella farmacia.
*eh leh meh-dee-*CHEE-*neh* NEHL-*lah fahr-maht-*CHEE-*ah.*
and medicine at a drug store.

Noi compriamo i fiori dal fioraio.
*Noy kohm-pr'*YAH-*moh ee f'*YOH-*ree dahl f'yoh-*RAH-*yoh.*
We buy flowers at the florist's.

Il pizzicagnolo vende prosciutto, sardine, salami.
*Eel peet-tsee-*KAHN-*n'yoh-loh* VEHN-*deh proh-*SHOOT-*toh, sahr-*DEE-*neh,*
*sah-*LAH-*mee.*
The delicatessen-keeper sells smoked ham, sardines, salami.

Nella latteria si prende il latte.
NEHL-*lah laht-teh-*REE-*ah see* PREHN-*deh eel* LAHT-*teh.*
In a dairy, we get milk.

Nella pasticceria si mangiano paste, dolci e gelato.
NEHL-*lah pahs-tee-cheh-*REE-*ah see* MAHN-*jah-noh* PAHS-*teh,* DOHL-*chee eh*
*jeh-*LAH-*toh.*
At the pastry shop we eat pastry, sweets and ice cream.

Nei grandi magazzini si trova un po' di tutto.
Nay GRAHN-*dee mah-gah-*DZEE-*nee see* TROH-*vah oon* POH *dee* TOOT-*toh.*
In the department stores, you find a little of everything.

Se Lei ci va per comprare un paio di scarpe,
*Seh Lay chee vah pehr kohm-*PRAH-*reh oon* PAH-*yoh dee* SKAHR-*peh,*
If you go there to buy a pair of shoes,

Lei dice, quando entra: **Buon giorno, signorina.**
Lay DEE-*cheh,* KWAHN-*doh* EHN-*trah:*   *b'*WOHN JOHR-*noh, seen-yoh-*REE-*nah.*
you say, when you go in: Good day, miss.

Dove si vendono le scarpe?
DOH-*veh see* VEHN-*doh-noh leh* SKAHR-*peh?*
Where are the shoes sold?

Essa glielo dice ed allora Lei si rivolge al commesso:
ESS-*sah l'yee-*EH-*loh* DEE-*cheh ehd ahl-*LOH-*rah Lay see ree-*VOHL-*jeh ahl*
   *kohm-*MEHS-*soh:*
She tells you and then you say to the clerk:

Mi mostri un paio di scarpe nere.
Mee MOHS-*tree oon* PAH-*yoh dee* SKAHR-*peh* NEH-*reh.*
Show me a pair of black shoes.

La mia misura è quaranta.
Lah MEE-*ah mee-*ZOO-*rah* EH *kwah-*RAHN-*tah.*
My size is forty.

 NOTE on Shoes: As you have no doubt guessed, shoe sizes in Italy are measured by a system other than ours.

Se il prezzo è troppo alto, Lei domanda:
Seh eel PREHT-*tsoh* EH TROHP-*poh* AHL-*toh, Lay doh-*MAHN-*dah:*
If the price is too high, you ask:

Non ne ha a minor prezzo?
Nohn neh AH *ah* MEE-*nohr* PREHT-*tsoh?*
Aren't there any cheaper?

Se l'articolo Le conviene, Lei dice: Va bene, lo prendo.
*Seh lahr-*TEE-*koh-loh Leh kohn-v'*YEH-*neh, Lay* DEE-*cheh: Vah* BEH-*neh, loh*
   PREHN-*doh.*
If you like the article, you say: All right, I'll take it.

Lo impacchi, lo prendo con me.
*Loh eem-*PAHK-*kee, loh* PREHN-*doh kohn meh.*
Wrap it up, I'll take it with me.

THINKING IN ITALIAN

(Answers on page 293)

1. Quali sono le più grandi città d'Europa?
2. È Bologna al nord di Roma?
3. È la Svizzera al nord o al sud dell'Italia?
4. Che paese è al sud della Svizzera?
5. È Londra lontana da Tokio? 6. È lontano da qui il Suo albergo?
7. Viaggiano molto gli americani? 8. Viaggia Lei in estate?
9. Viaggiano molti inglesi in Italia?
10. In quanti giorni si va dall'Europa in America?
11. In quante ore si va da Roma a Genova?
12. Quanto tempo adoperiamo per andare da casa Sua alla stazione?
13. Che cosa mette nella Sua valigia?
14. Porta la Sua valigia Lei stesso? 15. Che cosa dice al facchino?
16. Prende Lei un taxi per andare alla stazione?
17. Da dove partono i treni?
18. Che cosa fa Lei prima di salire nel vagone?
19. Dove prende i biglietti? 20. Capisce Lei bene l'italiano?
21. Che cosa dice se non capisce? 22. Che cosa c'è nelle strade?
23. Che cosa dice dopo esser entrato in un negozio?
24. Che cosa si mangia nelle pasticcerie?
25. Le piacciono le paste, il gelato, i dolci?
26. Dove si va a bere il latte?
27. Dove si va a comprare prosciutto, salami, ecc?

LEZIONE 36

L'invito al viaggio
Leen-VEE-toh ahl vee-AH-djoh
The invitation to the trip

DE ROSSI: **Mio caro amico Miller! Come sta?**
Deh ROHS-see: MEE-*oh* KAH-*roh* ah-MEE-*koh Miller!* KOH-*meh* STAH?
DE ROSSI: My dear friend Miller! How are you?

Venga, venga, si accomodi. Che bella sorpresa!
VEHN-*gah,* VEHN-*gah,* *see* ahk-KOHM-*moh-dee!* Keh BELL-*lah*
sohr-PREH-*zah!*
Come in, come in. Make yourself comfortable. What a fine surprise.

A USEFUL EXPRESSION: *Si accomodi:* You will notice
that this expression covers a variety of meanings, everything from "make yourself at home" to "come in" or "sit
down". It is a good example of a polite and quite idiomatic
expression which you will often hear.

MILLER: **Grazie dell'accoglienza; come sta Lei?**
MILLER: GRAHTS-*yeh dehl-lahk-kohl-*YEHN-*tsah;* KOH-*meh* STAH *Lay?*
MILLER: Thank you for the reception. How are you?

DE ROSSI: **Benone, grazie. E quale buon vento La conduce qui?**
*Beh-*NOH-*neh,* GRAHTS-*yeh. Eh* KWAH-*leh b'*WOHN VEHN-*toh Lah kohn-*DOO-*cheh kwee?*
Fine, thank you. And what good wind brings you here?

A TYPICAL ITALIAN EXPRESSION: *Bene* is "well"; *benissimo*—"very well"; *benone* is the approval of a very satisfying condition, meaning: "It couldn't be better."

MILLER: **Mi trovo in Italia da una settimana.**
Mee TROH-*voh een Ee-*TAHL-*yah dah* OO-*nah set-tee-*MAH-*nah.*
I have been in Italy for a week.

IDIOM TO REMEMBER: *Trovare* means "to find", but *trovarsi* (reflexive), "to find oneself", means "to be".

Sono venuto per concludere un contratto col
SOH-*noh veh-*NOO-*toh pehr kohn-*KLOO-*deh-reh oon kohn-*TRAHT-*toh kohl*
I came to close a contract with the

Governo Italiano, ma ho voluto prima visitare
*Goh-*VEHR-*noh Ee-tahl-*YAH-*noh, mah* OH *voh-*LOO-*toh* PREE-*mah vee-zee-*TAH-*reh*
Italian Government, but I wanted first to visit

i cantieri navali di Genova, di cui ho tanto
*ee kahn-t'*YEH-*ree nah-*VAH-*lee dee* JEH-*noh-vah, dee* KOO-*ee* OH TAHN-*toh*
the naval shipyards of Genoa, of which I have

sentito parlare; e prima di proseguire il mio
*sehn-*TEE-*toh pahr-*LAH-*reh; eh* PREE-*mah dee proh-seh-*GWEE-*reh eel* MEE-*oh*
heard so much, and before continuing my

viaggio sono venuto a Milano per farle una visita.
*vee-*AH-*djoh* SOH-*noh veh-*NOO-*toh ah Mee-*LAH-*noh pehr* FAHR-*leh* OO-*nah* VEE-*zee-tah.*
trip, I came to Milan to visit you.

DE ROSSI: **La ringrazio di tutto cuore!**
*Lah reen-*GRAHTS-*yoh dee* TOOT-*toh k'*WOH-*reh!*
I thank you with all my heart!

Ma allora Lei si recherà a Roma!
*Mah ahl-*LOH*-rah Lay see reh-keh-*RAH *ah* ROH*-mañ!*
But then you are going to Rome!

NOTE: *Recherà* is from *recare* meaning "to bring"; *recarsi* (reflexive) means "to go".

MILLER: Precisamente. Parto domani,
*Preh-chee-zah-*MEHN*-teh.* PAHR*-toh doh-*MAH*-nee.*
Exactly. I leave tomorrow.

DE ROSSI: Ma guarda che coincidenza! Anch'io vado a Roma
Mah GWAHR*-dah keh koh-een-chee-*DEN*-tsah! Ahn-*KEE*-oh* VAH*-doh ah*
ROH*-mah*
But look, what a coincidence! I too am going to Rome

domani; ho già prenotato il posto sull'aereo.
*doh-*MAH*-nee;* OH JAH *preh-noh-*TAH*-toh eel* POHS*-toh sool-lah-*EH*-reh-oh.*
tomorrow; I have already reserved a seat on the plane.

Perchè non parte con me?
*Pehr-*KEH *nohn* PAHR*-teh kohn meh?*
Why don't you leave with me?

MILLER: L'idea mi piace, ma farò in tempo a
*Lee-*DEH*-ah mee p'*YAH*-cheh, mah fah-*ROH *een* TEHM*-poh ah*
I like the idea, but will I make it in time to

prenotare il posto sull'aereo?
*preh-noh-*TAH*-reh eel* POHS*-toh sool-lah-*EH*-reh-oh?*
reserve a seat on the plane?

DE ROSSI: Andiamo subito all'ufficio della compagnia
*Ahn-d'*YAH*-moh* soo*-bee-toh ahl-loof-*FEET*-ch'yoh* DEHL*-lah*
*kohm-pahn-n'*YEE*-ah*
Let's go at once to the airline office

di aviazione e dopo andremo a colazione insieme.
*dee ah-vee-ah-ts'*YOH*-neh eh* DOH*-poh ahn-*DREH*-moh ah*
*koh-lah-ts'*YOH*-neh een-s'*YEH*-meh.*
and then we shall go to lunch together.

IMPIEGATO: Buon giorno, signori. In che posso servirli?
*Eem-p'yeh-*GAH*-toh:*   *b'*WOHN JOHR*-noh, seen-*YOH*-ree. Een keh* POSS*-soh*
                  *sehr-*VEER*-lee?*
EMPLOYEE: Good morning, gentlemen. What can I do for you?

Oh! Scusi, signor De Rossi, non l'avevo riconosciuto.
OH! SKOO-*zee, seen*-YOHR *Deh* ROHS-*see, nohn lah*-VEH-*voh*
ree-koh-noh-SHOO-*toh.*
Oh, excuse me, Mr. De Rossi, for not having recognized you.

DE ROSSI: **Il mio amico, il signor Miller, americano,**
Eel MEE-*oh ah*-MEE-*koh, eel seen*-YOHR *Miller, ah-meh-ree*-KAH-*noh,*
My friend, Mr. Miller, an American,

desidera ottenere un posto sull'aereo che parte
deh-ZEE-*deh-rah oht-teh*-NEH-*reh oon* POHS-*toh sool-lah*-EH-*reh-oh keh*
PAHR-*teh*
wishes to obtain a seat on the plane which leaves

per Roma domani alle sedici. Può accomodarlo?
þehr ROH-*mah doh*-MAH-*nee* AHL-*leh* SEH-*dee-chee. p'*WOH
ahk-koh-moh-DAHR-*loh?*
for Rome tomorrow at 4 P.M. (1600). Can you accommodate him?

IMPIEGATO: **Mi dispiace, signor De Rossi, ma l'aereo delle**
*Mee dees-p'*YAH-*cheh, seen*-YOHR *Deh* ROHS-*see, mah lah*-EH-*reh-oh*
DEHL-*leh*
I am sorry, Mr. De Rossi, but the plane at

sedici è al completo. Abbiamo però dei posti
SEH-*dee-chee* EH *ahl kohm*-PLEH-*toh. Ahb-b'*YAH-*moh þeh*-ROH *day*
POHS-*tee*
1600 is full. But we have some seats

sull'aereo delle undici antimeridiane.
sool-lah-EH-*reh-oh* DEHL-*leh* OON-*dee-chee ahn-teh-meh-ree-d'*YAH-*neh.*
on the 11 A.M. plane.

EXPRESSIONS to Remember: *Completo*—"complete".
Al completo—"Filled to capacity".
Antimeridiane—"A.M." (Ante-meridiem), before noon.
Pomeridiane—"P.M." (Post-meridiem), after noon.

DE ROSSI: **In questo caso parto anch'io alle undici.**
Een KWESS-*toh* KAH-*zoh* PAHR-*toh ahn*-KEE-*oh* AHL-*leh* OON-*dee-chee.*
In that case, I'll leave at 11 too.

Lei, signor Miller, è disposto a partire alle undici?
Lay, seen-YOHR *Miller,* EH *dees-*POES-*toh ah þahr*-TEE-*reh*
AHL-*leh* OON-*dee-chee?*
Are you willing to leave at 11, Mr. Miller?

MILLER: **Per me va benissimo.**
*Pehr meh vah beh-*NEES-*see-moh.*
That is fine for me.

DE ROSSI: (all'impiegato): **Allora ci dia due biglietti.**
*(ahl-leem-p'yeh-*GAH-*toh): Ahl-*LOH-*rah chee* DEE-*ah* DOO-*eh bee-l'*YET-*tee.*
(To the employee): Then give us two tickets.

IMPIEGATO: **Andata e ritorno?**
*Ahn-*DAH-*tah eh ree-*TOHR-*noh?*
Round trip?

MILLER: **Non per me. M'imbarcherò a Napoli perchè desidero**
*Nohn pehr meh. Meem-bahr-keh-*ROH *ah* NAH-*poh-lee pehr-*KEH
*deh-*ZEE-*deh-roh*
Not for me. I'll leave by ship from Naples because I wish

passare un paio di settimane in quella città
*pahs-*SAH-*reh oon* PAH-*yoh dee set-tee-*MAH-*neh een* KWELL-*lah cheet-*TAH
to spend a couple of weeks in that city

prima di lasciare l'Italia.
PREE-*mah dee lah-*SHAH-*reh lee-*TAHL-*yah.*
before leaving Italy.

DE ROSSI: (all'impiegato): **Allora, un biglietto di andata**
*(ahl-leem-p'yeh-*GAH-*toh): Ahl-*LOH-*rah, oon bee-l'*YET-*toh dee*
*ahn-*DAH-*tah*
(to the employee): Then, (give me) a round trip ticket

e ritorno per me ed uno di andata solamente per il signor Miller.
*eh ree-*TOHR-*noh pehr meh ehd* OO-*noh dee ahn-*DAH-*tah*
*soh-lah-*MEHN-*teh pehr eel seen-*YOHR *Miller.*
and a one way only for Mr. Miller.

IMPIEGATO: **Vuole favorirmi il Suo indirizzo, signor Miller?**
*v'*WOH-*leh fah-voh-*REER-*mee eel* SOO-*oh een-dee-*REE-*tsoh, seen-*YOHR
Miller?
Will you kindly give me your address, Mr. Miller?

MILLER: **Sono alloggiato al Grande Albergo, ma ricevo la**
SOH-*noh ahl-loh-*DJAH-*toh ahl* GRAHN-*deh Ahl-*BEHR-*goh, mah*
*reet-*CHEH-*voh lah*
I am staying at the "Grande Albergo" but I get my

posta presso l'American Express.
POSS-*tah* PRESS-*soh lah-*MEH-*ree-kahn Eks-*PRESS.
mail care of American express.

IMPIEGATO: **Ecco i biglietti, signori; il Suo, signor Miller,**
ECK-*koh ee bee-l'*YET-*tee, seen-*YOH-*ree; eel* SOO-*oh, seen-*YOHR *Miller,*
Here are the tickets, gentlemen; yours, Mr. Miller,

costa esattamente seimila lire, ed il Suo,
KOHS-*tah eh-zaht-tah*-MEHN-*teh* say-MEE-*lah* LEE-*reh, ehd eel* SOO-*oh,*
costs exactly 6000 lire, and yours,

signor De Rossi, ammonta a diecimila e cinquecento lire.
seen-YOHR *deh* ROHS-*see, ahm*-MOHN-*tah ah d'*YEH-*chee*-MEE-*lah eh*
cheen-kweh-CHEHN-*toh* LEE-*reh.*
Mr. De Rossi comes to 10,500 lire.

L'automobile partirà da qui alle 10 in punto;
Laou-toh-MOH-*bee-leh pahr-tee*-RAH *dah kwee* AHL-*leh d'*YEH-*chee een*
POON-*toh;*
The car will leave from here at 10 sharp;

abbiano la bontà di trovarsi in questo ufficio
AHB-*b'yah-noh lah bohn*-TAH *dee troh*-VAHR-*see een* KWESS-*toh*
oof-FEET-*ch'yoh*
please be in this office

qualche minuto in anticipo.
KWAHL-*keh mee*-NOO-*toh een ahn*-TEE-*chee-poh.*
a few minutes in advance.

MILLER: **Dura un'ora il viaggio da qui all'aeroporto?**
DOO-*rah oo*-NOH-*rah eel vee*-AH-*djoh dah kwee ahl-lah-eh-roh*-POHR-*toh?*
Does the trip to the airport take an hour?

EXPRESSION to Remember: *In punto*—"On the dot".
"Just on time".

MPIEGATO: **No, signore, è un viaggio di 25 minuti,**
Noh, seen-YOH-*reh,* EH *oon vee*-AH-*djoh dee vehn-tee*-CHEEN-*kweh*
mee-NOO-*tee,*
No, sir, it is a trip of 25 minutes,

ma ci vuole del tempo per pesare i bagagli.
*mah chee v'*WOH-*leh dehl* TEHM-*poh pehr peh*-ZAH-*reh ee bah*-GAH-*l'yee.*
but it takes time to weigh the luggage.

DE ROSSI: **Oltro a ciò, la compagnia d'aviazione vuole**
OHL-*troh ah* CHOH, *lah kohm-pahn-n'*YEE-*ah dah-vee-ah-ts'*YOH-*neh*
*v'*WOH-*leh*
Besides, the airline company wants

evitare ritardi di partenza causati da passaggeri dormiglioni.
eh-vee-TAH-*reh ree*-TAHR-*dee dee pahr*-TEHN-*tsah kaou-*ZAH-*tee*
dah pahs-sah-DJEH-*ree dohr-meel-l'*YOH-*nee.*
to avoid delays in departure caused by sleepy-head passengers.

THINKING IN ITALIAN

(Answers on page 294)

1. Dove si trovano i signori De Rossi e Miller?
2. Di dov'è il signor Miller?
3. Da quanto tempo è in Italia?
4. Che cosa fa a Milano il signor Miller?
5. È il signor De Rossi americano?
6. Di dov'è il signor De Rossi?
7. Dove andrà il signor Miller quando lascia Milano?
8. Partirà anche il signor De Rossi?
9. Che invito riceve dal signor De Rossi il signor Miller?
10. Accetta il signor Miller l'invito del signor De Rossi?
11. Dove vanno i due amici per prenotare i posti?
12. È facile ottenere posti sull'aereo delle 16?
13. Che dice Lei all'impiegato della compagnia di aviazione?
14. Perchè i due amici si decidono di prendere l'aereo delle 11?
15. Prende il signor Miller un biglietto di andata e ritorno?
16. Dove andrà il signor Miller prima di lasciare l'Italia?
17. Vive Lei in una città?
18. Qual'è il suo indirizzo?
19. Quanto dura il viaggio in automobile fino all'aeroporto?
20. A Lei piace viaggiare?

LEZIONE 37

La partenza dall'aeroporto
*Lah pahr-*TEHN*-tsah dahl-lah-eh-roh-*POHR*-toh*
The departure from the airport

(Suona il telefono.)
(*Soo-*OH*-nah eel teh-*LEH*-foh-noh.*)
(The telephone rings.)

MILLER: **(risponde)—Pronto. Chi parla?**
(*rees-*POHN*-deh)—*PROHN*-toh. Kee* PAHR*-lah?*
(answering)—Hello! Who is it?

HOW TO ANSWER THE TELEPHONE: "Hello! Who is it?" is translated in Italian by: *Pronto! Chi parla?* meaning: "Ready! Who speaks?"

TELEFONISTA: **Sono le 9,15, signor Miller.**
*Teh-leh-foh-*NEES*-tah:* SOH*-noh leh* NOH*-veh eh* KWEEN*-dee-chee, seen-*YOHR
Miller.
OPERATOR: It is 9:15, Mr. Miller.

219

MILLER: **Ma io ho chiesto di essere svegliato alle 8,30.**
Mah EE-*oh* OH *k'*YESS-*toh dee* EHS-*seh-reh svehl-l'*YAH-*toh* AHL-*leh*
OHT-*toh eh* TREHN-*tah.*
But I asked to be awakened at 8:30.

TELEFONISTA: **L'ho già chiamato prima, signore,**
LOH JAH *k'yah-*MAH-*toh* PREE-*mah, seen-*YOH-*reh,*
I have already called you before, sir,

ma forse si è riaddormentato.
mah FOHR-*seh see* EH *ree-ahd-dohr-mehn-*TAH-*toh.*
but perhaps you fell asleep again.

NOTE: *Addormentarsi*—"to fall asleep".
Riaddormentarsi—"to fall asleep again".

MILLER: **Per bacco! Il signor De Rossi m'aspetta all'ufficio**
Pehr BAHK-*koh! Eel seen-*YOHR *Deh* ROHS-*see mahs-*PEHT-*tah*
*ahl-loof-*FEE-*ch'yoh*
Great Heavens! Mr. De Rossi expects me at the

della compagnia d'aviazione alle 9,30.
DEHL-*lah kohm-pahn-n'*YEE-*ah dah-vee-ah-ts'*YOH-*neh* AHL-*leh* NOH-*veh*
eh TREHN-*tah.*
airline office at 9:30.

Dica al cassiere di prepararmi il conto, per favore.
DEE-*kah ahl kahs-s'*YEH-*reh dee preh-pah-*RAHR-*mee eel* KOHN-*toh, peh*
*fah-*VOH-*reh.*
Tell the cashier to prepare my bill, please.

TELEFONISTA: **Benissimo, signore. Manderò il facchino**
*Beh-*NEES-*see-moh, seen-*YOH-*reh. Mahn-deh-*ROH *eel fahk-*KEE-*noh*
Very well, sir. I'll send the porter

a prendere i Suoi bagagli.
ah PREHN-*deh-reh ee s'*WOY *bah-*GAH-*l'yee.*
to take your luggage.

(Nell'ufficio dell'albergo.)
*(Nehl-loof-*FEE-*ch'yoh dehl-lahl-*BEHR-*goh.)*
(At the hotel desk.)

CASSIERE: **Ecco il Suo conto, signor Miller.**
*Kahs-s'*YEH-*reh:* ECK-*koh eel* SOO-*oh* KOHN-*toh, seen-*YOHR *Miller.*
CASHIER: Here is your bill, Mr. Miller.

Ottomilacinquecento lire.
OHT-*toh-mee-lah-cheen-kweh-*CHEHN-*toh* LEE-*reh.*
8,500 lire.

MILLER: **Tutto è incluso nel conto?**
TOOT-*toh* EH *een-*KLOO-*zoh nehl* KOHN-*toh?*
Is everything included in the bill?

CASSIERE: **Tutto, signore. Include i pasti, le telefonate e le mance.**
TOOT-*toh, seen-*YOH-*reh.* Een-KLOO-*deh ee* PAHS-*tee, leh*
*teh-leh-foh-*NAH-*teh eh leh* MAHNT-*cheh.*
Everything, sir. It includes meals, telephone calls and tips.

EXPRESSIONS to Remember: *Chiedere*—"To ask". "To
request".
Per bacco!—"Great Heavens!" ("By Bacchus")
Il conto—"The bill".
Facchino—"Porter". "Red Cap".
Mancia—"Tip". "Gratuity".

MILLER: **Non ho sufficienti lire, posso pagare in dollari?**
*Noh-*NOH *soof-fee-ch'*YEHN-*tee* LEE-*reh,* POSS-*soh pah-*GAH-*reh een*
DOHL-*lah-ree?*
I haven't enough lire, can I pay in dollars?

CASSIERE: **Naturalmente, sono esattamente quattordici dollari.**
*Nah-too-rahl-*MEHN-*teh,* SOH-*noh eh-zaht-tah-*MEHN-*teh*
*kwah-*TOHR-*dee-chee* DOHL-*lah-ree.*
Naturally, it is exactly 14 dollars.

MILLER: **Ecco il danaro; la chiave l'ho lasciata in camera.**
ECK-*koh eel dah-*NAH-*roh; lah k'*YAH-*veh* LOH *lah-*SHAH-*tah een*
KAH-*meh-rah.*
Here is the money; I left the key in the room.

CASSIERE: **Grazie, signor Miller.**
GRAHTS-*yeh, seen-*YOHR *Miller.*
Thank you, Mr. Miller.

Faccia un buon viaggio. Giovanotto!
FAHT-*chah oon b'*WOHN *vee-*AH-*djoh.* Joh-vah-NOHT-*toh!*
Have a good trip. Boy!

Metta i bagagli del signor Miller in un taxi.
MEHT-*tah ee bah-*GAH-*l'yee dehl seen-*YOHR *Miller een oon tahs-*SEE.
Put Mr. Miller's luggage in a taxi.

MILLER: **Grazie; arrivederci. (al Facchino)**
GRAHTS-*yeh, ahr-ree-veh*-DEHR-*chee. (ahl Fahk*-KEE-*noh)*
Thank you, goodbye. (to the Porter)

No, non prenda quella valigetta; la porterò io
Noh, nohn PREHN-*dah* KWELL-*lah vah-lee-*JEHT-*tah; lah pohr-teh-*ROH
EE-*oh*
No, don't take that small bag; I'll carry it

stesso perchè contiene tutti i miei documenti, e non voglio perderli.
STEHS-*soh pehr*-KEH *kohn-t'*YEH-*neh* TOOT-*tee m'*YAY *doh-koo-*MEHN-*tee,*
eh nohn VOHL-*l'yoh* PEHR-*dehr-lee.*
myself because it contains all my documents and I don't want to lose
them.

> **(All'ufficio della compagnia di aviazione)**
> *(Ahl-loof-*FEE-*ch'yoh* DEHL-*lah kohm-pahn-n'*YEE-*ah dee*
> *ah-vee-ah-ts'*YOH-*neh)*
> (At the airline office)

MILLER: **Mi perdoni, mi caro De Rossi, sono in ritardo....**
Mee pehr-DOH-*nee,* MEE-*oh* KAH-*roh Deh* ROHS-*see,* SOH-*noh een*
*ree-*TAHR-*doh....*
Excuse me, my dear De Rossi, I am late....

DE ROSSI: **Non cerchi di scusarsi, non c'è tempo;**
Nohn CHEHR-*kee dee skoo-*ZAHR-*see, nohn* CHEH TEHM-*poh;*
Don't try to excuse yourself, there isn't time;

dobbiamo partire subito per l'aeroporto.
*dohb-b'*YAH-*moh pahr*-TEE-*reh* SOO-*bee-toh pehr lah-eh-roh-*POHR-*toh.*
we must leave at once for the airport.

> **(In automobile)**
> *(Een aou-toh-*MOH-*bee-leh)*
> (In the car)

DE ROSSI: **Non ha un viso molto allegro stamani.**
*Noh-*NAH *oon* VEE-*zoh* MOHL-*toh ahl-*LEH-*groh stah-*MAH-*nee.*
You haven't a very happy face this morning.

Si sente male?
See SEHN-*teh* MAH-*leh?*
Do you feel bad?

MILLER: **No, sto benissimo, ma ho fame....e con il mio**
*Noh, stoh beh-*NEES-*see-moh, mah* OH FAH-*meh....eh kohn eel* MEE-*o*
No, I'm fine, but I am hungry....and by my

ritardo ho privato anche Lei della colazione.
*ree-*TAHR-*doh* OH *pree-*VAH-*toh* AHN-*keh Lay* DEHL-*lah koh-lah-ts'*YOH-*neh*
delay I have deprived you too of your breakfast.

DE ROSSI: **Ma non ci pensi nemmeno.**
Mah nohn chee PEHN-*see nehm-*MEH-*noh.*
But don't even think of it.

Io non mangio mai la mattina, ed in quanto a
EE-*oh nohn* MAHN-*joh migh lah maht-*TEE-*nah, ehd een* KWAHN-*toh ah*
I never eat in the morning, and as for you,

Lei vedrà che prima di salire in aereo avrà tempo
*Lay veh-*DRAH *keh* PREE-*mah dee sah-*LEE-*reh een ah-*EH-*reh-oh ah-*VRAH
TEHM-*poh*
you will see that before we take off in the plane you will have time

di mangiare un elefante, se vuole.
*dee mahn-*JAH-*reh oon eh-leh-*FAHN-*teh, seh v'*WOH-*leh.*
to eat an elephant, if you wish.

MILLER: **E Lei, De Rossi, va a Roma per affari?**
Eh Lay, Deh ROHS-*see, vah ah* ROH-*mah pehr ahf-*FAH-*ree?*
And you, De Rossi, are you going to Rome on business?

EXPRESSIONS to Remember:

Essere in ritardo—"To be late".
Cercare—"To try". "To look for".
Non ci pensi nemmeno—"Don't give it a thought!"
In quanto a Lei—"As far as you are concerned".
Andare per affari—"To go on business".

DE ROSSI: **Oh no. Io vivo a Roma con la mia famiglia.**
OH *noh.* EE-*oh* VEE-*voh ah* ROH-*mah kohn lah* MEE-*ah fah-*MEEL-*l'yah.*
Oh no. I live in Rome with my family.

L'ufficio di Milano è una succursale della
*Loof-*FEE-*ch'yoh dee Mee-*LAH-*noh* EH OO-*nah sook-koor-*SAH-*leh* DEHL-*lah*
The Milan office is a branch of

mia ditta che ha sede nella capitale.
MEE-*ah* DEET-*tah keh* AH SEH-*deh* NEHL-*lah kah-pee-*TAH-*leh.*
my firm, which has its main office in the capital.

MILLER: **Sì? Allora Lei forse mi potrà indicare le cose**
*See? Ahl-*LOH-*rah Lay* FOHR-*seh mee poh-*TRAH *een-dee-*KAH-*reh leh*
KOH-*zeh*
Really? Then perhaps you will be able to tell me the most

più importanti da vedere durante il mio soggiorno a Roma.
*p'*YOO *eem-pohr-*TAHN-*tee dah veh-*DEH-*reh doo-*RAHN-*teh eel* MEE-*oh*
*soh-*DJOHR-*noh ah* ROH-*mah.*
important things to see during my stay in Rome.

DE ROSSI: **Sarò felice di farle da guida.**
*Sah-*ROH *feh-*LEE-*cheh dee* FAHR-*leh dah* GWEE-*dah.*
I will be happy to serve as your guide.

(**All'aeroporto**)
(*Ahl-lah-eh-roh-*POHR-*toh*)
(At the airport)

DE ROSSI: **Siamo i signori De Rossi e Miller**
*s'*YAH-*moh ee seen-*YOH-*ree Deh* ROHS-*see eh Miller*
We are Messrs. De Rossi and Miller

ed andiamo a Roma con l'aereo delle 11.
*ehd ahn-d'*YAH-*moh ah* ROH-*mah kohn lah-*EH-*reh-oh* DEHL-*leh*
OON-*dee-chee.*
and we are going to Rome on the 11 o'clock plane.

IMPIEGATO: **Benissimo, signori, i Loro nomi sono sulla lista.**
*Beh-*NEES-*see-moh, seen-*YOH-*ree, ee* LOH-*roh* NOH-*mee* SOH-*moh* SOOL-*lah*
LEES-*tah.*
Very good, gentlemen, your names are on the list.

Sono questi i loro bagagli?
SOH-*noh* KWESS-*tee ee* LOH-*roh bah-*GAH-*l'yee?*
Is this your luggage?

MILLER: **Sono tutti...**
SOH-*noh* TOOT-*tee...*
They are all...

DE ROSSI: **Questa grande valigia è mia,**
KWESS-*tah* GRAHN-*deh vah-*LEE-*jah* EH MEE-*ah,*
This big bag is mine,

il resto è del signor Miller.
eel RESS-*toh* EH *dehl seen-*YOHR *Miller.*
the others belong to Mr. Miller.

IMPIEGATO: (**dopo avere pesato le valige**)
(DOH-*poh ah-*VEH-*reh peh-*ZAH-*toh leh vah-*LEE-*jeh*)
(after having weighed the bags)

Il peso va bene: è dentro i limiti.
Eel PEH-*zoh vah* BEH-*neh:* EH DEHN-*troh ee* LEE-*mee-tee.*
The weight is all right: it is within the limit.

MILLER: (**a De Rossi, sottovoce**) **Scusi,**
(*ah Deh* ROHS-*see, soht-toh-*VOHT-*cheh*) SKOO-*zee,*
(to De Rossi, in a low voice) Excuse me,

perchè ha dichiarato che la grande valigia è sua?
pehr-KEH AH *dee-k'yah*-RAH-*toh keh lah* GRAHN-*deh vah*-LEE-*jah* EH
SOO-*ah?*
why did you declare that the big bag was yours?

DE ROSSI: **Perchè ogni passeggero ha diritto**
Pehr-KEH OHN-*yee pahs-seh*-DJEH-*roh* AH *dee*-REET-*toh*
Because each passenger has the right

al trasporto gratis di 25 chili di bagaglio;
ahl trahs-POHR-*toh* GRAH-*tees dee vehn-tee*-CHEEN-*kweh* KEE-*lee dee*
bah-GAH-*l'yoh;*
to free transportation of 25 kilos of luggage;

e siccome io non ne ho, e Lei invece
eh seek-KOH-*meh* EE-*oh nohn neh* OH, *eh Lay een*-VEH-*cheh*
and since I haven't any, and you on the other hand

ne ha oltre il limite, ho voluto evitarle
neh AH OHL-*treh eel* LEE-*mee-teh,* OH *voh*-LOO-*toh eh-vee*-TAHR-*leh*
have above the limit, I wanted to avoid your

il pagamento della sopratassa.
eel pah-gah-MEHN-*toh* DEHL-*lah soh-prah*-TAHS-*sah.*
having to pay the extra charge.

MILLER: **Lei è un genio! In compenso Le offro un**
Lay EH *oon* JEH-*n'yoh!* *Een kohm*-PEHN-*soh Leh* OHF-*froh oon*
You are a genius! As a reward I offer you a

elefantino, mentre io ne mangerò
eh-leh-fahn-TEE-*noh,* MEHN-*treh* EE-*oh neh mahn-jeh*-ROH
baby elephant, while I could eat

uno ben nutrito; perchè muoio di fame.
OO-*noh behn noo*-TREE-*toh; pehr*-KEH *m'*WOY-*oh dee* FAH-*meh.*
a well nourished one because I am dying of hunger.

NOTE to Student: The diminutive of nouns is formed by
substituting the last vowel with *-ino* (masculine), or *-ina*
(feminine). Ex: *Elefante—elefant-ino; bicchiere—bicchier-
ino; camicia—camic-ina; scatola—scatol-ina.* The augmenta-
tive is formed by using *-one,* instead of *-ino* or *-ina.* Ex:
Elefant-one, bicchier-one, camici-one, scatol-one. Notice that the augmenta-
tive form makes all nouns masculine. There are exceptions to these rules,
. . . as you will find out!

DE ROSSI: **Accetto. Il ristorante è sopra.**
*Aht-*CHEH*-toh. Eel rees-toh-*RAHN*-teh* EH SOH-*prah.*
I accept. The restaurant is upstairs.

ANNUNZIATORE: **Passeggeri per Roma, salgano a bordo.**
*Ahn-noon-ts'yah-*TOH*-reh:*   *Pahs-seh-*DJEH*-ree pehr* ROH-*mah,* SAHL-*gah-noh*
                       ah BOHR-*doh.*
ANNOUNCER: Passengers for Rome, on board.

   Apparecchio 2-24. Passeggeri per Roma.
   *Ahp-pah-*REHK*-k'yoh* DOO-*eh-vehn-tee-*KWAHT*-troh. Pahs-seh-*DJEH*-ree*
   pehr ROH-*mah.*
   Flight 2-24. Passengers for Rome.

MILLER: **Che disdetta! Adesso sarò a dieta d'aria!**
   *Keh dees-*DEHT*-tah! Ah-*DEHS*-soh sah-*ROH *ah d'*YEH*-tah* DAH-*r'yah!*
   What a shame! Now I shall be on a diet of air.

DE ROSSI: **Non si preoccupi. A bordo servono**
   *Nohn see preh-*OHK*-koo-pee. Ah* BOHR-*doh* SEHR-*voh-noh*
   Don't worry. They always serve something

   sempre qualche cosa da mangiare.
   SEHM-*preh* KWAHL-*keh* KOH-*zah dah mahn-*JAH-*reh.*
   to eat on board.

   EXPRESSIONS to Remember:
   Una succursale—"A branch". (Business only.)
   Sopratassa—"Extra charge".

THINKING IN ITALIAN

(Answers on page 294)

1. Sta dormendo il signor Miller quando il telefono suona?
2. Chi lo chiama?
3. Che cosa esclama il signor Miller quando pensa che il signor De Rossi lo aspetta?
4. Come mai il signor Miller ha così poco tempo?
5. Chi porterà i bagagli del signor Miller al taxi?
6. Con chi parla il signor Miller nell'ufficio dell'albergo?
7. Dove ha lasciato la chiave?
8. Perchè non permette al facchino di prendere la valigetta?
9. Dove lo aspetta il signor De Rossi?
10. Si è svegliato presto il signor Miller?
11. Perchè il signor Miller non ha un viso allegro?
12. Mangia la mattina il signor De Rossi?
13. Potrà il signor De Rossi servire da guida al signor Miller?
14. Dov'è la sede della ditta del signor De Rossi?
15. Qual'è il limite di peso del bagaglio che può essere trasportato gratis?
16. Perchè ha fame il signor Miller?
17. Ha avuto il tempo di mangiare all'aeroporto?
18. Perchè non mangia al ristorante dell'aeroporto?
19. Si serve da mangiare sugli aeroplani?
20. A Lei piace di viaggiare in aereo?

LEZIONE 38

L'arrivo a Roma
*Lahr-*REE-*voh ah* ROH-*mah*
The arrival in Rome

(In aeroplano)
(*Een ah-eh-roh-*PLAH-*noh*)
(In the airplane)

MILLER: **Arriveremo presto? Quanto tempo ci vuole ancora?**
*Ahr-ree-veh-*REH-*moh* PRESS-*toh?* KWAHN-*toh* TEHM-*poh chee v'*WOH-*leh*
*ahn-*KOH-*rah?*
Will we be arriving soon? How much longer does it take?

NOTE: Do not confuse *ci vuole*—"it takes" with *egli vuole*—"he wishes" or "he wants".

DE ROSSI: **Non ci vuole molto tempo.**
Nohn chee v'woh-leh mohl-toh tehm-poh.
It won't be long.

Si cominciano già a vedere i colli Albani.
See koh-MEENT-chah-noh JAH ah veh-DEH-reh ee KOHL-lee Ahl-BAH-nee.
The Alban hills can already be seen.

Vede laggiù la bellissima campagna romana?
VEH-deh lah-DJOO lah bell-LEES-see-mah kahm-PAHN-n'yah roh-MAH-nah?
Do you see the very beautiful Roman countryside?

MILLER: **È strano! Malgrado il mio tremendo appetito**
EH STRAH-noh! Mahl-GRAH-doh eel MEE-oh treh-MEHN-doh ahp-peh-TEE-toh
It is strange! Despite my tremendous appetite,

io sento una certa emozione al pensiero che
EE-oh SEHN-toh OO-nah CHER-tah eh-moh-ts'YOH-neh ahl pehn-s'YEH-roh keh
I feel a certain emotion at the thought that

mi avvicino alla Città Eterna.
mee ahv-vee-CHEE-noh AHL-lah cheet-TAH Eh-TEHR-nah.
I am approaching the Eternal City.

DE ROSSI: **Caput mundi!**
KAH-poot MOON-dee!
Caput mundi!

MILLER: **Come dice? Non ho capito.**
KOH-meh DEE-cheh? Noh-NOH kah-PEE-toh.
What do you say? I didn't understand.

DE ROSSI: **Caput mundi. È latino, e significa:**
KAH-poot MOON-dee. EH lah-TEE-noh, eh seen-n'YEE-fee-kah:
Caput mundi. It is Latin, and it means:

la capitale del mondo.
lah kah-pee-TAH-leh dehl MOHN-doh.
the capital of the world.

MILLER: **Io spero che nella "caput mundi"**
EE-*oh* SPEH-*roh keh* NEHL-*lah* "KAH-*poot* MOON-*dee*"
I hope that in the "caput mundi"

troverò un buon ristorante.
*troh-veh-*ROH *oon b'*WOHN *rees-toh-*RAHN-*teh.*
I will find a good restaurant.

DE ROSSI: **Lei oggi vede tutto con lo stomaco, ma stia**
Lay OH-*djee* VEH-*deh* TOOT-*toh kohn loh* STOH-*mah-koh, mah* STEE-*ah*
Today you see everything through your stomach, but don't worry

tranquillo che a Roma si mangia bene dappertutto.
*trahn-*KWEEL-*loh keh ah* ROH-*mah see* MAHN-*jah* BEH-*neh*
*dahp-pehr-*TOOT-*toh.*
because in Rome one can eat well anywhere.

MILLER: **Che paese è quello? Là, su quel colle.**
*Keh pah-*EH-*zeh* EH KWELL-*loh? Lah, soo kwell* KOHL-*leh.*
What town is that? There, on that hill?

DE ROSSI: **È Frascati, famoso per i suoi vini eccellenti.**
EH *Frahs-*KAH-*tee, fah-*MOH-*zoh pehr ee s'*WOY VEE-*nee eht-cheh-*LEHN-*tee.*
It is Frascati, famous for its excellent wines.

Un po' più a destra è Albano.
Oon POH *p'*YOO *ah* DEHS-*trah* EH *Ahl-*BAH-*noh.*
A little more to the right is Albano.

L'apparecchio sta girando,
*Lah-pah-*REHK-*k'yoh stah jee-*RAHN-*doh,*
The plane is making a turn,

stiamo per arrivare. Ecco Roma!
*st'*YAH-*moh pehr ahr-ree-*VAH-*reh.* ECK-*koh* ROH-*mah!*
we are about to arrive. There is Rome!

EXPRESSION to Remember: *Ecco*—"behold", "there is".

MILLER: **Che città grande! Com'è bella!**
*Keh cheet-*TAH GRAHN-*deh! Koh-*MEH BELL-*lah!*
What a large city! How beautiful it is!

(All'aeroporto)
*(Ahl-lah-eh-roh-*POHR-*toh)*
(At the airport)

L'ispettore d'immigrazione:
*Lees-peht-*TOH-*reh deem-mee-grah-ts'*YOH-*neh:*
The immigration inspector:

"I passeggeri sono pregati di mostrare
*"Ee pahs-seh-*DJEH-*ree* SOH-*noh preh-*GAH-*tee dee mohs-*TRAH-*reh*
"Passengers are kindly requested to show

il loro passaporto o tessera di riconoscimento."
eel LOH-*roh pahs-sah-*POHR-*toh oh* TEHS-*seh-rah dee
ree-koh-noh-shee-*MEHN-*toh."*
their passports or identification cards."

DE ROSSI: **Ecco la mia tessera.**
ECK-*koh lah* MEE-*ah* TEHS-*seh-rah.*
Here is my identification card.

ISPETTORE: **Benissimo. Passi pure.**
*Ees-peht-*TOH-*reh:*   *Beh-*NEES-*see-moh.* PAHS-*see* POO-*reh.*
INSPECTOR: Very well. Pass along.

MILLER: **Io sono americano, ecco il passaporto**
EE-*oh* SOH-*noh ah-meh-ree-*KAH-*noh,* ECK-*koh eel pahs-sah-*POHR-*toh*
1 am an American, here is my passport

ed altri documenti.
ehd AHL-*tree doh-koo-*MEHN-*tee.*
and other papers.

ISPETTORE: **Quanto tempo si fermerà a Roma?**
KWAHN-*toh* TEHM-*poh see fehr-meh-*RAH *ah* ROH-*mah?*
How long will you be staying in Rome?

 **EXPRESSIONS to Remember:**
Significare—"To signify" or "to mean".
Stare tranquillo—"Not to worry".
Stia tranquillo!—"Don't worry!" ("Be calm!")
Passi pure—"Go ahead".
Fermarsi—"To stay" "To stop".

MILLER: **Non so ancora, forse un mese.**
*Nohn soh ahn-*KOH-*rah,* FOHR-*seh oon* MEH-*zeh.*
I don't know yet, perhaps a month.

ISPETTORE: **(restituendo le carte) Prego, passi alla dogana.**
*(rehs-tee-too-*EHN-*doh leh* KAHR-*teh)* PREH-*goh.* PAHS-*see* AHL-*lah
doh-*GAH-*nah.*
(returning the papers) Please, go to the customs.

MILLER: **Scusi, dove posso cambiare dei dollari in lire?**
SKOO-*zee,* DOH-*veh* POHS-*soh kahm-b'*YAH-*reh day* DOHL-*lah-ree een*
LEE-*reh?*
I beg your pardon, where can I change dollars into lire?

ISPETTORE: **C'è un ufficio di cambio nell'aeroporto,**
CHEH *oon oof-*FEE-*ch'yoh dee* KAHM-*b'yoh nehl-lah-eh-roh-*POHR-*toh,*
There is an exchange office in the airport,

e.... stia attento ai borsaneristi.
eh.... STEE-*ah aht-*TEHN-*toh igh bohr-sah-neh-*REES-*tee.*
and.... watch out for black marketeers.

EXPRESSION to Remember: *Borsaneristi*—"Black marketeers" comes from *borsa*—"market" and *nero*—"black"; a
postwar word.

MILLER: **Grazie dell'avviso.**
GRAHTS-*yeh dehl-lahv-*VEE-*zoh.*
Thanks for the warning.

(Fuori)
(*f'*WOH-*ree*)
(Outside)

BAGAGLIERE: **I Suoi scontrini, signore?**
*Bah-gahl-l'*YEH-*reh: Ee s'*WOY *skohn-*TREE-*nee, seen-*YOH-*reh?*
LUGGAGE CLERK: Your checks, sir?

MILLER: **Eccoli. Quelle due valige brune e quella nera sono mie.**
ECK-*koh-lee.* KWELL-*leh* DOO-*eh vah-*LEE-*jeh* BROO-*neh eh* KWELL-*lah*
NEH-*rah* SOH-*noh* MEE-*eh.*
Here they are. Those two brown valises and that black one are mine.

BAGAGLIERE: **Un momento, signore, il doganiere**
*Oon moh-*MEHN-*toh, seen-*YOH-*reh, eel doh-gah-n'*YEH-*reh*
Wait a moment, sir, the customs inspector

deve ancora ispezionarle.
DEH-*veh ahn-*KOH-*rah ees-peh-ts'yoh-*NAHR-*leh.*
still has to inspect them.

MILLER: **(fra sè) Che seccatura! Devo continuamente**
(*frah seh*) *Keh sehk-kah-*TOO-*rah!* DEH-*voh kohn-tee-noo-ah-*MEHN-*teh*
(to himself) How annoying! I am constantly being obliged

aprire e chiudere le valige.
*ah-*PREE-*reh eh k'*YOO-*deh-reh leh vah-*LEE-*jeh.*
to open and close my bags.

DOGANIERE: **Apra le valige.**
*Doh-gah-n'*YEH-*reh:* AH-*prah leh vah-*LEE-*jeh.*
CUSTOMS INSPECTOR: Open the bags.

MILLER: **Ma esse sono già state ispezionate a Genova,**
Mah EHS-*seh* SOH-*noh* JAH STAH-*teh ees-peh-ts'yoh-*NAH-*teh ah*
JEH-*noh-vah,*
But they have already been inspected in Genoa,

al mio arrivo dagli Stati Uniti!
ahl MEE-*oh ahr-*REE-*voh* DAHL-*yee* STAH-*tee Oo-*NEE-*tee!*
upon my arrival from the U.S.A.

DOGANIERE: **Non lo dubito, signore, ma io non**
NOHN *loh* DOO-*bee-toh, seen-*YOH-*reh, mah* EE-*oh nohn*
I don't doubt it, sir, but I cannot

posso cambiare il regolamento.
POHS-*soh kahm-b'*YAH-*reh eel reh-goh-lah-*MEHN-*toh.*
change the regulations.

Ha tabacco, profumi o liquori da dichiarare?
AH *tah-*BAHK-*koh, proh-*FOO-*mee oh lee-k'*WOH-*ree dah dee-k'yah-*RAH-*reh?*
Do you have tobacco, perfumes or liquor to declare?

MILLER: **Sì, ho molte sigarette, ma ho già pagato la dogana.**
See, OH MOHL-*teh see-gah-*RET-*teh, mah* OH JAH *pah-*GAH-*toh lah*
*doh-*GAH-*nah.*
Yes, I have many cigarettes, but I have already paid the duty.

DOGANIERE: **Mostri la ricevuta, per favore.**
MOHS-*tree lah ree-cheh-*VOO-*tah, pehr fah-*VOH-*reh.*
Show the receipt, please.

(Miller mostra la ricevuta) Grazie.
(Miller MOHS-*trah lah ree-cheh-*VOO-*tah)* GRAHTS-*yeh.*
(Miller shows the receipt) Thank you.

DE ROSSI: **Miller, Miller!**

Mi scusi se mi sono assentato, ma
Mee SKOO-*zee seh mee* SOH-*noh ahs-sehn-*TAH-*toh, mah*
Excuse me for having gone away, but

ho voluto telefonare a mia moglie.
OH *voh-*LOO-*toh teh-leh-foh-*NAH-*reh ah* MEE-*ah* MOH-*l'yek.*
I wanted to telephone to my wife.

Essa è sempre preoccupata quando io viaggio in aereo.
ESS-*sah* EH SEHM-*preh preh-ohk-koo-*PAH-*tah* KWAHN-*doh* EE-*oh*
*vee-*AH-*djoh een ah-*EH-*reh-oh.*
She is always worried when I travel by air.

MILLER: Perchè? È tanto difficile, in Italia, per una donna
*Pehr-*KEH? EH TAHN-*toh* deef-FEE-*chee-leh, een Ee-*TAHL-*yah, pehr* OO-*nak*
DOHN-*nah*
Why? Is it so difficult, in Italy, for a lady

trovare un nuovo marito?
*troh-*VAH-*reh oon noo-*OH-*voh* mah-REE-*toh?*
to find a new husband?

DE ROSSI: No. Ma è difficile trovare un marito come me!
Noh. Mah EH dee-FEE-*chee-leh troh-*VAH-*reh oon* mah-REE-*toh* KOH-*meh*
meh!
No. But it is difficult to find a husband like me!

MILLER: Ben detto! Prima di lasciarmi può Lei
Behn DEHT-*toh!* PREE-*mah dee lah-*SHAHR-*mee p'*WOH *Lay*
Well said! Before leaving me can you

raccomandarmi un buon albergo?
*rahk-koh-mahn-*DAHR-*mee oon b'*WOHN *ahl-*BEHR-*goh?*
recommend a good hotel to me?

DE ROSSI: Sì. L'Albergo degli Ambasciatori.
*See. Lahl-*BEHR-*goh* DEHL-*yee Ahm-bah-shah-*TOH-*ree.*
Yes. The Ambassador Hotel.

Si trova in via Veneto, che è una strada
See TROH-*vah een* VEE-*ah* VEH-*neh-toh, keh* EH OO-*nah* STRAH-*dah*
It is on the via Veneto, which is a very

elegante e centrale. È fornito di
*eh-leh-*GAHN-*teh eh chehn-*TRAH-*leh.* EH *fohr-*NEE-*toh dee*
fashionable and central street. It is furnished with

tutte le comodità moderne.
TOOT-*teh leh koh-moh-dee-*TAH *moh-*DEHR-*neh.*
all modern conveniences.

MILLER: Benissimo. Andro là. Quando ci vedremo?
*Beh-*NEES-*see-moh. Ahn-*DROH LAH. KWAHN-*doh chee veh-*DREH-*moh?*
Excellent. I shall go there. When shall we see each other?

DE ROSSI: Passerò il pomeriggio in ufficio e questa
*Pahs-seh-*ROH *eel poh-meh-*REE-*djoh een oof-*FEE-*ch'yoh eh* KWESS-*tah*
I'll spend the afternoon at the office and this

sera dovrò restare in casa. Verrò a prenderla
SEH-*rah doh-*VROH *rehs-*TAH-*reh een* KAH-*zah. Vehr-*ROH *ah*
PREHN-*dehr-lah*
evening I must stay home. I'll come to get you

all'albergo domattina.
*ahl-lahl-*BEHR-*goh doh-maht-*TEE-*nah.*
at the hotel tomorrow morning.

Le mostrerò parte della capitale.
*Leh mohs-treh-*ROH PAHR-*teh* DEHL-*lah kah-pee-*TAH-*leh.*
I'll show you part of the capital.

MILLER: Benone! Allora arrivederci, De Rossi.
*Beh-*NOH-*neh! Ahl-*LOH-*rah ahr-ree-veh-*DEHR-*chee, Deh* ROHS-*see.*
Fine! Then goodbye, De Rossi.

DE ROSSI: A domani.
*Ah doh-*MAH-*nee.*
Till tomorrow.

NOTE on "Goodbye". Remember these expressions:
A rivederci—"Until we see each other".
A rivederla—"Until I see you".
A domani—"Until tomorrow".

(All'albergo)
(*Ahl-lahl-*BEHR-*goh*)
(At the hotel)

MILLER: Buon giorno. Desidero una camera con bagno.
*b'*WOHN JOHR-*noh. Deh-*ZEE-*deh-roh* OO-*nah* KAH-*meh-rah kohn*
BAHN-*n'yoh.*
Good morning. I wish a room with bath.

IMPIEGATO: La vuole a giornata o a settimana, signore?
*Lah v'*WOH-*leh ah johr-*NAH-*tah oh ah set-tee-*MAH-*nah, seen-*YOH-*reh?*
Do you want it by the day or by the week, sir?

MILLER: Mi fermerò qui parecchie settimane.
*Mee fehr-meh-*ROH *kwee pah-*RECK-*k'yeh set-tee-*MAH-*neh.*
I shall stay here several weeks.

IMPIEGATO: In questo caso Le do la camera 518,
Een KWESS-*toh* KAH-*zoh Leh doh lah* KAH-*meh-rah*
CHEEN-*kweh-*CHEHN-*toh-dee-chee-*OHT-*toh.*
In that case I shall give you room 518;

è molto grande e tranquilla.
EH MOHL-*toh* GRAHN-*deh eh trahn*-KWEEL-*lah.*
it is very large and quiet.

MILLER: E quanto costa?
Eh KWAHN-*toh* KOHS-*tah?*
And how much does it cost?

IMPIEGATO: Duemila lire, oltre le tasse.
DOO-*eh*-MEE-*lah* LEE-*reh,* OHL-*treh leh* TAHS-*seh.*
2000 lire, plus tax.

MILLER: (calcolando mentalmente)
(*kahl-koh*-LAHN-*doh mehn-tahl*-MEHN-*teh*)
(calculating mentally)

Duemila lire sono circa tre dollari.
DOO-*eh*-MEE-*lah* LEE-*reh* SOH-*noh* CHEER-*kah treh* DOHL-*lah-ree.*
2000 lire are about 3 dollars.

(All'impiegato) Va bene. Faccia portare
(*Ahl-leem-p'yeh*-GAH-*toh*) *Vah* BEH-*neh.* FAHT-*chah pohr*-TAH-*reh*
(To the employee) Good. Have my luggage

le mie valige in camera, e mi dica, per piacere,
leh MEE-*eh vah*-LEE-*jeh een* KAH-*meh-rah, eh mee* DEE-*kah, pehr*
p'yah-CHEH-*reh,*
brought up to the room, and tell me, please,

dov'è la sala da pranzo.
doh-VEH *lah* SAH-*lah dah* PRAHN-*tsoh.*
where is the dining room.

Non ho mangiato da ieri sera.
Noh-NOH *mahn*-JAH-*toh dah* YEH-*ree* SEH-*rah.*
I haven't eaten since yesterday evening.

THINKING IN ITALIAN
(Answers on page 295)

1. Che cosa vede Lei da un aeroplano?
2. Qual'è il paese che il signor De Rossi indica al signor Miller?
3. Perchè è famoso Frascati?
4. Capisce il signor Miller le parole: caput mundi?
5. Sono queste parole francesi?   6. Che parole sono?
7. Che documenti vuole vedere l'ispettore d'immigrazione?
8. Quanto tempo si fermerà a Roma il signor Miller?
9. Perchè il signor Miller cerca un ufficio di cambio?
10. Che avviso gli dà l'ispettore d'immigrazione?
11. Piace al signor Miller di aprire e chiudere le valige?
12. Le valige erano già state ispezionate?   13. Dove?
14. Che cosa mostra al doganiere il signor Miller, per non pagare la dogana una seconda volta?
15. A chi telefona il signor De Rossi?   16. Perchè?
17. In quale albergo andrà il signor Miller?
18. Dove passerà il pomeriggio il signor De Rossi?
19. Dove s'incontreranno i signori De Rossi e Miller?
20. Perchè il signor De Rossi raccomanda l'Albergo degli Ambasciatori?
21. Trova il signor Miller una buona camera?   22. Quanto costa?
23. Perchè il signor Miller vuole sapere dov'è la sala da pranzo?
24. A Lei piace la cucina italiana?

Per le strade ed i negozi di Roma

Pehr leh STRAH-*deh ehd ee neh-*GOH-*tsee dee*
ROH-*mah*

In the streets and stores of Rome

DE ROSSI: **Buon giorno, caro. Ha fatto colazione?**
*b'*WOHN JOHR-*noh,* KAH-*roh.* AH FAHT-*toh koh-lah-ts'*YOH-*neh?*
Good morning, my dear friend. Have you had breakfast?

MILLER: **Sì, grazie. Ma a proposito: vuole spiegarmi**
See, GRAHTS-*yeh. Mah ah proh-*POH-*zee-toh: v'*WOH-*leh sp'yeh-*GAHR-*mee*
Yes, thank you. But by the way: could you explain to me

come mai in italiano si usa la stessa paroia, colazione,
KOH-*meh migh een ee-tahl*-YAH-*noh see* OO-*zah lah* STEHS-*sah*
pah-ROH-*lah, koh-lah-ts'*YOH-*neh,*
why they sometimes use the same word, *colazione,*

per indicare il pasto del mattino e
*pehr een-dee-*KAH-*reh eel* PAHS-*toh dehl maht*-TEE-*noh eh*
in Italian to express the meal in the morning and

quello del mezzogiorno.
KWELL-*loh dehl meh-dzoh-*JOHR-*noh.*
the one at noon?

MY DEAR FELLOW! *Caro,* meaning "dear", is very much used in conversation among men as an expression of friendly affection. It corresponds to "my dear fellow", "my dear chap" or simply "old boy".

DE ROSSI: **Le dirò, Miller. Secondo le regole della lingua**
*Leh dee-*ROH, *Miller. Seh-*KOHN-*doh leh* REH-*goh-leh* DEHL-*lah* LEEN-*gwah*
I'll tell you, Miller. According to the rules of the language,

il pasto del mattino si chiama colazione,
eel PAHS-*toh dehl maht*-TEE-*noh see k'*YAH-*mah koh-lah-ts'*YOH-*neh,*
the morning meal is called *colazione,*

quello del mezzogiorno è il pranzo
KWELL-*loh dehl meh-dzoh-*JOHR-*noh* EH *eel* PRAHN-*tsoh*
the one at noon is the *pranzo*

e quello della sera è la cena; ma molti
eh KWELL-*loh* DEHL-*lah* SEH-*rah* EH *lah* CHEH-*nah;* *mah* MOHL-*tee*
and that in the evening is the *cena;* but many

italiani prendono solamente caffè, al mattino,
ee-tahl-YAH-*nee* PREHN-*doh-noh soh-lah-*MEHN-*teh kahf*-FEH, *ahl maht*-TEE-*noh.*
Italians take only coffee in the morning,

quindi chiamano colazione il loro pranzo
KWEEN-*dee k'*YAH-*mah-noh koh-lah-ts'*YOH-*neh eel* LOH-*roh* PRAHN-*tsoh*
and therefore call their lunch *colazione*

e pranzo la loro cena. È chiaro?
eh PRAHN-*tsoh lah* LOH-*roh* CHEH-*nah.* EH *k'*YAH-*roh?*
and their dinner *pranzo.* Is that clear?

MILLER: **Chiarissimo! E adesso sono a sua disposizione.**
K'yah-REES-see-moh! Eh ah-DEHS-soh SOH-noh ah soo-ah
dees-poh-see-tz'YOH-neh.
Perfectly clear! And now I am at your disposal.

DE ROSSI: **Il tempo è bellissimo; vuole fare una**
Eel TEHM-poh EH bell-LEES-see-moh; v'WOH-leh FAH-reh oo-nah
The weather is most beautiful; do you want to take a

passeggiata verso il centro della città?
pahs-seh-DJAH-tah VEHR-soh eel CHEHN-troh DEHL-lah cheet-TAH?
stroll toward the center of the city?

MILLER: **Sono nelle Sue mani.**
SOH-noh NEHL-leh soo-eh MAH-nee.
I am in your hands.

DE ROSSI: **Andiamo. (Essi escono)**
Ahn-d'YAH-moh. (EHS-see EHS-koh-noh)
Let's go. (They go out)

Eccoci già in piazza Barberini;
ECK-koh-chee JAH een p'YAH-tsah Bahr-beh-REE-nee;
Here we are already on Barberini Square;

adesso, scendendo per la via del Tritone
ah-DEHS-soh, shehn-DEHN-doh pehr lah VEE-ah dehl Tree-TOH-neh
now, if we go down Tritone street

irriveremo al Corso Umberto,
ahr-ree-veh-REH-moh ahl KOHR-soh Oom-BEHR-toh,
we shall come to Umberto avenue,

che è considerato il centro della città.
keh EH kohn-see-deh-RAH-toh eel CHEHN-troh DEHL-lah cheet-TAH.
which is considered the center of the city.

 **CAN A SQUARE BE ROUND?** The word *piazza* in Italian describes "a public square", "plaza" or "circle". Therefore a wide space surrounded by buildings, regardless of its shape, is called a *piazza*.

MILLER: **Mi dica, De Rossi; i romani celebrano oggi**
Mee DEE-kah, Deh ROHS-see; ee roh-MAH-nee CHEH-leh-brah-noh OH-djee
Tell me, De Rossi, are the Romans celebrating

qualche evento speciale?
KWAHL-keh eh-VEHN-toh speh-ch'YAH-leh?
some special event today?

DE ROSSI: **Certamente! Oggi si celebra l'arrivo**
*Chehr-tah-*MEHN-*teh!* OH-*djee see* CHEH-*leh-brah lahr-*REE-*voh*
Certainly! Today they celebrate the arrival

in città di un grande personaggio.
*een cheet-*TAH *dee oon* GRAHN-*deh pehr-soh-*NAH-*djoh.*
of a great personage in the city.

MILLER: **Ah sì? E chi è?**
Ah see? Eh kee EH?
Oh yes? And who is that?

DE ROSSI: **È il signor John Albert Franklin Miller,**
EH *eel seen-*YOHR *John Albert Franklin Miller,*
It is Mr. John Albert Franklin Miller,

di Boston, Massachusetts!
dee Boston, Massachusetts!
of Boston, Massachusetts!

MILLER: **Lei è sempre in vena di scherzare;**
Lay EH SEHM-*preh een* VEH-*nah dee skehr-*TSAH-*reh;*
You are always in a joking mood

ma ancora non mi ha detto che cosa si celebra.
*mah ahn-*KOH-*rah nohn mee* AH DEHT-*toh keh* KOH-*zah see* CHEH-*leh-brah.*
yet you have not told me what is being celebrated.

DE ROSSI: **Non si celebra niente, mio caro Miller.**
Nohn see CHEH-*leh-brah n'*YEHN-*teh,* MEE-*oh* KAH-*roh Miller.*
They are not celebrating anything, my dear Miller.

È il sole d'Italia, è l'umore degli italiani
EH *eel* SOH-*leh dee-*TAHL-*yah,* EH *loo-*MOH-*reh* DEHL-*yee ee-tahl-*YAH-*nee*
It is just the Italian sun, it is the humor of the Italians

che danno al paese questo colore di festività.
keh DAHN-*noh ahl pah-*EH-*zeh* KWESS-*toh koh-*LOH-*reh dee*
*fehs-tee-vee-*TAH.
which gives this country that festive air.

EXPRESSIONS to Remember:
Scendere per una via—"To go down a street".
Salire per una via—"To go up a street".
Essere in vena—"To be in the mood", "to be in the spirit".
Umore—"Humor", "mood". *Essere di buon umore—*"To be
in a gay mood".
Essere di cattivo umore—"To be in a sad mood" or "to be ill-tempered".

MILLER: **Che movimento per le strade!**
*Keh moh-vee-*MEHN-*toh pehr leh* STRAH-*deh!*
What movement in the streets!

Ce n'è quasi più che a New York.
Cheh NEH KWAH-*zee p'*YOO *keh ah New York.*
There is almost more than in New York.

DE ROSSI: **Ecco a destra la Piazza Colonna con la famosa colonna**
ECK-*koh ah* DEHS-*trah lah p'*YAH-*tsah Koh-*LOHN-*nah kohn lah*
*fah-*MOH-*zah koh-*LOHN-*nah*
Here on our right Colonna Square with the famous column

in onore di Marco Aurelio.
*een oh-*NOH-*reh dee* MAHR-*koh Aou-*REH-*l'yoh.*
in honor of Marcus Aurelius.

MILLER: **Non ho mai visto una colonna così alta!**
*Noh-*NOH *migh* VEES-*toh* OO-*nah koh-*LOHN-*nah koh-*ZEE AHL-*tah!*
I have never seen such a tall column!

DE ROSSI: **È alta cento piedi romani, oltre al piedistallo.**
EH AHL-*tah* CHEHN-*toh p'*YEH-*dee roh-*MAH-*nee,* OHL-*treh ahl*
*p'yeh-dees-*TAHL-*loh.*
It is 100 Roman feet high, in addition to the base.

MILLER: **Parlando di antichità Lei mi ricorda che il mio cappello**
*Pahr-*LAHN-*doh dee ahn-tee-kee-*TAH *Lay mee ree-*KOHR-*dah keh eel*
MEE-*oh kahp-*PEL-*loh*
Speaking of antiquities, you remind me that my hat

è molto sciupato e desidero comprarne uno nuovo.
EH MOHL-*toh shoo-*PAH-*toh eh deh-*ZEE-*deh-roh kohm-*PRAHR-*neh* OO-*noh*
*noo-*OH-*voh.*
is very much worn out and I want to buy a new one.

A WORD WITH TWO MEANINGS: *Ricordare* means "to remember" as well as "to remind".

DE ROSSI: **Ecco qui a sinistra un negozio di cappelli.**
ECK-*koh kwee ah see-*NEES-*trah oon neh-*GOH-*ts'yoh dee kahp-*PEL-*lee.*
Here on our left is a hat store.

Entriamo.
*Ehn-tr'*YAH-*moh.*
Let's go in.

(Nel negozio)
*(Nehl neh-*GOH*-ts'yoh)*
(In the store)

COMMESSO: **I signori desiderano?**
*Kohm-*MEHS*-soh: Ee seen-*YOH*-ree deh-*ZEE*-deh-rah-noh?*
CLERK: The gentlemen wish?

MILLER: **Desidero un cappello di feltro grigio,**
*Deh-*ZEE*-deh-roh oon kahp-*PEL*-loh dee* FEHL*-troh* GREE*-joh,*
I want a gray felt hat

proprio come quello che è in vetrina.
PROH*-pree-oh* KOH*-meh* KWELL*-loh keh* EH *een veh-*TREE*-nah.*
exactly like the one in the window.

COMMESSO: **Benissimo, signore. La sua misura?**
*Beh-*NEES*-see-moh, seen-*YOH*-reh. Lah* SOO*-ah mee-*ZOO*-rah?*
Very well, sir. Your size?

MILLER: **Sette e un quarto.**
SET*-teh eh oon* KWAHR*-toh.*
Seven and a quarter.

COMMESSO: **Ecco, signore; vuole provarselo?**
ECK*-koh, seen-*YOH*-reh; v'*WOH*-leh proh-*VAHR*-seh-loh?*
Here you are, sir; will you try it on?

NOTE to Student: *Proprio* means "proper", "one's own", "exactly". Ex: *Un nome proprio*—"a proper name". *La mia propria lingua*—"my own language". *Proprio come quello*—"exactly like that one". *Proprio così*—"exactly so". *Proprio!*—"Exactly!"

Provare means "to try", "to prove", "to taste".

Provarsi (reflexive) *un cappello, un vestito, una camicia* means "to try on a hat, a suit, a shirt".

MILLER: **La misura va bene, ma la qualità non mi soddisfa.**
*Lah mee-*ZOO*-rah vah* BEH*-neh, mah lah kwah-lee-*TAH *nohn mee sohd-*DEES*-fah.*
The size is right but the quality does not satisfy me.

COMMESSO: **Eccone uno di qualità superiore, ma costa**
ECK*-koh-neh* OO*-noh dee kwah-lee-*TAH *soo-peh-r'*YOH*-reh, mah* KOHS*-tah*
Here is one of better quality, but it costs

un po' di più. Seimila lire.
oon POH *dee p'*YOO*. Say-*MEE*-lah* LEE*-reh.*
a bit more. Six thousand lire.

MILLER: (A De Rossi) È molto caro?
(Ah Deh ROHS-*see)* EH MOHL-*toh* KAH-*roh?*
(To De Rossi) Is it very expensive?

DE ROSSI: Non è caro, considerando la buona qualità del feltro.
*Noh-*NEH KAH-*roh, kohn-see-deh-*RAHN-*doh lah b'*WOH-*nah kwah-lee-*TAH
dehl FEHL-*troh.*
It is not expensive, considering the good quality of the felt.

MILLER: (al commesso) Va bene; prendo questo.
*(ahl kohm-*MEHS-*soh) Vah* BEH-*neh;* PREHN-*doh* KWESS-*toh.*
(to the clerk) Very well; I (shall) take that one.

COMMESSO: Desidera avere le Sue iniziali incise nella benda?
*Deh-*ZEE-*deh-rah ah-*VEH-*reh leh* SOO-*eh ee-nee-ts'*YAH-*lee een-*CHEE-*zeh*
NEHL-*lah* BEHN-*dah?*
Do you wish to have your initials stamped in the band?

MILLER: Sì! Sì! Per piacere! J. M.
*See! See! Pehr p'yah-*CHEH-*reh! Ee* LOON-*gah.* EHM-*meh.*
Yes! Yes! If you please: J. M.

COMMESSO: Dobbiamo mandarlo, signore,
*Dohb-b'*YAH-*moh mahn-*DAHR-*loh, seen-*YOH-*reh,*
Shall we send it, sir,

o desidera portarlo con sè?
*oh deh-*ZEE-*deh-rah pohr-*TAHR-*loh kohn* SEH?
or do you wish to take it with you?

MILLER: No. Lo metto subito perchè voglio
Noh, Loh MEHT-*toh soo-bee-toh pehr-*KEH VOHL-*l'yoh*
No. I (shall) put it on right away because I want to

buttare via quello vecchio.
*boot-*TAH-*reh* VEE-*ah* KWELL-*loh* VEHK-*k'yoh.*
throw away this old one.

COMMESSO: I cappelli che i nostri clienti scartano
*Ee kahp-*PEL-*lee keh ee* NOHS-*tree klee-*EHN-*tee* SKAHR-*tah-noh*
The hats which our customers discard

noi li puliamo e li mandiamo al ricovero dei vecchi.
*noy lee poo-l'*YAH-*moh eh lee mahn-d'*YAH-*moh ahl ree-*KOH-*veh-roh*
day VEHK-*kee.*
we clean and send over to the Old People's Home.

MILLER: Ottima idea!
OHT-*tee-mah ee-*DEH-*ah!*
Excellent idea!

COMMESSO: **Ecco il cambio. Grazie, signore.**
ECK-*koh eel* KAHM-*b'yoh.* GRAHTS-*yeh, seen-*YOH-*reh.*
Here is your change. Thank you, sir.

(De Rossi e Miller escono dal negozio)
(*Deh* ROHS-*see eh Miller* ESS-*koh-noh dahl neh-*GOH-*ts'yoh*)
(De Rossi and Miller leave the store)

DE ROSSI: **Adesso stiamo per arrivare in Piazza Venezia.**
*Ah-*DEHS-*soh st'*YAH-*moh pehr ahr-ree-*VAH-*reh een p'*YAH-*tsah*
*Veh-*NEH-*ts'yah.*
Now we are about to reach Venezia Square.

Ecco, in fondo, il colossale Monumento
ECK-*koh, een* FOHN-*doh, eel koh-lohs-*SAH-*leh Moh-noo-*MEHN-*toh*
There in the background (is) the huge monument

a Vittorio Emanuele II.
*ah Veet-*TOH-*r'yoh Eh-mah-noo-*EH-*leh Seh-*KOON-*doh.*
to Vittorio Emanuele II.

MILLER: **Stupendo! Ma,... scusi, dove hanno potuto**
*Stoo-*PEHN-*doh! Mah,...* SKOO-*zee,* DOH-*veh* AHN-*noh poh-*TOO-*toh*
Stupendous! But,... excuse me, where were they able

trovare tutto quel marmo bianco?
*troh-*VAH-*reh* TOOT-*toh kwell* MAHR-*moh b'*YAHN-*koh?*
to find all this white marble?

DE ROSSI: **A Carrara, in Toscana, dove da molti secoli**
*Ah Kahr-*RAH-*rah, een Tohs-*KAH-*nah,* DOH-*veh dah* MOHL-*tee* SEH-*koh-lee*
At Carrara in Tuscany, where for many centuries

si scava marmo finissimo che viene
see SKAH-*vah* MAHR-*moh fee-*NEES-*see-moh keh v'*YEH-*neh*
they have been cutting the finest marble, which

spedito in tutte le parti del mondo.
*speh-*DEE-*toh een* TOOT-*teh leh* PAHR-*tee dehl* MOHN-*doh.*
is shipped to all parts of the world.

MILLER: **E quel palazzo a destra, così severo ma**
*Eh kwell pah-*LAH-*tsoh ah* DEHS-*trah, koh-*ZEE *seh-*VEH-*roh mah*
And that palace on the right, so austere yet

tanto elegante, che cosa è?
TAHN-*toh eh-leh-*GAHN-*teh, keh* KOH-*zah* EH?
so elegant, what is it?

DE ROSSI: **È il Palazzo Venezia; e a sinistra, in fondo**
EH *eel Pah-*LAH-*tsoh Veh-*NEH-*ts'yah; eh ah see-*NEES-*trah, een* FOHN-*doh*
It is the Palazzo Venezia; and to the left, at the end

a quel maestoso viale, Lei vede il Colosseo.
*ah kwell mah-ehs-*TOH*-zoh vee-*AH*-leh, Lay* VEH*-deh eel Koh-lohs-*SEH*-oh.*
of this majestic boulevard, you see the Colosseum.

MILLER: Prima d'ora non avevo mai veduto delle
PREE-*mah* DOH-*rah nohn ah-*VEH*-voh migh veh-*DOO*-toh* DEHL-*leh*
Never before have I seen such large

piazze così grandi, nè così belle.
*p'*YAH-*tseh koh-*ZEE GRAHN-*dee,* NEH *koh-*ZEE BELL-*leh.*
and such beautiful squares.

DE ROSSI: Non dimentichi che questa è la prima volta che
*Nohn dee-*MEHN-*tee-kee keh* KWESS-*tah* EH *lah* PREE-*mah* VOHL-*tah keh*
Do not forget that this is the first time that

Lei viene a Roma, Caput Mundi!
*Lay v'*YEH-*neh ah* ROH-*mah,* KAH-*poot* MOON-*dee!*
you come to Rome, Caput Mundi!

MILLER: Questi posti meravigliosi meritano di essere
KWESS-*tee* POHS-*tee meh-rah-vee-l'*YOH-*zee* MEH-*ree-tah-noh dee*
EHS-*seh-reh*
These marvelous places deserve to be

fotografati. Dove posso comprare delle film a colori
*foh-toh-grah-*FAH-*tee.* DOH-*veh* POSS-*soh kohm-*PRAH-*reh* DEHL-*leh feelm*
*ah koh-*LOH-*ree*
photographed. Where can I buy some color film

per la mia macchina cinematografica?
pehr lah MEE-*ah* MAHK-*kee-nah chee-neh-mah-toh-*GRAH-*fee-kah?*
for my movie camera?

Desidero anche comprare delle cartoline illustrate
*Deh-*ZEE-*deh-roh* AHN-*keh kohm-*PRAH-*reh* DEHL-*leh kahr-toh-*LEE-*neh*
*eel-loos-*TRAH-*teh*
I want also to buy some illustrated post cards

e dei francobolli.
*eh day frahn-koh-*BOHL-*lee.*
and some stamps.

DE ROSSI: Qui, a sinistra, c'è la Via Nazionale,
*Kwee, ah see-*NEES-*trah,* CHEH *lah* VEE-*ah Nah-ts'yoh-*NAH-*leh,*
Here, on the left, is the Via Nazionale,

dove vi sono molti negozi che vendono tutto ciò
DOH-*veh vee* SOH-*noh* MOHL-*tee neh-*GOH-*tsee keh* VEHN-*doh-noh* TOOT-*toh*
CHOH
where there are many stores which sell all

che Lei ha di bisogno, ma prima entriamo in
keh Lay AH *dee bee-*ZOHN*-yoh, mah* PREE*-mah ehn-tr'*YAH*-moh een*
you need; but first let us go into

questo ristorante per fare colazione.
KWESS*-toh rees-toh-*RAHN*-teh pehr* FAH*-reh koh-lah-ts'*YOH*-neh.*
this restaurant to have our lunch.

(Dopo)
(DOH*-poh*)
(Later)

MILLER: Dica, De Rossi, il Teatro dell'Opera
DEE*-kah, Deh* ROHS*-see, eel Teh-*AH*-troh dehl-*LOH*-peh-rah*
Tell me, De Rossi, is the Opera House

è aperto in questo periodo dell'anno?
EH *ah-*PEHR*-toh een* KWESS*-toh peh-*REE*-oh-doh dehl-*LAHN*-noh?*
open at this time of the year?

DE ROSSI: Sì. La stagione lirica è cominciata
*See. Lah stah-*JOH*-neh* LEE*-ree-kah* EH *koh-meent-*CHAH*-tah*
Yes. The opera season started

lunedì scorso. Questa sera danno
*loo-neh-*DEE SKOHR*-soh.* KWESS*-tah* SEH*-rah* DAHN*-noh*
last Monday. Tonight they are playing

la Tosca, di Puccini....
lah TOHS*-kah, dee Poo-*TCHEE*-nee ....*
Tosca, by Puccini....

MILLER: Allora, mi permette d'invitare Sua moglie e Lei a teatro?
*Ahl-*LOH*-rah, mee pehr-*MEHT*-teh deen-vee-*TAH*-reh* SOO*-ah* MOH*-l'yeh*
*eh Lay ah teh-*AH*-troh?*
Well then, will you permit me to invite your wife and you to the
theatre?

 EXPRESSIONS to Remember: *Questa sera danno la Tosca di Puccini,* means literally: "Tonight they will give Puccini's Tosca". What this sentence actually expresses is: "A performance of Puccini's Tosca will be given tonight". When you want to know what's playing in a theatre, whether it is a drama, an opera or a comedy, the common Italian question form is: *Che cosa danno questa sera al teatro?*

DE ROSSI: Al contrario, mia moglie desidera che Lei venga
*Ahl kohn-*TRAH*-r'yoh,* MEE*-ah* MOH*-l'yeh deh-*ZEE*-deh-rah keh Lay*
VEHN*-gah*
On the contrary, my wife wishes you to come

a cena da noi e dopo andremo a teatro.
ah CHEH-*nah dah noy eh* DOH-*poh ahn*-DREH-*moh ah teh*-AH-*troh.*
for supper at our home and afterward we shall go to the theatre.

Non dica di no. Verrò a prenderla all'albergo alle 7.
Nohn DEE-*kah dee* NOH. *Vehr*-ROH *ah* PREHN-*dehr-lah ahl-lahl*-BEHR-*goh*
AHL-*leh* SET-*teh.*
Don't say no! I shall come to pick you up at your hotel at 7 o'clock.

E adesso l'accompagno al Ministero degli
Eh ah-DEHS-*soh lahk-kohm*-PAH-*n'yoh ahl Mee-nees*-TEH-*roh* DEHL-*yee*
And now I'll accompany you to the Ministry of

Affari Esteri, dove Lei ha il suo appuntamento.
Ahf-FAH-*ree* ESS-*teh-ree,* DOH-*veh Lay* AH *eel* SOO-*oh*
ahp-poon-tah-MEHN-*toh.*
Foreign Affairs, where you have your appointment.

Eccoci arrivati. A questa sera, caro, e....
ECK-*koh-chee ahr-ree*-VAH-*tee. Ah* KWESS-*tah* SEH-*rah,* KAH-*roh, eh....*
Here we are. Till tonight then, dear friend, and....

in bocca al lupo!
een BOHK-*kah ahl* LOO-*poh!*
lots of luck!

EXPRESSIONS to Remember: *Venga a cena con noi,* means "Come to supper with us". But if you invite somebody to have supper at your house, you must say: *Venga a cena da noi.*

In bocca al lupo is an expression that you may use to wish an Italian success in a business enterprise, a romance, a performance, etc. The phrase means "I wish you to fall in the mouth of the wolf", and superstitious Italians use this form of well-wishing. More formal equivalents are: *Auguri!* and *Buona fortuna!*

THINKING IN ITALIAN
(Answers on page 295)

1. Come si chiamano i tre pasti giornalieri?
2. Verso dove vanno i signori?
3. Come si chiama la via che è considerata il centro di Roma?
4. Si celebra qualche cosa quel giorno, a Roma?
5. Che cosa è che dà all'Italia il colore di festività?
6. Che cosa vediamo nelle vie di una grande città?
7. Il cappello del signor Miller è nuovo o sciupato?
8. Dove compra egli il nuovo cappello?
9. Perchè non compra egli il primo cappello che vede?
10. Quanto costa il secondo cappello?
11. Che cosa dice il signor De Rossi a proposito del prezzo?
12. Che cosa incide il commesso nella benda del cappello nuovo?
13. Che cosa fa il cappellaio con i cappelli che i clienti scartano?
14. Che cosa vedono i signori in Piazza Venezia?
15. Che cosa si vede in fondo al viale, a sinistra di piazza Venezia?
16. Che desidera comprare il signor Miller?
17. Quando Lei viaggia, manda delle cartoline illustrate ai suoi amici?
18. Acceta il signor De Rossi l'invito a teatro del signor Miller?
19. Dove passerà la serata il signor Miller?
20. Che opera danno al teatro quella sera?
21. Dove accompagna il signor Miller, dopo la colazione, il signor De Rossi?
22. Qual'è l'ultima frase che il signor De Rossi dice al signor Miller?

LEZIONE 40

Turista e guida
*Too-*REES*-tah eh* GWEE*-dah*
Tourist and guide

MILLER: **Cocchiere, mi conduca alle Terme di Diocleziano.**
*Kohk-k'*YEH*-reh, mee kohn-*DOO*-kah* AHL*-leh* TEHR*-meh dee*
*Dee-oh-kleh-ts'*YAH*-noh.*
Coachman, drive me to Diocletian's baths.

COCCHIERE: **Salga in carrozzella, Commendatore.**
*Kohk-k'*YEH*-reh:* SAHL*-gah een kah-roh-*TSEHL*-lah, Kohm-mehn-dah-*TOH*-reh.*
COACHMAN: Get into the coach, Commendatore.

 NOTE on Politeness: *Commendatore* is an honorary title that the Italian Government gives to prominent citizens in recognition of some accomplishment of public interest. Porters, coachmen, shoe-shine boys, taxi-drivers, etc. use the title very freely to flatter their patrons and consequently make them more generous with their tips.

MILLER: **Che fontana meravigliosa! Come si chiama?**
*Keh fohn-*TAH*-nah meh-rah-veel-*YOH*-zah!* KOH*-meh see k'*YAH*-mah?*
What a marvelous fountain? What is it called?

COCCHIERE: **Confesso che non lo so, Commendatore.**
*Kohn-*FESS*-soh keh nohn loh soh, Kohm-mehn-dah-*TOH*-reh.*
I confess that I don't know, Commendatore.

Sono passato da questa piazza stamattina
SOH*-noh pahs-*SAH*-toh dah* KWESS*-tah p'*YAH*-tsah stah-maht-*TEE*-nah*
I passed this plaza this morning

e la fontana non c'era ancora.
*eh lah fohn-*TAH*-nah nohn* CHEH*-rah ahn-*KOH*-rah.*
and the fountain wasn't there yet.

MILLER: **(Guardando il cocchiere a bocca aperta)**
*(Gwahr-*DAHN*-doh eel kohk-k'*YEH*-reh ah* BOHK*-kah ah-*PEHR*-tah)*
(Looking at the coachman with open mouth)

Ma che cosa mi racconta Lei?
Mah keh KOH*-zah mee rahk-*KOHN*-tah Lay?*
But what tale are you telling me?

Ciò che dice non è possibile!
CHOH *keh* DEE*-cheh noh-*NEH *pohs-*SEE*-bee-leh!*
What you say is not possible!

COCCHIERE: **Eh! Lo so che non è possibile, Commendatore,**
EH! *Loh soh keh noh-*NEH *pohs-*SEE*-bee-leh, Kohm-mehn-dah-*TOH*-reh,*
Eh! I know it's not possible, Commendatore,

ma sa, stamattina conducevo un turista americano
*mah sah, stah-maht-*TEE*-nah kohn-doo-*CHEH*-voh oon too-*REES*-tah ah-meh-ree-*KAH*-noh*
but, you know, this morning I was driving an American tourist

in giro per la città, e quando gli ho detto che
een JEE*-roh pehr lah cheet-*TAH*, eh* KWAHN*-doh l'yee* OH DEHT*-toh keh*
around the city and when I told him that

impiegarono più de vent'anni per costruire
*eem-p'yeh-*GAH*-roh-noh p'*YOO *dee vehn-*TAHN*-nee pehr kohs-troo-*EE*-reh*
they took more than twenty years to construct

il Colosseo mi ha risposto che in America una
*eel Koh-lohs-*SEH*-oh mee* AH *rees-*POSS*-toh keh een Ah-*MEH*-ree-kah oo-nah*
the Colosseum, he replied that in America a

costruzione simile si può completare in pochi mesi.
*kohs-troo-ts'*YOH-*neh*   SEE-*mee-leh   see   p'*WOH   *kohm-pleh-*TAH-*reh
een POH-*kee* MEH-*zee.*
similar building could be completed in a few months.

Poi mi ha detto che una chiesa come quella di
Poy mee AH DEHT-*toh keh* OO-*nah k'*YEH-*zah* KOH-*meh* KWELL-*lah dee*
Then he told me that the Americans could

San Pietro gli americani la possono
*Sahn p'*YEH-*troh l'yee ah-meh-ree-*KAH-*nee lah* POHS-*soh-noh*
construct a church like St. Peter's

costruire in meno di un anno, e così adesso
*kohs-troo-*EE-*reh een* MEH-*noh dee oon* AHN-*noh, eh koh-*ZEE *ah-*DEHS-*soh*
in less than a year, and therefore

io volevo rivendicare l'onore dei romani.
EE-*oh voh-*LEH-*voh ree-vehn-dee-*KAH-*reh loh-*NOH-*reh day roh-*MAH-*nee.*
I wished now to vindicate the honor of the Romans.

MILLER: That's a good joke!

COCCHIERE: **Come dice, Commendatore?**
KOH-*meh* DEE-*cheh, Kohm-mehn-dah-*TOH-*reh?*
What did you say, Commendatore?

MILLER: **Oh, scusi. Dicevo che è una buona barzelletta.**
OH, SKOO-*zee. Dee-*CHEH-*voh keh* EH OO-*nah b'*WOH-*nah*
*bahr-dzehl-*LET-*tah.*
Oh, excuse me. I was saying that it is a good joke.

COCCHIERE: **Simpatica, non è vero? Eccoci alle Terme.**
*Seem-*PAH-*tee-kah, noh-*NEH VEH-*roh?* ECK-*koh-chee* AHL-*leh* TEHR-*meh.*
Pleasant, isn't it? Here we are at the Baths.

 AN IMPORTANT WORD: *Simpatico* or *simpatica,* from
simpatia—"sympathy". Technically it has the same meanings as in English, but it is more generally used to express a
sentiment of attraction, appeal, etc. If a person appeals to
you or a girl is attractive you may say that the person or
the girl is *simpatica.* As you can see in this lesson the same word can be
applied to an expression.

(Miller paga la corsa)   **Grazie, Commendatore.**
(Miller PAH-*gah lah* KOHR-*sah)*   GRAHTS-*yeh, Kohm-mehn-dah-*TOH-*reh.*
(Miller pays the fare)   Thank you, Commendatore.

MILLER: **È però vero che in America si fa tutto rapidamente.**
EH *peh-*ROH VEH-*roh keh een Ah-*MEH-*ree-kah see fah* TOOT-*toh*
*rah-pee-dah-*MEHN-*teh.*
But it's true that in America everything is done rapidly.

COCCHIERE: **Ma ... forse i costruttori americani del primo**
Mah ... FOHR-*seh ee kohs-troo-*TOH-*ree ah-meh-ree-*KAH-*nee dehl*
PREE-*moh*
But ... perhaps the American builders of the first

secolo dell'era Cristiana non amavano
SEH-*koh-loh dehl-*LEH-*rah Krees-tee-*AH-*nah nohn ah-*MAH-*vah-noh*
century of the Christian era didn't like

attraversare l'oceano.
*aht-trah-vehs-*SAH-*reh loh-*CHEH-*ah-noh.*
to cross the ocean.

MILLER: **Vedo che Lei vuole avere l'ultima parola. Arrivederci.**
VEH-*doh keh Lay v'*WOH-*leh ah-*VEH-*reh* LOOL-*tee-mah pah-*ROH-*lah.*
*Ahr-ree-veh-*DEHR-*chee.*
I see you want to have the last word. Goodbye.

MILLER: **(Alla guida) Vuole farmi girare le Terme?**
(AHL-*lah* GWEE-*dah) v'*WOH-*leh* FAHR-*mee jee-*RAH-*reh leh* TEHR-*meh?*
(To the guide) Will you take me around the Baths?

Ma l'avverto che non ho molto tempo.
*Mah lahv-*VEHR-*toh keh noh-*NOH MOHL-*toh* TEHM-*poh.*
But I warn you I haven't much time.

GUIDA: Very well, sir. Here you see ...

MILLER: **La prego di parlare in italiano.**
Lah PREH-*goh dee pahr-*LAH-*reh een ee-tahl-*YAH-*noh.*
Please speak in Italian.

GUIDA: **Come vuole, signore. Dicevo che la grande**
KOH-*meh v'*WOH-*leh, seen-*YOH-*reh. Dee-*CHEH-*voh keh lah* GRAHN-*deh*
As you wish, sir. I was saying that the great

piazza dell'Esedra, che Lei ha veduto prima, era,
*p'*YAH-*tsah dehl-leh-*SEH-*drah, keh Lay* AH *veh-*DOO-*toh* PREE-*mah,* EH-*rah,*
square of Esedra, which you saw before, was

ai tempi antichi, parte delle terme.
igh TEHM-*pee ahn-*TEE-*kee,* PAHR-*teh* DEHL-*leh* TEHR-*meh.*
in ancient times, part of the baths.

In quella piazza i giovani facevano i loro
Een KWELL-*lah p'*YAH-*tsah ee* JOH-*vah-nee faht-*CHEH-*vah-noh ee* LOH-*roh*
In this square the young men had their

giuochi sportivi, mentre i vecchi sedevano
*joo-*OHK-*kee spohr-*TEE-*veh,* MEHN-*treh ee* VEHK-*kee seh-*DEH-*vah-noh*
games of sport, while the old men used to sit

sotto i colonnati, che circondano la piazza stessa,
SOHT-*toh ee koh-lohn*-NAH-*tee, keh cheer*-KOHN-*dah-noh lah* p'YAH-*tsah*
STEHS-*sah,*
under the colonnades which surround the square itself

ed assistivano ai giuochi, o parlavano di
ehd ahs-sees-TEE-*vah-noh igh joo*-OHK-*kee, oh pahr*-LAH-*vah-noh dee*
and watched the sports or spoke about

filosofia, di letteratura o di politica.
fee-loh-zoh-FEE-*ah, dee let-teh-rah*-TOO-*rah oh dee poh*-LEE-*tee-kah.*
philosophy, literature or politics.

MILLER: Allora, questa piazza era la palestra delle Terme.
Ahl-LOH-*rah,* KWESS-*tah* p'YAH-*tsah* EH-*rah lah pah*-LESS-*trah* DEHL-*leh*
TEHR-*meh.*
Then, this square was the gymnasium of the baths.

GUIDA: Proprio così. Ecco, entriamo nella chiesa di
PROH-*pr'yoh koh*-ZEE. ECK-*koh, ehn-tr'*YAH-*moh* NEHL-*lah* k'YEH-*zah deе*
Exactly so. Here we are entering the church of

Santa Maria degli Angeli. Questa era una delle
SAHN-*tah Mah*-REE-*ah* DEHL-*yee* AHN-*jeh-lee.* KWESS-*tah* EH-*rah* OO-*nah*
DEHL-*leh*
Saint Mary of the Angels. This was one of the

sale delle Terme, che il grande Michelangelo ha
SAH-*leh* DEHL-*leh* TEHR-*meh, keh eel* GRAHN-*deh Mee-kehl*-AHN-*jeh-loh* AH
rooms of the Baths, that the great Michelangelo has

trasformato in una delle più belle chiese d'Italia.
trahs-fohr-MAH-*toh een* OO-*nah* DEHL-*leh* p'YOO BELL-*leh* k'YEH-*zeh*
dee-TAHL-*yah.*
transformed into one of the most beautiful churches in Italy.

MILLER: Ma se questa chiesa non era che una delle sale
Mah seh KWESS-*tah* k'YEH-*zah noh*-NEH-*rah keh* OO-*nah* DEHL-*leh* SAH-*leh*
But if this church was only one of the rooms,

quanto era grande tutto l'edificio?
KWAHN-*toh* EH-*rah* GRAHN-*deh* TOOT-*toh leh-dee*-FEE-*ch'yoh?*
how big was the whole building?

GUIDA: Un quarto di miglio quadrato.
Oon KWAHR-*toh dee* MEEL-*l'yoh kwah*-DRAH-*toh.*
A quarter mile square.

MILLER: Quanti capolavori d'arte in questa chiesa!
KWAHN-*tee kah-poh-lah*-VOH-*ree* DAHR-*teh een* KWESS-*tah* k'YEH-*zah!*
How many masterpieces of art there are in this church!

GUIDA: **Eh, sì. Bastano a riempire un grande museo.**
EH, *see.* BAHS-*tah-noh ah ree-ehm-*PEE-*reh oon* GRAHN-*deh moo-*ZEH-*oh.*
Oh, yes. There are enough to fill a big museum.

Venga, usciamo da questa porta.
VEHN-*gah, oo-sh'*YAH-*moh dah* KWESS-*tah* POHR-*tah.*
Come, let's go out this door.

MILLER: **Che cosa sono tutti questi sedili di marmo?**
Keh KOH-*zah* SOH-*noh* TOOT-*tee* KWESS-*tee seh-*DEE-*lee dee* MAHR-*moh?*
What are all these marble seats?

GUIDA: **Erano per l'uso dei bagnanti, e ve n'erano**
EH-*rah-noh pehr* LOO-*zoh day bahn-n'*YAHN-*tee, eh veh* NEH-*rah-noh*
They were for the use of the bathers and there were

oltre 3.000. Nel centro di questa corte Lei vede
OHL-*treh treh-*MEE-*lah. Nehl* CHEHN-*troh dee* KWESS-*tah* KOHR-*teh Lay*
VEH-*deh*
over 3,000. In the center of this court you see

gli avanzi di ciò che a quei tempi era una piscina,
*l'yee ah-*VAHN-*tsee dee* CHOH *keh ah* KWAY-*ee tehm-*PEE *eh-rah* OO-*nah*
*pee-*SHEE-*nah,*
the remains of what in that time was a swimming pool,

lunga 200 piedi. Come Lei vede, era tutta in mosaico,
LOON-*gah* DOO-*eh-*CHEHN-*tee p'*YEH-*dee.* KOH-*meh Lay* VEH-*deh,* EH-*rah*
TOOT-*tah een moh-*ZIGH-*koh,*
200 feet long. As you see, it was all in mosaic,

circondata di statue di marmo,
*cheer-kohn-*DAH-*tah dee* STAH-*too-eh dee* MAHR-*moh,*
surrounded by marble statues,

e l'acqua calda originava da una sorgente naturale.
eh LAHK-*kwah* KAHL-*dah oh-ree-jee-*NAH-*vah dah* OO-*nah sohr-*JEHN-*teh*
*nah-too-*RAH-*leh.*
and the hot water came out of a natural spring.

MILLER: **Il sapone era già conosciuto in quell'epoca?**
*Eel sah-*POH-*neh* EH-*rah* JAH *koh-noh-*SHOO-*toh een kwell-*LEH-*poh-kah?*
Was soap known at that time?

GUIDA: **No, signore. I ricchi usavano degli olii e delle**
*Noh, seen-*YOH-*reh. Ee* REEK-*kee oo-*ZAH-*vah-noh* DEHL-*yee* OH-*lee-ee eh*
DEHL-*leh*
No, sir. The rich used oils and

pomate, mentre i poveri usavano farina di lenticchie.
*poh-*MAH-*teh,* MEHN-*treh ee* POH-*veh-ree oo-*ZAH-*vah-noh* faĥ-REE-*nah*
*dee lehn-*TEEK-*k'yeh.*
salves, while the poor used lentil flour.

NOTE on the Imperfect: The imperfect tense is used for the descriptive form and to denote something that *was happening* at a specific time in the past or to describe an action that *used to happen repeatedly.* This is the only Italian form for "used to". Ex: "When I was living in Florence, I used to eat always at the restaurant."—*Quando io abitavo a Firenze, mangiavo sempre al ristorante.*

To form the imperfect use the endings *-avo, -ava, -avamo, -avano,* attached to the root of the first conjugation verbs; in the second conjugation use the endings *-evo, -eva, -evamo, -evano.* In the third conjugation use the endings *-ivo, -iva, -ivamo, -ivano.* This rule cannot be applied to the auxiliary *essere*—"to be"; the imperfect of which is as follows: *ero, era, eravamo, erano.*

MILLER: **Mi dispiace dovere interrompere questa visita**
*Mee dees-p'*YAH-*cheh doh-*VEH-*reh een-tehr-*ROHM-*peh-reh* KWESS-*tah*
VEE-*zee-tah*
I am sorry to interrupt such an

interessante; cercherò di riprenderla domani,
*een-teh-rehs-*SAHN-*teh; chehr-keh-*ROH *dee ree-*PREHN-*dehr-lah*
*doh-*MAH-*nee,*
interesting visit; I shall try to take it up again tomorrow

ma adesso debbo andar via perchè ho un'appuntamento.
*mah ah-*DEHS-*soh* DEHB-*boh ahn-*DAHR *vee-ah* pehr-KEH OH
*oo-nahp-poon-tah-*MEHN-*toh.*
but now I must leave because I have an appointment.

(Miller paga la guida e si allontana.)
(Miller PAH-*gah lah* GWEE-*dah eh see ahl-lohn-*TAH-*nah.)*
(Miller pays the guide and goes off.)

THINKING IN ITALIAN

(Answers on page 296)

1. Come si chiama la piazza in cui si trovano le Terme di Diocleziano?
2. Che cosa era quella piazza ai tempi degli antichi romani?
3. Che cosa facevano i giovani romani in quella piazza?
4. Dove si sedevano gli anziani?
5. Qual'è il nome della chiesa dove la guida ed il signor Miller entrano?
6. Che cosa vede il signor Miller uscendo dalla chiesa?
7. Quanti erano i sedili di marmo?
8. Chi usava i sedili?
9. Che cosa si vede nel centro della corte?
10. Quanto era lunga la piscina?
11. Da dove originava l'acqua per la piscina?
12. Usavano sapone gli antichi romanti?

LEZIONE 41

Si accomodi
*See ahk-*KOH-*moh-dee*
Make yourself at home

MILLER: **La Sua casa è veramente bella, De Rossi.**
Lah SOO-*ah* KAH-*zah* EH *veh-rah-*MEHN-*teh* BELL-*lah, Deh* ROHS-*see.*
Your house is really beautiful, De Rossi.

DE ROSSI: **Grazie, è a Sua disposizione.**
GRAHTS-*yeh,* EH *ah* SOO-*ah dees-poh-zee-ts'*YOH-*neh.*
Thank you, it is at your disposal.

 NOTE on Politeness: If an Italian tells you that his house is at your disposal please don't move in it with your furniture. It is only an expression of politeness corresponding to the English: "Make yourself at home".

Oh! Ecco mia moglie.—Giovanna, ho il piacere
OH! ECK-*koh* MEE-*ah* MOH-*l'yeh.—Joh-*VAHN-*nah,* OH *eel p'yah-*CHEH-*reh*
Oh! Here is my wife.—Giovanna, I have the pleasure
258

di presentarti il mio caro amico John Miller,
*dee preh-zehn-*TAHR-*tee eel* MEE-*oh* KAH-*roh ah-*MEE-*koh John Miller,*
to present my dear friend John Miller,

di cui ti ho tanto parlato.
dee KOO-*ee tee* OH TAHN-*toh pahr-*LAH-*toh.*
of whom I have so often spoken to you.

SIGNORA DE ROSSI: **Sono veramente felice di fare,**
SOH-*noh veh-rah-*MEHN-*teh feh-*LEE-*cheh dee* FAH-*reh,*
I am really happy to make

finalmente, la Sua conoscenza.
*fee-nahl-*MEHN-*teh, lah* SOO-*ah koh-noh-*SHEHN-*tsah.*
your acquaintance at last.

MILLER: **Lei è molto buona, signora, e debbo aggiungere**
Lay EH MOHL-*toh b'*WOH-*nah, seen-*YOH-*rah, eh* DEHB-*boh*
*ah-*DJOON-*jeh-reh*
You are very kind, madam, and I must add

che il piacere è tutto mio.
*keh eel p'yah-*CHEH-*reh* EH TOOT-*toh* MEE-*oh.*
that the pleasure is all mine.

SIGNORA DE ROSSI: **Prego, si accomodi. Le piace Roma?**
PREH-*goh, see ahk-*KOH-*moh-dee. Leh p'*YAH-*cheh* ROH-*mah?*
Please, make yourself at home. Do you like Rome?

MILLER: **Ne sono affascinato, signora, e nel breve tempo**
Neh SOH-*noh ahf-fah-shee-*NAH-*toh, seen-*YOH-*rah, eh nehl* BREH-*veh*
TEHM-*poh*
I am fascinated with it, madam, and in the short time

che starò qui mi prometto di approfittare di tutte
*keh stah-*ROH *kwee mee proh-*MEHT-*toh dee ahp-proh-feet-*TAH-*reh dee*
TOOT-*teh*
that I shall be here I promise myself to make use of all

le mie ore libere per meglio conoscere la città.
leh MEE-*eh* OH-*reh* LEE-*beh-reh pehr* MEH-*l'yoh koh-*NOH-*sheh-reh lah*
*cheet-*TAH.
my free hours to know the city better.

SIGNORA DE ROSSI: **Ma dove ha imparato Lei a parlare**
Mah DOH-*veh* AH *eem-pah-*RAH-*toh Lay ah pahr-*LAH-*reh*
But where did you learn to speak

l'italiano così bene?
*lee-tahl-*YAH-*noh koh-*ZEE BEH-*neh?*
Italian so well?

DE ROSSI: **Non te lo dicevo, Giovanna, che Miller**
*Nohn teh loh dee-*CHEH-*voh, Joh-*VAHN-*nah, keh Miller*
Didn't I tell you, Giovanna, that Miller

parla benissimo l'italiano?
PAHR-*lah beh-*NEES-*see-moh lee-tahl-*YAH-*noh?*
speaks Italian extremely well?

MILLER: **L'italiano m'è sempre piaciuto, e l'anno scorso,**
*Lee-tahl-*YAH-*noh* MEH SEHM-*preh p'yah-*CHOO-*toh, eh* LAHN-*noh*
SKOHR-*soh,*
I have always liked Italian and last year,

quando ho cominciato a trattare affari con il Governo
KWAHN-*doh* OH *koh-meen-*CHAH-*to ah traht-*TAH-*reh ahf-*FAH-*ree kohn*
*eel Goh-*VEHR-*noh*
when I began to do business with the Italian

Italiano, ho deciso di prendere un corso alla
*Ee-tahl-*YAH-*noh,* OH *deh-*CHEE-*zoh dee* PREHN-*deh-reh oon* KOHR-*soh*
AHL-*lah*
Government, I decided to take a course at

Scuola Berlitz, di Boston, e debbo confessare che il
*sk'*WOH-*lah* BEHR-*leets, dee Boston, eh* DEHB-*boh kohn-fehs-*SAH-*reh keh*
eel
the Berlitz School of Boston, and I must confess that the

risultato è stato più che soddisfacente
*ree-zool-*TAH-*toh* EH STAH-*toh p'*YOO *keh sohd-dees-fah-*CHEHN-*teh.*
result was more than satisfactory.

DE ROSSI: **Dica piuttosto che il risultato è stato sbalorditivo!**
DEE-*kah p'yoot-*TOSS-*toh keh eel ree-zool-*TAH-*toh* EH STAH-*toh*
*sbah-lohr-dee-*TEE-*voh!*
Say rather that the result has been astounding!

PEPPINO: **Papà, è questo il signore che viene**
*Pah-*PAH, EH KWESS-*toh eel seen-*YOH-*reh keh v'*YEH-*neh*
Papa, is this the gentleman who comes

dall'America ed ha sempre appetito?
*dahl-lah-*MEH-*ree-kah ehd* AH SEHM-*preh ahp-peh-*TEE-*toh?*
from America and who is always hungry?

DE ROSSI: **Peppino! Chi ti ha dato il permesso di entrare**
*Pehp-*PEE-*noh! Kee tee* AH DAH-*toh eel pehr-*MEHS-*soh dee ehn-*TRAH-*reh*
Peppino! Who gave you permission to enter

in salotto? (A Miller) Scusi, sa....
*een sah-*LOHT-*toh? (Ah Miller)* SKOO-*zee, sah ....*
the living room? (To Miller) Excuse us, you see ....

MILLER: (Ridendo di tutto cuore) Ma non si preoccupi!
(*Ree-*DEHN-*doh dee* TOOT-*toh k'*WOH-*reh*) *Mah nohn see
preh-*OHK-*koo-pee!*
(Laughing wholeheartedly) But don't worry!

È il Suo bambino?
EH *eel* SOO-*oh bahm-*BEE-*noh?*
Is this your youngster?

DE ROSSI: Questo è il più piccolo dei nostri tre bambini.
KWESS-*toh* EH *eel p'*YOO PEEK-*koh-loh day* NOHS-*tree treh bahm-*BEE-*nee.*
This is the smallest of our three children.

Ha solamente quattro anni e parla più di un
AH *soh-lah-*MEHN-*teh* KWAHT-*troh* AHN-*nee eh* PAHR-*lah p'*YOO *dee oon*
He is only four years old and talks more than a

avvocato in tribunale. Ma Le assicuro che io non
*ahv-voh-*KAH-*toh een tree-boo-*NAH-*leh. Mah Leh ahs-see-*KOO-*roh keh
ee-oh nohn*
lawyer in court. But I assure you that I have

ho mai detto che Lei ha sempre appetito; solamente
OH *migh* DEHT-*toh keh Lay* AH SEHM-*preh ahp-peh-*TEE-*toh;
soh-lah-*MEHN-*teh*
never said that you were always hungry; I only

ho raccontato a mia moglie come Lei abbia
OH *rahk-kohn-*TAH-*toh ah* MEE-*ah* MOH-*l'yeh* KOH-*meh Lay* AHB-*b'yah*
told my wife how you

sofferto la fame durante il viaggio da Milano a Roma.
*sohf-*FEHR-*toh lah* FAH-*meh doo-*RAHN-*teh eel vee-*AH-*djoh dah
Mee-*LAH-*noh ah* ROH-*mah.*
suffered from hunger during the trip from Milan to Rome.

MILLER: In fondo, signora De Rossi, è proprio vero
Een FOHN-*doh, seen-*YOH-*rah Deh* ROHS-*see,* EH PROH-*pree-oh* VEH-*roh*
To tell the truth, Mrs. De Rossi, it's really true

che da quando sono in Italia ho sempre appetito.
keh dah KWAHN-*doh* SOH-*noh een Ee-*TAHL-*yah* OH SEHM-*preh
ahp-peh-*TEE-*toh.*
that since I've been in Italy, I'm always hungry.

SIGNORA DE ROSSI: Sarà effetto del cambiamento d'aria.
*Sah-*RAH *ehf-*FEHT-*toh dehl kahm-b'yah-*MEHN-*toh* DAH-*r'yah.*
It is probably the effect of the change of air.

MILLER: O della buona cucina! . . . . Vieni, vieni Peppino,
Oh DEHL-*lah b'*WOH-*nah koo-*CHEE-*nah! . . . . v'*YEH-*nee, v'*YEH-*nee
Pehp-*PEE-*noh,*
Or of the good food! . . . . Come, come Peppino,

diamoci la mano. Vuoi venire con me in America?
*d'*YAH-*moh-chee lah* MAH-*noh. v'*WOY *veh-*NEE-*reh kohn meh een
Ah-*MEH-*ree-kah?*
let's shake hands. Do you want to come with me to America?

PEPPINO: **Se mi farai giocare coi cow-boys. Ma forse la mamma**
*Seh mee fah-*RIGH *joh-*KAH-*reh koy cow-boys. Mah* FOHR-*seh lah*
MAHM-*mah*
If you let me play with the cowboys. But perhaps my mother

non mi lascerà venire. Io ho una bella pistola,
*nohn mee lah-sheh-*RAH *veh-*NEE-*reh.* EE-*oh* OH OO-*nah* BELL-*lah*
*pees-*TOH-*lah,*
will not let me come. I have a beautiful pistol,

tutta d'argento col manico di madreperla.
TOOT-*tah dahr-*JEHN-*toh kohl* MAH-*nee-koh dee mah-dreh-*PEHR-*lah.*
all of silver with a mother of pearl handle.

DE ROSSI: **Bene, bene. Adesso vai a chiamare le tue**
BEH-*neh,* BEH-*neh. Ah-*DEHS-*soh vigh ah k'yah-*MAH-*reh leh* TOO-*eh*
All right, all right. Now go to call your

sorelline e di' loro di venire in salotto.
*soh-rehl-*LEE-*neh eh* DEE LOH-*roh dee veh-*NEE-*reh een sah-*LOHT-*toh.*
sisters and tell them to come into the parlor.

MILLER: **Oh! Che belle bambine! Dimmi, bella biondina, come ti chiami?**
OH! *Keh* BELL-*leh bahm-*BEE-*neh!* DEEM-*mee,* BELL-*lah b'yohn-*DEE-*nah,*
KOH-*meh tee k'*YAH-*mee?*
Oh! What beautiful children. Tell me, my beautiful blonde one, what
is your name?

 NOTE to Student: "What is your name" can be translated
by: *Qual'è il Suo nome?* but the most popular form is:
Come si chiama Lei? The literal translation would be:
"How do you call yourself?" Ex: "My name is Giovanni."—
Mi chiamo Giovanni.

ROSABIANCA: **Mi chiamo Rosabianca De Rossi.**
*Roh-zah-b'*YAHN-*kah: Mee k'*YAH-*moh Roh-zah-b'*YAHN-*kah Deh* ROHS-*see.*
I am called Rosabianca De Rossi.

MILLER: **Che bel nome! E tu, bella bruna, come ti chiami?**
Keh bell NOH-*meh! Eh too,* BELL-*lah* BROO-*nah,* KOH-*meh tee k'*YAH-*mee?*
What a beautiful name! And you, my beautiful brunette, what is your
name?

ROSALBA: **Mi chiamo Rosalba, signore.**
*Roh-*ZAHL*-bah: Mee k'*YAH*-moh Roh-*ZAHL*-bah, seen-*YOH*-reh.*
I am called Rosalba, sir.

MILLER: **E quanti anni hai?**
Eh KWAHN*-tee* AHN*-nee igh?*
And how old are you?

REMEMBER: "How old are you?" is translated by: *Quanti anni ha?*—"How many years have you?"

ROSALBA: **Otto anni, signore.**
OHT*-toh* AHN*-nee, seen-*YOH*-reh.*
Eight years old, sir.

SIGNORA DE ROSSI: **E Lei, signor Miller, ha figli?**
*Eh Lay, seen-*YOHR *Miller,* AH FEE*-l'yee?*
And you, Mr. Miller, have you children?

MILLER: **No, signora, io sono scapolo. Dovrei essere sposato,**
*Noh, seen-*YOH*-rah,* EE*-oh* SOH*-noh* SKAH*-poh-loh. Doh-*VRAY EHS*-seh-reh spoh-*ZAH*-toh,*
No, madam, I am a bachelor. I should be married,

ma non ho mai avuto il tempo d'innamorarmi.
*mah noh-*NOH *migh ah-*VOO*-toh eel* TEHM*-poh deen-nah-moh-*RAHR*-mee.*
but I have never had the time to fall in love.

(I bambini si allontanano)
*(Ee bahm-*BEE*-nee see ahl-lohn-*TAH*-nah-noh)*
(The children go out)

NOTE on the Conditional: This verb form is used to express whatever is not absolute, but dependent on a condition. It applies in Italian sentences in the same manner in which the words "would", "should" and "could" apply in English sentences. Ex: "I would like"—*Mi piacerebbe.* "I should refuse it"—*Io dovrei rifiutarlo.* "I couldn't possibly come"—*Non potrei assolutamente venire.*

DE ROSSI: **Non si scoraggi; è ancora in tempo.**
*Nohn see skoh-*RAH*-djee;* EH *ahn-*KOH*-rah een* TEHM*-poh.*
Don't be discouraged; there is still time.

Le piacerebbe bere un vermouth o un americano?
*Leh p'yah-cheh-*REHB-*beh* BEH-*reh oon* VEHR-*moot oh oon ah-meh-ree-*KAH-*noh?*
Would you like to drink a vermouth or an "americano"?

MILLER: **Preferirei un americano, grazie.**
*Preh-feh-ree-*RAY *oon ah-meh-ree-*KAH-*noh,* GRAHTS-*yeh.*
I would prefer an "americano", thank you.

DE ROSSI: **(alla moglie) Tu, cara, che vorresti?**
(AHL-*lah* MOH-*l'yeh) Too,* KAH-*rah, keh vohr-*REHS-*tee?*
(to his wife) You, dear, what would you like?

IMPORTANT NOTE: The pronouns *tu,* instead of *Lei,* and *te* and *ti,* instead of *se* and *La,* are used when addressing children, members of your own family and very intimate friends. The verb form accompanying these pronouns can be constructed by following these rules: When the verb form used with *Lei* ends with an *a* and the accent falls on the last syllable of the verb you simply add an *i.* Ex: *Lei dà, tu dai. Lei fa, tu fai. Lei va, tu vai. Lei scriverà, tu scriverai.* etc. If it ends with *ia* you eliminate the *a.* Ex: *Lei mangia, tu mangi. Lei viaggia, tu viaggi,* etc. In all other cases change the last vowel into an *i.* Ex: *Lei scrive, tu scrivi. Lei prende, tu prendi. Lei viene, tu vieni. Lei cammina, tu cammini,* etc.
In addressing Mr. Miller, Peppino uses *tu* instead of *Lei* because he is too young to know the difference.

SIGNORA DE ROSSI: **Anch'io vorrei un americano.**
*Ahn-*KEE-*oh vohr-*RAY *oon ah-meh-ree-*KAH-*noh.*
I too would like an "americano".

DE ROSSI: **Debbo prepararne uno anche per Amalia?**
DEHB-*boh preh-pah-*RAHR-*neh* OO-*noh* AHN-*keh pehr Ah-*MAH-*l'yah?*
Should I make another one for Amalia?

SIGNORA DE ROSSI: **Se vuoi. Intanto io vado a chiamarla.**
*Seh v'*WOY. *Een-*TAHN-*toh* EE-*oh* VAH-*doh ah k'yah-*MAHR-*lah.*
If you wish. Meanwhile I'll go to call her.

DE ROSSI: **Amalia è mia cognata, una sorella di mia moglie,**
*Ah-*MAH-*l'yah* EH MEE-*ah kohn-n'*YAH-*tah,* OO-*nah soh-*REHL-*lah dee* MEE-*ah* MOH-*l'yeh,*
Amalia is my sister-in-law, a sister of my wife,

che è rimasta vedova durante l'ultima guerra.
keh EH *ree-*MAHS-*tah* VEH-*doh-vah doo-*RAHN-*teh* LOOL-*tee-mah* GWEHR-*rah.*
who became a widow during the last war.

Signora De Rossi: (entrando con Amalia)
(*ehn*-TRAHN-*doh kohn Ah*-MAH-*l'yah*)
(entering with Amalia)

Amalia, permettimi di presentarti il
Ah-MAH-*l'yah, pehr*-MET-*tee-mee dee preh-zehn*-TAHR-*tee eel*
Amalia, permit me to introduce to you

signor Miller, un vecchio amico di Giorgio.
seen-YOHR *Miller, oon* VEHK-*k'yoh ah*-MEE-*koh dee* JOHR-*joh.*
Mr. Miller, an old friend of George's.

Amalia: (a Miller, che si è alzato)
(*ah Miller, keh see* EH *ahl*-TSAH-*toh*)
(to Miller, who has risen)

Tanto piacere, signor Miller; si accomodi, La prego.
TAHN-*toh p'yah*-CHEH-*reh, seen*-YOHR *Miller; see ahk*-KOH-*moh-dee, Lah*
PREH-*goh.*
A great pleasure, Mr. Miller, sit down please.

(Miller, che non ha saputo nascondere la sua sorpresa,
(*Miller, keh noh*-NAH *sah*-POO-*toh nahs*-KOHN-*deh-reh lah* SOO-*ah*
sohr-PREH-*zah,*
(Miller, who hasn't been able to hide his surprise

rimane muto e guarda Amalia, estatico.)
ree-MAH-*neh* MOO-*toh eh* GWAHR-*dah Ah*-MAH-*l'yah ehs*-TAH-*tee-koh.*)
remains silent and looks at Amalia ecstatically.)

De Rossi: (a Miller) Le piace...
(*ah Miller*) *Leh p'*YAH-*cheh*...
(to Miller) Do you like...

Miller: (sottovoce) Altro che! Non ho visto una donna
(*soht-toh*-VOH-*cheh*) AHL-*troh keh! Noh*-NOH VEES-*toh* OO-*nah* DOHN-*nah*
(in a low voice) More than that! I haven't seen such a beautiful

così bella dall'ultima volta che ho guardato
koh-ZEE BELL-*lah dahl*-LOOL-*tee-mah* VOHL-*tah keh* OH *gwahr*-DAH-*toh*
lady since I last looked at

le illustrazioni in un libro di fate.
*leh eel-loos-trah-ts'*YOH-*nee een oon* LEE-*broh dee* FAH-*teh.*
the pictures in a book of fairy tales.

De Rossi: Ma no! Io Le domando se Le piace l'americano.
Mah noh! EE-*oh Leh doh*-MAHN-*doh seh Leh p'*YAH-*cheh*
*lah-meh-ree-*KAH-*noh.*
But no! I asked you if you liked the "americano."

MILLER: **L'americano? Che americano? .... Oh, sì, è buonissimo.**
*Lah-meh-ree-*KAH*-noh? Keh ah-meh-ree-*KAH*-noh? .... *OH*, see,*
EH *b'woh-*NEES*-see-moh.*
The "americano"? What "americano"? .... Oh yes, it is very good.

CAMERIERA: **Signora, la cena è servita.**
*Kah-meh-r'*YEH*-rah:* Seen-YOH-rah, lah CHEH-nah EH sehr-VEE-tah.
MAID: Madam, dinner is served.

DE ROSSI: **Andiamo a mangiare. (a Miller) E speriamo che**
*Ahn-d'*YAH*-moh ah mahn-*JAH*-reh. (ah Miller) Eh speh-r'*YAH*-moh keh*
Let us go in and dine. (to Miller) And let's hope

Le piaccia la nostra cucina.
*Leh p'*YAH*-chah lah* NOHS*-trah koo-*CHEE*-nah.*
you like our cooking.

MILLER: **Dagli odori che sento non posso dubitare**
DAHL*-yee oh-*DOH*-ree keh* SEHN*-toh nohn* POHS*-soh doo-bee-*TAH*-reh*
From the odor I smell I cannot doubt

della bontà dei cibi.
DEHL*-lah bohn-*TAH *day* CHEE*-bee.*
that the food is good.

SIGNORA DE ROSSI: **In questo caso voglio sperare che gli**
Een KWESS*-toh* KAH*-zoh* VOHL*-l'yoh speh-*RAH*-reh keh l'yee*
In this case I hope that the

odori non siano solamente un'illusione.
*oh-*DOH*-ree nohn s'*YAH*-noh soh-lah-*MEHN*-teh oon-eel-loo-z'*YOH*-neh*,
odor is not only an illusion.

(Le due signore vanno avanti)
(Leh DOO*-eh seen-*YOH*-reh* VAHN*-noh ah-*VAHN*-tee)*
(The two ladies go first)

NOTE on the Subjunctive: The present tense form of the subjunctive is the same as the imperative form, but instead of expressing a direct command it expresses your desire, your wish, your hope for some condition to materialize. Ex: "I wish you to come with me"—*Io desidero che Lei venga con me.* "I wish you a quick recovery"—*Le auguro che guarisca presto.* "I hope that he succeeds"—*Spero che egli riesca.* This form is also used after expressions of feeling, emotions and moods in general. Ex: "I am sorry that you don't feel well"—*Mi dispiace che Lei non si senta bene.* "What a shame that you should leave so soon"—*Che peccato che Lei debba andar via così presto.* "I fear that his illness is very serious"—*Temo che la sua malattia sia molto grave.* "I am glad that you like it"—*Sono contento che Le piaccia.*

DE ROSSI: **Sono contento che mia cognata abbia preparato**
SOH-*noh* *kohn*-TEHN-*toh* *keh* MEE-*ah* *kohn-n'*YAH-*tah* AHB-*b'yah*
*preh-pah-*RAH-*toh*
I am happy that my sister-in-law made

il dolce, che è una delle sue specialità.
eel DOHL-*cheh, keh* EH OO-*nah* DEHL-*leh* SOO-*eh* *speh-ch'yah-lee-*TAH.
the dessert, which is one of her specialties.

MILLER: **Dev'essere la torta degli angeli.**
*Deh-*VESS-*seh-reh lah* TOHR-*tah* DEHL-*yee* AHN-*jeh-lee.*
It must be angel cake.

DE ROSSI: **Che cosa sarebbe la torta degli angeli?**
Keh KOH-*zah sah-*REHB-*beh lah* TOHR-*tah* DEHL-*yee* AHN-*jeh-lee?*
What could that be, angel cake?

MILLER: **Non so se in Italia esista questa specialità,**
*Nohn so seh een Ee-*TAHL-*yah eh-*ZEES-*tah* KWESS-*tah speh-ch'yah-lee-*TAH.
I don't know whether this specialty exists in Italy

ma negli Stati Uniti abbiamo una torta
mah NEHL-*yee* STAH-*tee* On-NEE-*teh ahb-b'*YAH-*moh* OO-*nah* TOHR-*tah*
but in the United States we have a cake

chiamata: Angel-Food Cake.
*k'yah-*MAH-*tah Angel-Food Cake.*
named "Angel-Food Cake."

DE ROSSI: **Ma scusi, che cosa Le fa credere che Amalia**
Mah SKOO-*zee, keh* KOH-*zah Leh fah* KREH-*deh-reh keh Ah-*MAH-*l'yah*
Excuse me, what makes you think that Amalia

abbia preparato il dolce che Lei dice?
AHB-*b'yah preh-pah-*RAH-*toh eel* DOHL-*cheh keh Lay* DEE-*cheh?*
made the kind of cake you mention?

MILLER: **Il fatto che essa sembra un angelo disceso sulla terra.**
Eel FAHT-*toh keh* ESS-*sah* SEHM-*brah oon* AHN-*jeh-loh dee-*SHEH-*zoh*
SOOL-*lah* TEHR-*rah.*
The fact that she seems to be an angel come down to earth.

DE ROSSI: **Bravo Miller! Ed io che non sospettavo**
BRAH-*voh Miller! Ehd* EE-*oh keh nohn sohs-peht-*TAH-*voh*
Bravo Miller! And I, who didn't suspect such

tanto romanticismo in un uomo d'affari,
TAHN-*toh roh-mahn-tee-*CHEES-*moh een oon oo-oh-moh dahf-*FAH-*ree,*
a romantic nature in a business man,

ed americano per giunta! Comincio a credere
*ehd ah-meh-ree-*KAH*-noh pehr* JOON*-tah!* *Koh-*MEENT*-choh ah*
KREH*-deh-reh*
and an American besides! I begin to think

che Lei sia peggio dei latini.
Keh Lay SEE*-ah* PEH*-djoh day lah-*TEE*-nee.*
that you are worse than the Latins.

MILLER: Caro De Rossi, le grandi ispirazioni hanno
KAH*-roh Deh* ROHS*-see, leh* GRAHN*-dee ees-pee-rah-ts'*YOH*-nee* AHN*-noh*
My dear De Rossi, great inspirations have

creato i grandi poeti . . . . Dica, Amalia
*kreh-*AH*-toh ee* GRAHN*-dee poh-*EH*-tee* . . . . DEE*-kah, Ah-*MAH*-l'yah*
created great poets. . . . Tell me, will

verrà con noi all'opera dopo cena?
*vehr-*RAH *kohn noy ahl-*LOH*-peh-rah* DOH*-poh* CHEH*-nah?*
Amalia come with us to the opera after dinner?

DE ROSSI: Certamente!
*Chehr-tah-*MEHN*-teh!*
Certainly!

MILLER: Meno male.
MEH*-noh* MAH*-leh.*
Thank goodness!

IDIOMS TO REMEMBER:
In fondo, meaning "at the end of this", or "at the bottom
of this".
Diamoci la mano.—"Let's shake hands".
Meno male.—"Thank goodness". (An understatement mean-
ing literally "Less bad".)
Altro che!—"And how!", "More than that", "Emphatically
yes!"

THINKING IN ITALIAN
(Answers on page 296)

1. Che cosa dice la signora De Rossi al suo invitato?
2. Come si chiama la signora De Rossi?
3. Quanti figli hanno i signori De Rossi?
4. Come si chiama il più piccolo?
5. Quante sorelle ha Peppino?
6. Come mai il signor Miller parla così bene l'italiano?
7. È il signor Miller offeso di ciò che dice Peppino?
8. Perchè non è sposato il signor Miller?
9. Come si chiama un uomo che non sia sposato?
10. Che cosa preferisce bere il signor Miller?
11. Come si chiama la cognata del signor De Rossi?
12. Come si chiama una donna che ha perduto il marito?
13. Come rimane il signor Miller quando vede Amalia?
14. È Amalia bella o brutta?
15. Che cosa annuncia la cameriera?
16. Andrà Amalia all'opera con gli altri?

Povera Tosca!
POH-*veh-rah* TOHS-*kah!*
Poor Tosca!

(In macchina, andando a teatro)
(*Een* MAHK-*kee-nah, ahn-*DAHN-*doh ah teh-*AH-*troh*)
(In the car, going to the theatre)

MILLER: **Che macchina è questa, De Rossi?**
Keh MAHK-*kee-nah* EH KWESS-*tah, Deh* ROHS-*see?*
What kind of car is this, De Rossi?

Non ne ho mai veduta una simile.
Nohn neh OH *migh veh-*DOO-*tah* OO-*nah* SEE-*mee-leh.*
I never saw one like it.

DE ROSSI: **È una Isotta Fraschini. Le piace?**
EH OO-*nah Ee-*ZOHT-*tah Frahs-*KEE-*nee. Leh* p'YAH-*cheh?*
It is an Isotta Fraschini. Do you like it?

MILLER: È splendida! È di quest'anno?
EH SPLEHN-*dee-dah!* EH *dee* KWESS-TAHN-*noh?*
It is splendid. Is it this year's?

DE ROSSI: Ma che! La comprai 7 anni fa, ma questo
*Mah keh! Lah kohm-*PRIGH *set-*teh AHN-*nee fah, mah* KWESS-*toh*
Of course not! I bought it 7 years ago, but this

è un tipo di macchina che si conserva in
EH oon TEE-*poh dee* MAHK-*kee-nah keh see kohn-*SEHR-*vah een*
is a type of car that stays in

buone condizioni per molti e molti anni.
*b'*WOH-*neh kohn-dee-ts'*YOH-*nee pehr* MOHL-*tee eh* MOHL-*tee* AHN-*nee.*
good condition for many, many years.

MILLER: Troverà posto per stazionare la macchina
*Troh-veh-*RAH POHS-*toh pehr stah-ts'yoh-*NAH-*reh lah* MAHK-*kee-nah*
Will you find a place to park the car

vicino al teatro?
*vee-*CHEE-*noh ahl teh-*AH-*troh?*
near the theatre?

DE ROSSI: Anche se vi fosse posto, non si potrebbe
AHN-*keh seh vee* FOHS-*seh* POHS-*toh, nohn see poh-*TREHB-*beh*
Even if there were a place we couldn't

lasciarla vicino al teatro perchè è proibito.
*lah-*SHAHR-*lah vee-*CHEE-*noh ahl teh-*AH-*troh pehr-*KEH EH
*proh-*EE-*bee-toh.*
leave it near the theatre because it is prohibited.

Ma Ennio, il nostro autista, si occuperà di ciò.
Mah EHN-*n'yoh, eel* NOHS-*troh aou-*TEES-*tah, see ohk-koo-peh-*RAH *dee*
CHOH.
But, Ennio, our chauffeur will take care of that.

AMALIA: Vede, signor Miller, quel grande edificio scuro
*VEH-*deh, *seen-*YOHR *Miller, kwell* GRAHN-*deh eh-dee-*FEE-*ch'yoh* SKOO-*roh*
Mr. Miller, do you see that large dark building

che si delinea nel chiarore lunare?
*keh see deh-*LEE-*neh-ah nehl k'yah-*ROH-*reh loo-*NAH-*reh?*
which stands out against the moonlight?

MILLER: Mi sembra un castello.
Mee SEHM-*brah oon kahs-*TELL-*loh.*
It seems to me to be a castle.

AMALIA: Per l'appunto. È il Castel Sant'Angelo; ed è lì
*Pehr lahp-*POON-*toh.* EH *eel Kahs-*TELL *Sahn-*TAHN-*jeh-loh; ehd* EH *lee*
Exactly. It is the Castle of St. Angelo, and there is

che si svolgono molte scene dell'opera
keh see SVOHL-*goh-noh* MOHL-*teh* SHEH-*neh dehl*-LOH-*peh-rah*
where many scenes of the opera which we

che sentiremo stasera.
keh sehn-tee-REH-*moh stah*-SEH-*rah.*
shall see this evening will take place.

(Arrivano a teatro)
(*Ahr*-REE-*vah-noh ah teh*-AH-*troh*)
(They arrive at the theatre)

MILLER: Dall'aspetto esterno di questo teatro non avrei
Dahl-lahs-PET-*toh ehs*-TEHR-*noh dee* KWESS-*toh teh*-AH-*troh nohn ah*-VRAY
From the outside view of this theatre I never would

mai sospettato tanto splendore nell'interno.
migh sohs-peht-TAH-*toh* TAHN-*toh splehn*-DOH-*reh nehl-leen*-TEHR-*noh.*
have suspected such splendor inside.

Sembra tutto d'oro; e quanta gente! Quanta eleganza!
SEHM-*brah* TOOT-*toh* DOH-*roh; eh* KWAHN-*tah* JEHN-*teh!* KWAHN-*tah
eh-leh*-GAHN-*tsah!*
It seems all of gold, and so many people! So much elegance!

DE ROSSI: Tutto è coperto con foglie d'oro zecchino.
TOOT-*toh* EH *koh*-PEHR-*toh kohn* FOHL-*l'yeh* DOH-*roh dzehk*-KEE-*noh.*
Everything is covered with fine gold leaf.

(L'orchestra intona l'inno nazionale americano
(*Lohr*-KEHS-*trah een*-TOH-*nah* LEEN-*noh nah-ts'yoh*-NAH-*leh
ah-meh-ree*-KAH-*noh*
(The orchestra strikes up the American national anthem

ed il pubblico scatta in piedi.)
ehd eel POOB-*lee-koh* SKAHT-*tah een p'*YEH-*dee.*)
and the public jumps to its feet.)

DE ROSSI: (Continuando, sottovoce a Miller)
(*Kohn-tee-noo*-AHN-*doh, soht-toh*-VOH-*cheh ah Miller*)
(Continuing, in a low voice to Miller)

Come fanno a sapere che Lei è in teatro?
KOH-*meh* FAHN-*noh ah sah*-PEH-*reh keh Lay* EH *een teh*-AH-*troh?*
How do they know that you are in the theatre?

(Miller, rigidamente sull'attenti,
(*Miller, ree-jee-dah*-MEHN-*teh sool-laht*-TEHN-*tee,*
(Miller, rigidly at attention,

risponde con uno sguardo
rees-POHN-*deh kohn* OO-*noh* SGWAHR-*doh*
replies with a look

che sembra dire: Questa volta non ci casco.
keh SEHM-*brah* DEE-*reh:* KWESS-*tah* VOHL-*tah nohn chee* KAHS-*koh.*
which seems to say: "I won't fall for it this time".

Finisce l'inno italiano che ha fatto
*Fee-*NEE-*sheh* LEEN-*noh ee-tahl-*YAH-*noh keh* AH FAHT-*toh*
The Italian hymn, which has followed

sequito a quello americano. Il pubblico applaude
SEH-*gwee-toh ah* KWELL-*loh ah-meh-ree-*KAH-*noh. Eel* POOB-*blee-koh*
*ahp-*PLAOU-*deh*
the American hymn, is finished. The public applauds

guardando in direzione del palco reale.)
*gwahr-*DAHN-*doh een dee-reh-ts'*YOH-*neh dehl* PAHL-*koh reh-*AH-*leh.)*
looking in the direction of the royal box.)

SIGNORA DE ROSSI: Questa rappresentazione è in onore
KWESS-*tah rahp-preh-zehn-tah-ts'*YOH-*neh* EH *een oh-*NOH-*reh*
This show is in honor

del Ministro degli Esteri americano
*dehl Mee-*NEES-*troh* DEHL-*yee* EHS-*teh-ree ah-meh-ree-*KAH-*noh,*
of the American Secretary of State,

che è ospite del Governo Italiano.
keh EH OHS-*pee-teh dehl Goh-*VEHR-*noh Ee-tahl-*YAH-*noh.*
who is the guest of the Italian Government.

MILLER: Lei, De Rossi, coglie tutte le occasioni
Lay, Deh ROHS-*see,* KOHL-*yeh* TOOT-*teh leh ohk-kah-z'*YOH-*nee*
You, De Rossi, seize every opportunity

per burlarsi di me.
*pehr boor-*LAHR-*see dee meh.*
to make fun of me.

(Le luci si abbassano, incomincia lo spettacolo)
(Leh LOO-*chee see ahb-*BAHS-*sah-noh, een-koh-*MEENT-*chah loh
speh-*TAHK-*koh-loh)*
(The lights go down, the show starts)

        (Finisce il primo atto.)
        *(Fee-*NEE-*sheh eel* PREE-*moh* AHT-*toh.)*
        (The first act finishes.)

AMALIA: (a Miller) Non le pare che Gigli sia veramente bravo
        (ah Miller) Nohn leh PAH-*reh keh* JEEL-*l'yee* SEE-*ah veh-rah-*MEHN-*teh*
        BRAH-*voh*
        (to Miller) Don't you think that Gigli is really good

nella parte di Mario Cavaradossi?
NEHL-*lah* PAHR-*teh dee* MAH-*r'yoh Kah-vah-rah-*DOHS-*see?*
in the part of Mario Cavaradossi?

MILLER: **Senza dubbio è veramente straordinario.**
SEHN-*tsah* DOOB-*b'yoh* EH *veh-rah-*MEHN-*teh strah-ohr-dee-*NAH-*r'yoh.*
Without a doubt he is really extraordinary.

La Maria Caniglia nella parte di Tosca è insuperabile.
*Lah Mah-*REE-*ah Kah-*NEEL-*yah* NEHL-*lah* PAHR-*teh dee* TOHS-*kah* EH
*een-soo-peh-*RAH-*bee-leh.*
Maria Caniglia in the role of Tosca is unsurpassable.

Che bella voce pastosa, drammatica!
Keh BELL-*lah* VOH-*cheh* pahs-TOH-*zah, drahm-*MAH-*tee-kah!*
What a mellow and dramatic voice!

DE ROSSI: **Andiamo tutti al bar a bere un cognac?**
*Ahn-d'*YAH-*moh* TOOT-*tee ahl bahr ah* BEH-*reh oon kohn-*YAHK?
Let's all go to the bar to have a cognac?

MILLER: **Se non fosse proibito fumare in palco**
Seh nohn FOHS-*seh proh-*EE-*bee-toh foo-*MAH-*reh een* PAHL-*koh*
If it weren't prohibited to smoke in the box

preferirei rimanere qui ad ammirare
*preh-feh-ree-*RAY *ree-mah-*NEH-*reh kwee ahd ahm-mee-*RAH-*reh*
I would prefer to remain here to admire

la decorazione di questa bellissima sala.
*lah deh-koh-rah-ts'*YOH-*neh dee* KWESS-*tah bell-*LEES-*see-mah* SAH-*lah.*
the decorations of this beautiful hall.

AMALIA: **Andiamo al bar adesso; resterà in palco durante**
*Ahn-d'*YAH-*moh ahl bahr ah-*DEHS-*soh; rehs-teh-*RAH *een* PAHL-*koh*
*doo-*RAHN-*teh*
Let's go to the bar now; you can stay in the box during

il prossimo intermezzo ed io Le terrò compagnia.
eel PROHS-*see-moh een-tehr-*MEH-*dzoh ehd* EE-*oh Leh tehr-*ROH
*kohm-pahn-n'*YEE-*ah.*
the next intermission and I shall keep you company.

MILLER: **I Suoi desideri sono ordini, signora,**
*Ee s'*WOY *deh-zee-*DEH-*ree* SOH-*noh* OHR-*dee-nee, seen-*YOH-*rah,*
Your wishes are commands, madam,

ed io li ubbidisco ciecamente.
ehd EE-*oh lee oob-bee-*DEES-*koh ch'yeh-kah-*MEHN-*teh.*
and I obey them blindly.

AMALIA: **Lei è molto galante, e la sua galanteria mi lusinga.**
Lay EH MOHL-*toh gah-*LAHN-*teh, eh lah* SOO-*ah gah-lahn-teh-*REE-*ah mee loo-*ZEEN-*gah.*
You are very gallant, and your gallantry flatters me.

MILLER: **Lei è molto bella ....e la sua bellezza mi affascina.**
Lay EH MOHL-*toh* BELL-*lah ....eh lah* SOO-*ah behl-*LEH-*tsah mee ahf-fah-*SHEE-*nah.*
You are very beautiful....and your beauty fascinates me.

AMALIA: **Mia sorella e mio cognato ci attendono al bar;**
MEE-*ah soh-*REHL-*lah eh* MEE-*oh kohn-n'*YAH-*toh chee aht-*TEHN-*doh-noh ahl bahr;*
My sister and my brother-in-law are waiting for us at the bar;

vogliamo andare, signor Don Giovanni?
*vohl-l'*YAH-*moh ahn-*DAH-*reh, seen-*YOHR *Dohn Joh-*VAHN-*nee?*
shall we go Mr. Don Juan?

MILLER: **Io, Don Giovanni? (con un sospiro) Andiamo!**
EE-*oh, Dohn Joh-*VAHN-*nee? (kohn oon sohs-*PEE-*roh) Ahn-d'*YAH-*moh!*
I, Don Juan? (with a sigh) Let's go!

NOTE on the Imperfect Subjunctive: This form is always preceded by the conditional conjunction *se*, "if", or any of its substitutes like: *In caso che*, or *caso mai*—"in case that". It expresses something which is not, because of a certain condition, or something which could be, if a certain condition existed. Therefore the subjunctive is invariably connected with the conditional form of another verb. Ex: "If I had a guitar I would sing a serenade."—*Se avessi una chitarra canterei una serenata*. In other words, if the condition of my having a guitar existed, I could sing a serenade. *Se avessi* is the imperfect subjunctive, and *canterei* is the conditional, thus called because it expresses an action that depends on a condition. More examples: "If I were rich I would travel a lot."—*Se fossi ricco viaggerei molto*. The same thought can be expressed by inverting the sentence, without changing its meaning: *Io viaggerei molto se fossi ricco*.

(Dopo il secondo atto Miller rimane
(DOH-*poh eel seh-*KOHN-*doh* AHT-*toh Miller ree-*MAH-*neh*
(After the second act Miller remains

nel palco con Amalia.)
nehl PAHL-*koh kohn Ah-*MAH-*l'yah.)*
in the box with Amalia.)

MILLER: **Non ho capito bene le parole di quest'atto,**
*Noh-*NOH *kah-*PEE*-toh* BEH*-neh leh pah-*ROH*-leh dee kwess-*TAHT*-toh,*
I didn't understand the words of this act too well

ma ho l'impressione che Tosca sia molto infelice.
mah OH *leem-prehs-s'*YOH*-neh keh* TOHS*-kah* SEE*-ah* MOHL*-toh*
*een-feh-*LEET*-cheh.*
but I have the impression that Tosca is very unhappy.

AMALIA: **Povera Tosca! Essa fu molto devota a Dio**
POH*-veh-rah* TOHS*-kah!* ESS*-sah foo* MOHL*-toh deh-*VOH*-tah ah* DEE*-oh*
Poor Tosca! She was very devoted to God

e fedele al suo Mario, ma pur di ottenere la di lui libertà
*eh feh-*DEH*-leh ahl* SOO*-oh* MAH*-r'yoh, mah poor dee oht-teh-*NEH*-reh*
lah dee LOO*-ee lee-behr-*TAH
and faithful to her Mario, but to obtain his freedom

accettò le dure condizioni
*aht-cheht-*TOH *leh* DOO*-reh kohn-dee-ts'*YOH*-nee*
she accepted the harsh terms

che Scarpia le impose.
keh SKAHR*-p'yah leh eem-*POH*-seh.*
that Scarpia imposed on her.

MILLER: **Mascalzone!**
*Mahs-kahl-*TSOH*-neh!*
Scoundrel!

AMALIA: **Più che mascalzone. Egli non mantenne la sua promessa**
*p'*YOO *keh mahs-kahl-*TSOH*-neh.* EHL*-yee nohn mahn-*TEHN*-neh lah*
SOO*-ah proh-*MESS*-sah*
More than a scoundrel. He didn't keep his promise

e fece fucilare Mario. Ecco perchè Tosca,
eh FEH*-cheh foo-chee-*LAH*-reh* MAH*-r'yoh.* ECK*-koh pehr-*KEH TOHS*-kah,*
and had Mario shot. That is why Tosca,

non potendo sopravvivere a tal grande dolore,
*nohn poh-*TEHN*-doh soh-prahv-*VEE*-veh-reh ah tahl* GRAHN*-deh*
*doh-*LOH*-reh,*
unable to survive such great sorrow,

si buttò nel fiume.
*see boot-*TOH *nehl f'*YOO*-meh.*
threw herself into the river.

MILLER: **Bisogna che io impari subito a nuotare**
*Bee-*ZOHN*-yah keh* EE*-oh eem-*PAH*-ree* SOO*-bee-toh ah n'woh-*TAH*-reh*
I must immediately learn how to swim

nel caso che una pena d'amore
nehl KAH-*zoh keh* OO-*nah* PEH-*nah dah*-MOH-*reh*
in case a romantic disappointment

dovesse costringermi a fare la stessa cosa;
doh-VEHS-*seh kos*-TREEN-*jehr-mee ah* FAH-*reh lah* STEHS-*sah* KOH-*zah;*
should force me to do the same thing;

ma Lei, Amalia, non sarà crudele con me, spero?
mah Lay, Ah-MAH-*l'yah, nohn sah*-RAH *kroo*-DEH-*leh kohn meh,*
SPEH-*roh?*
but you, Amalia, will not be cruel to me, I hope?

AMALIA: Ciò che Lei dice ha tutto il sapore d'una dichiarazione.
CHOH *keh Lay* DEE-*cheh* AH TOOT-*toh eel sah*-POH-*reh* DOO-*nah*
*dee-k'yah-rah-ts'*YOH-*neh.*
What you say has all the flavor of a declaration.

È dunque vero che
EH DOON-*kweh* VEH-*roh keh*
It is then true that

gli americani fanno tutto rapidamente.
l'yee ah-meh-ree-KAH-*nee* FAHN-*noh* TOOT-*toh rah-pee-dah*-MEHN-*teh.*
the Americans do everything rapidly?

MILLER: Le domando scusa, Amalia. Spero che nel mio
Leh doh-MAHN-*doh* SKOO-*zah, Ah*-MAH-*l'yah.* SPEH-*roh keh nehl* MEE-*oh*
I beg your pardon, Amalia. I hope that in my

entusiasmo non abbia detto più di quanto
ehn-too-zee-AHS-*moh nohn* AHB-*b'yah* DEHT-*toh p'*YOO *dee* KWAHN-*toh*
enthusiasm I haven't said more than

mi sia concesso dire.
mee SEE-*ah kohn*-CHEHS-*soh* DEE-*reh.*
I am permitted to say.

AMALIA: No, non è questo; ma io non desidero incoraggiarla.
Noh, noh-NEH KWESS-*toh; mah* EE-*oh nohn deh*-ZEE-*deh-roh*
een-kohr-rah-JAHR-*lah.*
No, it isn't that; but I don't wish to encourage you.

Anzitutto perchè non ci conosciamo che da poche ore,
Ahn-tsee-TOOT-*toh pehr*-KEH *nohn chee koh-noh-sh'*YAH-*moh keh dah*
POH-*keh* OH-*reh,*
First of all because we have known each other but a few hours,

poi perchè potrebbe darsi che il Suo entusiasmo
poy pehr-KEH *poh*-TREHB-*beh* DAHR-*see keh eel* SOO-*oh*
ehn-too-zee-AHS-*moh*
then because it could be that your enthusiasm

non sia che un fuoco di paglia, infine....
nohn SEE-*ah keh oon foo-*OH-*koh dee* PAHL-*l'yah, een-*FEE-*neh.* ...
is but a straw fire, and finally....

MILLER: Scusi se l'interrompo, ma che cosa
SKOO-*zee seh leen-tehr-*ROHM-*poh, mah keh* KOH-*zah*
Excuse me for interrupting, but what

c'entra il fuoco di paglia?
CHEHN-*trah eel foo-*OH-*koh dee* PAHL-*l'yah?*
brings up the straw fire?

AMALIA: La paglia produce una grande fiamma,...
Lah PAHL-*l'yah proh-*DOO-*cheh* OO-*nah* GRAHN-*deh f'*YAHM-*mah,*...
Straw produces a big flame,...

ma muore subito. Infine, dicevo, presto Lei
*mah moo-*OH-*reh* SOO-*bee-toh. Een-*FEE-*neh, dee-*CHEH-*voh,* PRESS-*toh Lay*
but dies quickly. Finally, I was saying, you will

lascerà l'Italia e probabilmente non avremo
*lah-sheh-*RAH *lee-*TAHL-*yah eh proh-bah-beel-*MEHN-*teh nohn*
*ah-*VREH-*moh*
soon leave Italy and we shall probably never

più l'occasione di rivederci.
*p'*YOO *lohk-kah-z'*YOH-*neh dee ree-veh-*DEHR-*chee.*
have the opportunity to see each other again.

MILLER: Al contrario! Oggi ho concluso il mio contratto con
*Ahl kohn-*TRAH-*r'yoh!* OH-*djee* OH *kohn-*KLOO-*zoh eel* MEE-*oh*
*kohn-*TRAHT-*toh kohn*
On the contrary! Today I closed my contract with

il Governo e, per conseguenza, dovrò ritornare
*eel Goh-*VEHR-*noh eh, pehr kohn-seh-*GWEHN-*tsah, doh-*VROH
*ree-tohr-*NAH-*reh*
the Government and, consequently, I shall have to return

presto a Roma e rimanervi a lungo. Le fa piacere ciò?
PRESS-*toh ah* ROH-*mah eh ree-mah-*NEHR-*vee ah* LOON-*goh. Leh fah*
*p'yah-*CHEH-*reh* CHOH?
to Rome soon and remain here a long time. Does that please you?

AMALIA: Risponderò a questa domanda al Suo prossimo viaggio in Italia.
*Rees-pohn-deh-*ROH *ah* KWESS-*tah doh-*MAHN-*dah ahl* SOO-*oh*
PROHS-*see-moh vee-*AH-*djoh een Ee-*TAHL-*yah.*
I shall answer this question on your next trip to Italy.

MILLER: Grazie, Amalia. Lei è più generosa di quanto
GRAHTS-*yeh Ah-*MAH-*l'yah. Lay* EH *p'*YOO *jeh-neh-*ROH-*zah dee* KWAHN-*toh*
Thanks, Amalia. You are more generous than

io speravo. In quanto al fuoco di paglia sia

EE-*oh speh*-RAH-*voh. Een* KWAHN-*toh ahl foo-*OH-*koh dee* PAHL-*l'yah*
SEE-*ah*

I had hoped. As to the straw fire, you may

certa che tutti i pompieri di Roma non potrebbero spegnerlo.

CHEHR-*tah keh* TOOT-*tee ee pohm-p'*YEH-*ree dee* ROH-*mah nohn*
*pohr-*TREHB-*beh-roh* SPEHN-*yehr-loh.*

be sure that all the firemen in Rome could not put it out.

NOTE ON PASSATO REMOTO: This tense is used to describe something that happened in the distant past and in a definite way. It differs from the imperfect past which, as you now know, describes something which *was* happening. Therefore it isn't unusual to find these two tenses being used in the same sentence. Ex: *Io incontrai il signor De Rossi quando viaggiavo in Italia.*—"I met De Rossi" is the action that happened at a definite time; "when I was traveling in Italy" is the action that *was happening.* In the first part of the sentence we use the definite past, *passato remoto;* in the second part of the sentence we use the imperfect tense, *imperfetto.*

(Davanti all'albergo, dopo lo spettacolo)
(*Dah-*VAHN-*tee ahl-lahl-*BEHR-*goh,* DOH-*poh loh speht-*TAH-*koh-loh*)
(Before the hotel after the show)

MILLER: Arrivederla signora Giovanna, buona notte Amalia,
*Ahr-ree-veh-*DEHR-*lah seen-*YOH-*rah Joh-*VAHN-*nah, b'*WOH-*nah*
NOHT-*teh Ah-*MAH-*l'yah,*
Good bye, madam Giovanna, good night Amalia,

a domani, caro De Rossi. Son Loro grato per
*ah doh-*MAH-*nee,* KAH-*roh Deh* ROHS-*see. Sohn* LOH-*roh* GRAH-*toh pehr*
until tomorrow, my dear De Rossi. I am grateful to you for

la bellissima serata che considero una delle
*lah bell-*LEES-*see-mah seh-*RAH-*tah keh kohn-*SEE-*deh-roh* OO-*nah*
DEHL-*leh*
the very beautiful evening, which I consider one of the

più dilettevoli della mia vita.
*p'*YOO *dee-leht-*TEH-*voh-lee* DEHL-*lah* MEE-*ah* VEE-*tah.*
most delightful of my life.

GLI AMICI, IN CORO: Buona notte, Miller. Si faccia vedere presto.
*L'yee ah-*MEE-*chee, een* KOH-*roh: b'*WOH-*nah* NOHT-*teh, Miller. See* FAHT-*chah*
*veh-*DEH-*reh* PREHS-*toh.*
THE FRIENDS, IN CHORUS: Good night, Miller. Let us see you soon.

THINKING IN ITALIAN

(Answers on page 296)

1. Qual'è il nome dell'opera che i De Rossi e Miller sentiranno?
2. Piace al signor Miller il Teatro dell'Opera di Roma?
3. Con che cosa è coperta la decorazione dell'interno del teatro?
4. Che cosa fa l'orchestra quando i nostri amici entrano in palco?
5. Dove vanno i nostri amici dopo il primo atto?
6. Perchè il signor Miller vorrebbe rimanere in palco?
7. Che cosa suggerisce Amalia?
8. Che nome dà Amalia al signor Miller?
9. Capisce il signor Miller tutte le parole dell'opera?
10. Che cosa non ha capito il signor Miller?
11. Di che cosa è grato ai signori De Rossi il signor Miller?
12. Perchè è egli grato?

ANSWERS

ANSWERS TO THE QUESTIONS OF LESSON 1 ON PAGE 3

È il libro.

Sì, è il libro.

No, non è la scatola, è il libro.

No, non è la tavola, è la scatola.

No, non è lo specchio, è la scatola.

È la scatola.

No, non è la lampada, è la chiave.

8. No, non è la sedia, è la chiave.

9. È la chiave.

10. È il lapis.

11. No, non è il quadro, è il lapis.

12. No, non è il libro, è il lapis.

13. No non è la porta, è la tavola.

14. No, non è la chiave, è la tavola.

15. È la tavola.

ANSWERS TO THE QUESTIONS OF LESSON 2 ON PAGE 6

È la scarpa.

È la scarpa.

Non è nè la cravatta nè il fazzoletto, è la scarpa.

È il guanto.

È il guanto.

No, non è il lapis, è il guanto.

7. È il cappello.

8. No, non è il vestito.

9. No, non è il soprabito.

10. Non è nè la giacca nè la camicia, è il cappello.

11. Sì, è il cappello.

12. No, non è la gonnella.

ANSWERS TO THE QUESTIONS OF LESSON 3 ON PAGE 11

No, non è gialla.

No, non è grigia.

È verde.

No, non è la penna rossa.

È la penna verde.

È il lapis.

Sì, è il lapis.

È giallo.

No, non è il lapis rosso.

No, non è verde.

11. No, non è la tavola, è la lampada.

12. No, non è la sedia.

13. È la lampada.

14. Sì, è la lampada.

15. È azzurra.

16. È il libro.

17. No, non è giallo.

18. No, non è bruno.

19. No, non è il libro nero.

20. È rosso.

281

ANSWERS TO THE QUESTIONS OF LESSON 4 ON PAGE 15

1. Sì, il libro rosso è lungo.
2. Sì, è largo.
3. Sì, è grande.
4. Sì, è corto.
5. Sì, è stretto.
6. Sì, è piccolo.
7. È rosso.
8. È verde.
9. Il vestito lungo è nero.
10. No, non è rosso.
11. Sì, è lungo.
12. No, non è corto.
13. Il vestito corto è giallo.
14. Non è nè nero nè verde, è giallo.
15. La finestra larga è azzurra.
16. È azzurra.
17. No, non è grigia.
18. No, la finestra rossa non è larga è stretta.
19. La finestra azzurra è larga.
20. Sì, la finestra azzurra è grande.
21. Sì, la finestra rossa è piccola.
22. La finestra piccola è rossa.
23. La finestra grande è azzurra.

ANSWERS TO THE QUESTIONS OF LESSON 5 ON PAGE 21

1. Io sono....
2. Sì, io sono americano. (No, io non sono americano.)
3. No, io non sono il professore.
4. No, io non sono italiano.
5. Sì, Lei è il Signor Berlitz.
6. Sì, Lei è il professore.
7. Sì, Lei è italiano.
8. No, Lei non è americano.
9. Sì, Arturo Toscanini è italiano.
10. No, Bing Crosby non è italiano.
11. No, Ingrid Bergman non è italiana.
12. Carmen Miranda è brasiliana.
13. Il generale MacArthur è americano.
14. Churchill è inglese.
15. Stalin non è spagnolo ma russo.
16. Hirohito è giapponese.

ANSWERS TO THE QUESTIONS OF LESSON 6 ON PAGE 27

1. Sì, il cappello del professore è nero.
2. Sì, è grande.
3. Il mio cappello è....
4. No, il Suo cappello non è verde.
5. No, la borsetta della signora Fibronia non è piccola, è grande.
6. No, la borsetta di Titina non è grande, è piccola.
7. Sì, è blu.
8. No, quel lapis non è grigio, verde.
9. Il mio fazzoletto è bianco.
10. La mia casa è piccola (è grande
11. Sì, è il mio libro. (No, non è il mio libro.)
12. Il cappello del professore è nero
13. Sì, la gonnella della signora Fibronia è lunga.
14. Sì la gonnella di Titina è corta.

ANSWERS TO THE QUESTIONS OF LESSON 7 ON PAGE 36

1. Il libro è sulla tavola.
2. No, il libro non è sotto la sedia.
3. No, la penna non è davanti alla tavola.

4. È sotto la tavola.
5. La sedia è sul pavimento.
6. Il professore è dietro alla tavola.
7. No, il professore non è sotto la tavola.
8. Sì, il professore è in piedi dietro alla tavola.
9. No, io non sono in piedi davanti alla porta.
10. Sì, io sono seduto sulla sedia.
11. Sì, la carta è dentro il libro.

12. No, la carta non è dentro la scatola.
13. La scatola è sotto la tavola.
14. No, la scatola non è sopra la tavola.
15. Sì, la penna è nella scatola.
16. No, la chiave non è sotto la sedia.
17. Quel lapis è nero.
18. Sì, è nero.
19. Questo lapis è rosso.
20. Questo libro è grande. (Questo libro è piccolo.)

ANSWERS TO THE QUESTIONS OF LESSON 8 ON PAGE 46

1. Il professore prende il libro.
2. Sì, il professore prende il libro.
3. No, egli non mette il libro sulla tavola.
4. No, egli non prende la scatola.
5. Il professore è in piedi.
6. No, il professore non chiude la finestra.
7. Il professore apre la finestra.
8. Egli apre la finestra.

9. No, io non apro la porta.
10. No, il professore non apre la porta.
11. No, il professore non va a New York.
12. No, egli non va a Parigi.
13. Il professore va a Pisa.
14. Roma è grande.
15. No, io non vado a Roma.
16. Il professore va a Pisa.

ANSWERS TO THE QUESTIONS OF LESSON 9 ON PAGE 52

1. Io conto da uno a dieci.
2. Lei conta: 1, 2, 3, ... ecc.
3. Il professore conta.
4. Vi sono ... sedie.
5. Sì, vi è una tavola.
6. Sulla tavola vi sono ... libri italiani.
7. Sei più cinque fanno undici.
8. Due più due non fanno cinque, fanno quattro.

9. Sette per tre fanno ventuno.
10. No, quattro per tre non fanno tredici, fanno dodici.
11. Un giornale americano costa cinque centesimi.
12. No, questo libro non costa mille dollari.
13. No, un dollaro non vale 300 lire.
14. No, una lira non vale un dollaro.
15. È il numero quindici.

ANSWERS TO THE QUESTIONS OF LESSON 10 ON PAGE 59

1. Il professore ha sotto il braccio un giornale.
2. Sì, sotto il braccio sinistro del professore c'è un giornale.
3. Sì, la pipa è nella tasca del professore.

4. La carta è sulla sedia.
5. No, la riga non è sotto il piede destro del professore.
6. Nella mano destra del professore vi sono delle penne.
7. Sì, nella scatola vi sono dei lapis.

8. Sì, sulla tavola vi sono delle chiavi.

9. I libri sono sulla tavola.

10. Sì, alla parete vi sono dei quadri.

11. Sì, sotto la tavola vi sono due cani.

12. Sulla tavola vi sono quattro lib

13. Sì, nella tasca del professore vi denaro. (No, nella tasca del pr fessore non c'è denaro.)

14. Sì, sulla sedia c'è un cappello.

ANSWERS TO THE QUESTIONS OF LESSON 11 ON PAGE 66

1. Io scrivo la lettera A sulla carta.

2. Lei scrive la parola "libertà".

3. Il signor Cerutti scrive l'alfabeto sulla lavagna.

4. Io leggo la frase: "Io sono americano."

5. In questa frase vi sono trentadue lettere.

6. Sì, io leggo questo libro. (No, io non leggo questo libro.)

7. Sì, il signor Berlitz legge l'italiano.

8. Sì, egli parla l'italiano.

9. No, il signor Galli non parla il russo.

10. Io parlo l'inglese.

11. No, la signora Guasti non parla spagnolo.

12. La parola "gentleman" non è tedesca nè francese, ma inglese.

13. Sì, Lei recita l'alfabeto.

14. No, io non recito l'alfabeto rus

15. Il professore d'italiano recita l'al beto italiano.

16. A New York si parla l'inglese.

17. Sì, a Roma si parla italiano.

18. No, a Madrid non si parla russ

19. A Berlino non si parla nè lo sp nolo nè l'italiano, si parla tedes

ANSWERS TO THE QUESTIONS OF LESSON 12 ON PAGE 71

1. Il professore scrive sulla lavagna.

2. No, la signora Fibronia non scrive.

3. Essa legge un giornale italiano.

4. Titina legge la sezione comica del giornale.

5. Il professore scrive sulla lavagna la parola "attenzione".

6. Il professore scrive col gesso.

7. No, il professore non scrive l'alfabeto, egli scrive una parola.

8. Sì, la signora Fibronia legge un giornale italiano.

9. Sì, il professore parla italiano.

10. No, il cane di Titina non par

11. Sì, io leggo l'italiano.

12. Sì, io parlo l'inglese.

13. Sì, il signor Berlitz parla il fr cese.

14. No, Titina non parla l'inglese.

15. Titina è seduta.

16. Nell'alfabeto italiano vi sono v tuna lettere.

17. Nell'alfabeto inglese vi sono v tisei lettere.

18. Nell'alfabeto italiano vi sono cinque vocali.

ANSWERS TO THE QUESTIONS OF LESSON 13 ON PAGE 78

1. Sì, signore, io ho un libro. (No, io non ho un libro.)

2. Sì, il professore Berlitz ha degli allievi.

3. Sì, Lei ha due occhi.

4. Io ho dieci dita.

5. I signori hanno i capelli corti.

Sì, io ho dei libri italiani. (No, io non ho libri italiani.)

I miei occhi sono ....

No, non sono dello stesso colore. (Sì, sono dello stesso colore.)

Sì, gli allievi hanno i loro libri. (No, gli allievi non hanno i loro libri.)

10. No, egli non mette la sua cravatta prima della camicia.

11. Egli mette le sue calze prima delle sue scarpe.

12. Sì, scrive bene. (No, non scrive bene.)

13. Sì, la Sua mano destra è più grande della Sua mano sinistra.

ANSWERS TO THE QUESTIONS OF LESSON 14 ON PAGE 84

Sì, le signore vanno al cinema. (No, esse non vanno al cinema.)

Sì, esse hanno il cappello in testa in chiesa.

Sì, noi andiamo alla scuola Berlitz.

Li mettono in tasca.

Sì, li aprono.

Sì, la chiudiamo. (No, non la chiudiamo.)

Sì, noi la apriamo.

Sì, loro scrivono sulla lavagna.

Sì, noi scriviamo delle parole ital-iane. (No, non scriviamo delle parole italiane.)

10. Sì, noi li mettiamo sulla tavola. (No, non li mettiamo. Li prendiamo con noi.)

11. Sì, gli allievi vengono a scuola.

12. Sì, essi leggono i loro libri.

13. No, noi non leggiamo il giornale in classe.

14. No, noi non le prendiamo.

15. Sì, io scrivo i miei compiti dopo la lezione. (No, non li scrivo.)

ANSWERS TO THE QUESTIONS OF LESSON 15 ON PAGE 89

Titina ha una lira.

No, non ha tanto danaro quanto il professore.

Il professore ha più danaro.

Sì, il professore ha dei lapis dietro l'orecchio.

Sì, egli ha più lapis di Titina.

No, Titina ha più libri del professore.

Titina ha più libri.

8. Titina ha meno danaro.

9. No, Titina non ha molto danaro.

10. Sì, il professore ha pochi libri.

11. Sì, io leggo molte parole italiane.

12. Sì, in questo libro vi sono molte pagine.

13. No, il "New York Times" non ha tante pagine quante questo libro.

14. Il professore ha più libri di me.

ANSWERS TO THE QUESTIONS OF LESSON 16 ON PAGE 93

Sì, vi sono dei cappelli sulla sedia.

C'è un fazzoletto.

Ci sono delle penne.

È bianco.

No, non c'è una scatola di penne sulla sedia.

6. No, non ci sono cappelli sulla tavola.

7. È sulla tavola.

8. No, non ci sono sigarette nella tasca del professore.

9. No, il professore non ha una sigaretta fra le labbra.
10. No, non c'è.
11. Sì, vi sono sigarette sulla tavola.

12. Sì, le sigarette sono sulla tavola.
13. No, sul pavimento non ci son cappelli.
14. Sono sulla sedia.

ANSWERS TO THE QUESTIONS OF LESSON 17 ON PAGE 98

1. Sì, il professore ha una sigaretta in mano.
2. Nella mano sinistra della signora Fibronia c'è un fazzoletto.
3. No, essa non ha niente nella sua mano destra.
4. Non c'è niente nella sua mano sinistra.
5. No, alla sinistra del professore non c'è nessuno.
6. Titina è fra il professore è la signora Fibronia.
7. Sì, il libro è nella mano destra della signora Fibronia.
8. Nessuno è seduto sulla sedia.

9. Sulla tavola non c'è niente.
10. Non c'è nulla sotto il braccio sinistro del professore.
11. La signora Fibronia e Titina son alla sua destra.
12. Non c'è niente sotto la sedia.
13. Sì, c'è qualcuno alla destra di Titina.
14. Il professore è alla sua sinistra.
15. Sì, il professore è dietro alla tavola.
16. No, il professore non ha un cappello in testa.
17. Il professore non ha nulla sul testa.

ANSWERS TO THE QUESTIONS OF LESSON 18 ON PAGE 104

1. Gina esce dalla stanza.
2. Sì, Sofia è seduta.
3. No, Arturo non si siede.
4. È Giuseppe.
5. Sì, egli entra.
6. No, essa non entra, ma esce.
7. No, egli non esce dalla stanza.
8. No, il professore non esce, egli entra.
9. Sì, sono in piedi.
10. Arturo entra.

11. No, il professore non è seduto.
12. Sì, io mi alzo dopo la lezione.
13. Sì, io mi siedo sulla sedia. (No, non mi siedo sulla sedia.)
14. Lei si siede sulla sedia.
15. Sì, gli allievi escono dopo la lezione.
16. Sì, noi ci sediamo al cinema.
17. No, io non mi siedo in chiesa. (Sì io mi siedo in chiesa.)

ANSWERS TO THE QUESTIONS OF LESSON 19 ON PAGE 110

1. Sì, le dà un libro.
2. Le dà una lira.
3. Essa dà una palla a Fido.
4. No, loro non gli danno un cappello.

5. Il professore.
6. Egli dice: "A rivederci, Titina."
7. No, essa non dice nulla a Fido.
8. Sì, dà una palla.
9. Fido non dice nulla.

10. Sì, essi gli parlano.

11. Sì, essi gli dicono "buon giorno" prima della lezione.

12. Egli dice loro: "A rivederci!".

13. C'è una palla nella mano sinistra della signora Fibronia.

14. Io Le dico che cosa c'è nella mano sinistra della signora Fibronia.

15. Essa gli dice: "Grazie, signore."

ANSWERS TO THE QUESTIONS OF LESSON 20 ON PAGE 117

1. L'odora col naso.
2. No, non ha buon odore.
3. Sì, la rosa ha buon odore.
4. La signora Fibronia odora una rosa.
5. No, non le vedo.
6. Sì, le vediamo.
7. Sì, noi lo sentiamo.
8. Sì, io lo sento.
9. Sì, noi mangiamo del pane.
10. Sì, noi vediamo il film.
11. Sì, noi mettiamo zucchero nel caffè.
12. Sì, gli americani mangiano del pane bianco.
13. Sì, essi bevono molto vino.
14. No, noi non mettiamo dello zucchero sulla carne.
15. Sì, io metto del latte nel tè. (No, io non metto del latte nel tè.)
16. La tagliamo con un coltello.
17. No, noi mangiamo i piselli con una forchetta.
18. Io scrivo con un lapis (con una penna).
19. No, noi non beviamo col naso.
20. Beviamo colla bocca.

ANSWERS TO THE QUESTIONS OF LESSON 21 ON PAGE 122

1. Tagliamo la carne con il coltello.
2. No, non la mangiamo col cucchiaio.
3. Col cucchiaio mangiamo la minestra.
4. Sì, l'odore della rosa mi piace.
5. No, l'odore del formaggio non mi piace.
6. Sì, il caffè con zucchero mi piace.
7. No, la minestra con lo zucchero non mi piace.
8. No, l'odore del cavolo non mi piace.
9. Sì, il sapore della fragola mi piace.
10. Sì, il formaggio mi piace. (No, il formaggio non mi piace.)
11. No, il tè senza zucchero non mi piace. (Sì, il tè senza zucchero mi piace.)
12. Sì, la birra mi piace. (No, la birra non mi piace.)
13. Sì, i fiori piacciono alle signorine.
14. Sì, mi piace parlare italiano.
15. Sì, la statua di Venere è bella.
16. Sì, i vestiti di Schiaparelli sono belli.
17. Sì, i suoi cappelli sono belli. Mi piacciono.
18. Sì, la sua cravatta è bella. Mi piace.
19. Il gufo è brutto.
20. Il pavone è bello.
21. Sì, la lingua italiana è bella.
22. Sì, mi piace di sentirla.

ANSWERS TO THE QUESTIONS OF LESSON 22 ON PAGE 126

1. Sì, Titina ne mangia. (No, essa non ne mangia.)

2. Sì, il professore ne beve. (No, egli non ne beve.)

3. Sì, la signora Fibronia ne mangia. (No, essa non ne mangia.)
4. Sì, io ne bevo. (No, non ne bevo.)
5. Sì, Lei ne beve. (No, Lei non ne beve.)
6. Sì, questi signori ne mangiano. (No, non ne mangiano.)
7. Sì, loro ne bevono. (No, non ne bevono.)
8. Sì, loro ne prendono. (No, non ne prendono.)
9. Sì, io ne bevo. (No, non ne bevo.)
10. Sì, loro ne prendono. (No, non ne prendono.)
11. Sì, io ne scrivo. (No, non ne scrivo.)

12. Sì, il mio professore ne legge. (No, non ne legge.)
13. Sì, ne ho. (No, non ne ho.)
14. Sì, io ne bevo. (No, non ne bevo.)
15. Sì, io ne bevo. (No, non ne bevo.)
16. Ne abbiamo dieci.
17. Ne ho molto. (Non ne ho molto.)
18. Sì, il signor Berlitz ne ha molti. (No, non ne ha molti.)
19. Sì, io ne ho poco. (No, non ne ho poco.)
20. Sì, ne abbiamo molti. (No, non ne abbiamo molti.)
21. Sì, io ne scrivo molte. (No, non ne scrivo molte.)
22. Sì, io ne leggo molti. (No, non ne leggo molti.)

ANSWERS TO THE QUESTIONS OF LESSON 23 ON PAGE 131

1. Sì, Titina tocca Fido.
2. No, essa non può toccare la mano destra del professore.
3. Sì, lo può toccare.
4. No, non lo tocca.
5. Sì, la lampada è bassa.
6. Sì, il professore può toccarla.
7. Non tocca niente.
8. Sì, egli porta occhiali.

9. No, egli non può vedere senza gli occhiali.
10. Sì, può uscire.
11. No, Lei non può scrivere.
12. No, noi non possiamo vederle.
13. No, essi non possono toccarlo.
14. Sì, lo posso rompere.
15. No, non la posso rompere.
16. Sì, la posso toccare.

ANSWERS TO THE QUESTIONS OF LESSON 24 ON PAGE 136

1. Sì, posso uscire. (No, non posso uscire.)
2. Sì, voglio uscire. (No, non voglio uscire.)
3. Sì, posso rompere la finestra.
4. No, non voglio romperla.
5. Sì, voglio parlare italiano qui.
6. Sì, voglio parlare inglese. (No, non voglio parlare inglese.)
7. Voglio leggere il libro (il giornale).
8. Sì, voglio mangiare qualche cosa. (No, non voglio mangiare nulla.)
9. Sì, voglio bere qualche cosa. (No, non voglio bere niente.)

10. Voglio bere dell'acqua, del vino, ecc.
11. Se la porta non è aperta, non possiamo uscire.
12. No, senza un cucchiaio non possiamo mangiare la minestra.
13. No, se non ho un coltello, non posso tagliare la carne.
14. Perchè non voglio romperlo.
15. Perchè essi non vogliono stracciarli.
16. Essi possono rompere la finestra con una palla.

ANSWERS TO THE QUESTIONS OF LESSON 25 ON PAGE 142

1. Sì, Titina vuole mangiar la mela.
2. No, essa non può toccarla.
3. No, il professore non dà la mela a Titina.
4. Perchè non vuole darla a Titina.
5. No, non vuole.
6. Sì, per uscire si deve aprire la porta.
7. Sì, se vogliamo vedere dobbiamo aprire gli occhi.
8. Per viaggiare si deve aver danaro.
9. Per scrivere dobbiamo aver una matita, o una penna, e della carta.
10. Devo aprire la porta.
11. No, il signor Berlitz non può leggere senza occhiali.
12. Per leggere egli deve avere degli occhiali.
13. Per andare all'opera dobbiamo avere biglietti.
14. No, io non posso mangiare la minestra con un coltello.
15. Per mangiare la minestra, devo avere un cucchiaio.
16. No, non si deve avere una forchetta ma un cucchiaio.
17. No, io non devo rompere il mio orologio.
18. No, Lei non deve andare al cinema se non vuole.

ANSWERS TO THE QUESTIONS OF LESSON 26 ON PAGE 151

1. Sì, vi sono degli orologi.
2. Sono sulla tavola e appesi alla parete.
3. Ne ho uno da tasca.
4. Lo metto in tasca.
5. È d'argento (d'oro, di nichelio, di acciaio).
6. Sì, segna i secondi. (No, non segna i secondi.)
7. Ventiquattro ore fanno un giorno.
8. In un minuto vi sono sessanta secondi.
9. No, non è avanti. (Sì, è avanti.)
10. È fatta di legno.
11. Sì, questa sedia è pure di legno.
12. Sì, la tavola è più grande della sedia.
13. No, il quadro non è più lungo della parete.
14. No, la finestra non è così grande come la porta. (No, la finestra è più piccola della porta.)
15. Sì, la Sua giacchetta è più lunga del Suo gilè.
16. Sì, la pesca è più buona della mela. (No, la pesca non è migliore della mela.)
17. Sì, io pronuncio bene il francese. (No, io non pronuncio bene il francese.)
18. Sì, i miei occhi sono buoni. (No, i miei occhi non sono buoni.)
19. Sì, vedo bene. (No, non vedo bene.)
20. No, il signor Berlitz non vede bene senza occhiali.
21. Sì, egli vede meglio cogli occhiali.

ANSWERS TO THE QUESTIONS OF LESSON 27 ON PAGE 156

1. In una settimana vi sono sette giorni.
2. Una settimana si compone di sette giorni.

3. L'anno comincia il primo di gennaio.

4. Finisce il trentuno di dicembre.

5. Il primo mese dell'anno è gennaio, il terzo è marzo ed il quinto è maggio.

6. Lunedì, martedì, mercoledì, giovedì, venerdì, sabato, domenica.

7. L'ultimo giorno della settimana si chiama domenica.

8. Oggi è lunedì (martedì, ecc).

9. Sì, ieri era domenica. (No, ieri non era domenica.)

10. Io vado in chiesa la domenica.

11. Sì, venerdì sarà il quindici. (No, venerdì non sarà il quindici.)

12. Oggi è il dodici.

13. Lunedì prossimo sarà il diciasette.

14. Lunedì scorso era il dieci.

15. Sì, domani sarà la fine del mese. (No, non sarà la fine del mese.)

16. Sono le cinque.

17. Noi lavoriamo durante cinque o sei giorni della settimana.

18. La domenica io non lavoro.

ANSWERS TO THE QUESTIONS OF LESSON 28 ON PAGE 162

1. Si dividono in due parti: le ore del giorno e le ore della notte.

2. Di giorno è chiaro.

3. No, non è buio ora. (Sì, è buio.)

4. Viene dal sole.

5. Il sole è nel cielo.

6. Di notte la luce elettrica illumina questa stanza.

7. Di notte per poter vedere noi accendiamo la luce.

8. Durante la notte nel cielo si vedono la luna e le stelle.

9. Il sole si leva da Levante.

10. In marzo il sole si leva alle sei di mattina.

11. I giorni sono lunghi in estate.

12. In estate le notti non sono più lunghe dei giorni.

13. Le notti sono lunghe in inverno.

14. Noi accendiamo la luce la sera.

15. Generalmente io vado a letto alle undici.

16. Io mi alzo alle sette di mattina.

17. Io faccio colazione alle otto.

18. Io comincio a lavorare alle nove.

19. Io lavoro fino alle sei.

20. Sì, mi piace lavorare. (No, non mi piace lavorare.)

ANSWERS TO THE QUESTIONS OF LESSON 29 ON PAGE 170

1. Quando fa brutto tempo il cielo è grigio.

2. È coperto di nuvole.

3. Sì, piove. (No, non piove.)

4. D'inverno la neve cade dal cielo.

5. No, non mi piace camminare per le strade quando piove.

6. Quando piove, porto in mano un ombrello.

7. Fa bel tempo. (Fa cattivo tempo.)

8. Sì, esco. (No, non esco.)

9. Sì, al Polo Nord fa freddo.

10. Nei mesi d'inverno.

11. Sì, in febbraio nevica spesso.

12. No, in aprile non nevica spesso.

13. La pioggia viene dalle nuvole.

14. No, non mi piace camminare quando piove.

15. Io porto dei vestiti pesanti nei mesi d'inverno.

16. A Napoli generalmente fa bel tempo.

17. Per scaldarmi mi siedo accanto al termosifone (accanto alla stufa.)

18. Il sole splende durante il giorno.

ANSWERS TO THE QUESTIONS OF LESSON 30 ON PAGE 177

1. Ieri ho fatto colazione alle otto di mattina.
2. Sì, ieri a mezzogiorno ho bevuto vino. (No, non ne ho bevuto.)
3. Ieri sera ho cenato alle nove.
4. Sì, stamattina ho mangiato qualche cosa.
5. Sì, ieri l'altro ne ho ricevute. (No, ieri l'altro non ho ricevuto delle lettere.)
6. Sì, ho letto "I promessi Sposi" del Manzoni. (No, non li ho letti.)
7. Ho messo il mio ombrello nel corridoio.
8. Sì, stamattina ho fatto una passeggiata. (No, non la ho fatta.)
9. Ieri ha fatto bel tempo. (Ieri ha fatto cattivo tempo.)
10. Sì, ne ho scritto una. (No, non l'ho scritta.)
11. Sì, ho letto il giornale. (No, non l'ho letto.)
12. Sì, la settimana scorsa ho visto il signor Berlitz. (No, non l'ho visto la settimana scorsa.)

13. Sì, nel millenovecentoquarantacinque ho visto il sindaco La Guardia. (No, non l'ho visto nel 1945.)
14. Sì, il mese scorso mi ha scritto una cartolina. (No, non mi ha scritto una cartolina.)
15. Sì, ieri ho avuto una lezione. (No, ieri non l'ho avuta.)
16. Sì, lunedì scorso ne abbiamo avuto una. (No, non ne abbiamo avuto una.)
17. Sì, ho sentito cantare Gigli. (No, non l'ho sentito cantare.)
18. Ieri ha fatto bel tempo. (Ieri ha fatto brutto tempo.)
19. La settimana scorsa abbiamo parlato d'un nuovo romanzo, che mi ha portato il mio professore.
20. Sì, l'ho visto. (No, non l'ho visto.)
21. Lei ha detto: buon giorno.
22. Sì, ho visto Roma. (No, non ho visto Roma.)

ANSWERS TO THE QUESTIONS OF LESSON 31 ON PAGE 182

1. Sì, il professore si è coricato nell' amaca.
2. Il professore ha bevuto una limonata.
3. Sì, egli si è tolta la giacchetta.
4. L'ha messa sulla sedia.
5. Sì, egli ha letto il suo giornale.
6. Sì, si è addormentato.
7. Sono andato al cinematografo ieri sera.
8. Sì, ci sono andato. (No, non ci sono andato.)
9. Sì, domenica scorsa sono uscito di casa. (No, non sono uscito di casa.)

10. Sì, lunedì scorso sono rimasto in casa. (No, non sono rimasto in casa.)
11. Sì, essa è partita per l'Europa. (No, non è partita per l'Europa.)
12. È partita in maggio (in luglio, ecc).
13. È arrivata in giugno.
14. Essa è rimasta in Europa fino al mese di ottobre.
15. Ieri mattina sono uscito di casa alle otto e mezzo.
16. Sono ritornato alle sei meno un quarto.
17. Sì, l'anno scorso ci sono andato. (No, non ci sono andato.)

18. Sì, qualcuno è venuto a vedermi. (No, nessuno è venuto.)

19. Sì, Lei é uscito alla stessa ora in cui sono uscito io. (No, Lei non è uscito alla stessa ora in cui sono uscito io.)

20. Sì, sono caduto quando sono uscito dall'ascensore. (No, non sono caduto.)

21. Sì, ci sono stato. (No, non ci sono stato.)

22. Vi sono salito due volte. (Non vi sono salito mai.)

23. Il Vulcania è arrivato a Genova venerdì.

24. È partito da New York lunedi (martedì, ecc).

25. Sì, vi sono salito spesso. (No, non vi sono salito mai.)

ANSWERS TO THE QUESTIONS OF LESSON 32 ON PAGE 187

1. Il professore stasera andrà alla casa della signora Fibronia.

2. Sì, essa sarà in casa.

3. Sì, avrò una lezione d'italiano. (No, non avrò lezione.)

4. Sì, stasera sarò in casa. (No, non sarò in casa.)

5. Stasera leggerò un libro.

6. Sì, potrò accompagnarla. (No, non potrò accompagnarla.)

7. Sì, potremo uscire.

8. Sì, vi andremo in automobile. (No, vi andremo a piedi.)

9. Partiremo alle otto.

10. Sì, dopo pranzo rimarrò in casa. (No, non rimarrò in casa.)

11. Sì, mi vedrà stasera. (No, non mi vedrà.)

12. Domani, andremo al cinema.

13. Sì, domattina leggerò il giornale, lo leggo ogni mattina.

14. Sì, stasera scriverò delle lettere, (No, non ne scriverò.)

15. Sì, stasera mangerò carne. (No, non ne mangerò.)

16. Sì, ne berrò. (No, non ne berrò.)

17. Sì, domani verrò qui. (No, non verrò qui.)

18. Sì, l'anno venturo andrò in Italia.

19. Sì, domani Lei mi vedrà. (No, non mi vedrà.)

20. Alla prossima lezione leggeremo il libro che Lei ci ha dato ieri.

21. Sì, alla prossima lezione parleremo italiano.

22. Sì, dopo la lezione usciremo.

23. Sì, ne avrò.

ANSWERS TO THE QUESTIONS OF LESSON 33 ON PAGE 196

1. Devono mangiare e respirare.

2. Per vivere noi abbiamo bisogno d'aria e di nutrimento.

3. Sono la vista, l'udito, l'odorato, il gusto ed il tatto.

4. Il cavallo, la vacca, il cane ed il gatto.

5. Lo stomaco ed i polmoni.

6. Stanno nell'acqua.

7. Il serpente si muove strisciando.

8. No, la rana non cammina, essa salta.

9. Sì, appartiene a me. (No, non appartiene a me.)

10. Perchè ci dà il miele.

11. I principali animali domestici sono: la vacca, il cavallo, il cane ed il gatto. I principali animali selvatici sono: la tigre, il leone, il lupo.

12. Il cane ha quattro zampe.
13. Un uccello ha due zampe.
14. Colle zampe camminano o saltano.
15. Colle ali volano.
16. Volano nell'aria.
17. Sì, nuota nel mare.
18. Senza mangiare e senza respirare non possiamo vivere.
19. Respiriamo coi polmoni.

20. I polmoni sono nel petto.
21. Il sangue è rosso.
22. Il cuore fa circolare il sangue.
23. È nel petto.
24. Sì, sto bene di salute. (No, non sto bene di salute.)
25. No, non si digerisce facilmente se si mangia troppo.

ANSWERS TO THE QUESTIONS OF LESSON 34 ON PAGE 203

1. Il professore è contento perchè egli ha molto danaro.
2. No, Titina non è felice.
3. Perchè ha rotto la sua bambola.
4. Sì, la signora Fibronia è triste.
5. Perchè nessuno l'ama.
6. No, l'uomo non è superiore agli animali in tutte le cose.
7. No, non si può parlare correttamente senza pensare.
8. Sì, ha freddo.
9. Adesso imparo l'italiano.
10. Sì, ho imparato la musica. (No, non ho imparato la musica.)
11. Sì, ho imparato a ballare.
12. Sì, io lo so.
13. No, Lei non lo sa.

14. No, noi non lo sappiamo.
15. Sì, egli lo sa. (No, non lo sa.)
16. Sì, io l'ho imparato.
17. Sì, io lo so ancora. (No, non lo so più.)
18. Sì, l'ho dimenticato. (No, non l'ho dimenticato.)
19. Sì, io ho buona memoria. (No, non ho buona memoria.)
20. Sì, si dimentica presto.
21. Sì, la conosco. (No, non la conosco.)
22. Sì, lo so (No, non lo so.)
23. Sì, desidero averne molto.
24. Sì, ne sono contento.
25. Sì, ne sono contento.
26. No, non l'ho conosciuto.

ANSWERS TO THE QUESTIONS OF LESSON 35 ON PAGE 211

1. Le più grandi città d'Europa sono: Londra, Parigi, Berlino, Mosca, Roma.
2. Sì, è al nord di Roma.
3. La Svizzera è al nord dell'Italia.
4. L'Italia è al sud della Svizzera.
5. Sì, è lontana.
6. Sì, il mio albergo è lontano da qui. (No, non è lontano.)
7. Sì, gli americani viaggiano molto.
8. Sì, io viaggio in estate. (No, non viaggio.)
9. Sì, in Italia viaggiano molti inglesi.

10. Dall'Europa si va in America in cinque giorni per mare e in un giorno in aereo.
11. Da Roma si va a Genova in dieci ore, in treno.
12. Per andare da casa mia alla stazione adoperiamo venti minuti.
13. Nella mia valigia metto tutto ciò che avrò di bisogno durante il mio viaggio.
14. No, non la porto io stesso; la porta il facchino.

15. Io dico: prenda questa valigia e la porti nella vettura.
16. Sì, prendo un taxi. (No, ci vado con l'autobus.)
17. Partono dalla stazione.
18. Prima di salire nel vagone compro un biglietto.
19. Li prendo allo sportello.
20. Sì, lo capisco bene. (No, non lo capisco bene.)
21. Dico: La prego, parli più adagio; io non capisco bene l'italiano.

22. Nelle strade ci sono dei negozi, c'è della gente che cammina e ci sono degli automobili.
23. Dico: Buon giorno, signore (signora).
24. Nelle pasticcerie mangiamo paste, gelati, dolci, ecc.
25. Sì, mi piacciono. (No, non mi piacciono.)
26. Sì, va in una latteria.
27. Dal pizzicagnolo.

ANSWERS TO THE QUESTIONS OF LESSON 36 ON PAGE 218

1. Si trovano a Milano.
2. Il signor Miller è americano di Boston.
3. È in Italia da una settimana.
4. Il signor Miller è venuto a Milano per far una visita al signor De Rossi.
5. Non, non è americano, è italiano.
6. È di Roma.
7. Andrà a Roma.
8. Sì, partirà anche il signor De Rossi.
9. Egli riceve l'invito di partire con lui.
10. Sì, egli accetta l'invito.
11. Vanno all'ufficio della compagnia di aviazione.

12. No, è impossibile, perchè l'aereo delle sedici è al completo.
13. Possono ottener un posto sull'aereo che parte per Roma alle dieci.
14. Perchè su questo aereo ci sono due posti.
15. No, il signor Miller non prende un biglietto di andata e ritorno.
16. Prima di lasciar l'Italia andrà a Napoli.
17. Sì, io vivo in una città. Vivo a New York.
18. Il mio indirizzo è ...
19. Il viaggio in automobile dura mezz'ora.
20. Sì, mi piace viaggiare. (No, non mi piace viaggiare.)

ANSWERS TO THE QUESTIONS OF LESSON 37 ON PAGE 227

1. Sì, egli sta dormendo.
2. La telefonista lo chiama.
3. Esclama: per bacco!
4. Perchè egli si e riaddormentato.
5. Il facchino li porterà al taxi.
6. Egli parla col cassiere.
7. Egli ha lasciato la chiave nella camera.
8. Perchè la valigetta contiene tutti i suoi documenti ed egli non vuole perderli.

9. Il signor De Rossi lo aspetta all' ufficio della compagnia di aviazione.
10. No, il signor Miller si è svegliato tardi.
11. Perchè ha fame.
12. No, non mangia mai la mattina.
13. Sì, il signor De Rossi potrà servire da guida al signor Miller.
14. La sede della sua ditta è nella capitale (è a Roma).

15. Il limite di peso del bagaglio trasportato gratis è 25 chili.
16. Perchè non ha fatto colazione la mattina.
17. No, non ha avuto il tempo.

18. Perchè l'annunziatore ha chiamato i passeggeri a bordo.
19. Sì, a bordo si serve da mangiare.
20. Sì, mi piace viaggiare in aereo. (No, non mi piace.)

ANSWERS TO THE QUESTIONS OF LESSON 38 ON PAGE 237

1. Da un aeroplano io vedo: monti, valli, città, paesi....
2. È Frascati.
3. È famoso per i suoi vini.
4. No, non le capisce.
5. No, non sono parole francesi.
6. Sono parole latine.
7. Egli vuole vedere il passaporto o la tessera di riconoscimento.
8. Si fermerà forse un mese.
9. Perchè vuole cambiare dei dollari in lire.
10. Gli dà l'avviso di star attento ai borsaneristi.
11. No, non gli piace.
12. Sì, le sue valigie erano già state ispezionate.
13. A Genova.

14. Gli mostra la ricevuta.
15. Telefona a sua moglie.
16. Perchè sua moglie è sempre preoccupata quando egli viaggia in aereo.
17. Va all'Albergo degli Ambasciatori.
18. Egli passerà il pomeriggio in ufficio.
19. S'incontreranno all'albergo.
20. Perchè questo albergo si trova in una strada elegante e centrale, e perchè è fornito di tutte le comodità moderne.
21. Sì, la trova.
22. Costa duemila lire oltre le tasse.
23. Perchè ha fame. Non ha mangiato da ieri sera.
24. La cucina italiana mi piace.

ANSWERS TO THE QUESTIONS OF LESSON 39 ON PAGE 249

1. Si chiamano colazione, pranzo e cena.
2. Vanno verso il centro della città.
3. Si chiama Corso Umberto I.
4. No, non si celebra nulla.
5. È il sole italiano e l'umore degli italiani.
6. Vediamo la gente che passa, automobili, negozi, ecc.
7. Il suo cappello è sciupato.
8. Lo compra in un negozio di cappelli.
9. Perchè non gli piace la qualità.
10. Costa seimila lire.
11. Dice che non è caro considerando la buona qualità del feltro.

12. Il commesso incide nella benda le iniziali del signor Miller.
13. Egli li manda al ricovero dei vecchi.
14. Vedono il colossale monumento a Vittorio Emanuele II.
15. Si vede il Colosseo.
16. Desidera comprare delle film a colori e dei francobolli.
17. Sì, ne mando ai miei amici.
18. No, non lo accetta.
19. La passerà in casa del signor De Rossi e al teatro.
20. Danno la Tosca di Puccini.
21. Lo accompagna al Ministero degli Affari Esteri.
22. La sua ultima frase è: In bocca al lupo!

ANSWERS TO THE QUESTIONS OF LESSON 40 ON PAGE 257

1. Si chiama piazza dell'Esedra.
2. Ai tempi dell'antichi romani quella piazza era la palestra delle terme.
3. Facevano i loro giuochi sportivi.
4. Loro si sedevano sotto i colonnati.
5. La chiesa si chiama Santa Maria degli Angeli.
6. Vede dei sedili di marmo.

7. Ve n'erano oltre tremila.
8. I bagnanti li usavano.
9. Nel centro della corte si vede una piscina.
10. Era lunga duecento piedi.
11. L'acqua originava da una sorgente naturale.
12. No, gli antichi romani non usavano sapone.

ANSWERS TO THE QUESTIONS OF LESSON 41 ON PAGE 269

1. La signora De Rossi dice: Prego si accomodi.
2. Essa si chiama Giovanna.
3. Ne hanno tre.
4. Il più piccolo si chiama Peppino.
5. Ne ha due.
6. Perchè egli ha preso un corso d'italiano alla Scuola Berlitz.
7. No, il signor Miller non ne è offeso.

8. Perchè non ha mai avuto il tempo di sposarsi.
9. Si chiama scapolo.
10. Preferisce bere un americano.
11. Si chiama Amalia.
12. Si chiama vedova.
13. Il signor Miller rimane muto.
14. Amalia è molto bella.
15. Essa annuncia che la cena è servita.
16. Sì, Amalia andrà all'opera.

ANSWERS TO THE QUESTIONS OF LESSON 42 ON PAGE 280

1. Il nome dell'opera è Tosca.
2. Sì, il Teatro dell'Opera gli piace molto.
3. È coperta con foglia d'oro zecchino.
4. L'orchestra intona l'inno nazionale americano.
5. Vanno al bar a bere un cognac.
6. Perchè vorrebbe ammirare la decorazione della sala.

7. Essa suggerisce di andare al bar.
8. Essa lo chiama signor Don Giovanni.
9. No, non le capisce.
10. Non ha capito il secondo atto.
11. È grato per la bellissima serata.
12. Perchè considera la serata una delle più dilettevoli della sua vita

GLOSSARY

A

a in, to, at
abbassare to lower
abbastanza enough
abitare to live, dwell
accanto next to, near
accendere to light
accento *m.* accent, stress
acerbo sour
accettare to accept
acciaio *m.* steel
accoglienza *f.* reception, welcome
accogliere to receive, to welcome
accomodare to accommodate
accomodi, si make yourself comfortable, sit down
acqua *f.* water
adagio slow

adesso now, at present
adoperare to use
aereo *m.* airplane
affare *m.* business
affari, uomo d' businessman
affascinare to fascinate
aggiungere to add
agosto *m.* August (month)
ala *f.* wing
albergo *m.* hotel
albero *m.* tree
alcuno somebody
alcuni, (-e) a few, some
alfabeto *m.* alphabet
allegro gay
allievo *m.* pupil, student
alloggiare to lodge

alloggiato, esser to be lodged
allora then, at that time
almeno at least
altare *m.* altar
alto tall, high
alunno *m.* pupil
altro other
alzare to raise
alzarsi to get up
amare to love
americano American
amico friend (male)
amica friend (female)
ammalato ill, in poor health
ammirare to admire
ammirazione *f.* admiration
ammontare (a) to amount (to)
amore *m.* love
anche also
ancora still, yet, again
andare to go
andata *f.* trip (to a destination)
andata e ritorno, biglietto d' round trip ticket
angelo *m.* angel
angolo *m.* corner
anello *m.* ring
anima *f.* soul
animale *m.* animal
anno *m.* year
annunciatore *m.* announcer
anticipo *m.* anticipation, advance payment
anticipo, in ahead of time
antico antique, old
antichità *f.* antiquity
anziano elder, elderly
ape *f.* bee
aperitivo *m.* aperitif
apparecchio *m.* apparatus, camera, airplane
appendere to attach, hang
appetito *m.* appetite
applaudire to applaud
appuntamento *m.* appointment
appunto, per l' exactly

approfittare to take advantage of
aprile *m.* April
aprire to open
aquila *f.* eagle
arabo Arabian, Arab
arancia *f.* orange
argento *m.* silver
aria *f.* air, melody, aria
arrivare to arrive
arrivo *m.* arrival
arrosto *m.* roast or broiled meat
arte *f.* art
ascensore *m.* elevator
asciutto dry
assistere to assist
asparago *m.* asparagus
aspettare to wait
aspetto *m.* aspect, view
assentarsi to leave, to be absent
assente absent
assicurare to assure, to insure
assomigliare to resemble
astro *m.* star
attendere to wait for, to attend
attenti, sull' at attention (milit.)
attento alert, attentive
attento, stia watch out
atto *m.* act, action
attraversare to cross
augurio *m.* good wish
autista *m.* driver, chauffeur
automobile *f.* automobile
autunno *m.* fall, autumn
avanti forwards, before
avanzo *m.* remnant, remainder, surplus, rest
avere to have
avere *m.* possession
aviazione *f.* aviation
avvertire to warn, to advise, to notice
avvicinarsi to get near
avvisare to advise, to warn
avviso *m.* warning
avvocato *m.* lawyer
azzurro (light) blue

B

baco da seta *m.* silk worm
Bacco *m.* Bacchus
Bacco, corpo di ⎱ good heavens!
Bacco, per ⎰
bagaglio *m.* luggage
bagnante *m.* bather
bagnare to bathe, wet
bagnarsi to take a bath, to get wet
bagnato wet
bagno *m.* bath, bath-tub
ballare to dance
bambina *f.* child (girl)
bambino *m.* child (boy)
banca *f.* bank
banco *m.* bench, bank
bar *m.* bar
barba *f.* beard
barba, far la to shave
barzelletta *f.* joke
basso low, bass (singer)
basta! that will do, enough!
bastare to suffice, to be enough
bastone *m.* stick
becco *m.* bill, beak, he-goat
bello beautiful
bene well
benissimo very well, all right
benone very well
bere to drink
Berlino *m.* Berlin
bevanda *f.* beverage
biancheria *f.* underclothes, linen
bianco white
biblioteca *f.* library
bicchiere *m.* glass (drinking glass)
biglietto *m.* ticket, note, short letter
birra *f.* beer
bisestile, anno leap-year
bisogno, aver...di to need something
bistecca *f.* beefsteak
blù blue, dark blue

bocca *f.* mouth
bordo, a aboard
borsanerista *m.* black marketeer
borsetta *f.* bag, pocket-book
bosco *m.* wood, forest
bottiglia *f.* bottle
braccio *m.* arm
bravo well done! bravo! brave
bravissimo! very well done
breve short, brief
bronzo *m.* bronze
bruciare to burn
bruno brown
bruttezza *f.* ugliness
brutto ugly
buio dark
buono good
buona, di...ora early
burlarsi (di) to make fun (of)
burro *m.* butter
bussare (alla porta) to knock (at the door)
busta *f.* envelop
buttare (via) to throw (away)

C

cacciare to hunt, chase
cadere to fall
caffè *m.* coffee, café
calamaio *m.* inkstand
calcolare to calculate, to compute
caldo warm, hot
calendario *m.* calendar, almanac
calore *m.* heat
calza *f.* stocking, sock
calzetta *f.* sock
calzoni *m.pl.* trousers
cambiamento *m.* change, alteration
cambiare to change, alter
cambiavalute *m.* money-changer
cambio *m.* change, exchange
cambio, ufficio di exchange office
camera *f.* room

cameriera *f.* chambermaid, house-maid
cameriere *m.* valet, servant, waiter
camicetta *f.* blouse
camicia *f.* shirt
camino *m.* chimney, fire-place, mantelpiece
caminetto *m.* small chimney, fire-place
cammello *m.* camel
camminare to walk
campagna *f.* country-side
cane *m.* dog
cantare to sing
cantiere (navale) *m.* shipyard
canto *m.* song
canzone *f.* song
capello *m.* hair
capelli *m.pl.* hair (s)
capire to understand
capitale *f.* capital (town)
capitale *m.* capital (money)
capolavoro *m.* masterpiece
cappello *m.* hat
carbone *m.* coal
cardinale cardinal
caricare to load, to wind up (a watch), to charge
carne *f.* meat, flesh
caro dear, expensive
carrozza *f.* carriage, coach
carrozzella *f.* cab, small carriage
carta *f.* paper, playing card
cartolaio *m.* stationer
cartoleria *f.* stationery shop
cartolina *f.* post-card
casa *f.* house, home
cascare to fall
caso *m.* case, circumstance
casseruola *f.* saucepan
cassetto *m.* drawer
cassiere *m.* cashier
castello *m.* castle
cattivo bad
causare to cause, bring about

cavallo *m.* horse
cavolo *m.* cabbage
cavolifiore *m.* cauliflower
celebrare to celebrate
cena *f.* supper
cenare to have supper
cenetta *f.* a little supper
cento hundred
centrale central
centro *m.* center
cercare to look for, to seek, to try
certo certain, sure
cervello *m.* brain
cessare to cease, stop
che what, that, than (with comparative)
chi who
chiamare to call
chiaro clear, light
chiarore *m.* light
chiave *f.* key
chiedere to ask
chiesa *f.* church
chilo *m.* kilogram
chilometro *m.* kilometer
chitarra *f.* guitar
chiudere to shut, to close
ci there, here
ci us, to us, each other
cibo *m.* food
cieco blind
cielo *m.* sky, heaven
cifra *f.* figure, cipher
Cina *f.* China
cinema *m.* ⎱cinema, movies
cinematografo *m.* ⎰
cinquanta fifty
cinque five
ciò this, that, it
cipolla *f.* onion
circolare to circulate
circolare *f.* circular, round, circular letter
circondare to surround
città *f.* city, large town

classe f. class
cocchiere m. coachman, driver
cogliere to gather, catch
cognata f. sister-in-law
coincidenza f. coincidence
col (con il) with the
colazione f. breakfast, luncheon
colle m. hill
colletto m. collar
collo m. neck, collar
colonnato m. colonnade
colossale huge, colossal
coltello m. knife
come how
cominciare to begin
commedia f. comedy
commendatore m. an honorary
  title bestowed by the Italian
  Government
commento m. comment
commessa f. salesgirl
commesso m. salesman
comodità f. comfort, convenience
comodo comfortable
compagnia f. company
compensare to compensate
compenso m. reward, compensa-
  tion
compito m. task, exercise
completare to complete
completo complete, full
complimentare to compliment
comporre to compose
composta f. compote, stewed fruit
comprare to buy
comprendere to understand, to
  comprehend, to include
comunicare to communicate, to
  inform
con with
concerto m. concert
concludere to conclude
condizione f. condition
condurre to conduct, to bring, to
  drive, to guide
confessare to confess

conoscere to know, to be ac-
  quainted with
conoscente m. acquaintance
conservare to preserve, keep, save
considerare to consider
consonante f. consonant
contare to count
contenere to contain, hold
contento satisfied, content, happy
continuare to continue
conto m. bill, account, calculation
contorno m. contour, outline
contorno, una costoletta con a
  chop with vegetables
contrario contrary
contratto m. contract
contro against
conversazione f. conversation
convincere to convince
coperto covered
coprire to cover
coraggio m. courage
coraggioso courageous, brave
coricarsi to go to bed, to lie
  down
coro m. chorus, choir
corpo m. body
correggere to correct
corretto correct, corrected
corridoio m. passage, corridor
corsa f. trip, run
corte f. court
cortile m. courtyard, yard
corto short
cosa f. thing, matter
così so, thus
costare to cost
costoletta f. cutlet, chop
costoletta di vitello veal-chop
costoletta di maiale pork-chop
cravatta f. neck-tie
credere to believe, to think
crema f. cream
cucchiaio m. spoon
cucina f. kitchen, cuisine
cuore m. heart

D

da from, to, by
danaro *m.* money
dappertutto everywhere
dare to give
data *f.* date (on calendar)
davanti before
delizioso delicious
decimo tenth
decorazione *f.* decoration
delineare to outline
delinearsi stand out against
dentro in, inside
desiderare to wish, to desire
desiderio *m.* wish, desire
destinazione *f.* destination
destro right (opp. of left), able
dicembre *m.* December
dichiarare to declare
dieta *f.* diet
dietro behind
difetto *m.* defect
differente different
differenza *f.* difference
digerire to digest
dilettevole delightful
dimensione *f.* dimension
dimenticare to forget
dire to say
dire bene to be right, to say the right thing
dirimpetto facing, in front of
diritto straight
discendere to descend, to get down
disdetta *f.* misfortune
dispiacere to displease
dispiacere *m.* displeasure, grief, sorrow
dispiace, mi I am sorry
disposizione *f.* disposal, disposition
disposto, esser to be willing
distanza *f.* distance
distinguere to distinguish

distinguersi to differ, to distinguish oneself
dito *m.* finger
ditta *f.* firm, business house
dividere to divide
dodici twelve
dogana *f.* customhouse, duty
doganiere *m.* customs inspector
dolce sweet
dolce *m.* dessert, pastry
dolci *m.pl.* sweets, candies
dolore *m.* pain, grief, sorrow
domanda *f.* question, request, application
domandare to ask, request, demand
domani tomorrow
domani l'altro day after tomorrow
domattina tomorrow morning
domenica *f.* Sunday
domestico domestic
domestico *m.* male servant
dopo after
dormiglione *m.* sleepy-head
dormire to sleep
dorso *m.* back (of something or someone)
dove where
dovere to owe, must, to be obliged to, to have to
dovere *m.* duty
dubitare to doubt
due two
dunque then, therefore, thus
durante during, while
durare to last
duro hard

E

ebbene well then!—well!
eccelente excellent
ecco here is, here are, there is, there are
eccoci here we are

edificio *m.* building
effetto *m.* effect
elefante *m.* elephant
elefantino *m.* little elephant
ella she
emozione *f.* emotion
entrare to enter
epoca *f.* epoch, time, period
equivalente *m.* equivalent
era *f.* era
esaminare to examine
esatto exact
esclamare to exclaim
esercizio *m.* exercise
esistere to exist
essa she
essere to be
essere *m.* being
Est east
estate *f.* summer
estatico enraptured, ecstatic
estendere to extend
età *f.* age, epoch, era
eterno eternal
evento *m.* event
evitare to avoid
evviva! hurrah! long live!
extra extra

F

facchino *m.* porter, vulgar, villain
faccia *f.* face
fagiolo *m.* bean
fame *f.* hunger
famiglia *f.* family
famoso famous
fanciulla *f.* (young) girl
fanciullo *m.* (young) boy
fare to make, to do
farfalla *f.* butterfly
farina *f.* flour, meal
farmacia *f.* pharmacy
fata *f.* fairy
favore *m.* favor

favore, per please (out of kind-
ness)
favorire to favor
favorisca please
fazzoletto *m.* handkerchief
febbraio *m.* February
fede *f.* faith
felice happy
feltro *m.* felt
fermarsi to stop, to stay
fermata *f.* stop
fermo still, fast, firm
feroce wild, ferocious
fiamma *f.* flame
fiammifero *m.* match
fiasco *m.* flask, bottle, failure
figlia *f.* daughter
figlio *m.* son
film *m.* film
film, a colori color-film
fine *f.* end
finestra *f.* window
finire to finish
fino (a) until, up to
fiore *m.* flower
fioraio *m.* florist
Firenze Florence
fisso fixed, firm
foglia *f.* leaf
foglio *m.* sheet (of paper)
fondo *m.* bottom, background
fondo, in basically, in the background
fontana *f.* fountain
forbici *f.pl.* scissors
forchetta *f.* fork
forma *f.* form
formaggio *m.* cheese
formare to form
formidabile formidable
fornire to furnish
forse perhaps
forte strong
fortuna *f.* luck, fortune
fotografia *f.* photo, picture
fra between

fragola *f.* strawberry
francese French, Frenchman, Frenchwoman
Francia *f.* France
francobollo *m.* stamp
frase *f.* sentence, phrase
fratello *m.* brother
freddo cold
fresco fresh, cool
fretta *f.* haste, hurry
frittura *f.* fried dish
fronte *f.* forehead
frutta *f.* fruit (literal)
frutto *m.* fruit (figurative & literal)
fumare to smoke
funzionare to function
fuoco *m.* fire
fuori outside
furtivo stealthy, furtive

G

galante gallant
gallina *f.* hen
gallo *m.* rooster
gamba *f.* leg
garofano *m.* carnation
gas *m.* gas
gatto *m.* cat
gelato *m.* ice-cream
generalmente generally
genere *m.* gender, kind, sort
genio *m.* genius
genitore *m.* father
genitori *pl.* parents
gennaio *m.* January
Germania *f.* Germany
gesso *m.* chalk
ghiaccio *m.* ice
già already
giacca *f.* coat, jacket
giacchetta *f.* jacket, coat
giallo yellow
Giappone *m.* Japan
gilè *m.* vest

ginocchio *m.* knee
giocare to play
gioiello *m.* jewel
giornale *m.* newspaper, journal
giornaliere daily
giornata *f.* day
giorno *m.* day
giuoco *m.* play, game
giovane *m.* young man
giovanotto *m.* young man, boy
giovedì Thursday
girare to turn, to tour
giro *m.* tour, turn
giù down
giugno *m.* June
giunta, per in addition
giusto just, right
gonnella *f.* skirt
governo *m.* government
gradevole pleasant, agreeable
gran ⎫
grande ⎬ great, large
grandemente largely
grato grateful
grazie! thanks! thank you!
Grecia *f.* Greece
gridare to shout, yell
grigio gray
grosso big, thick, fat
guanto *m.* glove
guardare to look
guardia *f.* guard, policeman
guarire to recover, to cure
guerra *f.* war
gufo *m.* owl
guida *m.* guide
gusto *m.* taste, savour

I

idea *f.* idea
ieri yesterday
ieri l'altro day before yesterday
illuminare to light, illuminate

imbarcarsi to go on board, to embark oneself
immaginare to imagine
immagine *f.* image
immigrazione *f.* immigration
impaccare to pack
imparare to learn
impermeabile *m.* rain-coat, impermeable
impiegato *m.* employee, official
importante important
inchiostro *m.* ink
incidere to engrave, to etch
inciso engraved
includere to include
incluso included, enclosed
incominciare to begin
indicare to indicate, show
indietro back, behind
indirizzo *m.* address
indossare to wear
indossarsi to put on
infelice unhappy
Inghilterra *f.* England
inglese English, Englishman, English (female)
iniziale *f.* initial
inno (nazionale) *m.* hymn, national anthem
innumerevole innumerable
inossidabile stainless
insalata *f.* salad
insegnare to teach
insetto *m.* insect
insieme together
insuperabile unsurpassable, insuperable
intanto meanwhile, while
intelligente intelligent
interessante interesting
intermezzo *m.* interlude, interval
interno *m.* interior, inside
interrompere to interrupt
intonare to intone, to strike-up (music)
inutile useless

invece instead
inverno *m.* winter
invitare to invite
invito *m.* invitation
io I
Irlanda *f.* Ireland
irlandese Irish
ispettore *m.* inspector
ispirazione *f.* inspiration
istrada (see strada)
Italia *f.* Italy
italiano Italian
italiano *m.* an Italian (man)
italiana *f.* an Italian (woman)

L

là there
labbro *m.* lip
labbra *f.pl.* lips
ladro *m.* thief
laggiù down there, yonder
lampada *f.* lamp
lampadina *f.* bulb (lamp)
lampone *m.* raspberry
lancetta *f.* hand (of a watch)
lapis *m.* pencil
largo wide
lasciare to let, to leave
latino Latin
latte *m.* milk
latteria *f.* dairy shop
lattuga *f.* lettuce
lavagna *f.* black board
lavare to wash
lavorare to work
lavoro *m.* work
leggere to read
leggero light (not heavy)
legna *f.* fire wood
legno *m.* wood
legume *m.* vegetable
Lei you
lei her, she
lenticchia *f.* lentil

leone *m.* lion
lettera *f.* letter
letteratura *f.* literature
letto *m.* bed
Levante *m.* East
levare to lift, to raise
levarsi to get up
lezione *f.* lesson
lì there, yonder
libraio *m.* book seller
libreria *f.* book shop
libro *m.* book
limite *m.* limit
limonata *f.* lemonade
limone *m.* lemon
lingua *f.* tongue, language
liquido *m.* liquid
liquore *m.* liquor
lista *f.* list
Londra *f.* London
lontano far
loro they, them, their
Loro you (pl.)
luce *f.* light
luglio *m.* July
lume *m.* light, lamp, candle
luna *f.* moon
lunedì *m.* Monday
lungo long
lungo, a for a long time
luogo *m.* place, spot
lupo *m.* wolf
lusingare to flatter, to allure

M

ma but
maccheroni *m.pl.* macaroni
macchina *f.* automobile, machine
macchina cinematografica *f.* movie camera
macellaio *m.* butcher
macelleria *f.* butcher shop
madre *f.* mother
madreperla *f.* mother of pearl

maestoso majestic, stately
maestra *f.* teacher (woman)
maestro *m.* teacher, master
magazzino *m.* department store
maggio *m.* May
magnifico magnificent
mai never, ever
malato sick, ill
malattia f. sickness illness
malcontento dissatisfied
malcontento *m.* dissatisfaction
male badly, bad
male *m.* evil
malgrado in spite of
malo bad
maltempo *m.* bad weather
mammola *f.* violet
mancare to be missing, to miss, to lack
mancia *f.* tip, gratuity
mandare to send
mandarino *m.* tangerine, mandarin
mangiare to eat
manico *m.* handle
maniera *f.* way, manner
mano *f.* hand
manto *m.* mantle
marciapiede *m.* side-walk
mare *m.* sea
marito *m.* husband
marmo *m.* marble
marrone brown, maroon
martedì *m.* Tuesday
marzo *m.* March
matita *f.* pencil
mattina *f.* ⎱
mattino *m.* ⎰ morning
maturo ripe
medesimo the same
mediante by means of
medicina *f.* medicine
medio middle, medium, average
meglio better
mela *f.* apple
melanzana *f.* egg plant
memoria *f.* memory

memoria, a   by heart
meno   less
mentalmente   mentally
mente f.   mind
mentre   while, whilst
mercoledì m.   Wednesday
meritare   to deserve
mese m.   month
metallo m.   metal
mettere   to put
mettersi   to put on, to put oneself
mezzanotte f.   midnight
mezzo   half
mezzo m.   means
mezzo, per   by means of
mezzodì m.
mezzogiorno m. } noon
mi,   to me, me
miele m.   honey
miglio m.   mile
migliore   better
milione m.   million
mille   thousand
minestra f.   soup
ministero m.   department, ministry
Ministero degli Affari Esteri   Ministry of Foreign Affairs
minore   smaller, less
minuto m.   minute
mio   mine, my
mischiare   to mix
miseria f.   misery, extreme poverty
misto   mixed
misura f.   size
moderno   modern
modo m.   way, manner
modo, in ogni   by all means
moglie f.   wife
molla f.   spring (in watch, etc.)
molle   soft
molto   much, very
momento m.   moment
mondo m.   world
montata, panna   whipped cream
montare   to climb
monumento m.   monument

morbido   soft, smooth
morire   to die
morto   dead, deceased
mosaico m.   mosaic
mosca f.   fly
Mosca f.   Moscow
mostra f.   exhibition
mostrare   to show
movimento m.   movement
mucca f.   cow
muovere   to move
muro m.   wall (outside)
museo m.   museum
musica f.   music
muto   silent, mute, dumb

N

Napoli f.   Naples
narrare   to tell, to relate
nascondere   to hide
naso m.   nose
naturale   natural
nave f.   ship, vessel
nazionale   national
nazionalità f.   nationality
nazione f.   nation
ne   of (him, her, it, them)
nè...nè   neither...nor
necessità f.   necessity, need
negare   to deny, to refuse
negli   in the (plur.)
negozio m.   shop
nemmeno   not even
neppure   neither, not even
nero   black
nervo m.   nerve
nessuno   nobody, no one
neve f.   snow
nevicare   to snow
nichelio m.   nickel
niente   nothing
nipote m.   nephew, niece
no   no
nocivo   noxious

noi we
nome *m.* name
nominare to name
non not
nonna *f* grandmother
nonno *m.* grandfather
nono (the) ninth
Nord *m.* North
nostro our, ours
notare to note, to notice
notte *f.* night
novanta ninety
nove nine
novembre *m.* November
nozione *f.* notion, idea
nube *f.* cloud
nuca *f.* nape
nulla nothing
numero *m.* number
numeroso numerous
nuotare to swim
nuovo new
nuovo, di again, once more
nutrimento *m.* nourishment, food
nutrire to nourish, to feed
nuvola *f.* cloud

O

o or
o...o either or
obbedienza *f.* obedience
obbligato obliged, compelled
occasione *f.* occasion, opportunity
occhiali *m.pl.* eye glasses
occhio *m.* eye
Occidente *m.* West
occupare to occupy
oceano *m.* ocean
odorare to smell
odore *m.* smell
oggetto *m.* object
oggi today
ogni every, each
oh! oh!

olio *m.* oil
oltre in addition to, besides
ombra *f.* shade, shadow
ombrello *m.* umbrella
omnibus bus
onde where, from where
onore honour
opera *f.* opera, work
ora *f.* hour
ora, di buon early
ora now
orario *m.* time-table
orchestra *f.* orchestra
ordinare to order
ordine *m.* order
orecchio *m.* ear
organismo *m.* organism
organo *m.* organ
Oriente *m.* East, Orient
originare to originate
ornamento *m.* ornament
oro *m.* gold
orologiaio *m.* watch-maker
orologio *m.* watch, clock
orologio da polso wristwatch
orso *m.* bear
oscuro dark, obscure
ospite *m.* or *f.* guest
ottanta eighty
ottavo (the) eight
ottenere to obtain, to get
ottimo best, very good, excellent
otto eight
ottobre *m.* October
Ovest *m.* West

P

pacco *m.* parcel, package
padre *m.* father
paese *m.* country, region, town village
pagare to pay
pagina *f.* page
paio *m.* pair

palato m. palate, taste
palco m. box (theatre)
palestra f. gymnasium
palla f. the ball
palazzo m. palace, large house
pane m. bread
panorama m. panorama
parco m. park
parecchi several
pare, mi it seems to me
parere to seem
parete f. wall (inside)
Parigi f. Paris
parlare to talk, speak
parmigiano m. Parmesan cheese, inhabitant from the city of Parma
parola f. word
parte f. part, share, role (theatre)
partenza f. departure
partire to depart, to leave
passare to pass, to spend time
passeggero m. passenger
passeggero passing, not lasting
passeggiata f. walk, ride, stroll
passeggio m. walk, promenade
passeggio, andar a to take a walk
passero m. sparrow
pasta f. pastry, tart, paste, dough
pasticceria f. pastry shop, assortment of pastry
pasto m. meal
pastoso mellow (voice)
patata f. potato
paura f. fear, dread
pavimento m. floor
pavone m. peacock
peggio ⎫
peggiore ⎬ worse
pelle f. skin, hide
pelo m. hair
pendolo m. pendulum
pendolo, orologio a pendulum clock
penna f. pen, feather

pensare to think
pensiero m. thought, idea
per for, because of
pera f. pear
percepire to perceive, to receive
perchè because
perchè? why?
perciò therefore
perdere to lose
perdonare to forgive
pericolo m. danger
pericoloso dangerous
periodo m. period
permanere to remain, to stay
permettere to allow, permit
però however
persona f. person
personaggio m. person, personage
personale personal
personalmente personally
pesante heavy
pesare to weigh
pesca f. peach
pesce m. fish
pescecane m. shark
pettinare to comb
pettine m. comb
petto m. chest, breast
piacere m. pleasure
piacere to please, to like
piacere, per please
piacevole pleasing, agreeable
piangere to weep
pianta f. plant
piatto m. plate, dish
piazza f. square, plaza
piccolo small, little
piede m. foot
piedi, in standing
piedistallo m. pedestal
pinna f. fin
pioggia f. rain
piovere to rain
pisello m. pea
piscina f. pool, swimming pool
pistola f. pistol

pittore *m.* painter
più more
piuma *f.* feather
piuttosto rather
pizzicagnolo *m.* delicatessen proprietor
po', un po' = un poco a little
poco a little
poi afterwards, then
poichè since
polizia *f.* police
pollo *m.* chicken
polmoni *m.pl.* lungs
Polo (Nord) (Sud) *m.* Pole, (North) (South)
polsino *m.* cuff
polso *m.* wrist, pulse
pomata *f.* pomade, salve
pomeriggio *m.* afternoon
pomodoro *m.* tomato
Ponente *m.* West
porco *m.* pig, pork, hog
porta *f.* door
portabagagli *m.* porter
portafoglio *m.* pocket book, portfolio, wallet
portalettere *m.* postman, letter-carier
portamonete *m.* purse
portare to carry, to bring, bear
portiere *m.* porter, janitor
Portogallo *m.* Portugal
porzione *f.* portion
posdomani the day after tomorrow
posizione *f.* position, situation
possedere to own, possess
posta *f.* post-office, mail
posto *m.* place, post, site
potere to be able, can
povero poor
pranzare to dine
pranzo *m.* dinner
preciso precise
preferire to prefer
pregare to ask, to beg, to pray

prelibato excellent, exquisite
prendere to take
preoccuparsi to worry, be concerned
preoccupato worried
preparare to prepare
presentare to present, to introduce
presente present
presidente *m.* president
presso near, beside, care-of
presto quick, quickly, early
presto, far to hurry
prezzo *m.* price
prima before
primavera *f.* Spring
primo first
principale principal
principio *m.* beginning, principle
privare to deprive
produrre to produce
professore *m.* professor, teacher
profumo *m.* perfume
progresso *m.* progress
proibire to prohibit
proibito prohibited, forbidden
pronto ready
pronuncia *f.* pronunciation
pronunciare to pronounce
proposito *m.* purpose, resolution
proposito, a! by the way!
proposta *f.* proposal
proprio own, one's own, proper
prosciutto *m.* ham
proprietario *m.* owner, proprietor
prossimo next
provare to try, to test, to feel, experience
pubblico *m.* public, audience
pulire to clean
punto *m.* point, stitch
punto cardinale cardinal point
punto esclamativo exclamation point
punto interrogativo question mark
pure also, too
purtroppo alas! unfortunately

Q

qua here
quaderno *m.* copy-book
quadrante *m.* dial
quadro *m.* painting, picture
quadrupede *m.* quadruped
qualche some
qualche volta sometimes
qualche cosa } something
qualcosa }
qualcuno somebody
quale which, who
qualità *f.* quality
quando when
quante, -i how many
quantità *f.* quantity
quanto how much
quaranta forty
quarto (the) fourth
quasi almost
quattordici fourteen
quattro four
quel } that
quello }
questo this
qui here
quindici fifteen
quinto (the) fifth

R

raccomandare to recommend
radersi to shave (oneself)
radio *f.* radio
raffreddarsi to catch cold, to get cold
ragno *m.* spider
rana *f.* frog
rapidamente quickly, rapidly
rappresentazione *f.* performance, show
raramente rarely, seldom
raro rare, scarce
recitare to recite

regalare to make a present
regalo *m.* present, gift
regolamento *m.* regulation
relativamente relatively
residenza *f.* residence
respirare to breathe
respirazione *f.* breathing
restare to remain
restituire to return, to give back
resto *m.* remainder, rest
rettile *m.* reptile
riaccendere to light again
ricevere to receive
ricevuta *f.* receipt
ricordare } to remember, to remind
ricordarsi }
ricovero dei vecchi *m.* old peoples home
ricco rich
ridere to laugh
riempire to fill, to fill again
rifiutare to refuse
riga *f.* line, ruler
rimandare to send back, postpone
rimanere to remain
rimettere to put again, to remit
rimunerare to reward, to remunerate
rincontrare to meet, encounter, to meet again
rincresce, mi I am sorry, I regret
ringraziare to thank
ripetere to repeat
riposarsi to rest
riposo *m.* rest
riprendere to take again
ripugnanza *f.* repugnance
riscaldare to heat, warm
rischiarare to illuminate, to light up
riso *m.* rice
riso *m.* laugh, laughter
rispondere to answer
risposta *f.* answer
ristorante *m.* restaurant
risultato *m.* result

ritardo *m.* retard
ritardo, essere in to be late
ritornare to return, come back
riuscire to go out again, to succeed
rivedere to see again, to revise
rivendicare to vindicate
rivolgersi to apply, to turn to
Roma *f.* Rome
romano Roman, inhabitant of Rome
romanzo *m.* novel, fiction, romance
rompere to break
rotto broken
rondine *f.* swallow
rosa *f.* rose
rosbiffe *m.* roast beef
rosso red
rumore *m.* noise
Russia *f.* Russia
russo Russian

S

sabato *m.* Saturday
sala *f.* hall, room
sala da pranzo dining room
salame *m.* salami
salire to mount, climb
salire le scale to go upstairs
salotto *m.* living room
salutare to greet, to salute
salutare healthy, wholesome
salute *f.* health
saluto *m.* greeting
saluti regards, salutations
sangue *m.* blood
santo saint
santo *m.* the saint
sapere to know
sapone *m.* soap
sapore *m.* taste
sardina *f.* sardine
sbagliare ⎱ to be mistaken
sbagliarsi ⎰

sbalorditivo amazing
sbarcare to land
scaldarsi to warm oneself, to grow angry
scapolo single, bachelor
scappare to escape, run away
scarpa *f.* shoe
scartare to discard
scatola *f.* box
scattare (in piedi) to spring up
scavare to excavate
scena *f.* scene
scendere to go downstairs
scherzare to joke
schiudere to open
sciampagna *m.* champagne
scimmia *f.* ape, monkey
sciupato worn, wasted
scontrino *m.* check, ticket
scoprire to discover, to uncover
scoraggiarsi to get discouraged
scorso past
scrittura *f.* writing, scripture
scrivere to write
scuola *f.* school
scuro dark
scusare to excuse
se if
sè oneself, himself, herself, itself, themselves
secolo *m.* century
secondo *m.* second
secondo (the) second
secondo according to
sedere to sit
sedersi to sit down, to take a seat
sedia *f.* chair
seduto, essere to be sitting
segnare to mark, note
segno *m.* sign
seguire to follow
sei six
selva *f.* forest, woods
selvatico wild
sembra, mi I think, it seems to me
sembrare to seem

sempre always
sensazione *f.* sensation
senso *m.* sense, meaning
sentimento *m.* sentiment, feeling
sentire to hear, to smell, to feel, to taste
senza without
sera *f.* evening
serata *f.* evening, evening party, soiree
serenata *f.* serenade
sereno clear, serene
serio serious, earnest
serpente *m.* snake
servire to serve
servirsi to make use
sessanta sixty
sesto (the) sixth
seta *f.* silk
sete *f.* thirst
settanta seventy
sette seven
settembre *m.* September
Settentrione *m.* North
settimana *f.* week
settimo (the) seventh
severo severe
sfortunato unfortunate, unlucky
sgradevole unpleasant
si each other, one another
si one, they
si oneself, himself, herself, itself, themselves
sì yes
Sicilia *f.* Sicily
sigaretta *f.* cigarette
sigaro *m.* cigar
signor *m.* Mr.
signora *f.* madam, Mrs.
signore *m.* gentleman
signorina *f.* young lady, Miss
silenzio *m.* silence
simile similar, alike
simpatico nice, agreeable, pleasant
sincero sincere, true
sindaco *m.* mayor

sinistro left (sinister, unlucky)
sipario *m.* curtain (theatre)
smarrirsi to get lost
soddisfare to satisfy
soddisfazione *f.* satisfaction
soffitto ceiling
soffrire to suffer
sole *m.* sun
solo alone
somigliare to look like, to be similar
sonno *m.* sleep
sonno, aver to be sleepy
sopra upon, on
soprabito *m.* overcoat
sopratassa *f.* surtax
sorella *f.* sister
sorellina *f.* little sister
sorpresa *f.* surprise
sospettare to suspect
sorgente *f.* spring, well
sotto under
sottovoce in a low voice
sovente often
Spagna *f.* Spain
spagnolo Spanish, Spaniard
spagnola Spanish (woman)
specialità *f.* specialty
spedire to send, to dispatch
spegnere to put out, extinguish
speranza *f.* hope
sperare to hope
spesso often, thick, dense
spiacevole unpleasant, disagreeable
spiaggia *f.* beach
spiegare to explain, to unfold
splendere to shine
sporco unclean, dirty
sportello *m.* ticket window
sposare to marry, to wed
squama scale
sta, come? how do you do?
stagione *f.* season
stamattina this morning
stanotte to-night

stanza *f.* room
stare to stand, remain, to be
stasera to-night, this evening
Stati Uniti U.S.
statua *f.* statue
stazionare to park
stazione *f.* station, railroad station
stella *f.* star
stesso same
sto bene I am well
stomaco *m.* stomach
stracciare to tear
strano strange
straordinario extraordinary
stretto narrow
strisciare to creep
struzzo *m.* ostrich
studente *m.* student
studiare to study
stufa *f.* stove
stupendo stupendous
su, sul, sulla on, upon
subito sudden, right away
succursale *f.* branch (office, store)
Sud *m.* South
suonare to sound, ring, to play (on the piano, etc.)
suono *m.* sound
superiore superior
sveglia *f.* alarm clock, reveille
svegliare ⎫
svegliarsi ⎭ to wake up
sviluppare to develop
Svizzera *f.* Switzerland
svizzero Swiss

T

tabella *f.* schedule, time table
tagliare to cut
tagliatelle *f.pl.* egg noodles
tale such, like, similar, John Doe
talvolta sometimes
tanto so much, so many, a lot
tardare to be late, to delay
tardi late

tasca *f.* pocket
taschino *m.* small pocket
tassa *f.* tax
tassametro *m.* taximeter
tassi *m.* taxi
tatto *m.* touch, feeling, tact
tavola *f.* table
taxi *m.* taxi
tazza *f.* cup, mug
te you
tè *m.* tea
teatro *m.* theatre
tedesca German (woman)
tedesco German (man)
tedesco German
telefonare to telephone
telefono *m.* telephone
temere to fear
temperamento *m.* temper, disposition, temperament
tempesta *f.* storm, tempest
tempo *m.* time, weather
teneramente tenderly
tenere to hold, keep
tenero tender, affectionate
tenore *m.* tenor
terme *f.pl.* hot baths
terminare to finish, to end, to terminate
termosifone *m.* radiator
terra *f.* land, ground, earth
terzo (the) third
tessera *f.* card, ticket
testa *f.* head
tigre *f.* tiger
tipo *m.* type
tirare to pull
toccare to touch
tocco *m.* touch, stroke of bell
tocco, al at one o'clock
togliere to take, to take off
toletta *f.* toilet, toilet articles, dressing table
topo *m.* mouse
torta *f.* cake
tornare to turn, to return

Toscana *f.* Tuscany
tra between
traggitto *m.* journey, trip
tramontare to set (sun)
tranquillo calm, quiet, tranquil
trasformare to transform
trasporto *m.* transport, conveyance
trattare (affari) to treat, to deal
  (business)
tre three
tredici thirteen
tremendo tremendous
treno *m.* train
trenta thirty
tribunale *m.* tribunal, court
triste sad
troppo too much
trovare to find
tulipano *m.* tulip
tuttavia yet, however
tutto all, whole
tutt'altro quite the contrary
tuttochè though, although

U

uccello *m.* bird
udire to hear
udito *m.* sense of hearing
ufficio *m.* office
ultimare to finish, to complete
umano human
umido humid (weather)
umore *m.* mood, humor
undici eleven
un a, an, one
una a, an, one
uno one
uomo *m.* man
uovo *m.* egg
usare to use
uscire to go out, leave
uso *m.* use
usualmente usually
utile useful, utility

utilità *f.* usefulness
uva *f.* grape

V

vacca *f.* cow
valere to be worth
valigetta *f.* small valise
valigia *f.* bag, valise, suit-case
valore *m.* value, valor
valuta *f.* money
vario various
ve see vi
vecchio old
vedere to see
vedova *f.* widow
vena *f.* mood
venerdì *m.* Friday
Venere *f.* Venus
Venezia *f.* Venice
venire to come
venire a trovare to visit, to come
  to see
venti twenty
vento *m.* wind
venturo future, next
veramente really
verde green
verdura *f.* green vegetables
vero true
verso *m.* verse, side
verso towards, near, about
vestiario *m.* clothes
vestire to dress
vestirsi to dress oneself
vestito *m.* dress, suit
vetrina *f.* shop-window
vetro *m.* glass
vettura *f.* carriage, vehicle, rail-
  road-car
vi there, in that place
vi to you
via away
via *f.* street
viaggiare to travel

viaggiatore *m.* passenger, traveller
viaggio *m.* travel, trip
viale *m.* boulevard, avenue
vicino near
vicino *m.* neighbour
vino *m.* wine
vino nero red wine
violetta *f.* violet
virgola *f.* comma
visibile visible
visita *f.* visit
visitare to visit
vista *f.* sight, sense of sight, view
vita *f.* life
vivente living, alive
vivo alive
vocabolario *m.* vocabulary
vocale *f.* vowel
voce *f.* voice

voi you
volare to fly
volere to want, desire, wish
volontieri gladly, willingly
volpe *f.* fox
volta *f.* time
volta, una once
volta, qualche sometimes

Z

zampa *f.* paw, leg
zampe di rane *f.pl.* frog's legs
zanzara *f.* mosquito
zia *f.* aunt
zio *m.* uncle
zucchero *m.* sugar
zuccheriera *f.* sugar-bowl